ISLAM
IDEOLOGY AND THE WAY OF LIFE

To
My dearest children,
who, I hope and pray, will
seek guidance from the Qur'an
and Sunnah of the Holy Prophet to
strengthen their faith (Iman) and to direct
their lives onto the Way of virtue, goodness and peace.

islam

IDEOLOGY AND
THE WAY OF LIFE

AFZALUR RAHMAN

Sponsored and published by:
THE MUSLIM SCHOOLS TRUST LONDON

Can also be had from

Muslim Information Services
233 Seven Sisters Road
London N4 2DA

Islamic Book Service
52 Field Gate Street
London E1

Islamic Book Centre
202 North Gower Street
London NW1 2LY

CONTENTS

Sponsor's Note

By the Grace and Blessing of God the Trust is publishing its fourth book 'Islam Ideology and the Way of Life' for the benefit of its English speaking readers.

This book Al Hamdu Lillah gives all the basic information about the faith of Islam, its various forms of worship, their significance in the practical life of man and the nature and scope of the systems which it wants to establish to bring virtue, goodness and peace in the lives of people.

Salem Azzam
Secretary General

In the name of God, Most Gracious, Most Merciful

Preface

"O you people! Adore your Guardian-Lord, Who created you and those who came before you, that you may have the chance to learn (and practise) righteousness." (Qur'an)

This book is written to provide elementary information about Islam to English speaking children . The book consists of two volumes. The first volume covers Tawhid and rights of Allah i.e., huquq Allah. It explains briefly the principles of Faith and various forms of ibadah and their effect on human behaviour.

The second volume deals with man's rights in society vis-a-vis his fellow-beings i.e., huquq al-ibad. It describes human society as Islam wants to establish and its essential features.

78 Gillespie Road,   Afzalur Rahman
London. N. 5.
9th April, 1980

INTRODUCTION

Islam embodies beliefs and concepts of great creativity, practicability and guidance for man in his relationship with his Creator and fellow-men. These beliefs serve as instruments of his mental culture, moral betterment, spiritual enlightenment, social justice and political tolerance. Belief is a great power. It strengthens one's faith in God and increases one's conviction of the truthfulness of His Messengers and their teachings. It prepares one mentally to believe in God with full knowledge and conviction and makes one ready to accept with complete responsibility the teaching of Islam. In short, it confirms one's complete acceptance of the ideology of Islam.

Ibadah (acts of devotion) bridges the spiritual gap between the Creator and oneself. It creates, develops and maintains one's relationship with God and brings one closer to Him. Thus belief and ibadah together form the basis of an ethical system in society. They make it easier for man to follow the Commandments of God and establish a system of justice and goodness in society. Aqa'id (Islamic doctrines) form the basis of iman (faith). These doctrinal beliefs are the basis and root of Islam. If they are strong, one's iman will be strong. If they are weak, one's iman will be weak. Thus the strength or weakness of the basis of Islam depends upon the strength or weakness of iman. It is, therefore, vital for every Muslim to have a clear understanding of the basic components of iman, which can only be derived from a thorough study of the Qur'an and the Hadith. It is equally important for a Muslim to observe certain ordained acts and codes (known as a'mal), which form the pillars of faith and, thus, of Islam. These can be divided into Acts of Devotion and Codes of Morality. The former consist of prayer, zakat (alms giving), fasting and the pilgrimage to Mecca, while the latter relates to ideals of character, social behaviour and justice. Both Acts of Devotion and Codes of Morality are included in the term ibadah. Codes of Morality are the principles of ibadah while Acts of Devotion are forms of ibadah.

VOL 1
FAITH AND WORSHIP

يَا أَيُّهَا الَّذِينَ آمَنُوا ارْكَعُوا وَاسْجُدُوا وَاعْبُدُوا رَبَّكُمْ وَافْعَلُوا الْخَيْرَ لَعَلَّكُمْ تُفْلِحُونَ ۩

O You who believe! Bow down and prostrate yourselves, and worship your Lord, and do good, that you may prosper (Qur'an).

1

Iman And Islam

Islam consititutes two basic complementary concepts, Iman (faith) and a'mal (actions). Iman unsupported by deeds, is fruitless, unauthentic and unreliable, while the reverse is meaningless and illogical. It is essential that both must be integrated to attain success in this world and the Hereafter. A person who has faith does not doubt the authenticity of the Message of Islam. He possesses an unshakable belief in God and His Attributes and is called mu'min (faithful). This strong faith leads him to a life of complete obedience and submission to the Will of God. Such a person is called a Muslim. Thus no person can be a true Muslim, without iman, the seed from which blossoms forth the flower and beauty of Islam. Just as one cannot grow a tree without a seed, in the same way one cannot become a Muslim without iman.

On the other hand, a person with iman but no belief in complete obedience in practice (a'mal) is not a true Muslim. He is guilty of weakness, but nevertheless remains a Muslim. The Holy Qur'an repeatedly warns us of these weaknesses and emphasises that only those who maintain goodness in their lives by acts of righteousness are true believers: "For believers are those who, when Allah is mentioned, feel a tremor in their hearts, and when they hear His Signs rehearsed, find their faith strengthened and put their trust in their Lord; who establish regular prayer, and spend freely out of the gifts We have given them for sustenance. Such in truth are the believers." (Qur'an 8: 4).

It is mentioned in Surah al -Baqarah:

"It is not righteousness that you turn your faces towards East or West; but it is righteousness to believe in Allah, and the Last Day, and the angels, and the Book, and the Messengers; to spend of your sustenance, out of love for Him, for your relations, for orphans, for the needy, for travellers, for those who ask and for the ransom of slaves; to be steadfast in prayer and practise regular charity; to fulfil the contracts you have made; and to be firm and patient in pain, suffering and adversity, and throughout all periods of panic; such are the People of Truth, the God-fearing." (Qur'an 2:177).

Iman in this verse includes practical actions *(a'mal)*. It implies verbal confession as well as good deeds. In fact, *iman* signifies verbal confession with full conviction of the Truth supported by actions. It may therefore be said that both *iman* and *a'mal* are essential qualities of a true Muslim. This is again confirmed in *Surah al-Baqarah:*

"This is a Book in which is sure guidance, without doubt, to those who fear *Allah;* who believe in the Unseen, and are steadfast in prayer, and spend out of what We have provided for them." *(Qur'an 2:2).*

The *Qur'an* here clearly states that only those with *iman* and *a'mal* can benefit from the guidance in it. It is important to note that the two qualities are always mentioned together in the Qur'an: "An Apostle, who rehearses to you the Signs of Allah containing clear explanations, that you may lead forth those who believe and do righteous deeds from the depths of darkness into light. And those who believe in Allah and work righteousness, He will admit to gardens beneath which rivers flow, to live therein forever." *(Qur'an 65:11).*

In the above verse, it is promised to lead the believers from the darkness of ignorance, that is, atheism, into light of knowledge and faith, but the promise is only for those who believe and do acts of righteousness.

The *Qur'an* brings good news to those who believe and do good deeds: "And give good news to the believers who work deeds of righteousness" *(Qur'an 17:9)*. Anyone, man or woman, who believes and submits to the Will of God is promised eternal happiness: "If any do deeds of righteousness, be they male or female and have faith, they will enter Paradise, and not the least injustice will be done to them." *(Qur'an 4:124)*.

And also they will be rightly rewarded and not rejected: "Whoever works any act of righteousness and has faith, his endeavour will not be rejected. We shall record it in his favour." *(Qur'an 21:94)*. This concept of the essential blend of *iman* and *a'mal* as a basis for a practising Muslim is further explained in the Hadith of the Holy Prophet (peace be upon him): "It is narrated by Abu Husayn that one day, while the Messenger of Allah was sitting in the company of some people, the Angel Gabriel came and asked the Messenger of Allah, "What is faith?" Allah's Messenger replied, "Faith is to believe in Allah, His Angels, His books, His Messengers and the Resurrection." Then he further asked, "What is Islam?" Allah's Messenger replied, "To worship Allah and none else, to establish prayer, to pay compulsory zakat, to fast in the month of Ramadan and to make the pilgrimage to the House." Thus *iman* embodies theoretical beliefs while *Islam* represents practical deeds.

Islam
Iman in practice is called *islam*. A believer who practises what he believes in is a true Muslim. *Islam* thus deals with all *those* deeds *(a'mal)* which are essential for the ultimate success of a believer. All good deeds are included in *ibadah* (devotion). A believer who does good is also indulging in an act of *ibadah* (devotion) to God. The acts of devotion which are considered vital for a Muslim are : *1. Salat* (prayer), 2. *Zakat* (alms giving), 3. *Sawm* (fasting), 4. *Hajj* (pilgrimage). The word *islam* means submission (to the Will of God). It means the total acceptance and implementation of the Commandments of God. *Islam* literally means peace.

Therefore the philosophy of *Islam* implies both obedience to God and peace while implementing His Commandments. It is this submission which brings the vital inner peace to individuals, and thus collectively to society and which in return guarantees real peace and lasting success.

Iman

Iman is the basis of all actions *(a'mal)* in *Islam*. *Islam* has based the foundation not only of its spirituality but also of its moral, political and social system on *iman*. *Iman* consists of belief in the five things mentioned in the following verses of the *Qur'an:* "The Messenger believes in what has been revealed to him from his Lord, as do men of faith. Each of them believes in Allah, His Angels, His Books and His Messengers." *(Qur'an 2:285).* And whoever refuses to believe in this is truly a non-believer: "O you who believe! Believe in *Allah* and His Messenger and the Scripture which He has sent to His Messenger and the Scripture which, He sent before him. Any one who denies *Allah*, His Angels, His Books, His Messengers and the Day of Judgement, has gone far, far astray. " *(Qur'an 4:136).*

The Holy Prophet defines the items of belief in the following Hadith: "I solemnly believe in *Allah*, His Angels, His Books, His Messengers and in the Day of Judgement, in the good and evil of fate and in life after death." Rejection or neglect of any one of the above components of *iman* consittutes a rejection of all. You cannot pick and choose in matters of faith; either you accept all or reject all. Once you have believed in the truthfulness of the Messenger of *Allah*, you must then accept everything he says without any reservations. Summing up, the essential components of *iman* are belief in : 1. God, 2. His Messengers, 3. His Books, 4. His Angels, and 5. the Day of Judgement.
1. Belief in God: The first component of *iman* is belief in God Who is the Sovereign, Lord and Master of the Universe,

Who knows what is hidden and what is seen. He is the end of all our desires and His Pleasure is the goal of all our actions. We abstaim from evil and adopt good ways of life in public and in private to win His Pleasure. We perform our actions with full knowledge of His Omniscence and Omnipresence. Thus all our actions and objectives are completely cleansed of impurity and selfishness. Our actions are subject to our ideas and ideas are shaped by our inner beliefs. Therefore to direct our ideas to right channels of purity and piety, it is absolutely necessary to improve and purify our beliefs. Purity of beliefs will lead to purity of action and far nobler actions will be performed through the strength of iman than we could otherwise do.

One who believes in God is expected to copy the perfect Atributes of God, or at least try to attain the highest moral qualities for the sake of his Lord. Belief in God and the knowledge of His Attributes helps to cultivate the noblest qualities in oneself and fashion one's life in virtue and purity. *Iman* makes man submit himself willingly to the Sovereignty of God and builds up a special kind of character in him which is essential for voluntary obedience of Divine Law and is the source of all unselfish and noble actions. Belief in the Oneness of God also leads to the unity and brotherhood of mankind and, as such, destroys the bonds of human slavery in all its forms.

2. Belief in the Prophet of God: Man cannot seek the pleasure of God unless he knows the likes and dislikes of God, and also cannot follow the Law of God unless he has full knowledge of it. He must therefore acquire knowledge of it. He must therefore acquire knowledge of Divine Law which is essential for his guidance. It is only Divine Guidance that can explain to him the reality of human existence and the universe; the purpose of his creation; and the principles on which he can build up strong foundation of morality, culture, civilization and social life.

Belief in prophets is essential because God's Law and His Guidance is received through them. It is through them that man has obtained detailed knowledge of the Law and ways which are prescribed for him and are liked by God. To believe in them and their teaching is to believe in God and His Teaching and *vice versa*. Thus *iman* in God's Prophets strengthens man's conviction in their truth and honesty and helps man to obey the ways and laws brought by them. Besides, Prophets are perfect examples of truthfulness, piety and nobility for men to follow.

3. Belief in God's Books: All Divine Teaching is contained in the Books of God, which are a source of Guidance for present and future generations. It is man's duty to learn, remember and spread the Guidance and Command of God as contained in His Books. Unless he believes in their truth, how can he obey them and preserve them for future generations? Belief in Divine Books in fact implies following and obeying the teaching contained in them.

4. Belief in the Angels of God: Angels are the link between man and God. All Prophets received the Divine Guidance through them. They are God's Messengers, who carry out His Commands on the earth and in the whole universe. Belief in them is a part of *iman* for they are the intermediaries between man and his Creator. Belief in Angels is belief in God and His noble and Truthful Teachings.

5. Belief in the Hereafter (Day of Judgement): Belief in the Hereafter is a corrective force. It makes man responsible for his actions in private and in public. It reminds him that he is not independent but answerable to God for all his actions on the Day of Judgement. This constant reminder makes him fully conscious and, therefore, responsible for his actions. He abstains from evil, not from fear of the human police but fear of punishment on the Day of Judgement. It is also a reminder to man that this life is a trial for a much nobler objective which is Eternal Life after death. Material life with all its

attractions is only a test for him. His real goal is the life in the Hereafter. Thus this belief in the Hereafter is the basis of goodness. It keeps man on the right course all his life.

Tawhid (Oneness of God)

The most important and fundamental teaching of Islam is belief in the Oneness of God - this is termed *Tawhid*. This is explained in the *Kalimah*, the first Article of Faith: there is no god but God; there is no one worthy of worship except God. This is the first article of Faith of the Muslim, who expresses it in these words: "There is no god but God and Muhammad is the Messenger of God."

Islam attaches great importance to this pillar of faith - concerning the Unity of God and the finality of the Prophethood. This is the foundation and bedrock of Islam. The expression of belief in this Article distinguishes a believer from a non-believer. Belief in one Supreme God is essential; knowledge of God and His Attributes is necessary for one to fashion one's life in virtue in accordance with the Divine Will. There is no room for polytheism (belief in more than one God) or atheism (belief in no God) in Islam. A true believer denounces all other kinds of deities and lowers his head in obedience to God, the Almighty. The believer, accepts and follows His Commands in word and deed .

Tawhid includes the following aspects:
(a) Concept of *Allah* (God)
The word *Allah* means, God. The *Kalimah* expresses the supremeness of God. All mortals are dependent on Him, while He is dependent on no one. No other being is worthy of worship on accout of his power save God. He is Unique and One in His Person and Attributes. The concept of *Tawhid* (Unity) was conveyed to all His Messengers, from Adam to Muhammad. All the Prophets, including Noah, Abraham, Moses and Jesus, taught the simple but absolute

concept of *Tawhid,* and finally it was taught by the last of them ,Muhammad.

The knowledge of God and His Attributes inspires and guides one on the Right Path, and removes all dubious ideas about the existence of one or many creators. It confirms God as the sole and supreme Planner, Designer, Controller and Creator of earth and the universe. For surely, such a magnificent world with infinite contrasts of colour, of light and darkness, of deep blue oceans and high green mountains and of silvery galaxies of stars with their strange unknown movements, could not have come into existence by itself or by some freak accident. Surely, the delicate discipline and balance of this unique system could only be maintained through the Grace, Knowledge and Power of the One God, *Allah.*

(b) Attributes of God
Surah al-Baqarah portrays the Glory of God in these words: *"Allah!* There is no deity but He, the Living, the Self-subsisting, Eternal. No slumber can seize Him nor sleep. His are all things in heaven and on earth. Who is there who can intercede in His presence except as He permits?

"He knows (what appears to His creatures as) before or after or behind them. Nor shall they compass anything of His Knowledge except as He wills. His throne extends over the heavens and the earth, and he feels no fatigue in guarding and preserving them. For He is the Most High, the Supreme (in Glory)." (Qur'an 2:255)

A glimpse of His Grandeur and Majesty can be seen in the following verse of the Qur'an: *"Allah* is He, then whom there is no other god: The Sovereign, the Holy One, the Source of peace and perfection, the Guardian of Faith, the Preserver of safety, the Exalted in Might, the Supreme. Glory to *Allah!* High is He above the partners they attribute to Him. He is

Allah the Creator, the Evolver, the Bestower of forms and colours. To Him belongs the most beautiful names. Whatever is in the heavens and on earth declares His praise and Glory. He is the exalted in Might, the Wise." (59:23).

God is free of weaknesses and frailties and needs no support of a friend , father or offspring: "He is *Allah,* the One and Only; *Allah,* the Eternal, Absolute; He begets not, nor is he Begotten. and there is none like Him." (Qur'an 112:1-4).

Muslims believe the Divine Attributes are synonomous only with God. These qualities are inherent only in God, and this belief is an integral part of *iman.* It is true that *Muslims* are unable to describe God because His Person is beyond human comprehension. However, the existence of God can be realised through His manifestations all round us and through His Attributes as foretold by His Messengers. Some of the more important Attributes are:

1. *al-Khaliq.* God is the Creator, the Designer and Controller of the universe. He is the Master of all.
2. *al-Qadim* and *al-Qayyum.* He is Infinite and Eternal. He has no beginning nor end. He was when there was nothing and He will be when there will be nothing.
3. *al-Aziz* and *al-Qadir.* He is All-Powerful and Omnipotent.
4. *Al-Hakim.* He is All-Wise. All His decisions are based on Supreme Wisdom and there is nothing in the universe which is futile.
5. *Al-Alim* and *al-Basir.* He is All-Knowing and All-seeing. Nothing is unknown to Him nor hidden from Him, for His Vision and Knowledge includes everything.
6. *ar-Rahim* and *ar-Rahman.* He is most Merciful and Most Gracious. His Mercy and Grace extends over all creatures beyond Measure.
7. *as-Samad.* He is the Eternal and Absolute. He is dependent on nothing, but everything is depend on Him.
8. *al-Malik.* He is the Sovereign and His Sovereignty reigns

over all the worlds. He is the undisputed Ruler who gives Commands and receives obedience.

9. *as-Subhan*. All Glory is to Him. He is the most Perfect, free from every flaw and weakness.

10. *al-Ghafur*. He is the Most Forgiving. He forgives those who repent and ask for His Forgiveness.

11. There is none like Him. He is incomparable to any person or thing.

12. He begets not, nor is He begotten. He has no son nor father.

(c) Huquq Allah

This verifies man's obligations to his Maker. Since God is the Creator and Sustainer of the universe, with all its beauty, men, as faithful and dutiful subjects, owe Him certain obligations, out of respect and reverence. These include: Worship of God *(Ibadah):* It is man's primary duty and obligation to worship God and no one else. He is reminded of this duty persistently in the Qur'an-:— "O you people! Worship your Guardian Lord, Who created you and those who came before you, that you may learn to do acts of righteousness; Who has made the earth your couch, and the heavens your canopy; and send down rain from the clouds and brought forth therewith fruits for your sustenance." (Qur'an 2:21-22).

And again in *Surah Zariya:* "I have only created jinn and men, that they may serve Me. No sustenance do I require of them, nor do I require that they should feed Me. For Allah is He Who gives sustenance to all - Lord of Power and Steadfast for ever. (Qur'an 51:56-58). Every Prophet commanded his people to worship and obey God. Prophet Noah exhorted his people to worship Allah alone: "He said, 'O my people! Worship Allah! You have no other deity but Him. Will you not fear Him?" (Qur'an 23:23).

Prophet Hud was sent to the people of 'Ad with the same Message: "To the 'Ad people, We sent Hud, one of their own brothers. He said: 'O my people! Worship *Allah;* you have no other deity but Him. Will you not fear Him?" (Qur'an 65). Prophet Salih came to the Thamud people: "To the Thamud people, We sent Salih, one of their own brothers, He said, 'O my people! Worship *Allah;* you have no other deity but Him.' " (Qur'an 7:73). Abraham (Ibrahim) said to his people, "Serve God and fear Him, that will be best for you - if you understand." (29:16). Jesus ('Isa) said to his followers: "O childern of Israel! Worship Allah, my Lord and your Lord. Whoever joins other deities with *Allah, Allah* will forbid him Paradise and the Fire will be his abode." (5:75). Messengers were sent to every nation with the same Message: "For We assuredly sent Messengers amongst every people, with the Command - Serve Allah and abstain from evil." (Qur'an 16:36).

(ii) Obedience
To obey and follow the Commandments of God is an obligation upon all *Muslims.* Obedience is also an integral part of *ibadah.* Those who claim to be *Muslims* and do not obey God are not true *Muslims.* For the believers are commanded to submit fully to the Law of *Allah* and thus enter into the fold of *Islam:* "O you who believe! Enter into *Islam* wholeheartedly; and follow not the footsteps of the evil one; for he is to you an open enemy." (Qur'an 2:208).

God advises His subjects to think before they act against Him: "Do they seek for other than the Way of *Allah,* while all creatures in the heavens and on the earth have, willingly or unwillingly, bowed to His Will?" (Qur'an 3:83). Again in Surah al-Nisa, the Lord advises: "Who can be better in religion than one who submits his whole self to *Allah,* does good and follows the way of Abraham, the true in faith?" (Qur'an 4:125). His guidance and Way is the best for all mortals; "Whoever submits his whole self to *Allah* and is a doer of good, has grasped indeed the most trustworthy hand. And with *Allah* rests the End and the Decision of all affairs." (Qur'an 31:22).

Muhammad was commanded, and through him the whole of mankind, to submit his entire life to the Will of God: "Say, I have been forbidden to invoke those whom you invoke besides *Allah,* seeing that the clear signs have come to me from my Lord; and I have been commanded to submit in *Islam* to the Lord of the Worlds." (Qur'an 40:66). For, undoubtedly, God's Guidance is the only true one: "Say, Allah's Guidance is the only guidance, and we have been directed to submit ourselves to the Lord of the Worlds." (Qur'an 6:71).

(iii) Love of God

Love for God follows naturally for obedient believers. Those who obey the Command of their Lord, gradually develop love and affection for Him. This process of gradual development of a feeling of love and affection towards God through obedience is the desire of all His faithful servants. In fact, worship of God out of love and reverence for Him is regarded by the true believers as real *ibadah,* while worship without love for Him is pointless: "Yet there are men who take for worship others besides *Allah,* as equal with Him. They love them as they should love *Allah.* But those who believe are overflowing in their love for *Allah." (Qur'an* 2:165).

There is no virtue in observing Islamic rituals without the genuine inner love for the Creator, for whose sake all these formalities are observed. For it is the love and affection behind religious devotion that is required and not only the outward rituals: "It is not righteousness that you turn your faces towards East or West, but it is righteousness to believe in *Allah* and the Last Day, and the Angels, and the Books, and the Messengers, and to spend of your wealth out of love for Him." (Qur'an 2:177). Surah al-Hajj emphasises the same principle when applied to the sacrifice of animals: "It is not their meat, nor their blood, that reaches *Allah*, it is your piety that reaches Him." (Qur'an 22:37). And again in Surah al-Baqarah: "It is no virtue if you enter your houses from the back. It is virtue if you fear *Allah*." (Qur'an 2:189).

(iv) Thanksgiving
Man is under obligation to God for all His bounties, for which he should be thankful: "It is He who brought you forth from the wombs of your mothers when you knew nothing; and He gave you hearing and sight and intelligence and love; that you may give thanks to Him." (Qur'an 16:78). And again in the same Surah: "It is He Who has made the sea subject, that you may eat thereof flesh that is fresh and tender, that you may extract therefrom ornaments to wear; and you see the ships therein that plough the waves, that you may seek thereof the bounty of Allah and that you may be grateful. " (Qur'an 16:14).

In these sublime verses, God reminds man of the favours He has bestowed upon him. Yet there are always those who are ungrateful: "It is We Who have placed you with authority on earth, and provided you therein with means for the fulfilment of your life. Small are the thanks that you give." (Qur'an 7:10). God in His infinite kindness and mercy suplies His subjects with endless bounty, to constantly remind them of His Grace and to make them realise the Truth and pay homage and thanks to Him: "But He provided a safe asylum for you, strengthened you with His aid, and gave you good things for sustenance, that you might be grateful." (Qur'an 8:26).

Gratefulness to God is always rewarded: "As a Grace from Us. Thus do We reward those who give thanks." And in Surah

Ibrahim: "And remember! Your Lord caused it to be declared publicly that if you are grateful, I will add more favours unto you, but if you show ingratitude, truly My punishment is terrible indeed." (Qur'an 14:7).

Ingratitude has many disguises: It may be a state or feeling, it may come in words or acts, or in other ways be a wilful rejection of God's Authority and a rebellion against His Law. In the end, the guilty one is always the loser, for God never loses. On gratitude, King Solomon (Sulayman) praised His Lord thus: "This is by the Grace of my Lord! To test me whether I am grateful or ungrateful! And if anyone is grateful, truly my Lord is free of all needs, Supreme in Honour." (Qur'an 27:40). And the righteous Luqman thanked his Lord: "We bestowed wisdom on Luqman; show your gratitude to Allah. Any who is grateful is so to the profit of his own soul; but if any is ungrateful, surely Allah is free of all wants, worthy of all praise." (Qur'an 31:12).

Man's goodness and gratitude has an effect only on his own character. It neither benefits God, nor does ingratitude harm Him, for He is above any need. In eulogising Him, man neither advances, nor by being ungrateful curtails, His Glory and Majesty, for these qualities are infinite in Him. By associating with Him through acts of devotion, man forwards his own moral wellbeing and piety. God loves His subjects more than parents love their offspring. He desires their betterment, but dislikes to see them destroy themselves through evil ways, for the real road to bliss is the road of obedience to the Lord. Those who are grateful and follow their Lord succeed, while those who are ungrateful and follow evil ways fail and ruin their own selves: "If you reject Allah, truly Allah has no need of you. But He does not like ingratitude from His servants. If you are grateful, He is pleased with you." (Qur'an 39:7).

(v) Seeking His Help

God is the Supreme Source of Knowledge and Mercy. Man is obliged to seek only His help under any circumstances. God is the Sustainer and Sovereign of all the Worlds; it is only He Who is capable of aiding man; and God has Himself taught man to seek His assistance: "Thee do we worship, and Thy Help do we seek." (Qur'an 1:5). All His Messengers have always sought His help in bygone days. Moses (Musa) advised his people to seek God's assistance: "Musa said to his people, 'Pray for help from God, and wait in patience, for the earth belongs to God, to give as a heritage to such of His servants as He pleases, and the end is best for the righteous." (Qur'an 7:128).

Humility and faith in God is strengthened when seeking His aid. Jacob (Yakub) prayed for help when he was in distress: "It is God alone Whose help can be sought." (Qur'an 12:18). Muhammad is taught to seek His help, "Our Lord most Gracious is the One Whose assistance should be sought against the blasphemies you (evildoers) utter." (Qur'an 21:112). The best and the right course for man is to seek His help, no matter what the problem, and the Lord will help. But if you turn away from Him, woe will strike you.

2

Angels of God

Belief in Angels is the Second Article of Faith in Islam. Muslims believe in the existence of Angels. They are invisible creatures created by God, and are neither sons nor daughters nor partners of Him. They are His servants and obey His Commands without hesitation. God transmitted His Messages to the Prophets through the Angels. Muhammad received his revelation from God through the Angel Gabriel (Jibra'il). So did many of the other Prophets before him.

God created numerous Angels. Each one is allotted a definte task. Some of them are mentioned in the Qur'an and the Hadith. They include Gabriel, Michael, Israfil, and Israel. It is essential for a Muslim to believe in the existence of Angels, who form the communication link between God and His subjects: "The Messenger believes in what has been revealed to Him from his Lord as do the men of faith. Each one of them believes in Allah, His Angels. . ." Qur'an 2:285).

Belief in the Angels is as important as belief in God, Himself. For anyone who denies the existence of Angels denies the existence of God: "Any who denies Allah, His Angels has gone far, far astray. " (Qur'an 4:136). However, there is nothing special about Angels, for God has the power to create anything He desires: "Praise be to Allah, Who created out of nothing the heavens and the earth, Who made the Angels messengers with wings." (Qur'an 35:1). They do not possess any divine power but were created to assist man in his capacity as vicegerent on earth: "And behold We said to the

Angels: 'Bow down to Adam;' and they bowed down."
(Qur'an 2:34). In a way man is superior to Angels. They are
pure creatures for they have no power and ability to sin.
Man, on the other hand, has the power and ability to disobey
God's Commands. If, in spite of this power, he obeys his
Lord out of love and reverence, he rises far above the Angels.

Books of God
The Qur'an and all the other Scriptures revealed to the
prophets before Muhammad, constitute the Third Article of
Faith in Islam. Belief in the Books of God, like belief in the
Angels, is an integral part of iman: "It is righteousness to
believe in Allah, and the Last Day, and the Angels and the
Books." (Qur'an: 2:177). God admonishes His last Prophet,
Muhammad, and thus the whole of mankind, to believe in the
Qur'an and the earlier Scriptures and not to doubt their
authenticity: "Say, We believe in Allah, and what has been
revealed to us and what was revealed to Abraham, Ishmael,
Isaac, Jacob and the Tribes; and in the Books given to Moses,
Jesus and the Prophets from their Lord. We make no
distinction between one and another, and to Allah do we
submit our will." (Qur'an 3:84).

To Prophet Abraham was revealed the Mushaf; to David the
Zabur (Psalms); to Moses the Tawrat (Torah) the Old
Testament; and to Jesus the Injil (New Testament). Since the
names of other religious Books have not been mentioned, we
cannot speculate on them. None of the revealed Books,
except the Qur'an, exists in its original form today. The
Mushaf of Abraham was lost by his people. Some of the
Books were changed and modified, such as the Books of
Moses and Jesus. God's words have been blended with those
of man; thus it is difficult to establish the authenticity of
various parts of these Books.

God reminds the people of the Books, the Jews and the Christians, not to alter His Message and to hide the Truth: "You people of the Book! Why do you clothe the Truth with falsehood and conceal the Truth, while you have knowledge?" (Qur'an 3:71). Muslim are ordered by God to believe in the earlier Books revealed before the Qur'an because they all came from the same Source - God. Because these earlier Scriptures were destroyed and distorted, so that God's original Message was no longer available in its original and pure form, God sent the Qur'an to mankind through Muhammad and that is why Muslims now follow only the Qur'an.

The Qur'an
The Qur'an is a Divine Book which was revealed to Muhammad for the guidance of mankind: "We have not sent down the Qur'an to you to be an occassion for distress, but only as an admonition to those who fear Allah. A revelation from Him Who created the earth and heavens on high." (Qur'an 20:2-4). And in Surah Yusuf: "We have sent it down as an Arabic Qur'an in order that you may learn wisdom." (Qur'an 12:2).

Its most distinguishing features as compared to the earlier Books are:
(i)   The old Books do not exist in their original forms. The text of most of them has been lost and only their translations exist today, whereas the Qur'an exists in its original form, as revealed to prophet Muhammad (peace be upon him) nearly 1400 years ago. There is historical evidence to prove its authenticity. God has promised to protect it from all kinds of peril at all times: "We have, without doubt, sent down the Message; and We certainly guard it (from corruption)". (Qur'an 15:9). God has preserved the purity of its text through centuries, and it will remain uncorrupted for ever for

He has Himself undertaken the task of protecting the purity of the Qur'an: "Move not your tongue concerning the Qur'an to make haste therewith. It is for Us to collect it and to promulgate it." (Qur'an 75:16-17). The Prophet Muhammad is urged in this verse not to hasten in learning the Qur'an for God would preserve it. Muslims have preserved it through memorising and copying it. People who memorise the Qur'an are called hafiz. Every year during the fasting month of Ramadan, the Qur'an is read in its entirety in mosques all over the world. Today there exist copies of the Qur'an dating back to the earliest Islamic times. The Qur'an, which was copied during the Caliphate of Uthman, still exists in the Library of Istanbul in Turkey.

(ii) The old Books consist of mixture of Divine Words and words of man. The Qur'an is free from such adulteration. Even the deadliest enemies of Islam admit the purity of the Qur'anic text.

(iii) There is no historical evidence to prove the authenticity of the Old Books, whereas there is ample proof about the authenticity of the Qur'anic text and even of the places and the occasions when they were revealed.

(iv) The languages of the old Books have been dead long ago. Even if the Books were in existence in their original forms, it would be virtually impossible to correctly comprehend and interpret them today. Arabic, the language of the Qur'an is a living one. It is spoken by millions all over the Arab world, understood by millions all over the world and is studied and taught in most of the world's foremost educational institutions. Today, it is also recognised as major language by the United Nations.

(v) The old Books were revealed by God to particular nations and people at a relevant time in history, but the Qur'an was revealed for the entire human race: "We sent Noah to his people with a mission: 'I have come to you with a clear warning - that you may obey none but Allah.' " (Qur'an 11:25-26).

Prophet Hud was sent to his people: "To the 'Ad people, We sent Hud, one of their own brethren. He said, "O my people! Serve Allah. You have no other deity but Allah'." (Qur'an 11:50). Moses was sent to deliver the people of Israel from the bondage of the Pharaohs and to guide them to the Way of God: "We gave Moses the Book, and made it a Guide to the children of Israel." (Qur'an 17:2). And Jesus was sent to gather the lost children of Israel and to guide them on the Right Path again: "And remember, Jesus, the son of Mary (Maryam), said, 'O children of Israel! I am the Messenger of God sent to you, confirming the Law which came before me.'" (Qur'an 61:6).

The Qur'an addresses all people, of all ages, irrespective of race and colour: "We have explained in detail in this Qur'an, for the benefit of mankind, every kind of similitude. But man is, in most things,contentious. And what is there to keep men back from believing, now that Guidance has come to them?" (Qur'an 18:54-55). It is an admonition and Guide for those who are not obstinate, but willing to accept and follow the Truth: "We have put forth for men, in this Qur'an, every kind of parable, in order that they may receive admonition." (Qur'an 39:27).

(vi) All the old Books contained Codes of Morality and of justice but none was comprehensive enough to contain a complete Code covering every aspect of human life. The Qur'an, on the other hand, provides the perfect Code for every branch of human activity so that people with wisdom can benefit from it: "A Book, whereof the verses are explained in detail, a Qur'an in Arabic, for people who understand." (Qur'an 41:3). A perfect Guidance, it also teaches unsurpassed principles of morality: "Ramadan is the month in which was sent down the Qur'an, as a guide to mankind, also clear Signs for guidance and judgement between right and wrong." (Qur'an 2:185).

God sent down His various Books from time to time as guidance. Now he has sent down the Qur'an so that men may proclaim His favours and praise Him: "But solemnly proclaim Allah's favours to you, and the fact that he sent you down the Book and Wisdom for your instruction." (Qur'an 2:231). The Qur'an confirms the Truth revealed by the previous Books: "It is He Who sent down to you in truth, the Book, confirming what went before it; and He sent down the *Tawrat* and the *Injil* before this, as a guide to mankind, and He sent down the criterion of judgement between right and wrong." (Qur'an 3:3). God's Message has now been completed with coming of the Qur'an, and those who wish to be guided by it should follow it: "This day I have perfected your religion for you, completed My favours upon you, and have chosen for you Islam as your religion." (Qur'an 5:4).

The Qur'an is the last and the most perfect Book of Allah. Its Message is real and practical for it comprehends all human actions. It explains the *Tawhid* doctrine effectively. It tells us how to live a virtuous life; how to conduct ourselves in public or at home; how to treat parents, relations, friends, strangers, the poor and orphans; it instructs us about economics and about our social, educational and political needs. It deals with internal and foreign affairs, in peacetime and during war. It provides advice in matters concerning marriage, divorce, birth and death, property, inheritance, buying and selling, trade and commerce, civil and criminal law and many other practical matters. In short, it is a Book of complete guidance covering life in general.

Some outstanding functions of the Qur'an include:
1. Guidance
The primary function of the Qur'an is to guide people on the Right Path: "And We have sent down to you the Book explaining all things as a Guide, a Mercy and Glad Tidings to Muslims." (Qur'an 16:89).

The Qur'anic revelation is universal; but only the righteous ones will take heed of it: "Surely, this Qur'an guides to that which is most right." (Qur'an 17:9). And the God-fearing ones: "This is the Book; in it is Guidance sure, without doubt, to those who fear Allah." (Qur'an 2:2).

2. Nur (Light)

It is the Divine Light of God which shows the clear path; the right from the wrong, the true from the false: "There has come to you from Allah a new light and a manifest Book." (Qur'an 5:17). And again in Surah Tagabun: "Believe, therefore, in Allah and His Messenger; and in the Light which We have sent down." (Qur'an 64:8).

3. Leading from Darkness to Light

The Qur'an leads people out of the ignorance of darkness and evil into the Light of goodness and piety: "A Book which We have revealed unto you, in order that you might lead mankind out of the depths of darkness into light - by the leave of their Lord." (Qur'an 14:1). This Divine Light offers a ray of hope to those who have lost their way in the wilderness of darkness: "He is the One Who sends to His servants manifest signs, that He may lead you from the depths of darkness into Light." (Qur'an 57:9).

4. Admonition

The Qur'an admonishes those who believe in God and fear Him: "We have sent down this Qur'an to you as an admonition to those who fear Allah." (Qur'an 20:2-3). Its admonition is plain and simple to understand: "And We have made this Qur'an easy to understand and remember; then is there any that will receive admonition?" (Qur'an 54:17). Thus there is no excuse for anyone to fail to accept the Divine Admonition.

5. Wisdom

The Qur'an contains unsurpassable wisdom and knowledge: "Yasin, by the Qur'an full of Wisdom." (Qur'an 36:1-2). The wisdom of the Qur'an can never mislead nor misguide: "For Allah has sent down to you the Book and Wisdom and you what you knew not." (Qur'an 4:113). Muhammad (peace be upon him) was taught the wisdom of the Qur'an, so that he in turn could divulge it to the rest of mankind.

6. Furqan (Criterion)

The Qur'an provides guidance on judgement and justice: "Ramadan is the month in which was sent down the Qur'an, as a guide to mankind, also clear Signs for guidance and judgement between right and wrong." (Qur'an 2:185). It is undoubtedly a manifest criterion between truth and falsehood: "It is He Who sent down to you, in truth, the Book as a guide to mankind, and He sent down the Criterion of judgement between right and wrong." (Qur'an 3:3).

7. Appeals to Reason

The Qur'an appeals to the inner reason of man to accept its Message: "We have sent it down as an Arabic Qur'an, in order that you may think, if you have wisdom." (Qur'an 12:2). Man is cautioned constantly to study and understand its Message: "We have revealed to you, O men, a Book in which is a Message for you. Will you not then understand?" (Qur'an 21:10).

8. Mercy

God promises mercy to those who follow the guidance of the Qur'an: "And this is a Book which We have revealed as a blessing; so follow it and be righteous, that you may receive Mercy. (Qur'an 6:155). This is the only hope for the spiritual future of man, a cure for the lost and hurt souls, a guide for the evil and misled ones, and a joy for those who repent." We sent down the Qur'an that which is a healing and a Mercy to those who believe." (Qur'an 17:82).

9. A Guard against Evil

The Qur'an develops fear of God, and reverence and love for Him; thus it guards those against evil: "It is a Qur'an in Arabic without any crookedness therein, in order that they may guard against evil." (Qur'an 39:28). A true believer is shielded by the powerful cover of the Qur'an against evil and wicked ways: "Thus does Allah make His Signs clear to men, that they learn self-restraint (and guard themselves against evil)." (Qur'an 2:187).

10. A Clear Explanation

Clarity is a distinguishing feature of the Qur'an: "This is a Book with verses basic or fundamental (of established meaning), further explained in detail— from One Who is Wise and Well-acquainted with all things." (Qur'an 11:1). The details of life are covered precisely: "And We have sent down to you the Book explaining all things." (Qur'an 16:89). Problems of life are explained from all points of view and by different ways, so as to elucidate its meaning to any layman: "We have explained things in various ways in this Qur'an, in order that they may receive admonition, but it only increases their flight from the Truth." (Qur'an 17:41). Divine Messages, no matter how simple, are always ignored and rejected by those who have strayed from their God.

11. Taqwa and Remembrance of God

Taqwa refers to the inner fear man must have for his Creator. This profound fear centralises the concept of God and His remembrance in the mind of the believer: "Thus We have sent this down — an Arabic Qur'an — and explained therein in detail some of the warnings, in order that they may fear Allah, or that it may cause their rememberance of Him." (Qur'an 20:113). God has clarified His Message aptly in the Qur'an for man to attain taqwa: "Thus does God make clear His Message to men, that they may fear Him." (Qur'an 187).

12. Good News

Those who are believers receive good news of the rewards due on the Day of Judgement: "We have sent down to you the Book explaining all things, a guide, a Mercy and good news to Muslims." (Qur'an 16:89). And again in Surah al-Naml: "These are verses of the Qur'an - a Book that makes things clear; a guide, a good news for believers." (Qur'an 27:1-2).

13. Warning to non-Believers

The Qur'an gives warning of severe punishment to those who reject its Message: "And this is a Book which We have sent down, bringing blessings (for believers) and confirming revelations which came before it, that you may warn the people of the mother of cities and all around her of the evil fate of those who reject it." (Qur'an 6:92). And in Surah al- Shura: "Thus We revealed to you an Arabic Qur'an, that you may warn the people of the mother of cities and all around her - and warn of the Day of Gathering, of which there is no doubt, when some will be in gardens for accepting the truth, and some in the blazing fire for rejecting it." (Qur'an 42:7).

14. Establishment of Justice

A vital function of the Qur'an is to guide in the establishment of balanced system of justice and equality: "We have sent down to you the Book in Truth, that you might judge between men, as guided by Allah." (Qur'an 4:105). Attempts will be made to defeat the system of justice. The Qur'an, therefore, warns the righteous to be on guard against such people, and exhorts them always to seek the help of God for protection: "It is God Who has sent down the Book in Truth, and the balance to judge between right and wrong." (Qur'an 42:17). Thus the Qur'an, being the last of the Revealed Books, provides the most comprehensive Code of Justice.

3

Messengers of God *(Risalat)*

Another vital aspect of the Islamic Creed is the belief in the Prophets of God. They range from Adam, the first human Messenger, to Muhammad, the last. Others include Noah, Abraham, Moses, David, Solomon and Jesus (peace be upon them all). All brought the same Message — Islam. God sent His Prophets to all nations in all ages before the advent of Muhammad. They were all men of enormous piety and virtue. They always practised what they preached, truly modelling themselves on the guidance of their Lord.

God mentions Abraham, a man of high calibre and noble character, and an example to all mankind: "There is, for you, an excellent example to follow in Ibrahim and those with him." (Qur'an 60:4). Also, he was a man of great faith and courage. He submitted his whole life to the Will of God, and sacrificed everything for His pleasure, almost including his son Ismael. His example is outstanding: "There was indeed in them an excellent example for you to follow — for those whose hope is in God, and in the Last Day." (Qur'an 60:6).

It is an example for those who believe and do righteous deeds. Any man who ignores the validity of this example and its message is surely the sole loser. In Muhammad, surely there is another glowing example of piety and devotion to God: "You have indeed in the Messenger of God a beautiful pattern of conduct for anyone whose hope is in God and the Final Day, and who engages much in the praise of God." (Qur'an 33:21).

Follow the steps of Muhammad, for his conduct was honest and brilliant: "And you are of an exalted standard of character." It may be remembered that equal belief in each respective Prophet is necessary, for there is no distinction between them: "Say you, We believe in Allah and the revelation given to us, and to Abraham, Ismael, Isaac, Jacob and the Tribes, and that given to Moses and Jesus, and that given to all other Messengers from their Lord. We do not differentiate between them and we bow to Allah in utter submission." (Qur'an 2:136). Every Muslim should study and recognise a Messenger of God, after verifying the truthfulness of his status, believe in him and in his teachings, and follow and obey him. This is the right approach and the way to Success and prosperity in both the worlds.

Prophethood — its Nature and Need

God has provided man with everything on earth to meet his physical and material needs. All the necessities of life including water, air, heat, light, etc. are freely available everywhere on earth. Vast quantities of natural resources are hidden in the earth, all awaiting their acquisition by man. He has but to look and make an effort in order to get them. God has also created man with vast ability and diverse capabilities in his struggle for survival. Because of his endless wants, God has blessed him with a passion for scientific curiosity, mathematical keenness, literary observation, and commercial intelligence. Thus man is equipped aptly to exploit the earth to meet his ever-increasing and insatiable needs in rapidly changing world.

There are experts in the fields of law and politics, finance and economics, engineering and mechanics, science and mathematics, administration and technical skill, technology and statistics — all trying hard to help man, in his earthly needs. But there are no mortals who can lead man to his eternal success and salvation, who can uncover all the secrets of nature and the origin of life, who can explain the meaning and existence of life, and the real values and end of life.

These are very difficult questions to answer but the answers are vital to building the foundations of a stable and healthy society. No reasonable person would ever believe that God, Who had made provisions even for the very ordinary and simple material needs of man, could have ignored his most important spiritual and moral need. But God in His Infinite Wisdom has not ignored this dire need. He has revealed through His Messengers the answers to all our needs. They were given knowledge of the purpose of human creation, the aim of life, and the laws of morality. They were shown the way of righteousness and prosperity in this life and the Hereafter. In other words, they were the experts in spiritual and moral matters just as the scientists, mathematicians, engineers, etc. are experts in physical matters. Messengers were sent to all nations to guide them on the right path: "Nor did We send before you as Messengers any but men, whom We did inspire, — living in human habitation." (Qur'an 12:109).

God sent men as His Messengers to introduce Him to His people. All the prophets taught the vital concept of Tawhid. They preached justice, truth and peity and talked about virtue, honesty and politeness. They spoke about individual accountability on the Day of Judgement and warned of the consequences for those who strayed from the fold of God: "The promise of Allah is true and sure; it is He Who begins the process of creation, and repeats it, that He may reward with justice those who believe and work righteousness; but those who reject Him will have draughts of boiling fluids and a grievous penalty, because they rejected Him." (Qur'an 10:4). And in Surah al-rum: "Those who reject Faith will suffer from that rejection; and those who work righteousness will spread their couch of repose for themselves in Paradise." "That He may reward those who believe and work righteous deeds out of His Bounty. For He loves not those who reject Faith." (Qur'an 30:44-45).

The fact that all the basic Messages of the prophets were identical, inspite of the vast time lapse, gives a clear indication that the source of the knowledge of the Prophets was the same, namely, God. God also provided man with the necessary tools for his moral and spiritual upkeep, uplift and enrichment, so that he might not complain on the Day of judgement of lack of adequate supply of the necessities of life. Therefore the mission of the Messengers was to educate and arm the physical and spiritual aspects of man on earth. If man fails, in spite of all this guidance, he has only himself to blame:"Messengers who gave good news as well as warning, that mankind, after the coming of the Messengers, should have no plea against Allah. For Allah is Exalted in Power, Wise." (Qur'an 4:165).

History of Prophethood

According to the Qur'an, man began his life on earth with full knowledge of tawhid. The first man — Adam — was also the first Messenger of God on earth. All mankind has descended from Adam and his wife, Eve (Hawa). Adam and his descendants started life with complete Guidance from the Lord. They were taught the rules of conduct and the codes of morality. They lived honest and righteous lives in the light of Revelation from God: "And He taught Adam the essential knowledge of everything; then He placed them before the Angels." (Qur'an 2:31). Adam was equipped with knowledge enough for his survival: "He Who taught the use of the pen taught man that which he knew not." (Qur'an 96:4-5).

Man was taught the use of the pen in his very first appearance on earth. He was given the knowledge of Tawhid and the principles of right and wrong, to implement them himself and spread them to his fellow men. Adam's descendants started off very well, but gradually strayed from the path of righteousness and justice. They began to adopt evil and wrong ways: "After them succeeded an evil generation; they inherited the Book, but they chose for themselves the vanities of this world." (Qur'an 7:169). And again in Surah Maryam: "But after them there followed a posterity who missed prayers and followed after lusts. Soon then, they will face destruction." (Qur'an 19:59).

God raised many Messengers from amongst the descendants of Adam to reform them. Many listened but many also rejected the call and followed the steps of the devil: "Mankind was one single nation, and Allah sent Messengers with good news and warnings; and with them He sent the Book in Truth, to judge between people in matters wherein they differed. But the people of the Book, after clear signs had come to them, did not differ among themselves except in selfish contumacy." (Qur'an 2:213).

God raised His Messengers among different people in all ages for human guidance: "To every people was sent a Messenger; when their Messenger comes before them, (on the Day of Judgement), their affairs will be judged between them with justice, and they will not be wronged." (Qur'an 10:47). Those who heed the advice of the Prophets will be rewarded on the Day of Judgement. Those who reject it will suffer the consequences. After the death of each Messenger, their followers gradually altered and aduterated their Messages and teachings, and people were lost to evil ways: "Then after him We sent many Messengers to their peoples. They brought them clear Signs, but they would not believe what they had already rejected before hand." (Qur'an 10:74). And again in Surah al-Nahl: "For We assuredly sent amongst every people a Messenger, with the Command, 'Serve Allah, and avoid evil.'Of the people, some were those whom Allah guided, and some were those who went astray." (Qur'an 16:36). God thus kept His promise and sent many Messengers to guide the people from the fetters of darkness into the light of glory of Islam: "The religion before Allah is Islam. Nor did the people people of the Book differ except through envy of each other, after knowledge had come to them." (Qur'an 3:19).

This Guidance was given to all the Prophets: "That was the reasoning about Us, which We gave to Abraham. We gave him Isaac and Jacob; all three We guided; and before him We guided Noah, and among his progeny, David, Solomon, Job, Joseph, Moses and Aaron and Zachariah and John and Jesus and Elias and Ismael and Elisha and Jonas and Lot. To them and to their fathers, and progeny and brethren: "We chose them and We guided them to a straight way — This is the Guidance of Allah: He gives that guidance to whom He pleases." (Qur'an 6:83-88). And constantly God's Messengers reminded their people to follow the Path of the Lord: "And We sent Noah and Abraham, and established in their line Prophethood and Revelation. Some of their people followed Right Guidance, but many of them became rebellious evildoers. Then, in their wake, We followed them with others of Our Messengers: We sent after them Jesus the son of Mary and gave him the Gospel." (Qur'an 57:26-27).

Although some followed the way of God, there were some who strayed away. But the Eternal Law of God, that good will prosper and evil will perish, in spite of its rejection by many, remains true to this day. And God continued to send His Messengers: "We have sent you Revelation (O Muhammad, the Last Messenger) as We sent it to Noah and the Messengers after him. We sent Revelation to Abraham, Ismael, Isaac, Jacob and the Tribes, Jesus, Job, Jonah, Aaron and Solomon, and to David We gave the Psalms . . . . Messengers who gave good news as well as warning that mankind, after the coming of the Messengers, should have no plea against Allah." (Qur'an 4: 163 and 165).

There is no excuse at all for any one who goes astray, for God's Prophets conveyed their Message clearly and simply : "O assembly of Jinn and men! Did there not come unto you Messengers from amongst you, setting forth unto you My Signs, and warning you of the meeting of this Day of yours?' They will say: 'We bear witness against ourselves.' It was the life of this world that deceived them. (The Messengers were sent) thus, for your Lord would not destroy for their wrongdoings men's cities whilst their occupants were unwarned." (Qur'an 6: 130-131).

In Surah al-Ma'idah, the people of the Book are reminded of this eternal truth: "O People of the Book! Now has come unto you, the series of Our Messengers, lest you should say: 'There came unto us no bringer of good news and no warner against evil.' (Qur'an 5:21). Old times witnessed the earlier Prophets. Modern times, when trade and industry and commerce are rapidly spreading, from East to West and North to South, and distances are closing owing to rapid progress in the means of transportation and communication, witnessed the coming of Muhammad in Arabic, to deliver the last Message of God to His people: "We have truly sent you as a witness, as a bringer of Good news, and as warner; in order that you, O men, may believe in Allah and His Messenger, that you may aid and honour him, and clebrate His praises morning and evening." (Qur'an 48: 8-9).

Status of the Messengers
God appointed His Prophets to undertake their Missions on earth to guide the people: "We sent not a Messenger except to teach in the language of his own people, in order to make things clear to them." (Qur'an 14: 4-5).

Again in Surah al-Anbiyah: "Before you also the Messengers
We sent were men, to whom We granted Revelation." (Qur'an
(Qur'an 21:7). and in Surah al-An-am: "We sent the
Messengers only to give Good News and to warn; so those
who believe and mend their ways — upon them shall be no
fear, nor shall they grieve. " (Qur'an 6:48).

Prophets had the proper authority and a clear mandate from
God. They executed this Message aptly and very often at the
risk of their own lives. They risked their social prestige and
wealth for their Divine Mission, but never hesitated nor tried
to adulterate or change the original Message of their Mission.
Prophets were assigned the duty of proclaiming good news to
the believers and warning to the unbelievers who rejected
their Message and went astray. All the Prophets honoured
their Missions, from Noah to Muhammad: "We sent Noah to
his people. He said, 'O people. Worship Allah. You have no
other diety but Him. I fear for you the punishment of a
dreadful Day!' " Noah fulfilled his Mission, although many
ignored his advice. "Noah said: 'I but fulfil toward you the
duties of my Lord's Mission; sincere is my advice to you,
and I know from Allah something that you know not.' "
(Qur'an 7:59-62).

And in Surah al-Shu'ara: "Behold, their brother Noah said to
them, 'Will you not fear Allah? I am to you a Messenger
worthy of all trust. So fear Allah and obey me." (Qur'an 26:
106-108). Prophet Hud came for the same reason: "Behold,
their brother Hud said to them, 'Will you not fear Allah? I
am to you a Messenger worthy of all trust. So fear Allah and
obey me. No reward do I ask of you for it; my reward is only
from the Lord of the Worlds.' " (Qur'an 26: 124-127). The
people of the Thamud reveived Salih: "Behold, their brother
Salih said to them, "Will you not fear Allah? I am to you a
Messenger Worthy of all trust. So fear Allah and obey me.' "
(Qur'an 26: 142-145).

Prophet Lot was sent to guide his people: "Behold, their brother Lot said to them, 'Will you not fear Allah? I am to you a Messenger worthy of all trust. So fear Allah and obey me.' " (Qur'an 26: 161-163). Prophet Shu'ayb came with the same Mission to his people: " 'Behold', Shu'ayb said to them, 'Will you not fear Allah? I am to you a Messenger worthy of all trust. So fear Allah and obey me.' " (Qur'an 26: 177-179). Moses was sent to Pharaoh: "And We sent Moses with Our Clear Signs and Authority, unto Pharaoh and his chiefs." (Qur'an 11: 96-97). And Jesus came with the same Mission: "Those Messengers We endowed with gifts, some above others. To one of them Allah spoke; others He raised to degree of honour; to Jesus, son of Mary, We gave clear Signs, and strengthened him with the Holy Spirit." (Qur'an 2: 253).

And the last of the Prophets, Muhammad, graced this world with the same purpose: "O mankind! The Messenger has come to you in truth from Allah; believe in him. It is best for you. But if you reject Faith, to Allah belong all things in the heavens and on earth." (Qur'an 4: 170). And again in Surah al-Nisa: "We have sent you Revelation, as We sent it to Noah and the Messengers after him. We sent Revelation to Abraham, Ishmael, Isaac, Jacob and the Tribes, to Jesus, Job, Jonah, Aaron and Solomon, and to David We gave the Psalms." (Qur'an 4: 163). It must be emphasized that "Muhammad is no more than an apostle" (Qur'an 3: 144) — a mere mortal, just like the other Prophets. He was to die as all of them did, but his message will remain to provide guidance for mankind.

They Demanded no Reward
History bears testimony that the Prophets of God were men of the highest quality — pious, honest and obedient. They were respected and revered in their own society. When God chose them for their office, they did not demand from the

people any reward for services. No matter how hard they worked, they were always aware of their Mission and their Lord. They obeyed the Command of God and struggled hard all their lives against the forces of evil and corruption. All this was to seek the pleasure of God.

Prophet Noah said to his people: "No reward do I ask of you for it. My reward is only from the Lord of the Worlds." (Qur'an 26: 109). Prophet Hud replied similarly to the 'Ad people: "No reward do I ask for it. My reward is only from the Lord of the Worlds." (Qur'an 26: 127). Prophet Salih repeated the same: "No reward do I ask of you for it. My reward is only from the Lord of the Universe." (Qur'an 26: 145). Prophet Lot spoke to his people thus: "No reward do I ask of you for it. My reward is only from the Lord of the Universe." (Qur'an 26: 164). And also Prophet Shu'ayb: "No reward do I ask of you for it. My reward is only from the Lord of the Universe." (Qur'an 26: 108).

The Divine Message was priceless and was not for the personal benefit of the Prophets. Muhammad confirmed this: "Those were the Messengers who reveived Allah's Guidance. Copy the Guidance they received. Say: 'Nor reward for this do I ask of you. This is but a Message for the nations'. " (Qur'an 6: 90). Muhammad, like those Prophets before him, told his people that his reward would be those who followed the path of truth and piety: "Say, 'No reward do I ask of you for it but this, that each one who desires may take a straight path to his Lord." (Qur'an 25: 57).

4

Functions of the Messengers

The main function of the Prophets was to introduce the doctrine of Tawhid. They were also to admonish people to realise their duties and responsibilities to God and their fellow men. Their functions are classified as:

1. Duty to God

All Prophets taught the concept of God, and exerted every effort to establish the Sovereignty of God over the people. "Further, We sent a long line of Messengers for your instructions. Now We sent Noah to his people. He said, 'O my people. Worship and obey Allah! You have no other deity but Him. Will you not fear Him.' " (Qur'an 23: 23).

"The same religion has He established for you as that which He enjoined on Noah — which We have sent by Revelation to you and that which We enjoined on Abraham, Moses and Jesus; namely, that you should remain steadfast in religion, and make no division therein. To those who worship other things than Allah, hard is the way to which you call them." (Qur'an 42: 13). "Behold! Abraham said to his father and his people, 'I do indeed clear myself of what you worship. I worship and obey only Him Who made me, and He will certainly guide me.' " (Qur'an 43: 26-27).

"Jesus said, 'O children of Israel! Worship and obey Allah, my Lord and Your Lord. Whoever joins other deities with Allah — Allah will forbid him Paradise, and the Fire will be his abode.' " (Qur'an 5: 75). And Muhammad said, "O my people! Worship and obey your Guardian — My Lord, Who created you and those who came before you, that you may have the opportunity to learn righteousness, ' " (Qur'an 2:21).

2. Duty to Fellow Men

The Prophet also emphasized the duties of man towards his fellow men. This duty they identified themselves with, in the service of Islam, and as an example to their people. Since they lived pious and honest lives, they could convert others by their standards and obedience. However, they constantly exhorted their people to follow the Path of God: "O you who believe! Enter into the fold of Islam wholeheartedly, and follow not the footsteps of the evil one, for he is to you an open enemy." (Qur'an: 2: 208).

For Islam is the only code of life which the Lord accepts: "The religion before Allah is Islam (submission to His Will). Nor did the people of the Book differ therefrom, except through envy of each other, after knowledge had come to them." (Qur'an 3: 19). Again in Surah al-Imran, "If anyone desires a religion other than Islam, never will it be accepted of him. Do they seek for other than the religion of Allah?: while all creatures in the heavens and on earth have bowed to His Will (accepted Islam). " (Qur'an 3: 83-85).Muhammad especially emphasized this point: "It is He Who has sent His Messenger with guidance and the Religion of Truth, to proclaim it over all religions." (Qur'an 48: 28). And in Surah al-Saff: "It is He Who has sent His Messenger with guidance and the Religion of Truth, that he may proclaim it over all religions." (Qur'an 61: 9).

Tawhid formed the crux of the Prophet's Mission. The practical consequence of this belief is to establish that God is the only source of value to man. Desires of God become values of man and goals of all his efforts. The man who strives to win the Pleasure of God recognizes no authority other than Him and accepts no guidance other than His. Thus Tawhid liberates man from idol-worship and hero-worship that is, from false gods and mortal heroes.

It liberates man's mind from all superstition and invites him to observe , analyse and draw conclusions from deductive reasoning for himself. This warrants a new relationship between man and nature. For God created the universe for the use of man, and man should try to harness the forces of nature to his advantage. This emancipation of man from polytheisn , and the preservation of his reason and independent judgment coupled with his acceptance of the Divine Guidance, constitutes the primary and most important function of God's Messengers.

Thus it was natural for the Prophets to encourage education. This they achieved by training chosen individuals whom they also helped to develop their characters. They fully realized that a system based on the Doctrine of Tawhid and commited to the establishment of Goodness, Truth and Justice in society can never be completely sound if organized by men of dubious and weak character. Ultimately, the feasibility and strength of such an order depends on the individuals who help to shape and nurture it.

First, the Prophets tried to nurture individual characters into the right channels. They emphasized that the objective of all human endeavour should be the Pleasure of God: "Thee do we worship and obey and Thy help do we seek." (Qur'an 1:5).

In the above verse, the emphasis is that not only should we obey God, but we should obey Him alone and seek His help only. This fundamental change in individual thinking and doing through the concept of Tawhid helps to channel human forces in the right direction. Instead of working to win vain glories for self, family or nation, he now works for the victory of Truth and Justice only for the Pleasure of God. Second, God's Prophets tried to strengthen basic human values and widen the scope of their operation. For it is easy to lose control of desire and greed on the one hand, and patience and perseverence on the other. Even basic values have a very limited and narrow field of operation in the eyes of materialists, whose main objective is the acquisition of worldly gain. There is a limit beyond which a materialist can never go in patience or perserverence. His patience will run out and he will break down. But a believer's patience and perseverence, which feeds on the Doctrine of Tawhid, will be unlimited. He will be able to bear everything for the Pleasure of God.

Again, the patience and tolerance of an unbeliever are very much limited. At times, he fights with courage and perseverence under a barrage of bullets, but at other times, he falls an easy prey to the desires of his self. He is unable to be consistent in his behaviour, whereas a believer is very consistent. Human values penetrate his whole life and constantly direct his course of actions. They prepare him to fight not only against a few hardships and dangers, but against every kind of pressure, greed or difficulty. In fact, the entire life of a believer is an example of patience and perseverence. He revels in patience, and his basic principle is that he should remain steadfast in the way of Truth and Justice under any circumstances.

The basic difference between a believer and a non-believer is that the former will thrive on Tawhid, while the latter will thrive on greed; the former works for the Pleasure of God and the latter for his personal greed. The Prophets ingrained in themselves fine qualities of Truth and Piety and wanted their followers to imitate this image of goodness, self-control and moral responsibility. They cleansed and purified themselves from the base and mean qualities of selfishness, greed and obscenity, and replaced them by self-sacrifice, truthfulness and goodness. These moral qualities account for the strength of character of the companions of Muhammad. The Prophet tried to achieve their objective of character-building in two basic ways: *by taqwa* and through *tazkiya*.

a. *Taqwa* (Godliness)

The word *taqwa* means 'Godliness' and 'devoutness'. A person who submits himself completely to the Will of God and His Law becomes His obedient servant; he is termed *'muttaqi'*. *Taqwa* can also be a condition of the heart when it is full of fear and reverence for God, so that it leads to external acts of piety and honesty. *Taqwa* is a very wide and comprehensive term and is applicable to almost every aspect of human life. Basically, it represents a feeling which is inherent but latent in man, corrective feeling that can be applied to all situations. It is like an inner warning system against moral danger and spiritual decay. Whenever anyone is straying, it puts him back on the right course; or whenever anyone is likely to outstrip the boundaries of God's Law, it warns of the danger and he retraces his steps.

The Messengers of God tried to nourish this quality among individuals through various forms of *ibadah* and through emphasis on their social obligations. They encouraged this quality in their followers through preaching the need of observing *ibadah:* "O you people! Worship and obey your Lord, Who created you and those who came before you, that you may attain *taqwa* (righteousness"). (Qur'an 2:21).

People are told to observe fasting for it will make them *muttaqi* (righteous): "O you who believe! Fasting is prescribed for you as it was prescribed for those before you, that you may attain *taqwa* (righteousness)." (Qur'an 2:183). God's Messengers taught that people should tread the Right Path to attain *taqwa*, for without sincerity, worship is useless: "It is not righteousness to turn your faces towards East or West — but it is righteousness to believe in Allah — and to be steadfast in prayer." (Qur'an 2: 177). Again, the essence of sacritice is explained: "It is not their meat nor their blood that reaches Allah; it is your *taqwa* that reaches Him." (Qur'an 22: 37).

Thus *ibadah* (or forms of *ibadah)* on its own, is not enough; it must be accompanied by pious acts *(i.e. taqwa)* which consist of complete submission to the Will and Law of God. It is an integral part of the doctrine of Islam, that *taqwa* should be attained by every Muslim: "Surely this is My Way leading straight; follow it. Follow not other paths, for they will scatter you about from His Great Path. Thus does He Command you, that you may be *muttaqi* (righteous)." (Qur'an 6: 153).

The Qur'an divides man into two thinking categories: the materially-orientated atheist and the pious believer. The former regards this life as the real and only life, in which material gains are his main criterion for determining his course of action. He recognizes no supreme authority to Whom he is accountable. The latter, however, considers worldly life as a preliminary stage to a better life in the Hereafter. He regards himself as accountable to his Lord on the Day of Judgement.

The temporal man considers moral values insignificant, while the lives of the pious revolve round the morals laid down by the Teaching of God. The former, when necessary, invents his own brand of moral code, while the latter has no need to and is not free to alter his code, which is given to him by the Prophets of God. In modern parlance, the two trends of thought are *fajur* (materialism, utilitarianism, pragmatism or opportunism — all leading to immoral ways of life) and *taqwa* (Godliness). These are diametrically opposed trends in human thought. A *fajir* people will have a *fajirin* culture, of which every aspect will be influenced by *fajur* and hence by immorality. On the other hand, a *muttaqi* people will have a permanent moral code to guide them on the Path of Truth in accordance with the Islamic way and tradition. They will not determine their policy by temporary or occasional gains, but will follow a definite unalterable objective, irrespective of material gain or loss.

Every community has a system of training for its individuals according to the nature of its objective. For example, the object of civil service in modern states is faithfully to maintain the administration of the country. Therefore all emphasis in the training of civil servants is on their faithfulness to the Government in power and on developing their administrative qualities. It is not concerned with *taqwa* or *taharat*. Any man, however corrupt or immoral in his private life, can enter civil service and achieve success for the Government is not concerned with the principle of justice or truthfulness in administration or politics.

Similarly, in military organizations, soldiers are trained to kill the enemy without being killed. They are not taught any high moral principles of life. If they obey the discipline of the army, they are good soldiers, even though they may be drunkards, adulterers or dishonest. Islam intends to establish a people whose objective is to establish justice and goodness in society. Each individual has to contribute by observing strictly the codes laid down by God, in trade, commerce, politics, sports and indeed in friendship.

In an Islamic society, the very purpose of life is fear and love of God. One has to be conscious of God's ever-present surveillance for nothing can remain hidden from His Knowledge. An individual may save himself, by various deceitful means, from the punishment of this world, but cannot escape from the punishment of God, Who knows both what is open and what is hidden. Islamic Faith and teachings prepare an individual to follow the Command of God and to obey His Law and to refrain from evil ways of life. And the ideology of Islam is strong enough to keep any willing individual, concerned for the betterment of humanity, on the path of Truth, Goodness and Justice.

Muhammad (peace be upon him) defined *taqwa* thus: "A man who is passing through a thick forest of thorny bushes tries to protect himself from the thorns by brushing off one, by moving to this side then to that side; all to guard him from the possible hurt. This caution is the quest for survival and protection from injury from the thorns is analogous with *taqwa.*" A *muttaqi* (devotee) should protect himself similarly from the thorns of life by *salah* and *taqwa. Salah* develops a kind of protection or immunization in the form of *taqwa* in a believer to guard him from evils, within and without. Islam honours only the righteous: "O mankind, We created you from a single male and a female, and make you into nations and tribes, that you may know each other. Verily the most honoured of you in the eyes of Allah is he who is the most righteous *(muttaqi)* of you." (Qur'an 49:13).

In Islam there is no distinction of colour or race. All men are equal in the eyes of God. They are all one before Him, and only the righteous and pious are honoured. Thus *taqwa* is the vital driving force in the inner strength of man. It is a great self-directive and self-corrective force which can provide drive as well as motivation to an individual for the right course of action. The Prophets of God, quite rightly, succeeded in making people observe their duty to their fellow men and in establishing a system of goodness and justive in society through the force of *taqwa*.

b. *Tazkiya* (Purification)

The second method used by the Prophets for individual character-building is *tazkiya*. The word *tazkiya* is used in a very wide sense and includes: (a) purification, (b) growth of personallity, (c) prosperity and success, and (d) moral integrity. It was through *tazkiya* that the Prophets were able to establish very strong and pious feelings in their followers. *Taqwa* protects man from the Displeasure of God,while *tazkiya* creates in him feelings of deep love and affection which make him work for the Pleasure of God. *Taqwa* keeps man within the limits of Law through fear of God, whereas *tazkiya* leads him to total submission for the Pleasure of God.

The difference between the two concepts can be better understood by an example: Government has two groups of exployees. One group of people do the duties which are assigned to them very honestly and conscientiously. They observe all rules and regulations and do not do anything which is against the wishes of the Government. They obey the command honestly but also literally. The other group consists of those sincere, faithful and dutiful people who are not exployees but well-wishers of the Government and are prepared to sacrifice everything, even their life and property, for its sake. They not only perform duties which are assigned to them, but always endeavour to find ways and means to increase the Government's efficiency and strength. The first type of people possess *taqwa* and constitue the *muttaqi* while the second type of people are termed *muhsin* (who do good for the Pleasure of God) and possess the quality of *ahsan*.

Islam enjoins its special forms of *ibadah* to train and inculcate those personal traits in men that are essential for the Islamic life. There is no doubt that consistent observance of *ibadah* help to develop a close relationship between an individual and his Lord. This gradually creates *taqwa* in him and it may be regarded as the first stage in building the character of an individual. It aids in laying the foundations of character while *tazkiya* strengthens it through development of qualities like sincerity and faithfulness. *Tazkiya* is training in character-building and development of the finer qualities of morality. It helps to overcome weaknesses in character left in the first stage: "A similar (favour have you already received) in that We have sent among you a Messenger of your own, rehearsing to you Our Signs, and purifying you, and teaching you the Scripture and Wisdom, that which you knew not." (Qur'an 2: 151).

In the above verse, three functions of a Prophet are mentioned. First, he rehearses the 'Signs of God'; second, he purifies you; third, he teaches you the Book and Wisdom. *Tazkiya* refers to the second function of purification. The Messenger cleanses the lives of people, removes every kind of evil and filth from their conduct, habits and dealings, and adorns them with high moral qualities. Thus they purified their hearts, ideas and actions of wrong and unhealthy elements and directed them into right channels. This exercise in mental culture and mental discipline gave so much personal power and strength to the individual that he was not only able to resist evil forces but was able to defeat them on all fronts very successfully and effectively. Thus character-building was the most important function of the Prophets and they achieved this objective through *taqwa* and *tazkiya*.

3. Justice and Truth

Messengers of God took great pains in training their followers and in removing the frailties in their character in order to prepare them for hard struggle against temptations and corruption. For it is easier to fight battles than to maintain a society free of corruption and decadence. It needs men of very high character who are capable of resisting all temptation. Islam abhors corruption, and Prophets of God were instructed to wipe out this evil at all costs and to establish a system of justice and goodness on earth: "We sent aforetime Our Messengers with Clear Signs and sent down with them the Book and the Balance of Right and Wrong, that men may stand forth in Justice." (Qur'an 57:25).

This verse clearly states the third objective of the Prophets, which was briefly mentioned in the previous verse; to establish justice and goodness in society. The Messengers were armed with three things: The Book of God, His Clear Signs, and the Balance of Right and Wrong *(mizan)* to establish such a system. They endeavoured to establish piety in the lives of individuals in order that Truth and justice should prevail in society. It is only Islam that can provide that guidance to a peaceful and blissful life: "It is He Who has sent Messengers with Guidance and Religion of Truth, that He may proclaim it over all religions." (Qur'an 61:9).

4. Guidance to the Right Way
Guidance was another vital function of a Prophet. There are hundreds of ideas and concepts that take man to different ways of life and it is hard to tell which one is the right one. Islam gives the only truthful guidance to overcome the ever-lasting numbers of temptations presented to human desire. And those who accept guidance will find the Right Way to prosperity and success: "And if, as is sure, there comes to you Guidance from Me, whosoever follows My Guidance, on them shall be no fear, nor shall they grieve. But those who reject Faith and reject Our Signs, they shall be companions of the Fire." (Qur'an 2: 38).

Every Messenger of God invited his people to the Right Way;

Moses did: "We did aforetime give Moses the Book of Guidance." (Qur'an 40: 53). And Muhammad followed suit: "Say, 'I but follow what is revealed to me from my Lord. This is nothing but advice from your Lord, and Guidance, and Mercy, for any one who has Faith.' " (Qur'an 7: 203).

God's Messengers tried to liberate men from the shackles of ignorance and darkness and show them the bright light of Islam: "Allah is the Protector of those who have faith; from the depths of darkness, He will lead them forth into Light. Of those who reject faith, their patrons are the devils; from Light they lead them forth into the depths of darkness." (Qur'an 2: 257). Again in Surah al-Hidid: "He is the One Who sends to His servants clear signs, that He may lead you from the depths of darkness into the Light. And surely, Allah is to you Most Kind and Most Merciful." (Qur'an 57: 9). But only the righteous, who accepted the Message of God's Messengers, benefited, while many others rejected and followed their evil ways.

5. Bringers of Good News and Warners

God sent His Messengers to spread His Word and warn those who rebel against it. No man can exuse himself by saying that he did not receive any bringer of Good News nor any warnings. Prophets of God did their duty by delivering God's Message to the People with great sincerity, enthusiasm and hardship. They also gave Good News to those who accepted, and warning to those who rejected them, in order that they might not complain of not receiving any Message of God: "O People of the Book! Now has come unto you, making things clear unto you, Our Messenger, after the break in the series of Our Messengers, lest you say, 'There came unto us no bringer of Good News and no warner from evil.' But now has come unto you a bringer of Good News and a warner from evil." (Qur'an 5: 21).

The Qur'an emphasizes that every Prophet was a bringer of Good News and warned of the consequences to evil-doers: "We sent the Messengers only to give Good News and to warn; so those who believe and mend their lives — upon them shall be no fear, nor shall they grieve. But those who reject Our Signs, them shall punishment touch, for they ceased not from transgressing." (Qur'an 6: 48-49). And no man can complain because of lack of a warning and guidance: "Messengers who gave Good News as well as warning, that mankind after the coming of the Messengers, should have no plea against Allah." (Qur'an 4: 165).

5

Messengers as Ideals

It is a natural tendency for man to have an exemplary personality to idolise. This is inherent in him for either hero-worship or for mere appreciation. Every man (and woman) and every boy (and girl) of today chooses for himself (or herself) ideal to follow. Some choose their heroes from film stars; some look for their heroes from the sports personalities: perhaps a footballer, a tennis player, or a boxing champion; other, more intellectual, types find their heroes from the annals of history.

Selection of an ideal hero is a very important decision in the life of an individual, for his success or failure may depend on it. In everyday life, young people choose their heroes and then change them very often, but it does not very much affect their life. On the other hand, selection of hero for finding the right course in life is a very serious business. You cannot afford to make a mistake in this field.

Hero-worship is essentially undesirable in Islam, except when you have God as your Hero; or when you idolise His Original and Divine Message. Since the Prophets of God taught His Message and Guidance, it is vital for Muslims to revere the Messengers of God. God admonishes His servants: "There is for you an excellent example to follow in Abraham and those with him." (Qur'an 60: 4). And again in the same Surah: "There was indeed in them an excellent example for you to follow — for those whose hope is in Allah and in the Last Day." (Qur'an 60: 6).

Abraham dissociated himself from his idol worshipping parents and people. He left his home in search of righteous people in another land and submitted wholeheartedly to Islam and struggled hard to live by God's ordained ideals: "Abraham was indeed a model, devoutly obedient to Allah, and true in Faith, and he joined not partners with Allah. He showed his gratitude for the favours of Allah, Who chose him, and guided him, to a Straight way." (Qur'an 16: 120-121). And again in Surah al-Imran: "Abraham was not a Jew nor a Christian; but he was true in Faith, and bowed his will to God's and he joined not partners with Allah." (Qur'an 3:67).

Indeed, Abraham was humanity personified. For who can be better in faith and in life than a man who submits his whole self to the Will of God and follows the example of Abraham? Who can be better in religion than one who submits his whole self to Allah, does good and follows the way of Abraham, the true in Faith? For Allah did take Abraham for a friend." (Qur'an 4: 125). His sacrifice for the cause of God, in those hostile surroundings, raised him far above other human beings. He was known as 'Friend of God'. And who could be better to follow than the friend of God?

All Prophets of God revelled in a life of goodness and piety. Since records of the lives of the past Prophets have been virtually lost and the details of their teachings forgotten, it would be wrong to speculate about them. Little is known about them, except names and few isolated acts; the major part of their lifestyles and habits are indeed unknown. It is true that they were pious and exemplary for their people and their teachings are a part of our belief, but their teachings and life history are lost, we cannot effectively follow their example.

The ray of light, which liberated their folk from the fetters of ignorance and evil, has dimmed and almost vanished over the centuries. Fortunately, God has provided man with another excellent example in the Prophet Muhammad, His Last Messenger: "You have indeed in the Messenger of Allah a beautiful pattern of conduct for anyone whose hope is in Allah and the Final Day, and who engages much in the praise of Allah." (Qur'an 33: 21). And again, in Surah al-Qalam: "And you, O Messenger, standest on an exalted standard of character." (Qur'an 68: 4).

The above verse shows the calibre and standing of Muhammad's conduct. For surely, his exalted character and moral fibre is an everlasting example for mankind and for those who seek the path of justice and Eternal Life. His guidance and Message is with us in its original form and his life-example is available to us in all its rich details.

Obedience to the Messengers

Once the status of a Prophet is established, by various indications of personal acts of piety and virtue, a person must accept his Message and follow in his footsteps. To deny him is, in fact, to deny Allah, and to disobey him is disobedience of Allah. Acceptance of the Messenger makes it obligatory to obey and follow his teachings. Human understanding has its limitation; thus the need for experts and specialists. To receive full benefit in any matter, you would consult a specialist in the relevant field, such as law, medicines, science, etc. The same applies to religious matters. You need expert advice on how to solve your moral problems and how to survive the pressures of the immediate future. For this purpose, the only course open is to seek the advice of God's Prophets, then accept and follow their way to goodness and piety.

Only a Messenger of God and no one else can provide guidance in this matter. It is, therefore, absolutely essential to believe in the guidance set forth by Prophets, accept their status and follow their teachings. The Qur'an repeatedly emphasises this point: "O you who believe! Believe in Allah, and the Book which he has sent to His Messenger and the Book which He sent to those before him." (Qur'an 4: 136). And again: "We sent not a Messenger but to be obeyed, in accordance with the Will of Allah." (Qur'an 4: 64). Prophets convey the Divine Message of God. To reject them would be to reject God: "But when Our Clear Signs are recited to them, those who rest not their hope on their meeting with Us, say, 'Bring us a Qur'an (reading) other than this, or change this.' Say, 'It is not for me, of my own accord, to change it. I follow nothing but what is revealed to me; if I were to disobey my Lord I should myself fear the penalty of a Great Day (to come,' " (Qur'an 10: 15).

God reveals His Message according to his own plan. Prophets were mere instruments for its execution. They neither add nor delete anything: "Your companion is neither astray nor being misled, nor does he say anything of his own desires. It is but Revelation sent down to him by his Lord." (Qur'an 53:23). And in Surah al-Kahf: "I am but a man like yourselves, but Revelation has come to me, that your God is one God; whoever expects to meet his Lord, let him work righteousness and in the worship of his Lord hold none as a partner." (Qur'an 18:110).

It is the duty of the Messenger to convey the Message of God to the people to the best of his ability and it is the duty of the people to accept his Message and follow his teachings. For the Lord warns: "He who obeys the Messenger obeys Allah, but if any turn away, We have not sent you to watch over their evil deed." (Qur'an 4: 80).The people are free to accept or reject the Prophets. If they accept their Message, it is they who will benefit from it, and if they reject it, it is they who will suffer. "O you who believe! Obey Allah, and obey the Messenger, and if you differ in anything among yourselves, refer it to Allah and His Messenger; if you believe in Allah and the Last Day. That is best and most suitable for final determination." (Qur'an 4: 59). The humblest of the believers join the company of great men who live in the perpetual Grace of God: "All who obey Allah and the Messenger are in the company of those on whom is the Grace of Allah — of the Prophets, the Sincere (lovers of truth), the witness (who testify), and the righteous. Ah! what a beautiful fellowship." (Qur'an 4: 69).

God also appeals to people to follow the Messengers, and in return He promises forgiveness and His Mercy to them: "Say 'If you love Allah, follow me, Allah will love you and forgive you your sins.' Say 'Obey Allah and His Messenger, but if they turn back, Allah loves not those who reject Faith." (Qur'an 3:31-32).

When the Truth is known, there is absolutely no excuse for a person to refuse to believe in it and follow it. The messenger of Allah has shown the Right Way to people who had lost their way and were wandering in the dark and deep valleys of barren and dry mountains and sandy deserts with very little or no hope of finding their way. How can such people refuse to accept the guidance of an expert who knows every inch of these valleys and deserts and can with certainty lead them to their proper destination?

The duty of the Messenger is to deliver the Message of God as revealed to him. As an authoritative representative of God, he simply gives the Message to the people. He neither changes nor adds to it. It is up to the people to accept or reject, and the Prophets cannot be blamed for the downfall of any man: "The Messenger's duty is but to proclaim the Message. But

Allah Knows all that you reveal and you conceal. Say, 'Not equal are things that are bad and things that are good, even though the abundance of the bad may dazzle you, so fear Allah, O people of understanding, that you may prosper.' " (Qur'an 5: 102).

This ultimate success and prosperity is promised to those who follow the Messenger of God. They choose the Truth, despite all the temptations and distractions. It is the duty of every believer to obey the Last Messenger and accept every one of his decrees without question, for he represents God: "It is not fitting for a believer, man or woman, when a matter has been decided by Allah and His Messenger, to have any option about their decision. If anyone disobeys Allah and His Messenger, he is indeed on a clearly wrong path." (Qur'an 33: 36). The test of true Faith is practical obedience and not mere lip service to the cause of God: "But no, by your Lord, they can have no real Faith, until they make you judge in all disputes between them, and find in their hearts no resistance against your decisions, but accept them with the fullest conviction." (Qur'an 4: 65).

Finality of Prophethood

The life and teachings of a Prophet linger on long after his death. The Messengers before Muhammad have 'died' because their teachings and their messages have been altered, adulterated or lost by their followers. Of the books given to Abraham, Moses, David, Jesus and other Prophets (peace be upon them), there is not a single Book in existence in its original form. We cannot even follow the example of the earlier Messengers, because their life-histories have been adulterated. But if we judge the life and teachings of Muhammad (peace be upon him), we can say with certainty that his teachings are still alive. His Book still exists in its original form, without any alteration in its letters, arrangements, syllables, title, text, or even punctuation.

Not only does his Book exist intact, but the entire account of his life private, as well as public, is preserved with complete accuracy. His sayings and actions and even minute details of his physical appearance are very accurately recorded. We can find guidance for ourselves from his Book, the Qur'an, and seek the practical examples from his life. Therefore, there is no need of any other Messenger after Muhammad (peace be upon him), because his message and his life are well preserved to guide man.

In fact, three fundamental things necessitate the advent of a new Messenger. First, when the teachings of the previous Messengers are changed or corrupted, there is a need for a new Messenger who can purify and restore the religion to its original form. Second, when the teachings of the previous Messengers are incomplete and do not provide a complete code of life necessary for a successful and prosperous life, there is a need for a new Messenger who can amend, improve, or add something to the old teachings. Thirdly, when the old Messengers were appointed for a particular people or country and their message was only for those people and was not universal, a new Messenger was needed for other people, nations, or countries.

As explained earlier, none of these conditions exists today. The Message of the Last Messenger has been fully preserved in the Last Book, the Qur'an. It provides complete and flawless guidance to mankind. All its sources are fully intact and even the details of the life and sayings of Muhammad are recorded in the pages of history. Second, his Message contains a complete code of life for mankind and there is no need of amendment, improvement, revision or addition to it. It has been perfected and completed by God, Who Knows best what is good for His creatures for all times to come. God has chosen this perfect religion for his servants and there is no other means of guidance to His Way for them but through

Islam:"This day I have perfected your religion for you,
completed My Favours upon you and have chosen for you
Islam as your religion." (Qur'an 5: 4). And in Surah al-Imran:
"The religion before Allah is Islam (submission to His Will)."
(Qur'an 3: 19). Again in the same Surah: "If any one desires
a religion other than Islam (submission to Allah), never will it
be accepted of him; and in the hereafter, he will be in the
ranks of those who have lost all spiritual good." (Qur'an
85).

It may, however, be pointed out that the Muslims do not
claim to have a religion peculiar to themselves, because Islam
is not a sectarian or ethnic religion. Islam is a religion of
nature, representing Truth, and as Truth is One, religion is
one. All the Messengers were given the same religion of
Truth — Islam — by God. All the Books contained the same
religion but the people changed this religion of Truth and
mixed falsehoods with it and formed their own versions:
"Behold! his (Abraham's) Lord said to him, 'Bow your will
to Me.' He said, 'I bow my will to the Lord and Cherisher of
the universe.' And this was the legacy that Abraham left to
his sons, and so did Jacob. 'O my sons! Allah has chosen the
Faith for you; then die not except in the Faith of Islam.' "
(Qur'an 2: 131-132).

And in the same Surah, Muhammad is Commanded to submit
himself to the religion of Islam: "Say you, We believe in
Allah, and the Revelation given to us, and to Abraham,
Ishmael, Isaac, Jacob and the Tribes, and that given to Moses
and Jesus, and that given to all the Prophets from their Lord.
We make no difference between one and another of them;
and we bow to Allah in Islam." (Qur'an 2: 136).

To sum up, the religion of Islam has been perfected and
exists with us in the same pure and perfect form as it was
revealed to Muhammad. Therefore, there is no need for any

new Messenger. Muhammad was sent for the whole of mankind and for all those to come, and not for the Arabs alone. He was the World Messenger: "We have not sent you but as a universal Messenger to men, giving them Good News, and warning them against sin, but most men understand not." (Qur'an 34: 28). And in Surah al-A'raf: "Say, O men! I am sent unto you all, as the Messenger of Allah to Whom belongs the dominions of the heavens and the earth." (Qur'an 7: 158).

The Qur'an has made it absolutely clear that Muhammad has not come for one race, tribe or country, or a particular people living at any particular time or place. His is a Message for all mankind. It is far above the limits of time and space, which are conditional, trivial and temporary. It is to last beyond time and space. Therefore, as long as we have this Message, there is no need for any other Book or Messenger of Allah. Muhammad was the Last Messenger, the real success and prosperity of the people depends on their following the right guidance. It is therefore, for the benefit of the people that they should accept and follow this Guidance: "O Mankind! The Messenger has come to you in Truth from Allah: believe in him; it is best for you. But if you reject Faith, to Allah belongs all things in the heavens and on earth; and Allah is All-Knowing, All-Wise." (Qur'an 4: 170).

And in Surah Yunus: "Say, O you men! Now Truth has come to you from your Lord! Those who receive Guidance, do so for the good of their own souls; those who stray, do so to their own loss." (Qur'an 10: 108). Truth has come to benefit mankind; those who accept its guidance, enjoy its benefits, while others who reject it, suffer their own loss. The Truth has come with convincing evidence of its authenticity from God, so that the people may apply its recipe to cure their mental and bodily ills: "O Mankind! Surely there has come to you a convincing proof from your Lord. For We have sent unto you a Light that is manifest." (Qur'an 4: 174). And in Surah Yunus: "O Mankind! There has come to you a direction and advice from your Lord and a healing for the diseases in your heart — and for those who believe, a Guidance and a Mercy." (Qur'an 10: 57).

In Muhammad and in the Qur'an people will find good advice and right direction. The final Commandment of God, finalising the institution of Prophethood, came after the completion and perfection of the mission of the Prophets, with the advent of Muhammad (peace be upon him), in the following words: "Muhammad is not the father of any of you men, but he is a Messenger of Allah, and the seal of the Prophets." (Qur'an 33: 40).

The line of Prophethood has come to an end, with its completion and perfection, and the document is sealed; now no further addition can be made to it. Muhammad's life and teachings exist to provide guidance, aspiration and light to those who seek assistance from them. The Holy Prophet himself said that there would not be any Prophet after him. He explained the finality of his mission in these words: "My relation to the long line of the Prophets can be understood by the parable of a building. The building was most beautifully built. Everything was complete therein except the place for one brick. I have filled that place and now the building has been completed." (Bukhari and Muslim).

Now the life of Muhammad (peace be upon him), his teachings and the Qur'an, are the only source of knowledge of Allah and His Message. If anyone is looking for this knowledge and way of life and Divine Guidance, he has to accept and follow the teachings of Muhammad (peace be upon him), the Last Prophet of Allah.

6

Life after Death

Muslims believe that life continues after physical death. All life must come to a physical end one day, the Day of Judgement. "Then fear Allah, and know that you will surely be gathered unto Him." (Qur'an 2: 203). And in Surah al-Hijr: "Surely it is your Lord who will gather them together. For He is Perfect in Wisdom and Knowledge." (Qur'an 15: 25).

The records of each man and woman, concerning their ethical, social and personal achievements, are preserved and will be presented to Allah on that fateful Day. He will judge their good and bad deeds and will reward them appropriately: with the Garden of Paradise or the Fire of Hell": "But Allah will judge between them in their quarrel on the Day of Judgement." (Qur'an 2: 113). And again: "And who believe in Allah and the Last Day and work righteousness shall have their reward with their Lord; on them shall be no fear, nor shall they grieve." (Qur'an 2: 62). Again in Surah al-Imran: "As to those who reject Faith, I will punish them with terrible agony, in this world and in the Hereafter, nor will they have anyone to help. As to those who believe and work righteousness, Allah will pay them in full their reward; but Allah loves not those who do wrong." (Qur'an 3: 56-57).

Allah is fully aware of the deeds of every person: "If there be but the weight of a mustard seed, and if it were hidden in a rock, or anywhere in the heavens or on earth, Allah will bring it forth; for Allah understands the finest mysteries, and is well-acquainted with them." (Qur'an 31: 16). Every deed will be sorted out in detail on that Day: "On that Day men will proceed in companies sorted out, to be shown the deeds they had done. Then shall anyone who has done an atom's weight of good, see it. And anyone who has done an atom's weight of evil shall see it."(Qur'an 99: 6-8)

Nothing can be hidden from Allah, warns the Qur'an: "Whatever deeds you may be doing, We are Witness thereof when you are deeply engrossed therein. Nor is hidden from your Lord so much as the weight of an atom on the earth or in heaven. Aand not the least and not the greatest of these things but are recorded in a clear record." (Qur'an 10: 61). God will judge the deeds justly: "Allah is never unjust in the least degrees; if there is any good done, He doubles it, and gives from His own Presence a great reward." (Qur'an 4: 40). All human beings, from Adam and Eve, will be restored to life on the Day of Judgement, to be judged and to answer for their actions: "In that is a Sign for those who fear the panalty of the Hereafter that is a Day for which mankind will be gathered together. That will be a Day of Testimony." (Qur'an 11: 103).

Importance of this Belief

Belief in the Hereafter is a vital component of a Muslim's Iman. The very concept of God and Islam becomes meaningless, if man, who is ordained to live by a strict code, cannot be judged, rewarded or punished, by the Ordainer, in this instance, God. The very concept of goodness and godliness breaks down, for there is no incentive for betterment nor a prospective goal. The finite nature of believing in a life only on earth removes the incentive to better oneself spiritually, and encourages the exploitive nature of man. Any individual who sincerely believes in the life after death, will strive harder in this world for a better life in the next world. For the Lord can surely distinguish between the good and the evil: "Nor can goodness and evil be equal. Repel evil with what is better." (Qur'an 41: 34). And in Surah al-Maidah: "Say, not equal are things that are bad and things that are good, even though the abundance of the bad may dazzle you. So fearAllah, O you that understand; that you may prosper." (Qur'an 5: 103). And again in Surah al-Sajdah: "Is then the man who believe no better than the man who is rebellious and wicked? They are not equal. For those who believe and do righteous deeds, are gardens as hospitable homes, for their good deeds; and as to those who are rebellious and wicked, their abode will be the Fire." (Qur'an 32: 18-19).

Main Viewpoints

Many viewpoints exist about the concept of life after death. First, there are those who believe that life ends with death. Their argument is that there is no scientific proof. But mere ignorance of anything is no proof that the thing does not exist. Science, however, is absolutely silent on the matter; it neither affirms nor rejects it.

Second, there are those who believe in the transmigration of souls. They say that man bears the consequences of his actions through rebirth. If he has done good, he will be born into a higher level; if he has sinned, he will be reborn into a lower kind of creation. This concept of a transmigratory circle is hazy in that there is no indication which form existed first or who or what controls the whole circle.

The third viewpoint represents the Islamic one — the concept of life continuing after death and the Day of Judgement. According to the Prophets of Islam, all life will one day cease and the universe will be destroyed. God will evolve a better life and a superior cosmos. Man will have developed to a greater intelligence and knowledge. Examples of the rebirth process are evident in nature, where rotted organic matter, plants and trees come to life in spring after being dormant in winter. If lower creatures enjoy this Divine process why cannot man, a higher creature in the eyes of God, enjoy it too? "And Allah sends down rain from the skies, and gives therewith life to the earth after its death. Surely in this is a sign for those who listen." (Qur'an 16: 65). And in Surah al-Rum:"And among His Signs He sends down rain from the sky and with it gives life to the earth after it is dead. Surely in that are signs for those who are wise." (Qur'an 30: 24).

In the following verse, the growth and reblossoming of leaves and flowers in spring is compared with the rising of the dead from their graves on the Day of Resurrection:" It is Allah who sends forth the winds, so that they raise up the clouds, and We drive them to a land that is dead, and revive the earth therewith after its death; even so will be the Resurrection." (Qur'an 35: 9).

And on that Day also the records of each individual will be presented: "But surely over you are appointed Angels, to protect you — kind and honourable — writing down your deeds; they know and understand all that you do." (Qur'an 82: 10-12). And on that Day also the good will be rewarded and the bad will be punished: "As for the righteous, they will be in bliss; and the wicked, they will be in the Fire, which they will enter on the Day of Judgement." (Qur'an 82: 13-15).

The concept of reward and punishment is justifiable . Physical actions are subject to spysical laws. For example, a man who puts his hand in the fire will burn his hand; or a man who drinks poison will suffer or die. In the same way those who commit evil will suffer the consequences, whereas those who do good will be rewarded.

But for these consequences man has to wait for life after death. First, because actions are completed after death. Second, the full and final implications of a person's actions will be clear then. In this world, a killer may ascape punishment, a brilliant scientist may starve, while a fool and idle layabout may live in luxury; thus reward can never be complete in this world, nor for that matter punishment. The concept of Paradise and Hell fits into these facts. Thus it is essential for a Muslim to believe in the Article of Faith (the Islamic Creed) which is embodied in *Kalimah-Tayyibah:* 1) there is no god but Allah and Muhammad is His Messenger; 2) belief in the Prophets of Allah; 3) belief in all the Books of Allah; 4) belief in His Angels; and 5) in life after death.

7

Ibadah **(Acts of Devotion)**

The word *ibadah* means obedience and submission to the will of God. It includes all actions which are performed in obedience and for the pleasure of Allah, in commerce, in social life, etc. Belief in Allah makes it obligatory for a man to obey and follow the teachings of His Messengers. One cannot just believe in the Sovereignty of God, and not accept and follow His Commands. The Holy Prophet said about the integration of acts and faith: Whoever says that faith is action is in fact referring to word of God. "And this is the Paradise which you are made to inherit because of the deeds which you used to do;" (Qur'an 43: 72).

And in the Qur'an in Surah al-Hijr: "So by your Lord, We will certainly call them to account for all their deeds." (Qur'an 15: 92-93). And again in Surah al-Saffat: "Surely this is the supreme achievement. For the like of this let all work who wish to work." (Qur'an 37: 60-61). God reminds us of the rewards for those with strong faith and who have done good: "As to those who believe and work righteousness, surely We shall not suffer to perish the reward of anyone who does a single righteous deed." (Qur'an 18: 30). And again in Surah al-Ra'ad: "For those who believe and work righteousness, is every blessedness, and a beautiful place of final return." (Qur'an 13: 29). And yet again: "It is He who begins the process of creation and repeats it, that He may reward with justice those who believe and work righteousness." (Qur'an 10: 4).

A'mal (good deeds) can be classified into two categories: (1) Acts of devotion, and (2) Good deeds to men. Through acts of devotion one fulfills obligations to Allah *(Huquq Allah),* and through good deeds to men, one fulfills obligations to towards his fellow beings *(Huquq al-'Ibad).* Iman denotes acceptance of Divine Truth. *'Ibadah* helps man to act according to the Truth he believes in. *Ibadah* is the most vital duty of man towards his Maker: "I have created only jinn and men, that they may serve and worship Me." (Qur'an 51: 56). In Surah al-Tawbah: "And they have been commanded no more than this: to worship (and serve) Allah, offering Him sincere devotion, being true in faith". (Qur'an 98: 5). And again in Surah al-Nisa'a: "O Mankind! reverence (and serve) your Lord, Who created you from a single person, created, of like nature, his mate, and from them scattered countless men and women; reverence (and serve) Allah through whom you demand your mutual rights." (Qur'an 4: 1).

Ibadah demands that man mould his entire life to the pattern of Islam (complete submission to God). In order to help achieve this high and noble objective, Islam has prescribed some forms of *Ibadah.* They are:
i)   *Kalimah ash-Shahadah*
ii) *Salat* (Prayer)
iii) *Zakat* (Poor Dues)
iv) *Sawm* (Fasting)
v)   *Hajj* (Pilgrimage)
These five represent the pillars of Islam.

Kalimah ash-Shahadah

'I bear witness that there is no diety but Allah, and I bear witness that Muhammad is the Messenger of Allah.' This is the first pillar of the Islamic Faith. When one believes and declares that there is no deity but Allah *(La ilaha illallah),* he denounces all other deities and accepts the sovereignty of Allah. When he declares his belief in the second part of the *kalimah (Muhammad-ur Rasulullah)*, he confirms and accepts the prophethood of Muhammad. And with this acceptance, belief in Allah, His Messengers, His Books, His Angels, and the Last Day, becomes obligatory.

Salat (Prayer)

Salat (prayer) is the second pillar of Islam and is compulsory for every adult man and woman. It is obedience in practice and a symbol of one's Faith, in God and His Message: "And We made them leaders, guiding men by Our Command, and We told them to do good deeds and to establish regular prayer." (Qur'an 21: 73). And again: "They only are believers whose hearts are full of fear, and those who establish regular prayer." (Qur'an 8: 2-3). Believers when they are given power on earth, become humble and God-fearing and establish regular *salat:* "Those who, if We establish them in the world, observe regular prayer." (Qur'an 22: 41).

Compulsory in All Ages

All the Messengers before Muhammad were commanded to establish the institution of prayer. Adam and his decendants, Noah and Abraham, were commanded to establish prayer: "These are they on whom Allah bestowed favours, from among the Messengers, of the seed of Adam, and of those whom We carried with Noah, and of the seed of Abraham and Israel. When the Messages of the Beneficent were recited to them, they fell down in submission, weeping." (Qur'an 19: 58). Abraham settled his son, Ishmael, and his mother, Hajirah, in Mecca and prayed for them thus: "Our Lord, I have settled a part of my offspring in a valley without cultivation by the Sacred House; in order, O our Lord, that they may keep up prayer. . . Our Lord, make me keep up prayer and my offspring too." (Qur'an 14: 37-40).

Isaac and Jacob were asked to establish prayer: "We made them leaders who guided (people) by Our Command, and We revealed to them the doing of good and the keeping up of prayer." (Qur'an 21: 73). Allah exhorted the Children of Israel to obey and worship Him: "Remember that We made a solemn covenant with the Children of Israel: you shall serve none but Allah. And do good to your parents and keep up prayer." (Qur'an 2: 83). and in Surah al-Maidah: "And certainly Allah made a covenant with the Children of Israel . . and Allah said: "Surely I am with you, if you keep up prayer. prayer." (Qur'an 5: 13).

And Ishmael commanded his people to observe prayer as he did: "And mention Ishmael in the Book. Surely he was truthful in promise – and he enjoined on his people prayer." (Qur'an 19: 54-55). Luqman advised his son thus: "O my son, keep up prayer and enjoin good and forbid evil." (Qur'an 31: 17). Shuayb asked his people to worship God: "And to Midian We sent their brother Shuayb. He said: O my people, worship Allah, you have no other God but Him." (Qur'an 11: 84). When Moses went to Mount Sinai, he heard the Voice of the Lord saying: "O Moses, surely I am thy Lord . . . I am Allah, there is no deity but I, so worship Me, and keep up prayer for My Remembrance." (Qur'an 20: 11-14). Zacharia was told by the Angels of God that his prayer was accepted by Allah: "So the Angels called to him as he stood praying in the sanctuary." (Qur'an 3: 39).

When Mary was told that she had been chosen from amongst all the women of the world, she was commanded to obey God thus: "O Mary, worship thy Lord devoutly and humble thyself and bow down (in prayer) with those who bow down (in prayer)." (Qur'an 3: 43). Mary was given the good news of the birth of Jesus. She was told that he would be a Messenger of God and would perform many miracles at the command of Allah, and that he would worship and obey his

Lord: "Surely Allah is my Lord and your Lord, so obey and worship Him." (Qur'an 3: 51). Jesus told his people that he was a servant of God: "I am indeed a servant of Allah. He has given me the Book and made me a Messenger — and He has enjoined on me prayer and almsgiving as long as I live." (Qur'an 19: 30-31). God has taught man to attain the highest honour through prayer: "Thee do we worship, and Thy Help we seek." (Qur'an 1: 5).

Importance of Prayer

Prayer is vital in Islam. The Qur'an has repeatedly emphasized this point: "Establish regular prayer, and be not among those who join partners with Allah." (Qur'an 30: 31).

Abstention from Prayer weakens the spirit of piety and faith. Muhammad warned time and again of the importance of prayer and called it a pillar of religion. It would be the first thing man would be questioned about on the Day of Judgement. On his death bed, Muhammad beseeched his followers to safeguard the institution of prayer. It is so important that it cannot be neglected or abandoned even when facing an enemy. This is because the chief objective of a believer is not fighting, but to create conditions where everyone can worship and obey God without fear. The literal meaning of *salat* is to pray and ask God for His Mercy and Blessings.

Muhammad was reported by Anas to have said: that prayer was the core of *Ibadah*. According to Nawman Bin Bashir Ansari, the Holy Prophet said that prayer was *Ibadah* and then in support of this he recited the following verse of the Holy Qur'an: "And your Lord says, 'Pray to me, I will answer your (prayer). But those who are too arrogant to serve Me will surely find themselve in Hell in humiliation.'" (Qur'an 40: 60). It was also reproted by Hakim that the Holy Messenger said that the best *Ibadah* was prayer.

God advises that those who worship Him will find peace and contentment: "The heart of those who believe find rest in the remembrance of Allah; now surely in the remembrance of Allah do hearts find rest." (Qur'an 13: 28). And again: "And seek assistance through patience and prayer." (Qur'an 2: 45). The Israelites were commanded to establish prayer in the Old Testament: "Seek ye the Lord while He may be found:; call ye, upon Him while He is near." (1s. 55: 6). A similar Commandment is found in the New Testament: "Watch ye therefore and pray always, that ye may be accounted worthy to escape all these things that shall come to pass." (Luke 21: 36)).

Philosophers have always recognized the great part played by prayer in the life of man. Macdonald said: "God, Himself the One, reveals Himself to man through the Prophets and otherwise, and man, in prayer, can come directly to God. This is Muhammad's great glory. The individual soul and its God are face to face."

Muhammad experienced the manifestation of the Glory of Allah on the Night of the Miraj (ascension). He experienced great joy and contentment in communion with God; there he was given the gift of prayer and the news that if Muslims observe the instition of prayer, they will enjoy the pleasure and satisfaction of being in the company of God. Muhammad said: "Prayer is Miraj for the believers."

"The real purpose of Islam in declaring that *Ibadah* embraces the total life of man is to make Faith play a practical and effective role in reforming human life and in developing in man an attitude of dignified patience and fortitude in the face of hardships and difficulties and in creating in him the urge to strive for the prevalence of good and extirpation of evil." In prayer, man finds the surest and quickest way of obtaining moral and spiritual perfection.

Benefits of Prayer

Prayer teaches simple rules of cleanliness and spiritual purification. It encourages punctuality, self-discipline, self-control and cleanliness. It develops high moral qualities of patience, perseverance, honesty and truthfulness. It makes people God-fearing and pious. It helps people to build strong characters. It brings them closer to God. Socially, it teaches equality, fraternity, tolerance, unity and co-operation.

Physical Cleanliness

Prayer develops neat and clean habits in man. If a person prays regularly, he has to keep his body clean by ablution, for there can be no prayer without ablution. Thus a believer must wash his hands, face, arms, and feet five times a day. He must also rinse his mouth, clean his nose and ears and eyes before every prayer. *Wudu* (ablution) is essential before every prayer: "O you who believe, when you rise up for your prayer, wash your faces, and your hands up to the elbows, and wipe your heads, and (wash) your feet up to the ankles. And if you are polluted, then wash yourselves. God desires not to place you in a difficulty, but He wishes to purify you." (Qur'an 5: 7).

The above verse also makes bathing obligatory for all Muslims who have had sexual relations. "According to Abdullah bin Umar, the Holy Prophet said that no prayer was accepted without proper ablution. And Abu Hyrairah reported the Messenger of Allah as saying, "The prayer of one who has annulled his state of ceremonial purity will not be accepted until he performs ablution.' Ali reported the Messenger of Allah as saying, 'The key of prayer is purification (through ablution).' And Ibn Abbas reported the Messenger of Allah as saying, 'Ablution is necessary for one who sleeps lying down, for when he lies down his joints are relaxed!"

It is therefore absolutely necessary that proper ablution is performed before every prayer. A Muslim performs prayer five times a day, thus he will perform ablution also five times a day. How can he possibly remain unclean? This regular cleanliness gradually develops very neat habits. "According to Jabir, the Messenger of Allah said, 'The key of Paradise is prayer, and the key of prayer is being purified.'" Abu Hurairah reported the Messenger of Allah as saying, "When a Muslim, or a believer, washes his face in the course of ablution, every sin he contemplated with his eyes will come forth from his face along with the water, or with the last drop of water. "When he washes his hands, every sin they wrought will come forth from his hands with the water, or with the last drop of water; and when he washes his feet, every sin towards which his feet have walked will come out with the water, or with the last drop of water, with the result that he will come forth purified from offences."

"Abdullah as-Sunabihi reported the Messenger of Allah as saying, 'When a believer performs ablution, then rinses his mouth, sins go out from his mouth; when he snuffs up water, sins go out of his nose; when he washes his face, they go out from under his eyelashes; when he washes his hands his hands, sins go out from his fingernails;when he wipes his head, sins go out from his ears and when he washes his feet, sins go out from his toenails. Then his walking to the mosque and the prayer will provide extra blessings for him'.

"Uthman said, 'If anyone performs ablution well, his sins will come out from his body, even coming out from under his nails.' " The word sins in the above passages can also be synonymous with physical dirt. "According to Abu Hurairah, the Messenger of Allah once asked his companions, 'Do you believe that dirt can remain on a person bathing five times a day in a stream running in front of his door?' The companions replied that no dirt can remain on his body. The Messenger of Allah then remarked: 'So exactly similar is the effect of prayer offered five times a day. With the grace of Allah, it washes away all sins.' "

Ablution wipes out physical dirt while prayer wipes out spiritual dirt. In fact ablution is a preface to spiritual regeneration through the performance of prayer.

Cleaning of Teeth

Muhammad also emphasized the necessity of cleaning teeth before every prayer. According to Abu Hurairah, the Messenger of Allah said, 'Were it not that it might distress my people, I would order them to delay the evening prayer and use the toothstick before every prayer.' 'A'isha said that Muhammad did not wake after sleeping by night or by day without using the toothstick before performing ablution. She also reported Allah's Messenger as saying: 'That prayer before which the toothstick is used is seventy times more excellent than that before which it is not used.' She also reported Allah's Messenger as saying, 'The toothstick is a means of purifying the mouth and is pleasing to the Lord.'

Bathing

Muhammad made bathing on Fridays obligatory for all Muslims. Ibn Umar reported that Allah's Messenger said, 'When any of you go to Friday prayer, he should bath.' Abu Sayd reported that Allah's Messenger said: 'Bathing on Friday is obligatory for every one who has reached puberty.' According to Abu Hurairah, Allah's Messenger said, 'It is a duty of every Muslim to bathe once a week, and wash his head and body.' Bathing is also obligatory on all those who have indulged in sexual relations and on women after menstruation. This is made clear in Surah al-Nisa: "O you who believe, go not near prayer after sexual relations until you have washed yourself." (Qur'an 4: 43). The injunction regarding menstruation is: "So keep aloof from women during menstrual discharge and go not near then until they are clean. But when they have cleaned themselves approach them as Allah has commanded you. Surely Allah loves those who turn much to Him, and He loves those who purify themselves." (Qur'an 2: 222).

Clothes

Muslims must wear clean clothes and use perfume on Fridays. It is vital for one to cover his body with clean clothes before he can offer prayer. "O children of Adam, take your adornment at every time and place of prayer." (Qur'an 7: 31). And again in Surah al-Maidah: "And thy garments purify and uncleanliness shun." (Qur'an 74: 4-5). Allah praises those who revel in cleanliness. "In it are men who love to purify themselves. And Allah loves those who purify themselves." (Qur'an 9: 108).

Taharat (Purification)

Taharat entails physical and spirutual purification. As far as physical purity is concerned, Islam differs much from Western habits. When bathing, you must wash your body with clean water and not the soapy water from the tub, which is full of body dirt. When going to the toilet for bowel movement you must use clean water to wash your body, and not just paper. One who is not physically clean will find it difficult to become spiritually clean: "Surely Allah loves those who turn much to Him, and He loves those who purify themselves." (Qur'an 2: 222). And again in Surah al-Nisa: "In it are men who love to purify themselves." (Qur'an 9: 108).

Muhammad's wives served as models of virtue and purity. They were told to establish regular prayer in order that they might be purified: "God only desires to take away uncleanliness from you, O people of the Household, and to purify you thoroughly." (Qur'an 33: 33). A'isha reported that the Messenger of Allah called 'Ali, Fatima, Hassan and Hussain and put a cloth over them and prayed, 'O Allah, these are the members of my household, take away uncleanliness from them and purify them."

Abu Malik Ashairi reported that the Messenger of Allah said that purity was equal to half the Faith. Musayd Bin Sayd reported from Abdullah bin Umar that he heard the Prophet saying: "Allah does not accept prayer without purification." Imam Nawvi says that this Hadith is a clear testimony to the fact that purification is essential for prayer.

8

Personal Benefits

1. **Punctuality:** Prayer teaches strict punctuality. A Muslim has to offer his prayer five times daily at appointed times. He has to learn to be punctual at every prayer or he will be late and lose the benefit of congregational prayer. This training is constant and consistent. You cannot postpone it, partly because it must be repeated five times a day, and partly because it must be performed in congregation, at stated times. "Establish regular prayer; for the prayer is enjoined on believers at stated times." (Qur'an 4: 103).

This regular attendance at congregational prayers will make one realize the importance of time and punctuality. This punctuality if kept up will soon creep into one's regular routine in ordinary life. This punctuality in prayer has far-reaching effects on the life of an individual. He learns to be regular to do things at proper times and within fixed times.

2. **Sense of Duty and Responsibility**
Prayer develops a sense of duty and responsibility in an individual, first towards his Creator and second towards his fellowmen. An individual cannot perform his duties properly and efficiently unless he is fully conscious of his obligations to other individuals and society. An individual who does not know what his duty is and what he stands for can hardly do any duty to other individuals or society.

It is therefore absolutely necessary that an individual who is appointed to a responsible post should be given adequate training to make him conscious of his duty and responsibility. Look at the army and its strict discipline. The soldiers have to follow a strict daily routine, including physical training, regular parading, etc. The object of all this training is to develop in them a sense of duty and a habit of doing everything in a systematic way.

A soldier of Islam is always on duty. He is constantly fighting the evil forces around him. Life for him is a constant battlefield. Islam is not merely an ideology. It is probably the most comprehensive religion, and it covers every aspect of human life.Therefore, for soldier of Islam, it is twenty four hour's service without any leave, holiday or rest.

Prayer is prescribed five times a day for this very purpose of supplementing and strengtheing the spirit of duty in a Muslim. God warns those who are not prepared to obey Him, "Seek Allah's help with patience and prayer; it is indeed hard except to those who bring a lowly spirit." (Qur'an 2: 45). One who regards prayer as a burden on him is himself a testimony to the fact that he is not willing to submit himself to the Command of God. Repetance, sincere prayer and paying *zakat* reiforce their status in the Islamic fraternity: "But (even so), if they repent, establish prayer, and pay *zakat*, they are your brothers in Faith." (Qur'an 9: 11).

The Qur'an is a guidance only for those who believe in the unseen (God) and establish prayer: "This is a Book; it is guidance sure, without doubt, to those who fear Allah, who believe in the Unseen , are steadfast in prayer." (Qur'an 2: 2-3). And the quality of hypocrites is that they are heedless of their prayer." "So woe to the worshippers who are neglectful of their prayer." (Qur'an 107: 4-5). If ever they offer their prayer, they offer it very unwillingly: "When they stand up to prayer, they stand without earnestness, to be seen of men." (Qur'an 4: 142).

3. Training in Self-Discipline

Great care is taken in the development of individual personality. 'Practise what you preach' is paramount. Prayer instils self-discipline into an individual. It becomes obligatory on every individual, man or woman, at the age of twelve. And this duty is not forgotten under any circumstance except when a woman is menstruating or in confinement. Whether you are on a journey, or sick, or fighting against your enemy, you have to fulfil your obligation of prayer. If you are so ill and weak that you cannot get up, offer your prayer in a sitting position; if you cannot sit, offer it in a lying position; and if you cannot even move your arms and legs, then offer it by signs. If water is not available, do the dry ablution *(tayyammum)* instead of water ablution; if you cannot find the correct direction of the Qibla, offer your prayer in the probable direction of the Qibla.When the time for prayer has come, a Muslim is duty bound under all circumstances to offer his prayer.

This strict regularity and discipline of prayer is a unique example and wonderful program of preparing individuals for the service of good and justice in the world. For a Muslim, there is no social or religous system other than Islam. The institution of prayer helps to remove weaknesses in individual character and strengthens the wall of the Islamic community with the cement of discipline, obedience and love.

4. Character-Building

The practical success of an individual depends on his perseverance and hard work. A man of character does his work persistently and constantly. This is called strength of character. Daily prayer is a duty which is performed with strict regularity five times a day and thus perseverance and persistence are its essential requisites. The Qur'an praises this quality in the Companions of Prophet Muhammad (peace be upon him) in these words: "Those who remain steadfast to their prayer." (Qur'an 70: 23).

And Muhammad, (peace be upon him), is reported to have said, "The dearest act in the eyes of Allah is that which is done constantly, even though it be small." And obviously no act is done with such strict persistency and regularity as daily prayer. This great discipline creates quality par excellence in the character of an individual and is known as *taqwa*. This is, in fact, the soul of Islamic character.

Those who work for Islam have *taqwa* and fear of God along with the strict discipline of society. They do not only administer the affairs of the world, but also try to establish truth and justice in the land. If you look at it in this way, you will notice that there is no restraint from evil better than prayer. The Qur'an refers to this, "Establish regular prayer, for it restrains from shameful and unjust deeds." (Qur'an 29: 45). Islamic character is a prerequiste to an Islamic life and is built on the institution of prayer. This is why, since ancient times, prayer has been an indispensable part of an Islamic community.

5. Self-Control

Along with character-building, prayer also develops the power of self-control in an individual. Character-building by itself can make an individual disciplined and cultured through the training of his human ego. But if the trained ego has no practical control over the powers of body and mind, which are its instruments, then the purpose of its training, i.e. right conduct, cannot be achieved. For example, when compared to a motor car, man combines the powers both of a motor and a driver. This combination can work rightly only if the motor and its powers are under the complete control of the driver, who is also properly educated and trained and fully knows his way.

If the driver is trained but the steering, brakes and accelerator are not under his control or only partially under his control, then the driver will not drive the motor but the motor will drive him. And as the motor knows only to run and has no sense of direction, it will take the driver in any direction and may even end in a crash. In this example, the powers of body and mind and the desires of the self of an individual are like a motor and his ego like the driver. These powers are as ignorant as the motor but, unlike the latter, are alive. They have desires, emotions and objectives and always try to lead the driver.

Prayer is prescribed to discipline these wild powers and desires of the body, mind and self. It provides ample opportunities of discipline to break the strength of their powers and thereby bring them under the control of the driver. There is constant struggle between the self and the ego. For example, early in the morning, one is called to the *salat al-Fajr* (dawn prayer) when one is warm and cosy in one's bed. One does not like to get out of bed and one's self advises one to stay in bed and enjoy sleep, but one's ego reminds one of the time of the prayer. If one has had intercourse with one's wife, one has to take a bath. If it is winter and there is no hot water, one has to bathe or do ablutions with cold water. There is a struggle between the self and the ego. If one obeys one's self, one becomes its slave, but, on the other hand, if one fulfils one's obligation of prayer, one tames one's self.

The same thing is experienced at other times of prayer, at noon, afternoon, evening and at night. The self is always looking of such occasions to exploit one's weaknesses. Prayer comes on every occasion to strengthen one's willpower and to resist the temptation of the self. This battle is daily fought at different times and under different conditions and in different ways. Sometimes at home, sometimes on a journey, sometimes in summer and sometimes in winter; during rest and during work; on holidays and on business; in grief and in suffering. Thus there is a constant struggle between the demands of the self and the call for prayer. One is constantly and continually put to the test; if one obeys one's self, one is defeated and one's own servant becomes one's master. But, if one fulfils the demand of prayer, one breaks the wild force of the self.

This is why the Holy Qur'an says that the immediate and irrevocable consequences of the neglect of prayer is that man becomes a slave to the desires and sensuous pleasures of life, strays away from the right course and, thereafter, falls deeper into the valleys of ignorance and darkness. (19: 59).

6. Patience and Perseverance

Prayer develops in man such qualities as patience, endurance, contentment and perseverance, which are needed in the service of justice and goodness and, above all, are a source of strength in face of the hardships and sufferings of life. The Holy Prophet is told to be patient in face of hardships and evil forces. "Therefore be patient with what they say, and celebrate (constantly) the praises of your Lord (through prayer)" (Qur'an 20: 130). The Holy Prophet is here told to bear every kind of hardship and oppression from enemies in the service of Islam with patience and endurance. He is further asked to establish prayer to strengthen his power of patience and endurance. This is because all good men must be patient with what seems to them evil around them. That does not mean that they should sit still and do nothing to destroy evil; for the fight against evil is one of the cardinal points in

Islam. What they are told is that they must not be impatient. They must come to God through prayer so that their patience and faith may be strengthened against the forces of evil. For through prayer they get not only strength but also spiritual joy.

This is the miracle of prayer, that it gives contentment and happiness to an individual: "Bear then, with patience, all that they say, and celebrate the praises of your Lord (through prayer)." (Qur'an 50: 39). The Holy Qur'an repeatedly advises people to obtain help and strength from prayer in all their troubles. "Nay, seek God's help with patience, perseverance and prayer." (Qur'an 2: 45).

The Arabic word *sabr* has many shades of meaning. It implies (i) patience in the sense of being thorough, not hasty; (ii) preserverance, constancy, steadfastness, firmness of purpose; (iii) systematic as opposed to spasmodic or haphazard action; (iv) a cheerful attitude of resignation and understanding in sorrow, defeat or suffering, as opposed to murmuring or rebellion, but saved from mere passivity or listlessness by the element of constancy or steadfastness.

The believers are again told to seek God's help through prayr: "O you who believe. Seek help with patience, perseverance and prayer; for God is with those who patiently persevere." (Qur'an 2: 153). The believers are told here to seek God's help in hardship with patience and perseverance and disciptine themselves through self-restraint in their struggle for the cause of their ideology. And to develop their powers of patience and perseverance, they are further advised to seek help through the establishment of prayer, which has the potentialities and ingredients needed in the formation and development of the former. Allah has therefore advised the believers again and again to establish prayer in order to strengthen their power of patience and perseverance.

The word *sabr* signifies strength of will, firmness of determination and organization of the desires of the self. God wants believers to develop such qualities in themselves to defeat both internal and external forces hostile to the establishment of truth and justice in society. As it is a very hard and nerve-wrecking job, so they are advised to strengthen themselves from outside through the establishment of regular prayer. It will assist in developing and strengthening their power of resistance and restraint on the one hand, and perseverance and steadfastness on the other.

7. Efficiency

Prayer is offered regularly five times daily, no matter where you are and what you are doing. This strict regularity strengthens an individual's self-discipline. Besides, observance of prayer creates and develops in man a sense of duty. He begins to realize his duty to his Creator and his fellow-beings. He considers it his duty to do everything nicely and perfectly because God Himself is Beautiful and Perfect and Likes His creatures to create beauty and perfection in their work. This realization on their part makes them most efficient workers in the community. Whether they are doctors, scientists, technologists, politicians, businessmen, industrialists or ordinary labourers, in whatever position they may be, their efficiency and hard work are examples to their colleagues, friends and others. And this is all due to prayer.

The Qur'an admonishes those who neglect their prayer. "So woe unto worshippers who are heedness of their prayer." (107: 4-6). Again in Surah al-Nisa: "When they stand up for prayer, they stand without earnestness, to be seen of men." (4: 142). Efficiency further increases with the realization on the part of an individual of the value of time. Regularity in prayer makes one fully conscious of the true value and importance of time. A true believer therefore works hard and does not waste a single moment of his life, which he regards as being as precious as gold, or more precious. And with increase in his efficiency, the product of his labour also increases.

8. Humility

God has promised success and prosperity for those who are humble, modest and lowly in the presence of their Lord: "Indeed, the believers are successful, who humble themselves in their prayer." (Qur'an 23: 1-2). Believers who offer regular prayer become conscious of their own insignificant position before the Grandeur and Majesty of their Creator. This Makes them every humble and modest in ordinary life. The Qur'an refers to this quality of the believers in these words: "Muhammad is the Messenger of Allah; and those who are with him are strong against unbelievers but compassionate amongst each other. You will see them bow and prostrate themselves in prayer, seeking Grace from God." (48: 29).

Humility is engraved in the hearts of believers through the establishment of prayer. Their faces show in them the Grace and Light of God; they are gentle, kind and forbearing. Examples of extreme humility and gentleness are found amongst the believers in the early period of Muslim history. This quality of the believers is again mentioned in the Qur'an: "Soon will Allah produce a people whom He will love as they will love Him — lowly with the believers, mighty against the unbelievers." (5: 57). Believers who have full faith in their Lord seek His Help through patience and prayer, while the hypocrites refrain from it because of their spiritual emptiness and apathy: "And prayer, indeed, is hard except to those who bring a lowly spirit, who bear in mind the certainty that they are to meet their Lord, and that they are to return to Him." (Qur'an 2: 45-46).

9

Social Benefits

1. Social Organization and Social Discipline
No nation or community can survive without proper organization and social discipline. Individual discipline and character alone cannot achieve it. An individual cannot achieve his ideal without co-operation with those co-existing with him, that is his community. A man cannot live alone. His whole life is reliant on other members of the community in multifarious ways.

It is a duty of every Muslim to promote fraternity in his community. This is achieved by spreading the Quranic teachings and establishing the law of God in their respective communities. The good must organize themselves to fight the cunning and powerful forces of evil.

It is therefore necessary that all worshippers organize themselves into one solid block. They must unite and help each other to achieve this objective. They must have unity in word and in deed. Prayer not only helps in building individual character but also in establishing a community structure and spirit. Daily prayer keeps the flame of this spirit going. This is why prayer in congregation is obligatory. The gathering of believers in the mosque five times daily is the basis of cummunity organization of the *Millat-i-Islamia*. A slight flaw in this structure shatters the creditability of the social and community spirit of the Muslims: "Then there came after them an evil generation who neglected prayer and followed lusts; soon then they will face destruction." (Qur'an 19: 59). The Prophet Moses was commanded to organize his community on a sound footing in order to combat the well-organized and powerful forces of his enemy, the Pharaoh of Egypt, by establishing regular prayer: "We inspired Moses and his brother with this Message . . . make your dwellings into places of worship, and establish regular prayer." (Qur'an 10: 87).

The Muslim community is disciplined into one solid unity through daily prayer. A Muslim hears the call for prayer, he leaves all his engagements and goes to the mosque to offer prayer with his brothers in Islam. It is a discipline more strict than that of the army but without any coercion. It is a voluntary discipline imposed from within to win the pleasure of God. In prayer, all Muslims stand in straight rows together, the rich and the poor, the black and the white, the employer and the employee, the servant and the master, all in front of their Lord. They all stand shoulder to shoulder together prostrating to the Lord. This voluntary gathering gives the Muslim community utmost mobility for action during the day or night. It gives them unity of purpose for they all have a common ideology and objective.

2. Mosques as Community Centres

Social gatherings on various occasions are natural in the life of organized communities. Islam has rightly recognized this and has provided Muslims with ample opportunities through the establishment of daily prayer, Friday prayer, and annual prayers at the Festival of *Id*. When the Muslims assemble in the mosque, they meet other people with one common objective. This unity of feeling, in spite of race, language, colour or nationality, moulds them into one homogeneous group. And it would be true to say that the establishment of the Muslim brotherhood is the greatest social ideal of Islam and prayer helps in achieving this.

When Muslims meet together for prayer; they feel and share one another's grief and suffering. They get the opportunity to know their brethren more closely and acquaint them of their needs and problems. This fraternity promotes sincerity, honesty, willingness to help and piety amonst them.

These assemblies also help the individual members of the community to overcome their shortcomings and weaknesses. In this way, the Islamic society is able to eradicate evil forces from within the person and the community. During the time of the Prophet and afterwards of the Caliphs, whenever any important event took place, whether political or social, or any Commandment was to be announced, a call for prayer was given and all the Muslims would assemble in the *Masjid-i-Nabwi* without dalay. The institution of prayer is thus really a community centre for the Muslims.

Prayer is the cardinal institution of Islam and reflects its religious social, cultural, political and moral objectives. The mosque is the centre of all Mulim gatherings. Prayer is the binding force between the Muslims; whoever breaks this bond goes to *kufr* (a state of unbelief).

3. Mutual Help and co-operation

This regular assembly for daily prayer also provides great opportunities for co-operation. People of different social and economic status meet one another in the mosque and learn each other's problems. In Islamic tradition, they will learn and cater for the needs of those in difficulty and suffering. Thus new fields of co-operation and mutual help between the sections of the community are found in these gatherings for the benefit of all its members: "Who believe in the unseen, are steadfast in prayer and spend out of what We have provided for them." (Qur'an 2: 3).

A believer provides whatever he can to meet the needs of his less fortunate fellow-beings whom he meets in the mosque. The institution of prayer cements their personal, social and cultural relationship and gradually creates and strengthens their co-operation in the economic as well as social fields of activities. They help each other in every possible way merely to seek the pleasure of God and give perference to the needs and requirements of other Muslim brothers over their own: "But those who before them, had homes (in Medina) and had adopted the Faith, show their affection to such as came to them for refuge, and entertain no desire in their hearts, for things given to the latter, but give them preference over themselves, even though poverty was their (own lot)" (Qur'an 59: 9).

This refers to the Ansars, who accepted Islam and invited the Holy Messenger and his Companions to join them in Medina. The Hijra (migration) was possible because of their goodwill and their generous hospitality. They entertained the Prophet and all the refugees (muhajrin) who came with him. All these feelings of brotherhood, co-operation and mutual help are daily being nourished and strengthened by prayer: "Who establish regular prayer and spend freely out of the gifts We have given them for sustenance. Such in truth are the true believers" (Qur'an 8: 3-4).This verse describes the qualities of true believers. They establish prayer and give generously out of their wealth to the poor and the needy in the community.

4. Equality and Brotherhood

Prayer in congregation is a training in brotherhood, equality and fraternity. All Muslims stand in prayer before their Lord as equals. There is no distinction between the rich and the poor, the white and the black, the Arab and non-Arab; they all stand together in rows to offer their prayer to God. If a sweeper comes first, he occupies the first row, and the one who comes last, be he a Duke, or head of the state, or the richest man in the community, he stands in the last row. No one can reserve his seat in the mosque. All Muslims, including governors, princes, capitalists and labourers stand together shoulder to shoulder as one people before the One Deity, God.

This is social democracy in action. Human distinctions are levelled down to the same status in prayer. The pride of the rich and humbleness of the poor are equalized and neutralized before God. All Muslims assemble in the mosque, devoid of any nationalistic or tribal barriers. In spite of linguistic and ethnic differences, they stand together as brothers for prayer. This daily practice in social democracy and human brotherhood is unique. It builds up social unity and international brotherhood: "The believers are but a single brotherhood; so make peace and reconciliation between your two contending brothers" (Qur'an 49: 10).

5. Training in *Jihad* (Holy War)
There seems to be a close relationship between prayer and *jihad* (Holy War). Any army must possess discipline to achieve any marked battle success. For without discipline the army spirit will distintegrate: Islam offers prayer as a training for discipline even in Holy war: "When you travel through the earth, there is no blame on you if you shorten your prayer for fear the unbelievers may attack you. For the unbelievers are unto you open enemies. When you, O Messenger, are with them, and stand to lead them in prayer, let one party of them stand up with you, taking their arms with them. When they finish their prostrations, let them take their positions in the rear. And let the other party come up which has not yet prayed. And let them pray with you, taking all precautions, and bearing arms. The unbelievers wish, if you were negligent of your arms and your baggage, to assult you in a single rush" (Qur'an 4: 101-102).

Thus the congregational prayer, even in danger in face of the enemy, is not ignored or neglected but performed with the same strictness. For in Islam, war is fought not for bloodshed or plunder, but to end the aggression and persecution *(fasad)* which is raised by the unbelievers to stop the servants of God from obeying His Commandments. Prayer is the real spirit of *jihad* and this makes it *ibadah* (worship). Devoid of this spirit, it would also be *fasad* on earth.

Importance of prayer in congregations is shown in the following verse: "If you fear (an enemy), pray on foot, or riding (as may be most convenient), but when you are in security, celebrate Allah's praises in the manner he has taught you." (Qur'an 2: 239). According to this verse, when conditions on the battlefield are extremely difficult and do not permit performance of prayer in congregation, mujahidin are allowed to offer their prayer individuallly, standing, or riding, or sitting, or running, or in any other position they find more convenient. Even the direction of the *Qibla* is relaxed, which shows that prayer in congregation is maintained, if the circumstances permit, even on the battlefield. The form of prayer the Qur'an mentions here achieves the objective of prayer as well as of defence.

Prayer throws light on the great importance of defence under conditions of war. The very fact that an important institution like prayer is shortened for this reason shows the importance of defence. The *mujahidin* are urged to take all precautions when offering prayer. This achieves a moderate and beautiful balance between human effort *(aml)* and trust in God *(tawwakkul);* between bravery and wisdom. This also reflects obedience of God through obedience to His Messenger.

6. Respect for the Rights of Others
Prayer also teaches respect for other people and their rights. The believers go to the mosque regularly five times daily and

meet all types of people who gather there for prayer. They stand together shoulder to shoulder like a solid cemented structure and present a striking example of discipline, cohesion and affection. This develops in them love and respect for other people and their rights. They gradually feel for them the same kind of regards and respect as for their own brothers.Whoever comes first, occupies the first row, matter what his social or political status may be; even the poorest and the humblest of the Muslims is fully conscious of this fact. This makes them realize the importance of time as well as the rights of others.

7. Tolerance

True believers also become tolerant through the daily routine of prayer. They have to prepare for prayer, perform ablution and then join other believers in the mosque for prayer. It needs a lot of endurance to stick to this rigorous discipline every day all the year round. They meet different sorts of persons, some poor and dirty, others rich and arrogant, but they learn to greet all with an open hearts as brothers and friends. They gradually become more tolerant to other people with lower social status and holding different views from their own.

It also enables an individual to endure and tolerate the hardships and sufferings he has to undergo in his life: "Nay, seek Allah's help with patient perseverance and prayer" (Qur'an 2: 45). Thus prayer will build up their endurance for hardship on the one hand, and their spirit of tolerance towards their enemies on the other. It will also help them to restrain their fear of, and anger against, the non-believers.

8. Unity

Prayer is the strength behind unity: "The believers are but a single brotherhood, so make peace and reconciliation between your two contending brothers"(Qur'an 49: 10). The establishment of unity is the greatest social ideal of Islam. It unites men of different languages, ethnic groups, colours and nationalities. When they hear the call of the *Muezzin,* they all gather together as brothers for prayer. It is, in fact, the most vital and effective way of uniting believers into one solid block: "Muhammad is theMessenger of Allah; and those who are with him are strong against unbelievers, but compassionate amongst each other" (Qur'an 48: 29).

Prayer is a constant reminder to the believers that they are brothers in Faith and so they must remain united as one single people, otherwise they will fall into dispute and their power and unity will shatter into pieces: "And obey Allah and His Messenger; and fall into no disputes, lest you lose heart and your power depart; and be patient and perservering" (Qur'an 8: 46).

Prayer as a Spiritual Link
Prayer is a wonderful gift of God. It offers a simple way to obtain unbroken concentration *(dhyan)* for the purpose of Divine Enlightenment *(giyan).* There is no need to go to unusual lengths to achieve concentration for meditation. Prayer provides opportunities for harmonious functioning of body and mind at the right level to achieve this concentration.

All the movements of the body, from the standing position to the prostration, are the expression of total submission of the physical self before the Supreme Being. Recitation of the Divine Words in prayer help to bring the mental attitude of man in line with his physical posture. This process of the body and the mind to the Divine Will help to ignite the latent forces in man and to strengthen his spiritual relationship with God.

In a way, this spiritual awakening of man completes the third side of the triangle and thereby gurantees his moral and spiritual elevation. Complete balance between the three faculties i.e., physical, mental and spiritual, in prayer helps man to achieve communion with God. Thus prayer is a means of creating a link between the Creator and the creature. And regularity in prayer can help to maintain and strengthen this link. Strong faith in God rests on the institution of prayer, which is also responsible for the formation of Muslim national character.

Rules for Performance of Prayer

In view of the great importance of prayer, it is absolutely necessary that it is performed properly in the way it was performed and taught by Prophet Muhammad (peace be upon him). It must be performed earnestly and humbly. "Successful indeed are the believers who are humble in their prayer" (Qur'an 23: 1-2). The word *khushya* means to show humility and make entreaties before God. This state of *khushya* of the heart instils a sense of fear into man in the presence of his Lord. In fact, *khushya* in prayer refers to a state of complete humility of body and mind. This is the essence and soul of prayer. The Holy Messenger once saw a man playing with his beard while offering his prayer. He said, "Had there been *khushya* in hs heart it would have shown on his body."

There are certain rules of prayer which, on the one hand, assist humility of the heart and, on the other, keep the performance of prayer, at least in the physical sense, to a certain standard. Some of the important rules of prayer are given below:

1. Prayer must be performed with ease, comfort and calmness.
2. There must not be any movements of hands, head, eyes or legs other than necessary in the performance of *Ruku, sujud*, etc.

3. Every part of prayer must be performed properly and quietly.

4. One part of a prayer must be completed before the next part is initiated.

5. Deliberate meditation on unrelated thoughts should be avoided.

6. One should constantly endeavour to understand the meaning of the words one is reciting in prayer.

7. Every prayer must be performed at its proper time as stated in the Holy Qur'an: "Prayer indeed has been enjoined on believers at fixed times" (Qur'an 4: 103).

The words *kitab mawqut* refers to the performance of each prayer at fixed times. The times pf prayer were fixed by the Holy Messenger under Divine Guidance, and the observance of each prayer at its proper time is an essential part of it. The Holy Qur'an condemns people who are careless and do not perform their prayer properly: "So woe to the praying ones, who are unmindful of their prayer" (Qur'an 107: 4-5). The word *sahun* is very comprehensive and refers to the prayer of those people who neglect or ignore it, or abstain from it, or perform it lazily and sluggishly.

Times of Prayer

Prayer in Islam is a part of the everyday life of man. A Muslim begins and ends his day with prayer. To pray five times a day is constant reminder to man that he is a servant of God and therefore he must not forget his duties and obligations to Him. Every day in the life of a Muslim is a day of remembrance and obedience. He starts his day with the morning prayer before sunrise *(salat al-fajr)*. Thus his day begins with remembrance of God. Then he starts his work but stops for the mid-day prayer *(salat al-zuhr)*. After the prayer, he goes back to work until the afternoon, when he offers his afternoon prayer *(salat al-asr)*.

At the end of the day, he once again prays to God at the time of the sunset *(salat al-maghrib)*. And before he goes to bed, he again remembers his Lord in his night prayer *(salat al-isha)*. Thus the whole day of a Muslim is spent in work and in the remembrance of God The five times daily prayers were prescribed by God for the Muslims at the time of the *Mi'raj* (Ascension): "Establish regular prayer at the sun's decline till the darkness of the light, and the morning prayer with reading from the Qur'an" (Qur'an 17: 78).

Four prayers — *zuhr, asr, maghrib* and *isha* — from the declination of the sun from the zenith to the darkness of the night; and the morning prayer *(fajr)*. In Surah Hud, God says: "And establish regular prayers at the two ends of the day and at the approaches of the night" (Qur'an 11: 114). "At the two ends of the day" refers to morning and evening prayers and "approaches of the night" to the night prayer. This Command either merely emphasizes the importance of these three prayers, or refers to the time when five prayers were not yet prescribed.

And in Surah Ta Ha: "And celebrate constantly the praises of your Lord, before the rising of the sun, and before its setting; you celebrate them for part of the hours of the night, and at the sides of the day" (Qur'an 20: 130). Again in Surah Rum: "So give glory to Allah, when you reach eventide and when you rise in the moring; to Him be praise in the heavens and on the earth; and in the late afternoon and when the day begins to decline" (Qur'an 30: 17). The timings of the five times daily prayers are further clarified by the Holy Messenger:
"Ibn Abbas reported Allah's Messenger as saying, 'Gabriel twice led me in prayer at the House (of Allah). He prayed the noon prayer with me when the sun had passed the meridian to the extent of the thong of a sandal; he prayed the afternoon prayer with me when everything's shadow was as

long as itself; he prayed the sunset prayer with me at the time when one who has been fasting breaks his fast; he prayed the night prayer with me when the twilight had ended; and he prayed the dawn prayer with me at the time when food and drink becomes forbidden to one who is fasting. On the following day, he prayed the noon prayer with me when his shadow was as long as himself; he prayed the afternoon prayer with me when his shadow was twice as long as himself; he prayed the sunset prayer with me at the time one who has been fasting breaks his fast; he prayed the night prayer with me when about a third of the night had passed; and he prayed the dawn (morning) prayer with me when there was clear daylight. Then turning to me he said, 'Muhammd, this is the time observed by the Prophets before you, and the time is anywhere between these two times' (Abu Dawd and Tirmidhi and Muslim).

Jabir bin Abdullah reported that the Prophet (peace be upon him) used to pray the *zuhr* prayer at midday and the asr prayer at a time when the sun was still bright, the *maghrib* prayer after sunset (at it stated time) and the *isha* at a variable time. Whenever he saw the people assembled for the *isha* prayer, he would pray earlier and if the people delayed, he would delay the prayer. And they or the Prophet (peace be upon him) used to offer the *fajr* prayer when it was still dark.

There are many sayings of the Holy Messenger (peace be upon him) which suggest the superiority of praying at the stated times. "it is reported by Abdullah that he asked the Holy Prophet (peace be upon him) which deed was the dearest to Allah. He replied: 'To pray in time.' (Muslim). Ali also reported that the Prophet said, "There are three things, Ali, which you must not postpone, (and the first is) prayer when its time comes."

10

Composition of Prayer

The number of *rakat, fardh* and *sunnah* to be offered in each prayer is prescribed by the Holy Prophet under instructions from God. These details of *rakat,* of *fardh,* as well as *sunnah* prayer can be found in books of *hadith.* Each prayer is composed of (a) *fardh,* prescribed prayers, (b) *sunnah* and (c) *nafillah,* additional, optional prayers. The Holy Prophet (peace be upon him) offered *sunnah* and additional prayers before and after the prescribed prayers *(fardh).* The composition and sequence of prayers is given below:

Name of prayer	Number of Sunnah before Fardh	Number of Fardh (prescribed)	Number of Sunnah after Fardh	Number of naffilah (optional)
Fajr (Dawn)	2	2	-	-
Zuhr (Midday)	4	4	2	2
Asr (Afternoon)	4	4	-	-
Maghrib (Sunset)	-	3	2	2
Isha (Night)	4	4	2	2+3w+2

Note: The three rakat prayer shown in nafillah between two *nafillah* prayers each consisting of two *rakat* in the *isha* prayer are called *witr.* These are considered *wajib* (necessary) according to Hanafi Muslims, but other sections of Muslims, regard them as *sunnah.* Details of *rakat,* of *fardh, sunnah* and *witr* prayers are also shown on the chart.

Mode of Prayer

The mode of Islamic prayer plays an important part in realizing the Divine Communion. Preliminary preparations of cleansing and ablution preceding prayer, and feelings of extreme humility and reverence in postures of standing, bowing down, sitting and prostration are essential for creating the necessary spirit in man to receive Divine Guidance and Divine Inspiration. There is no doubt that particular postures of the body do create feelings of pride and ego in man and are not conductive to Divine Communion, but the Islamic prayer contains reverential postures which make man feel very humble and low before the Supreme Being. This state of humbleness in combination with recitation of the Holy verses from the Qur'an help man to feel the Divine Presence in prayer.

1. Humility

It seems likely that there is a very close and intimate relationship between the prayer and the Divine Vision. The physical postures and the movements in prayer also play a very significant role in revitalizing and reigniting the potential and latent sources of power in man to enable him to open a channel between himself and the Creator. If the prayer is offered properly and the four main physical postures in it are performed perfectly, it helps man to rekindle his inner latent source of energy and to utilize it in rebuilding his past relationship with the Divine Power. It is a very effective means of developing the human self.

All the movements of the body, from the standing position to the prostration, are the expression of extreme humility of the body before the SUPREME BEING. It is in fact total submission of the physical self before the SUPREME AUTHORITY. Recitation of Divine Words and glorification of God in prayer help to bring the mental powers of man into complete obedience to His Will and Command. This process of submission of the body and the mind to the DIVINE WILL through the proper synchronization of physical postures and repeated utterance of Divine Words in prayer help to ignite the latent forces of man and to strengthen his spiritual powers.

It must, however, be emphasized that this link cannot be maintained without the establishment of regular prayer. The prayer is the means as well as the end. It helps man to establish and maintain his link with God. If the prayer or its proper performance is lost, the link with the spiritual world will automatically be cut off. The prayer is an occasion of great joy for a believer for he is raised to a position of excellence and elevation through it. He is called by his Lord to meet Him five times a day. Such an occasion demands great humility and reverence. A true believer really feels *Khushu* and *Khudhu* in the presence of his Lord. *Khashia* is a condition of the heart, the result of fear of God. *Khudhu* is the effect of this condition on the physical self of a believer, which is shown by humility and submission: "For believers are those who, when Allah is mentioned, feel a tremor in their hearts, and when they hear His Signs rehearsed, find their Faith strengthened . . . who establish regular prayer" (Qur'an 8: 2-3).

A believer stands facing his Lord in prayer full of emotion and feeling of solemn humility. The Presence of the Sublime Sovereign makes him all the more humble and low: "They fall down on their faces in prayer, in tears, and it increases their humility" (Qur'an 17: 109).

God promises rewards to those believers who maintain their prayer and humility in it: "The believers must eventually win through . . . those who humble themselves in prayer . . . and who strictly guard their prayer" (Qur'an 23: 1-2 and 9). The benefit of prayer is reaped by those who observe all its conditions and follow its directives in earnestness. In fact, the real benefit of the teachings of the Qur'an is reaped by those who establish regular prayer for fear of their Lord: "Thou canst but admonish such as fear their Lord unseen and establish regular prayer" (Qur'an 35: 18). And again: "Who feared Allah and brought a heart turned in devotion to Him." (Qur'an 50: 33).

There is a slight but delicate difference between fear and *khushia*. Fear shows one's helpnessness in relation to the other's strength and power; whereas *Khushia* is used to denote that awe and dread which affects the heart of an individual on seeing the grandeur and majesty of some authority. Here *Khushia,* instead of fear, is used to show that fear of Allah in the heart of a believer is produced not merely because he is afraid of His Punishment but because His Grandeur and Glory is a constant source of awe and dread of Him. *Khushia* does influence the physical movements and conditions of a believer in that it makes him very humble and devout: "Guard strictly your (habit of) prayer, and stand before Allah in a devout (frame of mind)" (Qur'an 2: 238).

In this verse, first, a believer is told to strictly guard the institution of prayer under all conditions and never to relax in its observance. Second, he is advised to be obedient, submissive and humble before his Lord. This shows that there is a close relationship between prayer and humility. Gradually regularity in prayer does teach an individual humility before God and obedience to His Command. A believer offers his prayer in extreme submission. The use of the word *qanut* is a clear indication that the Command "To strictly guard your prayer" includes obedience to God and humility in His Presence.

The prayer is a very solemn and serious occasion during

which a believer is fully absorbed in a dialogue with his Lord. He has no time to think about anything else or indulge in any act which might distract his attention or disturb his concentration.

2. Communion with God

Prayer is the means through which man is able to initiate and maintain his relationship with God. It takes him away from the struggle of this world and brings him closer to his Lord. It enables him to continue his economic activities without being forgetful of his duty to his Creator. In other words, prayer is the only effective means through which man can keep in constant companionship with God in the hustle and bustle of life.

One may be a doctor, a scientist, a teacher, a businessman, a labourer, a banker, a manager, or a capitalist, and may be all the time busy in his daily work; but so long as he practises regular prayer, he has the most effective and practical way of keeping his link with God. Prayer is a constant reminder of the reality of his servitude to Him. And this relationship can guard him and keep him on the path of righteousness and justice: "And if My servants ask you, O Messenger, concerning Me, tell them that I am quite close to them. I hear and answer the prayer of the humble petitioner, when he calls Me. Convey this to them, O Messenger; perhaps they may be guided aright" (Qur'an 2: 186).

This verse points to the close relationship of man with his Lord. It tells him in plain words that God, inspite of His Majesty and Grandeur, is very close to him. He can hear his prayer and He can answer him. He is never distant or remote from his servants. He is the most sincere friend and constant companion of His slaves. He always comes to their help whenever they ask for it. Though they cannot see Him, He always looks after them and guards them against evil. And He is always ready and willing to listen to their prayers and to help them.

He says, "Here am I, the Sovereign, the Absolute Ruler of the boudless universe and Possessor of all the Powers of Authority, and so close to you that I can answer your call for help. You need no recommendation or intercession for approaching Me. You can call Me anywhere and at any time you like, and I will be there with you to listen to you and help you. You should free yourself from the folly of running from door to door after false associates, and accept My invition and turn to Me and trust Me and submit to Me and become My servant: "It was We Who created man, and We Know what dark suggestions his soul makes to him: for We are nearer to him than (his) jugular vein" (Qur'an 50: 16).

"God created man, and gave him his limited free will. God knows the inmost desires and motives of man even better than man does himself. He is nearer to a man than the man's own jugular vein. As the bloodstream is the vehicle of life and consciousness, the phrase "nearer than the jugular vein" implies that God knows more truly the innermost state of our feeling and consciousness than does our own ego."

The Holy Messenger, peace be upon be him, explicitly described prayer as the *miraj* (ascension) of the believers. It was on the night of the *miraj* that the Holy Messenger (peace be upon him) had direct contact with Almighty God and experienced the great mysteries of the human soul. And it was on that very night that he was given the gift of daily prayer by God. The Holy Messenger advised his followers to perform the prayer properly and regularly so that they might also experience the Divine Mysteries. Anyone who is sincere in his prayer and is capable of communicating with the Divine Being has no obstacle in his way. It is a direct line between man and the Creator, and man needs no intermediaries.The Holy Messenger explained the significance of prayer in these words: "You pray to God in such a way as if you see Him, and if you cannot do so, think that He sees you."

If you offer your prayer regularly in this manner, you are sure to develop a very close relationship with God; the Holy Qur'an declares in clear words: "Put they trust in the Mighty, the Merciful, Who sees thee standing forth (in prayer), and thy movements among those who prostrate themselves. For it is He Who hears and knows all things" (Qur'an 26: 217-220).

The Holy Messenger is here told to put his entire trust in God Who knows and sees everything. Again in Surah Yunus, it is said: "And you are not engaged in any business nor do you recite any portion of the Qur'an, nor do you do any work, but We are witness over you when you are engaged therein. And not the weight of an atom in the heaven is hidden from thy Lord, nor anything less than that nor greater, but it is registered in a clear record" (Qur'an 10: 61). Nothing in the universe is hidden from its Creator, Who knows the smallest as well as the biggest thing. He even knows and hears what is spoken or hidden in the hearts of people. He is fully aware of what we conceal and of what we declare and pronounce: "If you speak the word aloud (it is no matter), surely, He knows the secret, and the most hidden" (Qur'an 20: 7).

God knows even the secrets of the subconscious mind, which are hidden even from ourselves: "He know the hidden and the manifest. . . It is the same to Him whether any of you conceal his speech or declare it openly; whether he hide himself by night or walk forth freely by day" (Qur'an 13: 9-10).

Once the Holy Messenger told a man not to spit in front of him while in prayer for at that time he is engaged in very private talk with his Lord. It is reported by Ibn Umar that one night, when the Holy Messenger was confined to the mosque (in *itakaf*), he peeped through the door and said, "O people. When a person is engaged in prayer, he is engaged in conversation with his Lord; he should know what he is talking about."

This shows what effect prayer should have on the person who is offering it, and what an intimate relationship it creates and develops between a man and his Lord. As prayer is a sort of formal conversation and dialogue between man and his Creator, it is essential that the former should stand solemnly and respectfully in prayer. The Holy Qur'an teaches the believers how to stand before their Lord in these words: "Observe strictly the prayer and take particular care to offer prayer in the most excellent way; stand before Allah like devoted servants" (Qur'an 2: 238).

"The guarding of prayers is not simply the observance of the outward form; it is both the form and the spirit to which attention is drawn. Prayers are to be offered at stated times and a particular method is to be observed, for if regularity and method had not been adopted, the institution of prayer, which is so helpful in keeping alive a true faith in God in the heart of a Muslim, would pass into mere idealism as it has in other religions. The fact is that to keep the spirit of man in touch with the Divine Spirit, an external form was neccessary. The external form is needed to bring the inner faculty into action. As regards the spirit of prayer, attention is called to it again and again in the Holy Qur'an. In the verse quoted, the injunction to guard the prayers is followed by the words: "Stand up truly obedient to Allah." These words aim at generating the spirit of obedience to God.

It is true, to a great extent, that the external behavour of a man is an index to his inner devotion or feeling towards God. If you really obey God and submit your whole life to His

Laws, you will feel pleasure and happiness in standing solemnly before Him and therefore showing your respect to Him. And the nearer and closer you are to the Lord, the greater will be the expression of solemnity and respect in your external behaviour.

Peace and Contentment

Peace and tranquility comes with *Dhikr Allah* (remembrance of God), and the best, most convenient and simplest form of this is prayer. You stand solemnly, bow and prostrate before the Creator and also recite a portion from the Holy Qur'an which is the best form of *Dhikr Allah*. The word dhikr is often used in the Holy Qur'an for prayer. And, as the essence of prayer is Remembrance of God, somtimes the latter phrase is used to convey the meaning of the former, so that an individual, while practising the form, may not lose sight of its spirit. "Guard strictly yoor (habit of) prayer.But when you are in security celebrate Allah's praises in the manner He has taught you" (Qur'an 2: 238-9).

Moses was commanded to establish prayer in order to remember Him: "verily, I am Allah: There is no deity but I; so Serve thou Me (only) and establish prayer for My Remembrance" (Qur'an 20: 14). A pleasant and noble state of the heart is attained through prayer and Remembrance of God: "Those who believe and whose hearts find satisfaction in the Remembrance of Allah: for without doubt, in the Remembrance of Allah do heart find satisfaction" (Qur'an 13: 28).

For it is prayer that provides an opportunity to human beings to come closer to their Lord and attain the highest and the noblest goal of their life – *Ridhwan Allah* (God's Pleasure). And there is no doubt that ultimate success and lasting peace of mind is only for those who establish regular prayer: "(To the righteous soul will be said): O (thou) soul, in (complete) rest and satisfaction! Come back thou to thy Lord, well pleased (thyself) and well-pleasing unto Him. Enter thou, then, among My servants! Yea, enter thou My heaven" (Qur'an 89: 27-30).

"The righteous enter into their inheritance and receive their welcome with a title that suggests freedom from all pain, sorrow, doubts, struggle, disappointments, passion, and even further desire: at rest, in peace, in state of complete satisfaction. In Muslim theology, this state of the soul is the final state of bliss . . . Good receives a warm welcome from the Lord of Goodness Himself. The climax of the whole is: 'Enter My Heaven'." (A. Yusuf Ali)

Righteousness and devoutness, which entitle a believer to such an ideal and heavenly bliss and tranquility come through the establishment of the institution of prayer: Abu Musa reported Allah's Messenger as saying, "When you are in anger (or in sorrow or grief) perform ablution and offer two rakat. It will cool down your temper and you will find peace and satisfaction in it." Once the Holy Messenger said: "I like such and such things most but prayer is the coolness of my eyes." In other words, he meant that the real peace and satisfaction of his heart was in prayer. Abu Hurairah reported Allah's Messenger as saying, "If people knew what blessing lies in the call to prayer and in the first row, then they would do nothing but cast lots for it; if they knew what blessing lies in going for prayer early, they would race to it; if they knew what blessing lies in the prayer after nightfall and in the morning prayer, they would come to them even if they had to crawl to do so."

He also reported Muhammad (peace be upon him) as saying; "No prayer is more burdensome to the hypocrites than the dawn and the evening prayers; but if they knew what blessing lies in them, they would come to them even if they had to crawl to do so." The Holy Qur'an and the Sunnah (custom) of the Holy Prophet give us a clear indication that the real and lasting peace *(itminan)* of the heart is in prayer.

Loss of Prayer
Believers who break up the institution of prayer lose their spirituality and goodness. The loss of prayer is the beginning of their end. The fact that the establishment of prayer had been the chief factor in organising and building up the broken and scattered power of the Israelites and other old nations is evident in history. The Holy Qur'an mentions in many chapters how the nations gradually rose to power and excellence with the establishment of the institution of prayer; and how they went to ruin and oblivion after the break up of this institution.

The Holy Qur'an describes the ruin of such people in these words: "Then there came after them an evil generation, who neglected (and missed) prayer and followed after lusts; soon then, they will face destruction" (Qur'an 19: 59).

Prayer is the first and foremost link between a believer and God. It keeps alive his close relationship with God by day and night. It keeps him close to the center of Godliness and does not let him break his active link. As soon as this link is broken, man goes further and further away from goodness and piety until his relationship with God is completely Thereafter he does not care for any values or the good things of life but follows only his carnal self. He becomes a slave to his self. He follows every vain desire that pleases him. This is the unavoidable consequence of the break up of this relationship with God. When man abstains from prayer, his heart loses its only link with God. As time passes, this gulf widens and man goes deeper and deeper into the depths of evil and lust. Gradually he developes hostility to goodness and righteousness. He opposes everything that is good and right in this world. This obedience to his self becomes stronger until every aspect of his moral and social life becomes subservient to his self instead of to God.

When the guilty are questioned on the Day of judgement about their evil deeds which led to their downfalls and degradation, they will admit their failure to keep up the institution of prayer: "And (ask) of the guilty, 'what has brought you to Hell?' They will say, 'We were not of those who established prayer.' " (Qur'an 74: 41-43). Abstention from prayer, infact, means disobedience to the Command of God. And obviously one who does not obey the Command of God and is not prepared to follow the code of life set by the Messenger of God is not a true believer.

People who do not perform prayer properly but observe only the outward form of it are like those who do not perform it at all. They consider it a burden on them and come for it lazily. Such people do not really perform prayer. The Holy Qur'an describes those people who merely observe the outward form of prayer and do not conform to its spirit in these words: "So woe to the worshippers who are neglectful of their prayer" (Qur'an 107: 4-5). This verse shows that worship does not consist merely of outward form. There is no doubt that outward form is an essential part and that without it there cannot be any prayer. But it must be accompanied by earnest desire to understand and follow the Command of God in word and in deed. Those believers who are not regular or who do not perform it earnestly and sincerely in obedience to the Command of their Lord, merely perform it to be seen by other people and to soothe their respective consciences.

Language of Prayer
Prayer is an obligatory form of worship prescribed by God

for His servants. Its rules of conduct and performance are strictly laid down by the Holy Messenger under instructions from his Lord. It is one of the essentials of prayer that it must be offered in the language of the Qur'an. The Holy Messenger and his companions offered prayer in Arabic and since then it has been offered in Arabic by all Muslims. All Muslim scholars, jurists and commentators agree on this. It is narrated by Anas bin Malik that God's Messenger said, "Whoever prays like us and faces the *Qibla* and eats our slaughtered animals is a Muslim."

In another Hadith, Anas bin Malik quotes God's Messenger as saying: "I have been ordered to fight with people till they say, 'None has the right to be worshipped but Allah.' And if they say so, pray our prayer, face our *Qibla* and slaughter as we slaughter, then their blood and property will be sacred to us and we will not interfere with them except legally and they will be reckoned with by Allah."

Obviously, our prayer must be like the prayer of the Holy Prophet in form and in content. Any change in form or content will make it different from the prayer of the Holy Prophet. It is a compulsory act of devotion and therefore must always be performed strictly in accordance with the instructions of the Holy Prophet (peace be upon him). Even a slight change in its form or content will render it null and void and it will cease to be an act of worship or *ibadah*. In order to keep it an act of *ibadah,* the original form and content must be maintained. In other words, it must always be offered in the Arabic language.

Recitation of *Surah Fatiha* is an essential part of prayer and no prayer can be complete without it. Ubada bin As-samat reported Allah's Messenger as saying: "He who does not recite *Fatiha-al-Kitab* is not credited with having observed prayer" (Bukhari and Muslim). Abu Hurairah, reported

Allah' Messenger as saying: "If anyone observes prayer in which he does not recite *Umm al-Qur'an*, it is deficient (he said three times) and incomplete." And Surah *Fatiha* cannot be translated into any other language without losing much of its elegance, beauty, grandeur and meaning. Even Western scholars admit that its translation can convey neither its recitational beauty and charm, nor the meaning, the impact and the full significance of the original Arabic texts. This *Surah* is the most essential part of the prayer. Translation of this Divine *Surah* loses many of the immeasurable effects it has on the observer of the prayer.

Above all, the Arabic text gives the impression of a direct contact with the Divine Being. The observer of prayer feels as if he is talking directly to his Lord. He feels great reverence and humility in his Presence. This effect is the direct result of the Arabic text recited in prayer. Each word of *Tasbih*, *Fatiha* and *Tashah-hud* has a magical effect which can never be achieved by its translation. In a standing position, you commence your prayer with *Allahu Akbar* and *Tasbih* of Allah. You glorify your Lord with His praises and enter into prayer. Your mind receives an impression of the Glory and Majesty of Allah and you assume an sttitude and posture of utter reverence and humbleness before Him. You change from one posture of the body to another with *takbir*, *Allahu Akbar* and the impression of your humbleness and His Grandeur and Greatness is renewed at every change of movement.

Then the expressions of complete reverence and humility in *Ruku* and *Sujud* (bowing and prostration) felt by the observer through the recitation of Arabic words cannot be produced by translations. These short phrases produce an immense effect on the attitude and posture of a person who is offering prayer. They remind him of the Divine Command which is to be observed in the Presence of his Lord.

Again the profound effect of *Surah Fatiha* can never be obtained by its translation. It will lose all its divine and miraculous effect. The ideas expressed by the small and simple Arabic words of *Surah Fatiha* can hardly be translated into any other language. Surely, the repetition and its immense spiritual effect, which is the essence of prayer, will lose its real purpose and significance in its translation.

In the sitting position, a believer recites *tashah-hud*. He promises before his Creator that all his prayers and acts of worship through words, action and sactity will be for Him alone. These words actually make him feel he is sitting in His Presence and presenting his petition to Him personally. Its translation into any other language will never achieve this effect and will therefore lose all its real purpose and significance.

Prayer is a great force of unification for the Muslim world. The uniformity of prayer among the Muslims strengthens their universal brotherhood. It greatly helps in the realisation of our goal that all Muslims are brothers. The bond of common laguage in prayer supplies us with a great force of unification,when all Muslims gather together, especially in Hajj (pilgrimage) in Mecca. There is no need of translations or explanations before the start of their prayer. They offer their prayer in form and in content in the same way. A call of the *Muezzin* bring them together and they offer their prayer behind one leader *(imam)* in a common language, Arabic. This infuses in them a spirit of universal brotherhood. They forget their colour, creed and race and come before their Lord to offer their prayers and thanks in one language. They feel as brothers and sisters and members of one great family of Islam.

Thus prayer through the bond of common language serves as a great unifying force among the Muslims. It brings them together in the most perfect state of equality with the deepest and most earnest feelings and ties of universal brotherhood among them. The diversification of language of prayer among the multitude of people coming from the four corners of the world, of varying colours and languages, would fail in the object of uniting the human race. In the Divine Service, the bond of Islam has brought the human race closer through the use of common language in prayer. And this common language can be no other than Arabic, the language of the Qur'an.

It is through ignorance that some people say that prayer must be offered in one's own language, so that a man is able to unfold his leart before his Lord and is able to express his innermost feelings before his Master. One can express one's heart's feelings to one's Lord in private whenever one wishes. There is no time or space fixed for such dialogue between the servant and his Master. But the compulsory prayer prescribed by Allah for His servants is an official Divine Service. It has to be performed with observation of the full Divine Command in form and content. It is not so difficult for a believer to memorise the prayer together with the meaning of the Arabic text.

The personal and social benefits of learning the short prayer in the original language are immense and beyond human comprehension. They far outweigh the narrow and personal benefit of self-expression of one's feelings in one's own language before Allah.

11

Zakat (Poor Due)

Zakat (poor due) is the third Pillar of Islam. It is obligatory but only on those Muslim men and women who possess wealth above a certain limit. The word *zakat* means to purify. It purifies and protects our soul from miserliness, selfishness and greed, and purifies our wealth from the evils of this world.

Zakat is neither a tax nor a voluntary contribution by individuals to the state treasury. It is an act of *ibadah* and worship like that of *salat* (prayer). Prayer is an act of worship through words and physical postures of the body, while the poor due is an act of worship through expenditure of wealth. A certain portion of wealth is given out to the poor in obedience to the Command of Allah. The Qur'an mentions the payment of poor due in the following verses: "Those who believe and do deeds of righteousness, and establish regular prayer and pay poor due will have their reward with their Lord" (Qur'an 2: 277). And in Surah Luqman: "These are verses of the Book full of Wisdom, a guide and mercy to the doers of good, those who establish prayer and pay poor due" (Qur'an 31: 2-4). And again: "And they have been commanded no more than this: to worship Allah, offering Him sincere devotion, being true in faith; to establish regular prayer; and give poor due" (Qur'an 98: 5). And in Surah al Nur: "So establish regular prayer, and give regular poor due;

and obey the Messenger that you may receive mercy" (Qur'an 24: 56).

The Prophet Muhammad (peace be upon him) explained the Commandment regarding poor due to his companions on various occasions: "And the statement of Allah, 'Establish prayer and pay poor due', Ibn Abbas reported that Abu Sufyan told him the Hadith of the Prophet (peace be upon him): He (the Prophet) ordered us to establish prayer, to pay poor due, to keep good relations with relatives, and to be chaste." According to Ibn Abbas, the Prophet (peace be upon him) sent Mu'adh to Yemen and said: "Invite people to certify that none has the right to be worshipped but Allah, and I am Allah's Messenger, and if they obey you to do so, then teach them that Allah has enjoined on them five prayers in every day and night, and if they obey you to do so, then teach them that Allah has made it obligatory for them to pay poor due from their property and it is to be taken from the wealthy among them and given to the poor."

Anas said that when Abu Bakr sent him to Bahrain he wrote him this letter: "In the name of Allah, most Gracious, most Merciful, there is the obligatory *sadaqa* which Allah's Messenger imposed on the Muslims on the Command of Allah."

1. A Basic Principle of Islam

Zakat and *salat* are the two most fundamental and basic principles of Islam. They have always been obligatory on Muslims in all ages. Prophet Abraham and his followers were commanded to observe these principles: "And We made them leaders, guiding (men) by Our Command, and We sent them Revelation to do good deeds, to establish regular prayer; and to pay poor due" (Qur'an 21: 73). And his son Ishmael obeyed the Command of his Lord and enjoined prayer and poor due payment on his people: "He used to enjoin on his people prayer and poor due, and he was most acceptable in the sight of his Lord" (Qur'an 19: 55). The people of Israel were commanded to observe the same principles: "And be steadfast in prayer; give regular poor due; and bow down your heads with those who bow down in worship" (Qur'an 2: 43). God made a Covenant with the people of Israel that they would obey His Commandment: "Allah did aforetime take a Covenant from the children of Israel, and We appointed twelve leaders among them. And Allah said; 'I am with you if you but establish regular prayer, give poor due. . . (Qur'an 5: 13).

Previous nations were also commanded to obey those two principles in good faith: "Have you not turned your vision to those who were told to hold back their hands from fighting, but establish regular prayer and pay regular poor due" (Qur'an 4: 77). The righteous and the pious have always been obedient to their Lord: "They are those who, if We establish them in the land establish regular prayer, and give regular poor due, enjoin the right and forbid wrong" (Qur'an 22: 41). And when Prophet Musa (peace be upon him) went with seventy men to meet his Lord, he was told: "That I shall ordain Mercy for those who do right, and give regular poor due, and those who believe in Our Signs" (Qur'an 7: 156).

And Prophet Isa (peace be upon him), who was a faithful servant of his Lord, received a similar Commandment: "And Allah has enjoined on me prayer and poor due as long as I live" (Qur'an 19: 31). Prophet Muhammad (peace be upon him) was given the same instructions: "He has chosen you, and has imposed no difficulties on you in religion; it is the cult of your father Abraham. It is He Who has named you Muslims, both before and in this Revelation . . . . so establish poor due, and hold fast to Allah" (Qur'an 22: 78).

All Prophets of God have always stressed the need for the

organisation of the institution of poor due for the prosperity and social betterment of all. Prophet Muhammad (peace be upon him) brought this institution, like other principles of Islam, to perfection: He gave it a proper place in society,both as a basic Pillar of Islam and as an act of worship and as an economic measure of great significance.

2. Purpose of *Zakat*

Zakat is not a charity but a compulsory payment by the rich to the state. It is a social claim, as a matter of right and not as charity, on the wealth of the rich. By paying poor due, the rich are, in fact, paying back their debt to the poor and society. If they fail to pay this social debt, they are committing a sin in the eyes of God and a crime against the law of the land. Thus by paying poor due, the rich are not doing any favour to the poor or society but are doing their normal moral as well as legal duty.

All wealth and riches belong to God. It is entrusted to us by Him, so that We may satisfy our needs and help our less fortunate brothers to satisfy their requirements. Thus the object of poor due is, first, to prove our faithfulness to our Master by making material sacrifice in obedience to His Command and for His Pleasure; second, to help the poorer section of the community to meet their basic needs without any hardship and inconvenience, in the best possible way; third, to achieve equitable distribution of wealth, along with the operation of the law of inheritance and the zero rate of interest, so that on one in the community is deprived of its benefits. Both the rich and the poor share the social wealth for the satisfaction of their needs.

Islam wants every man and woman to live in honour and dignity. It wants to build up the Community on very strong moral and economic foundations so that it can survive against all opposition. It can never tolerate poverty amid plenty, some indulging in extreme luxuries while others rot in extreme poverty. The institution of *zakat* is meant to correct such a situation and, instead, establish right and just balance between the two extremes. It is also a correcting force in that it never lets the situation go to extremes but keeps it in balance all the time.

It also helps in the development of a healthy and good spirit in the community. Though poor due is compulsory, Muslims pay it voluntarily and feel pleasure in paying it because they regard it as an act of *ibadah* and devotion, like prayer: "And establish regular prayer and give regular poor due; and loan to Allah a beautiful loan" (Qur'an 73: 20).

The words 'beautiful loan' fully express the spirit with which poor due is given by the Muslims. It is given with joy without expecting any monetary compensation. The Muslims feel great pleasure and gratitude for the Grace and Bounty of Allah, and for being able to help their brothers in need. This spirit of obedience, submission, gratitude, hope and mercy is behind all acts of devotion, including paying poor due.

In short, the institution of *zakat* purifies individuals as well as society and increases goodness in every heart. It makes the rich generous to the poor and makes the poor thankful and better off. It protects individuals and society from all evils — evils of poverty as well as of plenty. It protects the community from confusion and from the danger of conflict between the rich and the poor. Thus the poor due is a great blessing for all.

3. Importance of *Zakat*

Zakat is one of the basic fundamental ordinances of God and its observation is vital. Anyone who believes in God and establishes regular prayer but refuses to pay the poor due is not considered a true believer. The first Caliph, Abu Bakr, declared *jihad* against some people who called themselves Muslims but refused to pay the poor due. He quoted the following verse of the Qur'an in support of his action: "But even so, if they repent, establish regular prayer, and give regaular poor due, they are your brethren in Islam (Qur'an 9: 11). And God condemns those who do not pay poor due: "And woe to those who join partners with Allah — those who give no poor due and who deny the Heareafter" (Qur'an 41: 6-7). God and His Messenger promise forgiveness to those who believe in God, establish prayer and pay the poor due, in these words: "If, then, you do not do so, and Allah forgives you, then at least establish regular prayer; pay regular poor due; and obey Allah and His Messenger" (Qur'an 58: 13).

These verses of the Holy Qur'an clearly show the great importance of the institution of *zakat* in Islam. It is as fundamental as the institutions of *salat* and *sawm* (prayer and fasting). Its basic importance lies in the economic field, where it helps to eradicate poverty and hunger from the community.

This economic importance of the poor due is clearly shown by the following saying of the Holy Prophet (peace be upon him): "Ibn Abbas reported that when Allah's Messenger (peace be upon him) sent Mu'adh to Yemen, he said to him, "You are going to people of a Divine Book. First invite them to Allah's worship and when they come to know Allah, inform them that Allah has enjoined on them five prayers in every day and night, and if they start offering these prayers, inform them that Allah has enjoined on them *zakat*. And it is to be taken from the rich amongst them and given to the poor amongst them."

But its function in fostering qualities of sacrifice and goodness and in suppressing evil qualities of selfishness and greed among the people is no small contribution.

Another important function of the poor due is that it encourages investment and discourages the hoarding of wealth in the community.

4. *Zakat* as a State Institution

Zakat is not only obligatory but is a state institution. It is the duty of the state to calculate and collect it from its citizens. Individuals are not free to calculate and spend it where and how they like. Every penny of the poor due is to be calculated according to the state rate and collected in accordance with the instruction of the Qur'an. The Holy Prophet made it a state institution and appointed officials to calculate and collect it from the Muslims. Similar instructions were issued to the governors of various provinces. After the time of the Holy Messenger, his Caliphs followed in his footsteps. His first Caliph, Abu Bakr, even declared war against some tribes who refused to pay poor due to the *bait al-Mal* (state treasury).

The Holy Qur'an, while describing the main items of expenditure of the poor due fund, clearly refers to the expenditure on the officials responsible for collecting and distributing it. This makes *zakat* a public institution, controlled and managed by the public. The Holy Prophet (peace be upon him) and his Caliphs fully understood its implications and treated *zakat* as a state institution.

According to Abu Hurairah, when Allah's Messenger (peace be upon him) died and Abu Bakr became the Caliph, some Arabs refused to pay the poor due to the Treasury. Abu Bakr decided to declare war against them. Umar said to Abu Bakr, "How could you fight with these people when Allah's Messenger has said: 'I have been ordered to fight the people until they say that none has the right to be worshipped but Allah, and whoever said it then he saved his life and property from me except on trespassing against the law (rights and conditions), and their accounts will be with Allah.' " Abu Bakr replied, "By Allah! I will fight those who differentiate between prayer and poor due because poor due is the compulsory claim (of the state) from the property (of the wealthy). By Allah! If they withheld even a she-kid which they used to pay at the time of Allah's Messenger (peace be upon him), I would fight with them." Then Umar said, "By Allah, it was nothing, but Allah who gave Abu Bakr the true knowledge and later I came to know that he was right."

However, if there is no Muslim state, or any national institution for this purpose, it may be collected by individuals or institutions who are working for the cause of Islam. It is preferable to pay the entire sum of poor due to one deserving individual or institution rather than distrutute it among scores of people.

5. Goods Liable for *Zakat*
Zakat is levied on wealth which exists in the form of cash or which yields income. Two important commodities, gold and silver, which have always been the source of wealth and a form in which it can be hoarded, are subject to poor due levy. Whether people hoard it or invest it, they have to pay the levy on their gold and silver under all circumstances. And cash in any form, coins, notes or bank deposits, is treated in the same way. *Zakat* stimulates investment and discourages hoarding in the community. If people do not invest their wealth, hold it in cash or gold or silver, and pay *zakat* every year, their wealth will gradually be consumed by this annual levy. It is a very effective way of keeping wealth in circulation.

It is reported by Amr bin Shuaib, on his father's authority, that his grandfather told of Allah's Messenger (peace be upon him) addressing the people and saying: 'If anyone is guardian of an orphan who owns property, he must trade with (invest) it and not leave it till *sadaqa* (or *zakat)* consumes it.' "

(Tirmizi).

The Holy Prophet (peace be upon him) clearly foresaw the great function of the poor due in encouraging investment and discouraging the hoarding of wealth in the community. The importance of *zakat* has immensely increased in modern industrial society, wherein investment and employment are directly co-related and movements of precious metals exert tremendous influence and pressure on international currencies. Articles of merchandise and animals used for trade purposes are also subject to poor due. It is also levied on the produce of land, whether agricultural or gardening, in the form of *ushr*. There is no *zakat* payable on precious stones and immovable property or on the machinery or implements of an artisan or a farmer.

6. *Nisab* (the Exemption Limit)

The poor due is payable on wealth which remains in possession of a believer for a period of a whole year, and whose value has reached a certain level, known as *nisab*. Below this minimum level *(nisab)*, no *zakat* is charged. The level varies with different kinds of wealth, but for cash and precious metals including ornaments, it is 200 dirhams or 52½ tolas (about 21 oz.) of silver, and 28 mithqals or 7½ tolas (about 3 oz.) of gold. *Nisab* for merchandise of all kinds was calculated by the silver standard but can be fixed by other more convenient forms of evaluation. Such as the standard currency of any country through the conversion of the silver standard into the local currency of that particular country.

The *nisab* for animals varies with different species. It is five for camels, thirty for bulls or cows and forty for goats or sheep. In the case of horses, *nisab* is fixed by their price. For cereals, *nisab* is five *wasaq*, according to two different measurements. It is about 26 maunds and 10 seers or 2200 lbs approximately according to one count, and 18 maunds and 35½ seers according to the other. This is approximately one ton in the former, and two thirds of a ton in the latter case. Thus the poor due is payable on gold, silver, merchandise, cattle and other valuables, if their value, number or quantity, as the case may be, is above the exemption limit as explained above.

7. Rate of *Zakat*

Zakat is charged annually at a uniform rate of 2½% on all cash held at the end of the year. It is not levied on total capital but on annual savings which have remined with the person for the whole year. The details are given in books of hadith, as shown below. Ali reported Allah's Messenger as saying, "With regard to coins, however you must pay a *dirham* for every forty, but nothing is payable on a hundred and ninety. When the total reaches two hundered, five dirhams are payable.

"Regarding sheep, for every forty sheep up to a hundred and twenty, one sheep is payable. If there is one more, then up to 200 two sheep are payable. If there are more, then up to three hundred three sheep are payable, and if there are more than three hundred, a sheep is payable for every hundred. But if you possess only thirty-nine, nothing is payable on them. Regarding cattle, a male calf of a year old is payable for every thirty and a cow in its third year for forty, but nothing is payable on working animals."

Anas reported Abu Bakr's letter ordering him to charge *zakat* at this rate: for twenty four camels or less a sheep is to ge given for every five. When they reach twenty-five to thirty-five, a she-camel in her second year is to be given. When they reach thirty-six to forty-five, a she-camel in her fourth year which is ready to be covered by a stallion is to be given. When they reach forty-six to sixty, a she-camel in her fourth year which is ready to be covered by a stallion is to be given. When they reach sixty-one to seventy-five, a she-camel in her fifth year is to be given. When they reach seventy-six to ninety, two she-camels in their third year are to be given. When they reach ninety-one to a hundred and twenty, two she-camels in their fourth year which are ready to be covered by a stallion are to be given. When they exceed a hundred and twenty, a she-camel in her fourth year for every fifty. If anyone has only four camels, no *(zakat) sadaqa* is payable on them unless their owner wishes, but when they reach five, a sheep is payable on them.

Abdullah bin Umar reported Allah's Messenger as saying, "A tenth is payable in what is watered by rain or wells, or from underground moisture, and a twentieth on what is watered by draught camels." According to Abu Said Al-Khudhri, Allah's Messenger (peace be upon him) said: "There is no *zakat* on less than 5 camels and also there is no *zakat* on less than 5 *auqiyah* of silver (200 *dirhams*). And there is no *zakat* on less than 5 *wasq* of food grain or dates (about one ton)."

A careful study of these rates of poor due show that in spite of slight variations, the standard rate of 2½% has been maintained in principle for almost all forms of wealth. In the case of unearned incomes, like treasure-trove, which do not involve much labour, the share of the state is increased. Similarly with land farming, the share of the owner is determined according to the labour involved in the cultivation of crops. Irrigated lands cost more capital and labour to the owner, so the rate of poor due on the yield from such lands is lower than from that of unirrigated lands. In all these cases, the state share in the form of *zakat* is adversely related to the cost of cultivation.

8. Recipients of *Zakat*

All those who are eligible to receive some payment from the poor due fund are mentioned in the following verse of the

Qur'an: "Alms are for the poor and the needy, and those employed to administer the funds; for those whose hearts are to be reconciled, to free the captives and the debtors, in the cause of Allah; and for the travellers; a duty imposed by Allah. And Allah is full of Knowledge and Wisdom" (Qur'an 9: 60).

According to this verse of the Qur'an, the following people are entitled to receive help from the poor due fund.

1. The poor who are unable to support themselves and their families.
2. The needy who have lost their wealth and source of income due to various factors.
3. Those officials who are engaged in the collection or payment of the fund.
4. New converts to Islam who need help in order to re-establish and rehabilitate them in their new life.
5. Prisoners of war.
6. Those who have incurred debts in meeting their lawful and essential needs and cannot pay them back.
7. Travellers rendered helpless in a foreign country while in pursuit of lawful economic activities.
8. It is also spent on various kinds of activities undertaken in the service of Islam.

12

Sawm **(Fasting)**

Fasting, like prayer, is also an act of worship and is the Fourth Pillar of Islam. It is compulsory for all Muslims, both men and women , children; but pregnant women, the sick and travellers are exempted from fasting. But travellers have to observe fasting after the end of their journey, pregnant women after the delivery of their child and the sick when they become well. Women during the period of menstruation need not fast but have to make up the lost days afterwards.

People in distress, hardship, or inconvenience are exempt from fasting but have to make up the lost fasting days afterwards: "Fasting is for a fixed number of days; but if any of you is ill, or on a journey, the prescribed number should be made up from the days later. For those who can do it with hardship is a ransom, the feeding of one that is indigent. But he that will give more of his own free will, − it is better for him. And it is better for you that you fast" (Qur'an 2: 184). Obviously, this permission not to fast during sickness or journeys is given to avoid unnecessary inconvenience and hardship to believers.

1. An Institution of Islam
Fasting is another important institution of Islam. It has always been an obligatory duty on believers even before the advent of Prophet Muhammad (peace be upon him). All the

previous nations were commanded to observe fasting: "O you who believe! Fasting is prescribed to you as it was prescribed to those before you, that you many learn self-restraint" (Qur'an 2: 183).Fasting has been universally recognized by all Faiths. It was practised by people of all Faiths in one form or another. It is practised by Hindus and Jews. Prophets Musa and Isa practised fasting and enjoined it on their followers. Disciples of Isa fasted but this institution later lost its true significance.

Prophet Muhammad (peace be upon him) was asked to re-establish this institution in its proper place and form. He was ordered to fast during the month of Ramadan.

2. Month of Ramadan

Ramadan is the ninth month of the Islamic Calendar. The Qur'an was first revealed in this month: "Ramadan is the month in which was sent down the Qur'an, as a guide to mankind, also clear Signs for guidance and judgement between right and wrong" (Qur'an 2: 185). God selected this Holy Month for fasting and made it compulsory: "So every one of you who is present at his home during that month should fast in it. But if anyone is ill, or on a journey, the prescribed period should be made up by days later. Allah intends every facility for you; He does not want to put you to difficulties. He wants you to complete the prescribed period" (Qur'an 2: 185).

Muslims commence the Fast with the appearance of the moon for the month of Ramadan and end it with the new moon of Shawwal. Ibn Umar reported hearing Allah's Messenger saying: "When you see the new moon of Ramadan, start fasting, and when you see the new moon of the month of Shawwal, stop fasting; and if the sky is overcast and you cannot see it, then regard the month of Ramadan as of 30 days" (Bukhari).

God selected lunar months for the purpose of fasting for very obvious and significant reasons. The lunar months rotate and share all seasons and weathers in the course of time. The month of Ramadan would, accordingly, come in every weather and season and Muslims all over the world would have the experience of fasting in winter as well as summer, in shorter days as well as in longer days. Muslims living all over the globe will equally share the benefits and hardships of fasting during all weathers. This would not have been the case if fasting had been prescribed according to the solar months for the convenience of fasting in shorter days and cooler weather would have permanently gone to one part of the world, and the hardship of fasting in longer days and hotter weather permanently to the other part.

Sepcification of a particular time for fasting would have taken away much of its value. It would not have given diverse experience to people of all countries of fasting in all kinds of weather and seasons. Every year the month of fasting moves ten days backward and in 36 years, it moves a full calendar year backwards. During this period, all people have the pleasure and privilege of fasting in all kinds of weather and all seasons. This change of the fasting month through the seasons and various kinds of weather takes believers through a very rigorous form of training and discipline which could never have been achieved by fasting in a particular solar month or at a specified time each year. At the same time, it is fair and just for all people in all parts of the world.

3. Fasting Arrangements
Muslims make very elaborate preparations and arrangements for the month of fasting. They cancel business tours and try to stay at home during the month of Ramadan. They get up early in the morning before dawn and offer nafilla (optional) prayer before taking their sehri (morning meals). In Muslim countries, especially in India and Pakistan, people in groups

move about in the streets singing praises of Allah and *Darud* on His Holy Messenger (peace be upon him) to wake people up for sehri. Many people do not sleep at all during the night, but read the Qur'an and offer *nafilla* prayers. In Saudi Arabia most of the people do not sleep at night during the month of Fasting. They go to sleep after morning prayer.

Again in the evening at *iftari* (breaking of fast) people gather together in the mosques, or families assemble at home, and have plenty of fruit, sweets, salty dishes and cold drinks. Normally Muslims, according to the *Sunnah* (custom) of the Holy Messenger (peace be upon him), break their fast with a couple of dates and then take a light snack at sunset, followed by evening prayer *(salat al-maghrib)*.

The breaking of fast is called *iftari*. After the prayer, they have their full dinner. At the breaking of the fast, Muslims repeat the words of the Holy Messenger (peace be upon him) according to his *Sunnah:* Oh Allah! I have fasted for you , I have believed in you, and with your food I break the fast. In the name of Allah, most Gracious, most Merciful." It is also the *Sunnah* of the Holy Messenger (peace be upon him) to break fast soon after sunset without delay. Sahl reported Allah's Messenger said: "They will continue to prosper as long as they hasten the breaking of the fast."

When Muslims begin their fast at dawn, they take their meals, known as *Sahur* or *sehri* in the tradition of the Holy Messenger (peace be upon him). This event is described in the Holy Qur'an in these words: "And eat and drink, until the white thread of dawn appears to you distinct from its black thread; then complete your fast till the night appears" (Qur'an 2: 187).

It is the *Sunnah* of the Holy Messenger (peace be upon him) to eat before commencing fast early in the morning before dawn: According to Anas, Allah's Messenger (peace be upon him) said, "Take a meal a little before dawn for there is a blessing in taking a meal at that time." At the commencement of the fast, when Muslims take *sehri* (or *Suhur)* they pronounce their intention of fasting in these words, according to the *Sunnah* of the Holy Messenger (peace be upon him): "Oh Allah! I intend to fast today in obedience to your Command and only to seek your pleasure." There is an additional prayer, called *tarawih* prayer, of 8,12, or 20 *rakat,* with the night prayer, during the month of fasting.

4. Times of Fasting
The fast lasts from dawn to dusk, between which times a Muslim may neither eat nor drink anything, nor smoke, nor indulge in sexual intercourse. He should avoid hearing, seeing or doing anything evil or obscene. According to the Holy Messenger (peace be upon him), people who do even minor evils lose the good effects of fasting. Abu Hurairah reported Allah's Messenger (peace be upon him) as saying: "Whoever does not give up false speech and evil action, Allah is not in need of his leaving his food and water (i.e. Allah will not accept his fasting)."

Thus mere hunger and thirst does not consitute fasting. It consists in complete abstention from worldly things, including food, drink and evil-doing of every kind. This is the essence of fasting and of all forms of *ibadah.* It is not mere refraining from food and drink but from all kinds of foul speech, abusive words and evil deeds. The times of fasting are clearly laid down in the Qur'an in the following words: "And eat and drink, until the white thread of dawn appears to you distinct from its black thread; then complete your fast till the night appears." (Qur'an 2: 187). This verse of the Holy Qur'an clearly lays down the time limits of fasting. It does not, however, give times by the clock but mentions the clear and visible signs on the horizon which indicate the arrival of mornings and evenings in all parts of the world. This is the natural and simple method by which people can find times of fasting and prayer without much difficulty in any part of the world.

People living in some parts of the world face long periods of darkness but they still have their hours of sleep and work and hours of relaxation. They go to work at fixed hours and come back at fixed hours. They get up at certain hours in the morning for work and go to bed at fixed hours at night. They speak of their day activities and night engagements as do people living on or around the Equator. They may not have seen the sun for long periods of time, but every day, they observe the visible sign of the approaching day in the form of light on the eastern horizon, clearly differentiating day from night. They get up and go to work and, in the evening, they clearly observe the light fading away and darkness gradually spreading over the sky. Accordingly, they fix their times of work, play and other engagements.

They can fix their starting time for fasting from the approaching light on the Eastern horizon, separating it from darkness, at the end of their night; and the ending time from the approaching darkness at the end of their working day. This can be done with ease and without any difficulty. It needs little observation. And I am sure, people living in those extreme regions of the earth must have observed these natural geographical phenomenon many times in their lives. In the rest of the world, it is no problem. Fast begins at dawn and ends at sunset. There is no need to be very strict about the times. There can be a difference of seconds and even minutes in fixing actual times.

5. Purpose of fasting
A Muslim does not eat, drink or smoke and undergoes a severe and rigorous discipline during the month of fasting

because of his Faith in God, and for His Love and for fear of His punishment. This continuous rigorous discipline strengthens one's Faith in Allah and makes one sincere, faithful and obedient to His Command.

(a) Social Benefits

Hunger is, in fact, a great revealing experience. It shows people what it is like to be hungry. It helps them to feel and share other people's suffering in hunger and thirst. All Muslims, rich and poor, all over the world, go through this experience of hunger and thirst. They all are brought closer to each other through fasting. This is bound to renew their brotherly ties and awaken sympathy for the poor in the hearts of the rich.

During the month of *Ramadan,* all Muslims, rich and poor, gather in the mosques at the time of *iftari* (breaking of fast) and for additional, *tarawih* prayers at night. In fact, it is a time of great festivities in the mosques. The rich and the poor, all come to the mosque during this month at least and meet each other. This greatly helps to strengthen the feeling and ties of Muslim brotherhood among them. They feel, experience and see brotherhood in practice in the mosques every day during this month. Thus fasting can have immense social value.

Certainly it has great social impact when all Muslims, from every walk of life, fast together. They come to gether in large numbers for *iftari* and for *tarawih* prayers in the mosques and sit together. It helps to bring them closer to each other, thrilled and filled with sentiments of love and brotherhood.

(b) Physical Benefits

Fasting has also many great physical benefits for us. Abstention from food and drink for a full month of days does a lot of good to the physical health of the person. It gives the stomach a rest during the day when nothing is eaten or drunk and provides it with an opportunity to do an annual cleaning. During the year, many kinds of toxic matter and other unwanted chemicals are formed in the body, which, if left there, are likely to cause damage to the bodily system and thereby invite various kinds of diseases and sickness.

During the month of fasting, the stomach has plenty of time to do the annual cleaning and repairing of the body system. All toxic matter is dissolved, burnt or removed from the body during fasting. The whole system is cleansed of undesirable and unwanted material and is greatly strengthened after this annual overhauling through fasting. Even fatty substances in the body are eliminated in this process. After this, the body is completely restored to its natural condition ready to face with strength the journey of the next year.

Fasting also helps to strengthen one's will and determination to face the hardships of life. It is, in fact, a practial training in increasing and building up one's power of resistance.

(c) Moral Benefits
Fasting teaches a man moral discipline through practical training during the month of *Ramadan*. It is through fasting that he suffers and undergoes trials of hunger and thirst. He goes through this hard discipline day in, day out, for a full month. He abstains from food, drink and from all other pleasures of life and restrains himself from indulgence in enjoyment during the day. He does this willingly without any external pressure or coercion, merely in obedience to the Command of God, to seek His Pleasure. It helps in building up his moral character.

It also teaches him self-control and self-restraint, in order to overpower his sensual lusts and conquer his physical desires. He does not eat or drink when he wishes, or when his appetite is strong. He eats and drinks at intervals when he is allowed to do so. This enables him to be the master and not the slave of his desires and appetites. He becomes strong to control and rule his desires. His confidence in himself grows and his will power is strengthened. He has subdued his wishes and has become master of his self. A muslim learns to supperess his passions and his desires every day during the month of fasting, for the sake of God. Thus, through fasting, a man attains real moral greatness.

(d) Spiritual Benefits

Fasting has immense spiritual value for it is basically a spiritual exercise and discipline. It brings man closer to God and removes all barriers between him and his Lord: "O you who believe! fasting is prescribed to you — so that you may fear Allah (and gain your *taqwa)"* (Qur'an 2: 183).

The very purpose of fasting, in this verse of the Qur'an, is described as the attainment of *taqwa*. Believers are commanded to observe fasting in the month of *Ramadan* so that through it they may be able to attain nearness to God. As fasting is observed for God and only He Knows whether a person is really fasting or not, it brings a man very close to his Creator.

Abu Hurairah reported Allah's Messenger (peace be upon him) as saying: "All the deeds of Adam's sons are for them, except fasting which is for Me, and I will give the reward for it."

Fasting strengthens the spiritual powers of man and clarifies his mental and spiritual vision for seeing and experiencing the multifarious manifestations of his Lord. The fact that it is observed merely in obedience and for the pleasure of God, makes it more significant. It lifts man very high in the spiritual world.

Fasting protects man from all kinds of temptations of body and mind and keeps him on the path towards his Lord. No evil desires or carnal pleasures of the self can mislead or misdirect him from his goal. Fasting is a protective shield against all kinds of moral or spiritual dangers.

According to Abu Hurairah, Allah's Messenger (peace be upon him) said, "Fasting is a shield or shelter from committing sin. If one of you is fasting, he should avoid obscenity and quarrelling, and if somebody should fight or quarrel with him, he should say 'I am fasting.' "

Fasting reminds one throughout the day that he is abstaining from food and drink and other pleasures of life in obedience to the Command of God. There is none to see and check whether he is eating or drinking or enjoying other pleasures of life. He abstains from all these things with the full knowledge that God is always with him and always sees and hears him doing everything, and that nothing can be hidden from Him. Thus fasting develops a very strong sense of nearness and closeness to God and of His Presence everywhere. The rigid discipline of fasting for one month makes Divine Nearness and Presence a reality for the believers. They develop a new awareness of a higher spiritual life, far above the life of desires and passions. Here they can meet their Lord, talk to Him and enjoy His Companionship: "When My servants ask you concerning Me, I am indeed close to them. I listen to the prayer of every crier who calls on Me. Let them also, with a will, listen to My Call, and believe in Me, that they may walk in the right way." (Qur'an 2: 186).

This emphasises the spiritual significance of fasting and how it helps to bring man closer to his Lord and Sovereign. This experience is further elaborated in a hadith of the Holy Messenger (peace be upon him): "There are two pleasures for the fasting person, one at the time of breaking his fast, and the other at the time when he meets his Lord; then he will be pleased because of his fasting."

This hadith throws further light on the spiritual value of fasting. It also helps in strengthening one's spiritual power in another way. Abstention from food and drink all day long for a complete month definitely weakens one's physical strength and powers. In the past, people of all religions, Christials, Jews and Hindus, have tried to weaken their physical powers through stravation in order to strengthen their spiritual powers and to build up their relationship with their Lord. They tried to achieve nearness to Allah through complete annihilation and destruction of their physical powers by starvation. Muslims have found a short and effective recipe in fasting, without starving themselves, to seek closeness to God. There is no doubt that when you leave nourishment of your body and your carnal desires for the sake of God, your soul and your spiritual powers begin to receive more and more nourishment from your Lord. This process gradually develops and strengthens the spiritual powers of the person who is fasting and, by the end of the month of *Ramadan* gives him sufficient spiritual strength to attain a very close relationship with his Creator.

(e) Economic Benefits

Among other blessings, fasting brings enormous economic benefits for the Muslim community. During the month of *Ramadan,* the rich people spend very generously on the poor to win the Pleasure of God. Their generosity and charity enable the poor section of the community to receive sufficient funds during this month to meet their needs for at least a part of the year. Muslims make every effort to do more good in this month than during the rest of the year, in the hope that their efforts will be rewarded many times by God. The month of *Ramadan* is a month of blessing and the Muslims spend more, following the tradition of their Messenger (peace be upon him), in order to attain more goodness from their Lord.

Ibn Abbas reported that the Holy Messenger (peace be upon him) was the most generous amongst the people, and he used to be more so in the month of *Ramadan:* "Abu Hurairah reported Allah's Messenger (peace be upon him) as saying: "When the first night of *Ramadan* comes, the devils and rebellious jinn are chained, the gates of hell are locked and not one of them is opened; the gates of Paradise are opened and not one of them is locked, and a crier calls, You who desire what is good, come forward, and you who desire evil refrain." Salman al-Farsi told of Allah's Messenger as saying on the last day of *Sha'ban:* 'A great month, a blessed month. If someone draws near to Allah during it with some good act, he will be like one who fulfills an obligatory duty in another month . . . It is the moth of endurance, and the reward of endurance is Paradise. It is the month of sharing with others, and a month in which the believers provision is increased. If someone gives one who has been fasting something with which to break his fast, it will provide forgiveness of his sins and save him from hell . . . It is a month whose beginning is mercy, whose middle forgiveness, and whose end is freedom from hell."

The Muslims, especially those who are rich, give a share of their wealth to the poor in order to seek the Blessings and Pleasure of their Lord. Thus *Ramadan* helps all in obtaining something in it, the poor get some money to meet their economic needs from the overflowing charity of the rich, while the latter hope to get their reward from their Lord in many forms. Then peole who, owing to sickness or old age, cannot fast, are asked to feed the poor in compensation. Many rich people who are sick or too old to fast lavishly feed the poor in the month of *Ramadan:* "For those who can do it but with hardship, is a ransom, the feeding of one that is in need. But he that will give more, of his own free will, it is better for him. " (Qur'an 2: 184).

The Holy Prophet (peace be upon him) according to Abu Hurairah and Ibn Abbas, told those who could not endure fasting to feed a poor person for every day they did not fast. Permanently sick people are also permitted, according to the above-quoted verse of the Qur'an, to give *fidya* (food to the poor) in compensation.

At the end of *Ramadan,* there is the festival of *Id al-Fitr,* when Muslims gather together to offer a two *rakat Id* prayer as a token of gratitude and thanksgiving to their Lord for having successfully completed the month of fasting. But it is obligatory on every Muslim, man and woman, to pay *fitrana* to the poor for every member of the family, including babies and children, before going to *Id al-Fitr. Ramadan* and the Festival of *Id* will not benefit Muslims unless first they enable the poor members of the community to have enough money to celebrate the Festival. The Holy Messenger (peace be upon him) laid great stress on the payment of *Fitrana* (about 50 pence per person, it changes with change in the price of cereals) ,before the celebration of *Id al-Fitr.* He even told his followwers that non-payment of this poor due will render their fasting null and void.

In short, the month of fasting has great economic benefits for the Muslim community, especially for the poor. It brings the Blessing of God in the form of wealth and food into the homes of poor people.

13

Hajj (Pilgrimage)

Hajj is the fifth Pillar of Islam and is an act of *ibadah* (worship), like prayer and fasting. It is a religous duty and is obligatory, once in their lifetime, for all those Muslims who can afford to perform it. All the five pillars of Islam perform very important and specific functions in training a Muslim for the service of Islam. Prayer provides an exercise in mental culture; *zakat* gives training in spending wealth, fasting provides training in self-discipline and self-control over the body and its desires; and *hajj* is a form of *ibadah* which covers all aspects of human life. It trains a Muslim to sacrifice all his wealth, all his time, all his physical and mental energies and all his comforts and possessions in the way of Allah.

The *Ka'ba* and its History
The building called the *Ka'ba* stands in the centre of the city of Mecca in Saudi Arabia. It is about 45 feet high, 33 feet wide, and 50 feet long, and is covered with a black cloth decorated with verses from the Qur'an.
The *Ka'ba* was the first mosque on the earth to be appointed by God for His Worship. It is also called *Bait Ullah* (House of God); *Bait al-Haram* (the Forbidden House), and *Bait al Atiq* (the Ancient House).
It was the first House of Worship on the earth: "The first House of Worship appointed for men was that at *Bakka* (Mecca); full of blessing and of guidance for all." (Qur'an 3:

96). It is also an Ancient House: "Then let them complete the rites prescribed for them, perform their vows, and again circumambulate the Ancient House." (Qur'an 22: 29). It is also the Forbidden House *(Bait al-Haram)*, a place whose sanctity must not be violated: "Allah made *Ka'ba,* the Sacred House, an asylum of security for men." (Qur'an 5: 100). It is a place of sanctity and respect: "O My Lord! I have made some of my offspring to dwell in a valley without cultivation, by your sacred House." (Qur'an 14: 37).

There is no authentic record to show when the *Ka'ba* was first built, or who built it, but it was reconstructed by Abraham and Ishmael (peace be upon them): "And remember Abraham and Ishmael raised the foundations of the House with a prayer." (Qur'an 2: 127).

Though there is no historical record as to when and by whom the *Ka'ba* was built at Mecca, the Qur'an makes it clear that it was already there when Prophet Abraham (peace be upon him) left his wife Hajara with his baby Ishmael in the barren valley of Mecca: "O our Lord! I have made some of my offspring to live in a valley without cultivation, by Your Sacred House; in order, O My Lord, that they may establish regular prayer." (Qur'an 14: 37).

Probably the building of *Ka'ba* was then in a ruined condition. It was a dry and barren valley. There was no sign of water anywhere when Prophet Abraham (peace be upon him) left his wife and son in this uncultivated and barren valley. But God created a spring from under the feet of the baby boy Ishmael when his mother left him there on the sand and went to look for water. This spring still exists there and hundreds and thousands of pilgrims drink its water and take some back to their homes. It is known as zam zam.

When Ishmael grew up, his father came to see him and told

him that Allah had Commanded him to sacrifice him: "So We gave him the Good News of a patient and forbearing boy, then, when the son reached the age of serious work with him, he said, "O my son! I see in a vision that I offer you in sacrifice. Now say what is your opinion!" The son said, "O my father! Do as you are Commanded, you will find me, if Allah wills, one of the patient." (Qur'an 37: 101-2). So when they had both submitted their wills to Allah, and he had laid him prostrate on his forehead for sacrifice, We called out to him: "O Abraham! You have already fufilled the vision!" - thus indeed do We reward those who do right. For this was obviously a trial and We ransomed him with a momentous sacrifice." (Qur'an 37: 103-107).

Thus after Abraham (peace be upon him) had gone through the trial successfully, God made him leader of the nations: "And remember that Abraham was tried by His Lord with certain Commands, which he fulfilled. He said, 'I will make you an Imam to the nations.' " (Qur'an 2: 124).

Prophet Abraham (peace be upon him) again came back to Mecca, when Ishmael had grown into a man, and rebuilt the Ka'ba: "And remember Abraham and Ishmael raised the foundations of the House with this prayer: 'Our Lord! Accept this service from us; for you are the All-Hearing, the All-Knowing. Our Lord! Make of us Muslims, bowing to Your Will, and of our progeny a people Muslim, bowing to Your Will; and show us places for the celebration of due rites; and turn unto us in Mercy . . . Our Lord! Send amongst them a Messenger of their own." (Qur'an 2: 127-9).

God accepted their prayer and Commanded them not to obey anyone except Him: "Behold! We gave the site (at Mecca) to Abraham, of the Sacred House (Ka'ba), saying, 'Associate not anything in worship with Me; and sanctify My House for those who compass it round (tawaf) or stand up, or bow, or prostrate themselves in prayer." (Qur'an 22: 26).

Then Abraham (peace be upon him) prayed for the safety and prosperity of the place where he had settled his offspring and its people in these words: "And remember Abraham said, 'My Lord make this a city of peace, and feed its people with fruits.' " (Qur'an 2: 126).

When the building of the *Ka'ba* was completed and Ishmael had settled down with some other Arabs in that place, Prophet Abraham (peace be upon him) was commanded by God to proclaim pilgrimage to the House for the people: "And proclaim pilgrimage among men; they will come to you on foot and mounted on every kind of camel, lean on account of journeys through deep and distant mountain highways." (Qur'an 22: 27).

Abraham (peace be upon him) also prayed for God's Grace and His Mercy on his progeny and on all people that they might come to this House with love and affection: "So fill the hearts of some among men with love towards them, and feed them with fruits, so that they may give thanks." (Qur'an 14: 37).

The sanctity of the *Ka'ba* had made the city of Mecca a sacred place. The *Quraish*, who were the deadliest enemies of Prophet Muhammad (peace be upon him), had gained honour and prestige, wealth and security, owing to the sanctity of the *Ka'ba*. People all over the Arabian subcontinent respected them and did not even disturb their trade. They owed all their honour and wealth to the *Ka'ba* and to God. They are reminded of this fact in these words: "For the covenants (of security and safeguard enjoyed) by the *Quraish*, their covenants (covering) journeys by winter and summer; let them adore the Lord of this House, Who provides them with food against hunger, and with security against fear (of danger)." (Qur'an 106: 1-4).

In those days of insecurity, the sancity, of the *Ka'ba* enabled them to obtain agreements of security and safety from all the people around them. They carried on their trade freely and without fear. Their trade routes to Syria, Egypt and other places were undisturbed. All these benefits to the people of Mecca were the direct result of the sanctity of the *Ka'ba*.

Since those days of Prophet Abraham (peace be upon him), people have been coming to the *Ka'ba* either for a short visit *(umra)* or for the Pilgrimage. Today hundreds and thousands of Muslims come annually on aeroplanes, ships, coaches and camels from all parts of the world to Mecca for polgrimage. All the year round, people flock together to this place for visit *(umra)*. There are wars and fighting everywhere; nowhere is real peace and contentment, but go to Mecca and you will find there peace and contentment. The significance of this verse is realised at Mecca: "Remember We made the house a place of assembly for men and a place of safety." (Qur'an 2: 125).

People in hundreds and thousands all the year round go to Mecca and perform *tawaf* (circumambulation) with love and devotion to their Lord. Summer or winter, day or night, raining or fire, people flock around the *Ka'ba* to perform *tawaf* in extreme love and reverence. When the *Ka'ba* was flooded in 1969 and there was four or five feet of water in it, people were still performing *tawaf*. In the scorching heat of the sun at noon, when the temperature goes up to 120 degrees and even higher, and stones of the floor of the *Ka'ba* are burning hot, people continue their usual *tawaf* around the *Ka'ba* in extreme humility, love and devotion.

Importance and Significance of the Pilgrimage

In some ways, the Pilgrimage is the most signigicant of all forms of the *ibadah*. It is only in pilgrimage that a Muslim is required to give up all his work and leave all his near and dear ones for a number of days and undertake a journey to Mecca. He is to give up all the pleasures and amenities of life and live a simple asceitic life during the Pilgrimage. All this rigorous discipline and hard life is merely for the love of God.

During the Pilgrimage, a Muslim visits many holy and historical places in Mecca and Medina which leave an everlasting impresion of the glory of Islam on his mind. It is a practical experience of the history of Islam and a sort of refresher course for him. His Faith in God and in His Messenger is strengthened and his Knowledge of the truthfulness of His Message is increased. The Pilgrimage is, in a way, essential for every Muslim, for it refreshes and invigorates his Faith.

God forgives the sins of those who perform the pilgrimage and does not care for those who die without performing it: Abu Umama reported Allah's Messenger as saying: "He who is not prevented from performing the Pilgrimage by an obvious necessity, a tyrannical ruler, or a disease which confines him at hime, and dies without having performed the Pilgrimage, may die if he wishes as a Jew or if he wishes as a Christian." Abu Hurairah reported Allah's Messenger as saying: "Those who perform the Pilgrimage and those who perform the *umra* are people who have come to visit God. If they supplicate Him, He will respond to them, and if they ask Him for forgiveness, He will forgive them."

Social Benefits
One of the Pilgrimage's great social benefits is that it helps in levelling all kinds of distinctions of rank, colour and race. People of all colours, all nationalities, all races, and of all ranks, from all the four corners of the world come here and meet and live together. They have all come before their Lord in extreme humility, wearing two white sheets, as members of Universal Muslim Brotherhood, without any distinction between the high and the low. Kings and servants, employers and their employees, capitalists and wage earners, masters and slaves, all assemble as humble servants of their Lord.

They are all clad in one type of dress, assemble at one place, utter the same words, *Labbaika Allah humma labbaika* (Here am I, O God! Here am I in Your Presence) and move in one direction.

It is the Pilgrimage that makes all Muslims high or low, black or white, Arab or non-Arab, wear one dress, speak one language and assemble at one place in obedience to and for the Pleasure of God. They are all equal before their Lord. They have left their marks of distinction behind and have come to join once in their lifetime in this demonstration of equality of man. Thus it is a practical experience of equality and universality unparalleled.

Economic Benefits

The Pilgrimage has its economic benefits for Muslims. They come from various walks of life; some are traders or industrialists, others are capitalists or farmers. They can discuss the economic problems of their mutual benefits; exchange of technical know-how or skill, or exchange of goods and machinery between them. The rich countries can think of the ways to give financial aid or loans to the poor and underdeveloped Muslim countries. The poor countries can duscuss their economic problems with their brother pilgrims from the rich countries.

They can determine the nature and qualities of their imports and exports from each other on this occasion. They can formulate the basic principles of their economic measures for the next year in consultation with each other. Thus the Pilgrimage can provide a forum for discussion for the formation of common economic policies for mutual benefits and for the establishment of a Common Market for the Muslim World.

It is a great occasion and opportunity for discussing the day to day economic problems that face Muslim countries in the world of to day. Many Muslim countries may find it difficult or impossible, owing to financial weakness or lack of technical and scientific knowledge, to launch better industrial or agricultural schemes to improve their economic position. The Pilgrimage provides such countries with an opportunity to seek financial as well as technical aid from their sister Muslim countries who have the necessary skills, technical knowledge and capital for this purpose.

It is a great economic blessing in disguise. Muslims perform an act of *ibdah* and devotion and, at the same time, they make profit by trading in goods with their fellow Muslims from other countries. In Islam, *ibadah* is not divorced from worldly business as it is in other religions. Every act of a believer, whether prayer or business transaction is considered an act of *ibadah* if it is performed in obedience of God. So long as a believer is obeying the law of God, his every action is an act of *ibadah:* "It is not objectionable for you to seek the bounty of your Lord during the Pilgrimage." (Qur'an 2: 198). Trade is allowed during the pilgrimage in the interest of both, the trader, to meet his own journey expenses, and of other pilgrims in general, who would otherwise be put to great hardship and inconvenience for lack of the necessities of life.

Thus the pilgrimage is beneficial to the individual trader and to all other pilgrims in providing both for individual needs and the economic interests of the entire Muslim World.

Political Benefits
All the Muslims gather together at one centre, Mecca, for the Pilgrimage. They can discuss the current subject of their common interest and can formulate in general a common policy to be followed by All Muslim countries in the United Nation organisations and the Security Council. They

assemble on this holy and pious occasion every year, which gives them great chance of agreeing on many topics of common interest. This annual gathering certainly helps to bring them closer to each other.

Spiritual Benefits

Above all these benefits lies the higher spiritual experience which is made possible by this unparalleled gathering of men and women from all parts of the world. It is the experience of coming closer and closer to God until a pilgrim feels that all the barriers between him and his Lord are removed and nothing stands between them. He feels he is standing in the presence of his Lord, and in excitement and ecstacy he cries, *'Labbaika Allah humma labbaika'* (Here am I, O God! Here am I in Your Presence).

In the valley of *Arafat,* on this great occasion, hundreds and thousands of people are assembling, all of them in groups shouting "Here we are, O God! Here we are, in Your Presence!' This experience of a pilgrim cannot be described in words, it can only be felt by one who has gone through such an experience himself.

A pilgrim has left his home, his country, his business and his relatives and has come here to seek the pleasure of God. He has given up all the pleasures, comforts and amenities of life, and has undertaken this long journey to Mecca to go through all the hardships, inconveniences and sufferings of the pilgrimage. Here he is in the company of thousands of his Muslim brothers, all wearing one dress, answering the Call of their Lord in one language. He has even taken off his worldly dress and wrapped round him two white sheets and has come in the Presence of his Sovereign to seek His Pleasure and Goodwill. Having forsaken all the physical barriers which stand between him and his Lord, he is calling and crying, 'Here am I, God, here am I.' This extreme concentration of his ideas and mind on God in extreme humbleness brings him in reality into the Presence of God.

It is true that God is not confined to any one place, and the *Ka'ba* is no exception. But the higher experience of nearness to God is attained in the atmosphere of a multitude of people who lave left everything behind and have gathered together here for God, their only objective here is God and His Pleasure, all worldly comforts, wealth, engagements and relations, which are a veil hiding the spirtual realities of the other world, are left behind, and he can, during the pilgrimage, turn to God and feel his Presence in reality.

The great significance of this higher spiritual experience in a gathering may be expressed from another point of view. It is true that one's heart and mind can have a mysterious communion with another, as proved by telepathy. When you are in the company of a man who is inspired by the same thing and is underging the same spiritual experience, your spiritual experience will naturally get additional strength from him and will in return strengthen him.

When hundreds and thousands of people are gathered for the Pilgrimage, they are all inspired by the presence of the Divine Being. The objective of all is one and they are all concentrating on that objective. This internal unity of objective is further strengthened by their outward unity. They are all clad in the same way, all gathered together in the same place and uttering the same words again and again, *'Labbaika Allah humma labbaika'* (Here we are, O God! Here are we in Your Presence). Their appearance and their demeanour and their regular crying all give the impression that they are, in fact, standing in the Presence of their Lord. They are so absorbed in their dialogue with the Divine Being that they have lost all sense of time or space, or even of their own being. This spiritual experience in gatherings is many times intensified and heightened in its effect on each individual pilgrim by the accumulated effect of the of the experience of hundreds and thousands of other pilgrims. Though God is not confined to any one place, it is a reality that many of the people who are gathered at Mecca in the valley of *Arafat* on the 9th of the month of Dhu al-Hijjah do see Him and feel His Presence amongst themselves.

For Whom it is Compulsory

The Pilgrimage to Mecca once in a lifetime is a religious duty and an act of *ibadah* for a Muslim. It is obligatory on all adults who can afford to undertake a journey to Mecca: "Pilgrimage thereto is a duty men owe to Allah, – those who can afford the journey." (Qur'an 3: 97).

Thus there seems to be three conditions on the obligation to perform the pilgrimage to Mecca:
It is obligatory, first, only on adults and not children, second, second, only on those who have sufficient money to pay for the return journey to Mecca and to meet all the expenses during their stay in Mecca and elsewhere. Those who do not possess sufficient provision for this journey are not required to undertake it: "And take a provision with you for the journey." (Qur'an 2: 197).

It is essential that pilgrims should take sufficient provision with them so that they may perform the ceremonies of the pilgrimage with complete concentration and peace of mind and will not be forced to resort to begging.

Third, it is necessary only for those who are physically fit to undertake the journey. People who are sick or very old and are unable, due to their physical disability, to undergo the hardships of a long journey, are not required to undertake it. Fourth, danger to life, owing to war in certain areas in or around the Holy Land, or in one's own country, may also free a man from the obligatory undertaking of the Pilgrimage. The Holy Messenger (peace be upon him) and his companions could not perform pilgrimage for many years after migration to Medina owing to danger to their lives.

14

Ceremonies

The great Messenger of God, Abraham (peace be upon him), proclaimed annual pilgrimage to the Holy House of God (Qur'an 22: 27) and people began their journeys to the Holy Land and the *Ka'ba*. Gradually, this great institution of the Pilgrimage was established. Some un-Islamic ceremonies were later on introduced into it by the infidels of Mecca during the courcse of centuries after Abraham (peace be upon him), but Muhammad (peace be upon him) purified it of all adulteration.

The main events of the Pilgrimage are as follows:

1. *Ihram* (Ceremonial Dress)
The Pilgrims, on reaching the boundaries of the *Ka'ba,* take a bath and put on *ihram,* consisting of two sheets of cloth, preferably white, one on their shoulders and the other round their waist, covering the lower parts of the body. Women pilgrims do not put on *ihram* but are allowed to perform the Pilgrimage in their ordinary clothes, preferably white. Men must not cover their heads, while women must not cover their faces during the pilgrimage. The footwear of pilgrims should be below the ankles.
After *ihram,* the intention to perform the pilgrimage may be expressed in these words: "O Allah! I intend to perform the pilgrimage and I have put on *ihram.* Make it easy for me and accept it." Then a two-rakat prayer is offered before starting the journey to Mecca.

Miqat − It may be pointed out that *ihram* is put on at places called *miqat*. These are the boundary lines of *haram* (forbidden) areas and no pilgrim can go beyond *miqat* lines without *ihram*. Ibn Abbas said that Allah's Messenger (peace be upon him) appointed the following places for putting on *ihram (miqat);* Dhul Hulaifa for the people of Medina, Al − Juhfa for the people of Syria, Qarn al-Manazil for the people of Najd, and Yalamlam for the people of Yemen; so these spots are for those regions and for people of other regions who come to them intending to perform the Pilgrimage and *umra*. The place where those who live nearer to Mecca should put on *ihram* is where they live. According to A'isha, Allah's Messenger (peace be upon him) appointed Dhatulrq as the place where the people of Iraq should put on *ihram*. People who go to Pilgrimage by air or by ship put on *ihram* at Jeddah.

Forbidden Things in *Ihram*
The word *ihram* derives its root from *haram* which means forbidden. A pilgrim is forbidden even lawful pleasures on entering upon a state of *ihram*. Women must not put on jewellery or personal adornments or even scent. Pilgrims must not shave, trim their hair or nails, or have marital relations: Abdullah reported that Allah's Messenger (peace be upon him) was asked what sort of clothes a *muhrim* (one in a state of *ihram)* may wear. He replied: 'He should not wear a shirt, turban, trousers, a hooded cloak, or a dress perfumed with saffron or wars. If shoes are not available he can wear khuffs but he should cut them so that they reach below the ankles."

There should not be any fighting, rudeness, or even arguments during the state of *ihram*. It is a state of complete self-denial and submission to God. It is a symbol of renunciation of worldly pleasures, vanities and desires: "For the pilgrimage are the months well known. If anyone undertakes that duty therein, let there be no obscenity, nor wrangling in the pilgrimage." (Qur'an 2: 197).

These evils are condemned under all circumstances, but the severity of these sins increases many times when committed during the state of *ihram.*
According to Abu Hurairah, Allah's Messenger (peace be upon him) said: "If anyone performs the Pilgrimage for Allah's sake without talking immodestly or acting wickedly, he will return free from sin as on the day his mother bore him."

2. *Talbiya*
Miqat is also called *muhill* which means a place of raising voices with *talbiya.* On entering into the state of *ihram* at the appointed *miqat (Muhill),* the pilgrims raise their voices with *talbiya* in the tradition of the Holy Messenger of Allah. *Talbiya* consists in reciting the following words aloud: *Labbaika, Allah Hummah, Labbaika Labbaika* (Here am I, O God. Here am I, here am I in Your Presence). *La Shrika Lak Labbaika,* (You have no partner, here am I). *Inn al Hamda Wal ni'amata Lak* (Surely all Praise and Grace are for You). *Wal Mulka La Sharika Lak,* (and the Kingdom is Yours, You have no partners).

These words of *talbiya* are often recited again and again by the pilgrims on reaching Mecca and during their journey from Mecca to Mina and Arafat and back to Mina, until the throwing of stones on the 10th of Dhul Hijja, Khallad bin As-Saib on his father's authority reported Allah's messenger (peace be upon him) as saying: 'Gabriel came to me and commanded me to order my companions to raise their voices in *talbiya.*' " Ibn Umar said that Allah's Messenger (peace be upon him) used to perform two *rakat* in Dhul Hulaifa (Medina's *miqat),* then when the she-camel stood up with him on its back at the mosque of Dhul Halaifa, he shouted these words: *'Labbaika, Allah, hummah labbaika labbaika.'* "

3. *Tawaf* (Circumambulation) of the Ka'ba

After *ihram*, the pilgrims proceed to Mecca. On reaching Mecca, they leave their luggage at hotels or places of their *muallams*, as prearranged, and go to the *Ka'ba*. When they enter the building, they recite the following verse in accordance with the *sunnah* (tradition) of the Holy Prophet: "O Allah. You are Peace, and Peace comes from You. So greet us, O Allah with Peace."

Tawaf means going round the *Ka'ba*. It forms a very important part of the devotional acts of the Pilgrimage. It is the first act of the pilgrims on reaching Mecca and also their last act before leaving. The Qur'an commands the *tawaf* of the House of God in these words: "And let them complete the rites prescribed for them, perform their vows, and again go round the Ancient House." (Qur'an 22: 29).

The Prophet Muhammad (peace be upon him), on his arrival at Mecca, always performed *tawaf* of the *Ka'ba:* According to Ibn Umar, Allah's Messenger (peace be upon him) immediately on arriving, performed *tawaf* for the Pilgrimage or *umra;* he ran three circuits and walked four, then after making two prostrations (two *rakat* prayer), he would go between Safa and Marwa." Ibn Abbas reported Allah's Messenger (peace be upon him) as saying, *"Tawaf* of the House is like prayer, except that you speak while performing it, but he who speaks must speak only what is good."

The pilgrims go straight to the Black Stone *(Hajr-i-Aswad)* and kiss it, or touch it, unless prevented by the crowds, in which case, they raise their hands facing in the direction of the *Ka'ba* and say aloud: *"Allahu Akbar"* (God is Great). then, starting from the Black Stone, or from its corner, they begin their *tawaf.* Remember that *tawaf* begins from the Black Stone or from its corner; if the crowds prevent one going to the Black Stone and kissing it, then start *tawaf* from that corner. "Jabir reported that Allah's Messenger (peace be upon him) came to Mecca, went to the Stone and touched it, then moved to his right, running three circuits and walking four." "Ibn Abbas reported that Allah's Messenger (peace be upon him) went round the House on a camel, and as often as he came to the corner (of the Black Stone), he pointed to it with something in his hand and said, *'Allahu Akbar'* (God is Great)."

The pilgrims go round the *Ka'ba* seven times, starting and finishing each round at the corner of the Black Stone, kissing or touching it at the end of each round, if possible. If they are prevented from doing so, they raise their hands each time they reach the corner of the Black Stone, saying, *'Allahu Akbar'*. Certain prayers are repeated during *tawaf*. According to some traditions, *Kalimah al-Tamjid* is also recited. But between *Rukn al-Yamani* and the corner of the Black Stone, a famous Qur'anic verse is recited: *Rabbana atina fid dunniya hasanatanw wa fil akhirata hasna tanw wakina a'zab annar:* "O our Lord. Grant us the best of this world and the best of the Hereafter, and protect us from the punishment of the Fire."

During *tawaf* and the rest of the Pilgrimage in the *Ka'ba*, the pilgrims keep the middle of the upper sheet of cloth under their elbow, so that their right shoulder is bare and the left covered. After completion of *tawaf* of seven rounds, they stand between the Black Stone and the far end of the Gate of the *Ka'ba*, called *muqam-i-Multazim*. There they stand in front of the Gate of the *Ka'ba*, or touching it close to the wall of *Ka'ba*, and say their personal prayers, many in tears, weeping, before their Lord. Asking for forgiveness of their sins and for His Mercy and Blessing and requesting His Favours: Abis bin Rabia said that he saw Umar kissing the Stone and saying, "I know for sure that you are a stone which can neither benefit nor harm, and had I not seen

Allah's Messenger kissing you I would not have kissed you."

After this the pilgrims go to or near *Muqam-i-Ibrahim* to offer a two *rakat* prayer in accordance with the *sunnah* of the Holy Messenger: "In it are Signs manifest; for example, the station of Abraham; whoever enters it attains security; pilgrimage thereto is a duty men owe to Allah." (Qur'an 3: 97). And in Surat al-Baqarah: "Remember We made the House a place of assembly for men and a place of safety; and take you the station of Abraham as a place of prayer." (Qur'an 2: 125). It is a place of great blessing, where Prophet Abraham (peace be upon him) and his illustrous sons, Ishmael and Muhammad (peace be upon them) prayed.

The Black Stone *(Hajr-i-Aswad)*, according to Muslim tradition, was brought by the Angel Gabriel from Paradise, and was laid on the corner of the *Ka'ba* by Prophet Abraham under instruction from His Lord. And pilgrims kiss it following the traditions of the Great Messenger of God but do not worship it. The station of Abraham is also a Holy Place where Prophet Abraham publicly offered his prayers. And God has commanded the Muslims to make this a place of prayer. After this the *Muhrim* drinks *Zam Zam* from the Well of *ZamZam*.

4. *Sa'i* (Hastening)

After completing *tawaf,* pilgrims perform *sa'i* or running between *Safa* and *Marwa* seven times. Prophet Abraham (peace be upon him) left his few months old son, Ishmael, with his mother Hajara in the valley of *Faran* in *Mecca,* in obedience to the Command of Allah, with some food and water. After a couple of days, she found herself without water and food. She went on the Mount of *Safa* to look for water and left the baby boy on the sand. She ran in search of water between the mounts *Safa* and *Marwa* seven times but found nothing. She stood at Marwa and looked at her son who was lying on the sand. To her amazement, she heard a noise of gushing water through a narrow hole. When she went back to the place where she had left Ishmael, she found a spring of water was gushing out of the sand near the feet of of the baby.

God had opened up the spring miraculously at the feet of the baby, who was rubbing the sand with his feet, for their use and the use of the people of *Mecca* and the future pilgrims to this Holy Place.

In the memory of Prophet Abraham's wife Hajara's efforts between Safa and Marwa, in search of water for her son, God has made *sa'i* (running) between these mounts an important part of the pilgrimage and *umra*. After *tawaf,* the pilgrims and the visitors to the *Ka'ba* for *umra,* have to walk seven times between *Safa* and *Marwa,* starting from Safa and finishing the last round at *Marwa.* This is mentioned in the Qur'an in the following words: "Behold. *Safa* and *Marwa* are among the symbols of Allah. So if those who visit the House in the season of pilgrimage, or at other times (for *umra)* should compass round them." (Qur'an 2: 158).

The Prophet Muhammad (peace be upon him) used to do *sa'i* (or running) between Safa and Marwa whenever he visited Mecca for the Pilgrimage or *umra:* According to Ibn Umar, Allah's Messenger, after completing *tawaf* and a two *rakat* prayer, would go between As-Safa and al-Marwa. Qadama bin Abdullah bin Ammar said that he saw Allah's Messenger (peace be upon him) running between As-Safa and Al-Marwa on a camel without striking it, driving people away, or telling them to move aside."

Certain prayers are recited while going between these two places. When pilgrims, or those who go for *umra,* commence their running from *Safa* and again, when they reach *Safa* again, they recite loudly; *"Inna Safa wal Marwata* (behold

Safa and *Marwa) min sha'a'r Allah* (are the symbols of Allah." (Qur'an 2; 158).

The pilgrims recite many words glorifying their Lord and singing His Praises during this time between Safa and Marwa. According to some sources, it was a tradition of the Prophet Muhammad (peace be uon him) to recite *Kalimah at-tawhid* during *Sa'i*. In general, the pilgrims ascend Safa, face the *Ka'ba* and raise their hands in thanksgiving, singing aloud the Praises of their Lord. Then they walk down towards Marwa. On reaching Marwa, they ascend and raise their hands facing in the direction of the *Ka'ba* in thanksgiving, singing aloud the Praises of their Lord. They then come down and walk towards Safa and so on, repeating each time what they said in the first round. After completing seven rounds, they pray to God for forgiveness and ask for His Blessings.

5. Head-Shaving or Haircut

After the completion of ceremonies at Safa and Marwa, whether they can come out of the state of *ihram* or not depends on whether the person intends to do *umra* or the pilgrimage.

(a) *Umra*

Any Muslim who visits the *Ka'ba* at any time of the year other than the month of *Dhul Hijja* performs *umra,* the minor pilgrimage. This consists of all the ceremonies described above from number (1) tp (4). After completing the ceremonies at Safa and Marwa, he may have his head shaven or his hair cut and then come out of the state of *ihram*. He has performed *umra* in accordance with the Commandment of God. "Abu Hurairah reported Allah's Messenger as saying, "The performance of *umra* is an expiation for sins committed and the reward for *Hajj Mabrur* (the one accepted by Allah) is nothing other than Paradise."

(b) *Hajj at-Tammattu* **(Interrupted Pilgrimage)**

If a pilgrim comes to Mecca before the month of *Dhul Hijja,* or even a few days before the date of the Pilgrimage, he may perform *umra* only and complete all ceremonies described under numbers (1) to (4) and then come out of the state of *ihram* by having his head shaven or his hair cut. Women can come out of the state of *ihram* merely by cutting some of their hair. He (or she) has performed *umra* and waits for the specified dates of the Pilgrimage and then puts on *ihram* again for the Pilgrimage along with other pilgrims on the specified date, i.e. 8th of *Dhul Hijja.* This is called *Hajj at-Tammattu,* which literally means 'profitting' and it consists of combining *umrah* and the Pilgrimage. Before the Holy Prophet (peace be upon him), the pagans of Mecca had stopped this practice and the pilgrims were deprived of the benefits of *umra* with the pilgrimage unless they remained in the state of *ihram* between *umra* and the performance of the Pilgrimage itself. This may have meant days or even weeks in *ihram.*

The Holy Prophet, by the Command of Allah, made it quite lawful first to complete *umra* as described above and come out of the state of *ihram,* and then perform the Pilgrimage along with other pilgrims between the specified dates: "If any one wishes to continue *umra* on the pilgrimage, he must make an offering, such as he can afford, but if he cannot afford it, he should fast three days during the pilgrimage and seven days on his return, making ten days in all. This is for those whose household is not in the vicinity of the Sacred Mosque." (Qur'an 2: 196).

Those who reap the benefit of *umra* and the Pilgrimage are required to sacrifice a lamb or a goat, or share in the sacrifice of a camel or a cow with other pilgrims. If they cannot afford a sacrifice, they have to fast for ten days, three days during the Pilgrimage and seven days when they go back to their homes, as will be explained later.

According to Jabir, Allah's Messenger ordered his companions to perform *umra* with the *ihram* they intended for the Pilgrimage and to perform *tawaf*, and then cut short their hair and finish *ihram*. Ibn Abbas reported Allah's Messenger in the Farewell Pilgrimage as saying, "This is an *umra* which we have treated as a complete observance, so those who have no sacrificial animals may come completely out of the sacred state (of *ihram*), for the *umra* has become incorporated in the *Hajj* till the Day of Resurrection."

(c) *Hajj al-Qiran*
Qiran literally means uniting. It consists of entering into the state of *ihram* with the intention of performing both *umra* and *Hajj* together without leaving the state of *ihram* after *umra*, during the month of *Dul Hijja*.

Those who come in the month of *Dhul Hijja* on the specified date, or a day or two earlier with the intention of performing the Pilgrimage, perform all the ceremonies described above from (1) to (4), but do not have their heads shaven or their hair cut and remain in the state of *ihram*. They then join other pilgrims on 8th of *Dhul Hijja* in their journey to Mina, the next step in the performance of the Pilgrimage.

Thus the difference between *Qiran* and *Tammattu*, described under section (b), is that in the latter there is a break in the state of *ihram*, whereas in the former, the state of *ihram* is continuously maintained until the completion of all the ceremonies of the Pilgrimage.

6. Leaving Mecca for Mina
The pilgrims who had earlier performed *umra* and come out of the state of *ihram* put on their *ihram* for the pilgrimage on the 8th of *Dhul Hijja*. Then all pilgrims start together their

journey towards Mina, a place three or four miles from Mecca. They have to reach Mina before noon and offer their *zuhr, asr, maghrib* and *isha* prayers there. They sleep that night in Mina and offer the *fajr* prayer on the 9th of *Dhul Hijja* after sunrise, then all leave for Arafat. They all have to reach the plain of Arafat by noon in accordance with the tradition of the Prophet Muhammad, (peace be upon him).

7. *Wuquf* (halting) at *Arafat*

On the 9th of *Dhul Hijja,* all pilgrims leave Mina after sunrise and reach Arafat by noon or after noon. The Arafat plain is a valley surrounded by dry and barren mountains. It is said that Adam and Eve, after being thrown from Paradise, first met here. They recognized each other in this plain, which is therefore called Arafat, which means 'recognition'. It is about six miles from Mina and nine miles from Mecca.

The pilgrims in thousands set out towards Arafat in buses, coaches, cars, trucks, and on foot, reciting *talbiya* loudly, *'Labbaika, Labbaika, Allah humma Labbaika'* and *'Takbir Allahu Akbar'.* On reaching Arafat with their *mu'allams,* they stay in their camps and offer *zuhr* and *asr* prayers combined. It is a thrilling experience and a wonderful sight to watch hundreds and thousands of pigrims in *ihram* raise their hands in prayer and thanksgiving and repeat the words again and again in the valley of Arafat:
Labbaika! Labbaika Allah Humma Labbaika! Labbaika! La Sharika Lak Labbaika! Innal Hamda wal ni'mata lak wal Mulka la Sharik Lak
Here are We, Here are We, O our Lord! Here are we, here are we, You have no partner ,Here are we, Praise and Grace be Yours and Yours is the Sovereignty undivided.
Staying in the plain of Arafat is the essential part of the Pilgrimage. Any pilgrim who fails to reach Arafat has not performed the pilgrimage. Prophet Muhammad (peace be upon him) clearly told his companions that without the stay

in Arafat on the 9th of *Dhul Hijja,* there is no pilgrimage: "There is no pilgrimage without Arafat. He who comes on the night of Muzdalifa, before the dawn of the Day of Sacrifice (i.e. 10th *Dhul Hijja),* has fulfilled the essential rites."

On one side of the plain of Arafat is the Mountain of Mercy *(Jabal ar-Rahamat).* The pilgrims go up the mountain reciting *Talbiya* in thousands. It is said that Adam prayed on this mountain, a place of Blessing and Grace for the pilgrims: Jabir reported Allah's Messenger (peace be upon him) as saying, 'When the day of Arafat comes Allah descends to the lowest heaven and praises them to the angels saying: "Look at my servants who have come to me deshevelled, dirty and crying from every deep valley. I call you to witness that I have forgiven them.' "

Amr bin Sh'aib, on his father's authority, quoted his grandfather as saying that Allah's Messenger (peace be upon him) said, 'The best supplication is that on the day of Arafat.' " Jabir reported Allah's Messenger (peace be upon him) as saying: "The whole of Arafat is a place of standing." All the pilgrims are required to stay in the plain of Arafat until sunset and then they move towards Muzdalifa after sunset. But they must not offer their *maghrib* prayer in Arafat.

8. Night at *Muzdalifah*

After sunset, on the 9th of *Dhul Hijja,* all pilgrims set out to Muzdalifah, a place between Arafat and Mina. On reaching Muzdalifah, they offer their *maghrib* and *isha* prayers together. This place is also called *Mash'ar al-Haram:* "Then when you pour down from Mount Arafat, celebrate the Praises of Allah at the Sacred Monument *(Mash'ar al-Haram),* and celebrate His Praises as He has directed you . . . . Then pass on at quick pace from the place whence it is usual for the multitude so to do, and ask for forgiveness of Allah. . . . .

So when you have accomplished your holy rites, celebrate the Praises of Allah, as you used to celebrate the praises of your fathers – yea, with far more heart and soul." (Qur'an 2: 198-200).

The pilgrims are expected to remember God and recite His Praises as much as they can throughout the period of the Pilgrimage, but with greater vigour and zeal at this place. Muzdalifah is a narrow valley between two mountains and it was here that the armies of Abraha, Abyssinian governor of Yemen, who invaded Mecca in the year of the birth of the Holy Messenger (peace be upon him), were destroyed by the miracle of birds. This incident is mentioned in the Qur'an in Surah al-Fil in these words: "See you not how Your Lord dealt with the companions of the elephant? Did He not make their treacherous plans go astray? And sent against them a flight of birds, striking them with stones of baked clay." (Qur'an 105: 1-4).

The pilgrims spend all night at Mazdalifa, praying and reciting the Praises of their Lord, and offer their *fajr* prayer very early in the morning and then set out for Mina. But before starting their journey back to Mina each one is required to collect 70 stones or pebbles which they have to throw on fixed places at Mina. Jabir reported Allah's Messenger (peace be upon him) as saying: 'The whole of Arafat is a place of standing, the whole of Mina is a place of sacrifice, whole of Muzdalifa is a place of standing.'

Abdullah bin Masud said that he never saw Allah's Messenger (peace be upon him) observe a prayer out of its proper time with the exception of two, the sunset prayer *(maghrib)* and the night prayer, which he observed that day (at Muzdalifah) before its proper time. According to Ibn Umar, Allah's Messenger (peace be upon him) combined the sunset *(maghrib)* and night prayer, each with an iqama (at

Muzdalifah).

9. Return to Mina – The Day of Sacrifice

The pilgrims leave Muzdalifah for Mina in the morning after offering their *fajr* prayer very early on *Yawm an-Nahr* (Day of Sacrifice), the 10th of *Dhul Hijja*. It is the day which is celebrated as *Id-Adha* throughout the Muslim world and animals are sacrificed in commemoration of the Great Sacrifice of Prophet Abraham (peace be upon him).

On reaching Mina they go to *Jamra al-Aqba* and throw seven stones while reciting *takbir: Allahu Akbar*. The ceremony of throwing stones begins in the forenoon on 10th *Dhul Hijja* and ends before sunset. Ibn Abbas said: "Allah's Messenger (peace be upon him) sent us small boys of the bani Abd al-Muttalib ahead on asses on the night of al-Muzdalifah, and he patted our thighs and said: "My little children, do not throw pebbles at the *Jamra* till the sun rises." Jabir said that he saw Allah's Messenger throwing pebbles at *Jamra* on the Day of the Sacrifice in the forenoon, and next day when the sun had passed the meridian (afternoon).

The throwing of stones is symbolic, for the ceremony is observed in memory of the stones thrown by the Messenger Abraham (peace be upon him) at this place on Satan, who tried to misguide him from the path of Allah.

After the ceremony of stones, pilgrims offer their sacrifices. Thousands of sheep, goats, cows and camels are offered in sacrifice on that Day by the pilgrims and by Muslims all over the world to commemorate the Great Sacrifice of Ishmael by his father Prophet Abraham (peace be upon them both).

After this sacrifice, pilgrims have their heads shaven or their hair cut and then come out of the state of *ihram*. Women simply cut a few hair. Shaving is preferable to a hair cut: According to Ibn Umar, at the Farewell Pilgrimage, Allah's

Messenger (peace be upon him) said: "O Allah! Have mercy on those who have themselves shaved." The people suggested that he should add those who had clipped their hair. He again said the same words, and when they made the same request, he added: 'and those who clip their hair.' " Yahyah bin al-Hasain quoted his grandmother as saying she heard Allah's Messenger (peace be upon him) at the Farewell Pilgrimage: "make supplication three times for those who had their heads shaven and once for those who clipped their hair."

Ibn Umar said that Allah's Messenger (peace be upon him) had his head shaven at the Farewell Pilgrimage, as did some of his companions, but some had their hair clipped.

After this ceremony, the pilgrims proceed to Mecca, if possible, for *Tawaf al-Ifada* on that day and offer their *zuhr* prayer and come back to Mina.

The following are the main ceremonies which are observed on the 10th of the *Dhul Hijja*, the Day of Sacrifice and during the next two or three days and in the same order in Mina:

(a) *Ramy al-Jimar*

The pilgrims, on reaching Mina, first go to the ceremony of *Ramy al-Jimar* (throwing stones). They go to *Jamra al-aqaba* and throw seven stones, which they had picked up at Mazdalifa the previous night, reciting loudly with each pebble: *'Labbaika! Labbaika! Allahu Akbar.'* This ceremony lasts from forenoon till just before sunset.

(b) The Sacrifice

After *Ramy*, the pilgrims offer sacrifice of animals. The Qur'an mentions the sacrifice in these words: "And celebrate the Name of Allah, through the days appointed, over the cattle which He has provided for them for sacrifice." (Qur'an 22: 28). And again in the same Surah: "To every people did We appoint rites of sacrifice, that they might celebrate the name of Allah over the sustenance He gave them from animals fit for food." (Qur'an 22: 34). And again in the following words: "The sacrificial camels We have made for you as among the symbols from Allah; in them is much good for you; then pronounce the Name of Allah over them as they line up for sacrifice. When they are down on their sides after slaughter, eat thereof, and feed such as beg not but live in cententment; and such as beg with due humility." (Qur'an 22: 36). A'isha said that Allah's Messenger (peace be upon him) once brought sheep for sacrifice to the house and garlanded them. Jabir reported that in the year of al-Hudaibiya, we, along with Allah's Messenger (peace be upon him), sacrificed a camel for seven people and a cow for seven people.

(c) Shaving or Hair Cut
Then the pilgrims shave their heads, or have their hair cut. Women have only some of their hair cut or trimmed.

(d) Out of *Ihram*
The pilgrims, men only because women do not put on *ihram*, now come out of the state of *ihram*. They can have bath and wear normal clothes.

(e) *Tawaf al-Ifada*
Thereafter, they go to Mecca for *Tawaf al-Ifada* and go round the *Ka'ba* seven times, offer a two *rakat* prayer at, or near, the Station of Abraham, or at any convenient place in the *Ka'ba,* and then walk between Safa and Marwa *(Sa'i).*

Tawaf al-Ifada is an indispensable part of the Pilgrimage and it is best to perform it on the Day of Sacrifice, the 10th of *Dhul Hijja.* But nowadays, due to the great rush of people and jammed traffic conditions between Mina and Mecca on that day, when hundreds and thousands of people are packed in that valley, it is very difficult, especially for old people or women and children, to visit the *Ka'ba* for *Tawaf al-Ifada.* It is, therefore, permissible for such people to perform it later during the next three days of *Dhul Hijja*, commonly known as *Ayyam al-Tashriq*, or even later: "Then let them complete the rites prescribed for them, perform their vows, and again do *tawaf* of the Ancient House. Such is the pilgrimage, Whoever honours the sacred rites of Allah, for him it is good in the sight of his Lord." (Qur'an 22: 29-30).

It is reported by Jabir bin Abdullah as well as A'isha that the Holy Messenger (peace be upon him), after the sacrifice in Mina on the Day of Sacrifice, went to Mecca for *Tawaf al-Ifada* and prayed the *zuhr* prayer as well in Mecca and came beck to Mina.

(f) *Muqrim* **and** *Muttamati*

It may here be pointed out that pilgrims who are *muqrim* or *mufrid* (who remained in the sacred state of *ihram* after *tawaf* and *Sa'i* before the commencement of *Hajj)*, end their pilgrimage with *tawaf al-Ifada* and they may not repeat *Sa'i* between Safa and Marwa. But the *muttamati* (who had combined *umra* with the pilgrimage and had come out of the state of *ihram* after *tawaf* and *sa'i* between Safa and Marwa and had put on new *ihram* for the Pilgrimage on the 8th day of *Dhul Hijja,* have to perform *sa'i* between Safa and Marwa again after *tawaf* of the *Ka'ba*. After these ceremonies, the pilgrims return to Mina to complete the rest of *Ramy al-Jimar*.

(g) *Ayyam at-Tashriq*

The pilgrims come back to Mina after *tawaf al-Ifada* and remain there for two or three days *of Dhul Hijja* known as *Ayyam al-Tashriq* and complete the remaining ceremounies of the pilgrimage: "Complete the praises of Allah during the appointed days. But if anyone hastens to leave in two days, there is no blame on him, and if anyone stays on, there is no blame on him, if his aim is to do right." (Qur'an 2: 203).

These days are 11th, 12th, and 13th of *Dhul Hijja*.

(h) *Ramy al-Jimar*

The pilgrims stay for two or three days in Mina and complete the ceremonies of throwing stones during these days. The stone throwing is usually done after sunset. There are three places for throwing stones and each one is called *Jamra*. The pilgrims start from *Jamra Aqaba* on the 11th day of *Dhul Hijja* after sunset and throw seven stones, at the same time crying out, *'Allahu Akbar.'* Then they proceed to *jamra wusta* (the middle *jamra)* and throw seven stones, at the same time crying out, *'Allahu Akbar.'* They go to *jamra sughra* (the smallest *jamra)* and again throw seven stones, at the same time crying out, *'Allahu Akbar.'*

This is repeated on the 12th and 13th day of *Dhul Hijja* by the pilgrims, but those who leave for Mecca on the 12th of *Dhul Hijja* throw seven stones extra on each *jamra,* which they would have thrown on the 13th day of *Dhul Hijja* had they stayed in Mina. While throwing stones on these three places, the pilgrims cry out, *'Allahu Akbar.'* A'isha reported Allah's Messenger as saying, "Throwing bebbles at the jimar and running between As-safa and al-Marwa were appointed only for the remembrance of Allah." Jabir reported Allah's Messenger, as saying, while throwing pebbles on the Day of Sacrifice, "Learn your rites, for I do not know whether I am likely to perform the Pilgrimage after this occasion."

10. Return to Mecca

After staying in Mina for two or three days, the pilgrims return to Mecca on the 12th or 13th day of *Dhul Hijja* and make preparations for going back to their home countries by air, sea or land.

11. *Tawaf al-Wida*

Before leaving for their homes, pilgrims are required to perform farewell *(wida) tawaf* of the *Ka'ba,* when they go round the Ka'ba seven times and offer a two rakat prayer.

The Prophet Muhammad (peace be upon him) insisted that no pilgrim should leave Mecca without performing his final farewell *tawaf:* Ibn Abbas reported that the people were ordered (by the Holy Messenger) to perform *tawaf* of the *Ka'ba (tawaf al-wida)* as the last thing to do before leaving (Mecca), except the menstruating women who were excused."

Anas bin Malik reported that Allah's Messenger (peace be upon him) offered *zuhr, asr, maghrib* and *isha* prayers and slept for a while in a place called al-Mahassab (near Mecca) and then rode to the *Ka'ba* and performed *tawaf* round it *(tawaf al-wida)*.

With the completion of these ceremonies, the Pilgrimage proper is completed. But many of the pilgrims, after completing the rites of the Pilgrimage, leave Mecca for Medina to visit the Mosque of the Holy Prophet *(Masjid-i-Nabwi)* and his grave.

12. Visit to Medina

Muhammad (peace be upon him) was very fond of Medina, and urged people to visit it after pilgrimage: A man of the family of *Al-Khattab* reported Allah's Messenger (peace be upon him) as saying, "He who purposely comes to visit me will be under my protection on the Day of Resurrection." Ibn Umar traced the following back to Allah's Messenger (peace be upon him): "He who performs the Pilgrimage and visits my grave after my death will be like him who visited me in my lifetime."

Many pilgrims stay there for 8 to 10 days to complete at least 40 prayers, recommended in a tradition. They pay homage to the Prophet Muhammad (peace be upon him) for his great sacrifice for the cause of Islam. Many stand near his grave, with tears flowing from their eyes in love and excitement, reciting: "O the Messenger of Allah! Peace, Allah's Mercy and

Blessing be upon you and upon your family and your followers. I bear witness that you are the servant and the Messenger of Allah."

O Allah. Send Your Peace and Blessings upon Muhammad and upon his family and his followers, as you sent your Peace and Blessing upon Abraham, his family and his followers. You are worthy of all Praise full of all Glory."

General Rules of the Pilgrimage

Rules governing various abnormal and exceptional situations during the Pilgrimage are described briefly in the following:

1. If a pilgrim is forced to shave his head, due to illness or head trouble or is obliged to wear sewn or tailored clothes for fear of cold or heat during the state of *ihram* he has to offer a sacrifice of an animal, or fast three days, or feed six people: "If any of you is ill, or has an ailment in his scalp, he should in compensation either fast, or feed the poor, or offer sacrifice." (Qur'an 2: 196).

2. Any pilgrim who combines *umra* with the pilgrimage, *(mutamatti)* should make an offering of an animal. The sacrifice is to be made after he has entered into the state of *ihram* for the pilgrimage. It must not be made before his entering into the state of *ihram* for the Pilgrimage because he is not called *mutamatti* until he has actually combined *umra* with the pilgrimage by putting on *ihram* on the 8th day of *Dhul Hijja*. The sacrifice may be made on the 10th day of *Dhul Hijja*.

3. If a *mutamatti* is unable to offer a sacrifice, he has to fast for ten days – three days during the Pilgrimage, 8th, 9th, and 10th day of *Dhul Hijja,* and seven days when he gets back home, thus completing ten days: "If anyone wishes to continue *umra* on to the Pilgrimage, he must make an offering, such as he can afford, but if he cannot afford it, he must fast three days during the Pilgrimage, and seven days on his return, making ten days in all." (Qur'an 2: 196).

4. The facility of *muttamatti* is only for those who do not

live in Mecca. It does not apply to the inhabitants of Mecca: "This is for those whose household is not in the vicinity of the Sacred Mosque." (Qur'an 2: 196).

15

Jihad (Holy War)

The word *jihad* denotes a maximum struggle or effort towards a goal. According to Imam Razi, *jihad* is of three kinds. First, a struggle of maximum exertion against a visible enemy; second, a struggle against evil forces in all forms; and third, the struggle against the passions and carnal desires of the self. Thus *Jihad* covers all kinds of exertion or effort, physical, mental or material undertaken in the way of God.

Jihad is the most misunderstood Islamic concept. Non-Muslims always take it to mean war and fighting. Many orientalists understand *jihad* as a religious duty upon every Muslim to propagate Islam by means of arms and force. Hence the conclusion that Islam was spread by means of force. They also blame Muhammad our Prophet (peace be upon him), in that he was patient and forbearing at Mecca when he was weak and had few followers; but when he became strong and the number of his followers increased, he became warlike and declared *jihad* against non-Muslims.

Jihad is a very comprehensive term. It refers to the maximum struggle and sacrifice of a Muslim, physically, mentally and materially, in the cause of Islam.

Thomas Carlyle, in his book On Heroes and Hero-Worship, has rediculed the Western concept of *jihad* in these words:

"Much has been said of Muhammad's propagating his religion by the sword. It is no doubt far nobler what we have to boast of the Christian religion, that it propagated itself peaceably in the way of preaching and conviction. Yet withal, if we take this for an argument of the truth or falsehood of a religion there is a radical mistake in it. The sword indeed: but where will you get your sword! Every new opinion, at its starting, is precisely in a minority of one. In one's head alone, there it swells as yet. One man alone of the whole world believes it; there is one man against all men: That he take a sword, and try to propagate with that, will do little for him. You must first get your sword! On the whole a thing will propagate itself as it can. We do not find, of the Christian religion either, that it always disdained the sword, when once it had got one. Charlemegne's conversion of the Saxons was not by preaching.

"I care little about the sword: I will allow a thing to struggle for itself in this world, any sword, tongue or implement it has, or can lay hold of. We will let it preach, and pamphleteer, and fight, and to the uttermost bestir itself, and do, beak and claws, whatsoever is in it; very sure that it will, in the long run, conquer nothing which does not deserve to be conquered. What is better than itself, it cannot put away, but only what is worse. In this great Duel, Nature herself is umpire and can do no wrong: the thing which is deep-rooted in Nature, what we call truest, that thing and not the other will be found growing at last.

". . . . Islam devoured all these vain jangling sects and I think had right to do so. It was a Reality, direct from the great Heart of nature once more. Arab idolatries, Syrian formulas, whatsoever was not equally real, had to go up in flame, mere dead fuel, in various senses, for this was fire."

Islam spread because it was the voice of Nature and Truth; nothing could withstand its momentous onslaught. All false ideologies and theories faded before the Light of the Truth of Islam. It did not need any sword. Truth is more powerful and devastating in destroying falsefhood than the sword.

Jihad and Qital

Qital means fighting for the cause of God. When Muslims were persecuted by all and were threatened by the Quraish of Mecca who were now waging war against them, God gave permission to fight back in these words: 'To those against whom war is made, permission is given to fight, because they are wronged . . . they are those who have been expelled from their homes in defiance of right − for no cause except that they say: "Our Lord is Allah." (Qur'an 22: 39-40).

Clearly, this commandment to fight back was given to the Muslims only for self-preservation and self-defence. Under the circumstances, fighting becomes obligatory on all Muslims in order to protect not only their ideology and beliefs but their homes, lives, property and everything else.

Thus whenever a Muslim state is attacked by any other state or states, it becomes the religious duty of every Muslim of that state to join in fighting against the invaders. It is just like conscription in times of war by the modern Western states, the main difference being that *jihad* is fighting for the sake of God as a religious duty as an act of *ibadah*, whereas in conscription, people fight for nationalistic reasons under compulsion.

If the Muslim stae under attack is not strong enough to defend itself, it then becomes the religious duty of other neighbouring Muslim states to help. If they fail to protect and defend her properly, then it becomes the religious duty of all the Muslim states of the world to help her.

The Muslims are told to retaliate against those who fight against them in these words: "Fight in the cause of Allah those who fight you, but do not transgress limits; for Allah loves not transgressors." (Qur'an 2: 190). But Muslims never will be the first to attack any innocent and peaceful people. Peaceful co-existance between non-Muslims and Muslim states is urged in the Qur'an: "But the treaties are not dissolved with those Pagans with whom you have entered into alliance and have not subsequently failed you in aught, nor aided anyone against you. So fulfil your engagements with them to the end of their term: for Allah loves the righteous." (Qur'an 9: 4).

Muslim states must maintain their treaties and friendly relations with non-Muslim states as long as the latter continue to respect the rights and agreements reciprocately: "But if they violate their oaths after their agreements, and taunt you for your Faith — fight you the chiefs of Unfaith: for their oaths are nothing to them: that thus they may be restrained." "Will you not fight people who violated their oaths, plotted to expel the Messenger, and took the aggressive by being the first to assault you?" (Qur'an 9: 12-13).

Qital is one aspect of *jihad,* waging of holy war in the defence of Islam and of one's country against any aggressors. The Muslims fight only when it is essential for the maintenance of peace, and do not waste a moment in welcoming any proposals of peace which are likely to end hostilities: "And fight them on until there is no more disorder and oppression and there prevail justice and goodness and Faith in Allah; but if they cease let there be no hostility except to those who practise oppression." (Qur'an 2: 193).

This verse clearly lays down the basic principle of fighting. The Muslims are commanded to fight against aggression and persecution. When these conditions of fighting cease to exist and peaceful life returns to the state, they are required to cease their war operations. They fight to bring back justice, goodness, peace and order. When they have established peace and rule of law in the country and the enemy has agreed to abide by these conditions, they stop fighting.

Jihad does not mean fighting and killing for propagating Islam. Faith is a matter of conviction and conscience and no amount of force and coercion can ever bring a man to believe in something of which he is not convinced. Faith cannot, therefore, be thrust upon anyone by foce nor is this method recommended by Islam: "Let there be no compulsion in matters of Faith: Truth stands clear from error. Whoever rejects evil and believes in Allah has grasped the most trustworthy handhold, that never breaks." (Qur'an 2: 256).

VOL 2
FAITH AND PRACTICE

لَقَدْ أَرْسَلْنَا رُسُلَنَا بِالْبَيِّنَٰتِ وَأَنْزَلْنَا
مَعَهُمُ الْكِتَٰبَ وَالْمِيزَانَ لِيَقُومَ النَّاسُ بِالْقِسْطِ

We surely sent Our Messengers with clear
Signs, and revealed with them the Book
and the Balance (of Right and Wrong),
that mankind may establish (system of)
justice (on the earth) (Qur'an).

1

Faith and Practice

Tawhid (Unity)

Having discussed the relation of man to God and all the ingredients of this relationship, *(huquq Allah)*, in the first volume of this book, we shall deal with the second part of the faith,i.e., the rights of people *(huququl-'ibad)* or man's relationship with his fellow-beings. In other words, his deeds and actions *(a'ml)*, which form an essential part of his belief, will be the subject of this volume.

Man's duties towards his fellow-beings spring from his belief in the Unity of God *(Tawhid)*. In fact, these are the consequences of his belief in One God. The first essential ingredient of Islamic faith is the Doctrine of *Tawhid*, expressed in the first part of the article of Faith, 'There is no god but God' *(la ilaha illa' Llah)*. This tells man that there is no one worthy of worship and obedience except God. When this belief is deeply entrenched in the mind of a Muslim, the other Articles and aspects of Faith follow as a consequence of it. It is therefore absolutely necessary that the Islamic concept of Divinity, i.e., *Tawhid*, must first be thoroughly studied and discussed.

Tawhid is the basis of reliance on God. A believer puts his complete trust in God and God alone and does not rely on any other thing or person. However, this strength and excellence of belief is achieved gradually by an ordinary believer. In the first stage, he is required to utter the *Kalimah*, 'There is no god but One God *(la ilaha illa'Llah)* with his tongue and thereby enter the fold of Islam. He becomes a member of the Muslim Community. In the second stage, he confirms it with his heart and soul and really understands and believes in God with full conviction and sincerity. In the third stage, he sees God as the sole cause of everything in the universe. He believes with clear understanding that God alone is the Creator, Sovereign and Controller of all that exists over , on and beneath the earth. Thus, the basis of reliance on God is attained in this stage, which cannot be attained by mere faith. A believer now believes that God is in reality the Doer of all actions. He is the Creator as well as the Ultimate Cause of everything. He provides sustenance to all His creatures, ordaines life and death, poverty and plenty, and all things are under His full Control. And He is alone and has no one as His partner. At this stage, a believer will not look towards others but will rely on Him alone because He is the sole Master and Sovereign. This is the stage of those who are very close to God. In the fourth stage, a believer sees nothing but God. His heart is widened by the light of Islam: "And whomsoever it is Allah's Will to guide, He expands his bosom to Islam" (6: 125). And again in Surat Az-Zumar: "Is he whose bosom Allah has opened to Islam, so that he follows a light from His Lord, like the one who disbelieves?" (39: 22).

This is the stage of the Truthful *(siddiq)* who even forgets himself when he is fully absorbed in the Doctrine of *Tawhid*. (1) This strength of the belief is also called a state of absolute certainty *(Haqq-al-Haqq)* when the believer sees manifestations of His Lord in everything. All created phemon phenomana are for him the image of his Lord for they are all passing events while His Lord is Eternal.

This belief in *Tawhid* demands certain things from the believer. First, that he should not obey and worship *('ibadah)* anyone except God. All his acts of worship and sacrifices should be totally reserved for Him alone: "I created Jinn and men only that they may serve (worship) Me" (51: 56). This is clarified in Surah Ha Mim: "Adore not the sun and moon; but adore God, Who created them if it is in Truth Him you wish to serve (worship)" (41: 37). Again in Surah Az-Zumar: "So worship God, making religion purely for Him (only). Surely pure religion is for God alone" (39: 2-3). And again: "Say, O Muhammad, I am forbidden to worship those whom you invoke besides God" (40: 66).

Secondly, he is required to call for help to God only and to no one else. He must present all his demands and petitions to Him alone and ask for His help under all circumstances. He is the Lord and Master of the whole universe and has power over all things. Therefore a believer must always turn to Him for help for the fulfilment of all his needs and requirements. (2) This is expressed in Surah Al- Fatihah: "You alone we worship, and You alone we ask for help" (1: 5). In Surah Yunas: "And call not on any other than God, that which can neither profit you nor hurt you" (10: 106). And in Surah Al-Al-Qasas: "And call not on any other god, besides God. There is no god but He." (28: 88).

This is explained in Surah Al-Mu'min: "And your Lord says: Call on Me; I Will answer prayer. But those who scorn My service will enter hell, disgraced" (40: 60). And again in Surah Al-Baqarah it is in very clear words: "When My servants ask you concerning Me, I am indeed close to them. I

---

1. Imam Gazzali, *Ihya ulum-id-Din* English translation by M. Fazlul Karim, Book IV. pp. 237-39.
2. Abul Ala Maududi, *The Meaning of the Qur'an*, VOl: 1: 41: 141.

answer the prayer of the suppliant when he calls on Me" (2: 186). Though we cannot see Him and feel Him with our senses, we must not think that He is far from us. Indeed, He is so near to every servant of His that he can invoke Him and place his requests before Him whenever he likes and wherever he may be — so much so that He can hear and answer even those requests which are not expressed in words but made only in the innermost heart. In the above verse God addresses mankind directly: "Here am I the Sovereign, the Absolute Ruler of the boundless universe and Possessor of all powers and authority, so near to hear and answer you that you need no recommendation or intercession for making any request anywhere and anytime you like. Therefore you should free yourselves from the folly of running from door to door after false gods and accept My invitation and turn to Me and trust in Me and submit to Me and become My servant *('abd)."* (2)

Thirdly, a believer must also believe that God alone is the Knower of the Unseen the hidden and the unknown treasures of the earth and the heavens *('ilm al-gaib):* "Say, O Muhammad, no one in the heavens and the earth knows the Unseen except God" (27: 65). And in Surah Al-An'am: "And with Him are the keys of the Unseen. No one but He knows them. And He knows what is on the land and in the sea. Not a leaf falls but He knows it. There is not a grain in the darkness (or depths) of the earth, nor anything fresh or dry (green or withered) but is (noted) in a clear Record" (6: 59).

Fourthly, it also demands that a believer should in no circumstances sacrifice any animal or give anything in the name of any person other than God, nor mention any other name along with God when sacrificing. "This applies both to the flesh of that animal which is staughtered in name of anyone or anything other than that of God and also to that food which is to be offered to anyone or anything other than God. As a matter of fact, everything really belongs to God and is given by Him; therefore it should be offered in His Name alone as a mark of gratitude to Him. And if it is offered in any other name it means that that one is acknowledged as the supreme authority and the giver of favours or at least a partner with Him in those matters." (3) This is mentioned in many Surahs of the Qur'an: "He has forbidden you . . . that on which any other name has been invoked besides that of God" (2: 173). And in Surah Al-An'am: "Say; I find not in that which is revealed to me anything forbidden to anyone who wishes to eat thereof except . . . that on which the name of other than God has been invoked" (6: 145). " This point has been clearly emphasised in Surah Al-An'am when the believers are told to eat that over which the Name of God has been mentioned and not to eat that over which God's Name has not been mentioned: "So eat that on which God's Name has been pronounced . . . and eat not of that whereon God's Name has not been pronounced" (6: 118, 121).

Fifthly, it also demands that Sovereignty and Power over all the universe belongs to God alone. Therefore His Law should prevail over all the affairs of the people — from the cradle to the grave — covering every espect of their life. As He is the Sovereign and the Ruler, His Law stands supreme in the land and no other law-maker should be recognised besides Him. Whatever His Law allows is lawful and whatever His Law forbids is unlawful. There is no other authority to challenge His Sovereignty and His Law in the land. In other words, people should submit all their affairs to the Law of God: "And in whatever you differ, the verdict therein belongs to God" (42: 10). This is the natural and logical consequence of God's Sovereignty and Absolute Rule over the universe. When He is the Sovereign and the Lord, it is His domain to settle people's affairs and disputes in this world as well as in the Hereafter, no matter what they are. The Qur'an refers to this fundamental principle of law: "And if you have a dispute concering any matter, refer it to God and the Messenger if you are in truth believers in God." (4: 59). And in Surah Al-Al-Ahzab: "And it behoves not a believing man or a believing woman, when God and His Messenger have decided an affair (for them), that they should (after that) claim any say in the affair" (33: 36). In short, a believer must believe with full conviction and understanding that God has power over all things and has full control over all His creation all the time. And he should be grateful to Him, call on Him and prostrate before Him with love and sincerity; live as His slave and servant and not accept slavery of any kind, physical or spiritual, to any other being; and he should obey His and follow His Law and not his self nor any other person or persons.

Believers are exhorted not to follow any other Law than that of God: "Follow that which is sent down to you from your Lord, and follow, as protecting friends, none besides Him" (7: 3). This is explained in Surah At-Tawbah: "They have taken as Lords besides God their Rabbis and their monks and the Messiah, son of Mary, when they were commanded to worship only One God. There is no god except Him. Praise and Glory to Him. (Far is He) from having the partners they associate (with Him)" (9: 31).

According to a tradition, when Hadrat 'Adi bin Hatim, who was formerly a Christian, came to the Holy Prophet with the intention of understanding Islam, he asked several questions in order to remove his doubts. One of these was: "This verse accuses us of taking our scholars and monks as our Lords. What is its real mening, sir? For we do not take them as our Lords." As a reply to this, the Holy Prophet put a counter question to him: "Is it not a fact that you accept as unlawful

---

3. *The Meaning of the Qur'an*, VOl. 1. p. 134.
4. *The Meaning of the Qur'an*, VOl. 1V. 186-87.

what they declare to be unlawful and lawful what they declare to be lawful?" A'di confessed, "Yes, sir, it is so." The Holy Prophet replied, "This amounts to making them your Lords." This Hadith clearly shows "that those who themselves set limits to the lawful and the unlawful without the authority of God's Book, assume for themselves the rank of Godhead and those who acknowledge their right of making laws take them as their Lords. It should be noted that they have been charged with (a) attributing sons to God, and (b) giving the right of making laws to others than God. These are to prove that their claim, that they believed in God, is false, even though they should believe in His existence. But such a wrong conception of God makes their belief in God meaningless." (4) It is further clarified in Surah Yunus: "Say: Have you considered what provision God has sent down to you, how you have made of it lawful and unlawful? Say: Has God permitted you, or do you invent a lie concerning God? Such people are considered disbelievers, or rebels: "Whoso judges not by that which God has revealed, such are disbelivers; such are wrong-doers; such are evil-livers (5: 44-45-47). "

Thus people who do not judge by the Law of God are: (a) disbelievers (b) unjust and (c) transgressors or rebels. In other words, those who discard the Law of God and judge by the law formulated by themselves or by others are guilty of three crimes. First, they practise disbelief by their rejection of the Law of God. Second, they become guilty of injustice because they violate the Law of God which is perfectly just and equitable. Third, they become transgressors against God (fasiqin), because, in spite of being God's servants, they transgress against their Master's Law and adopt their own or that of others. Thus, in practice, they break away from allegiance and subjection to their Master and deny His Authority; this is fisq (transgression). "This disbelief and injustice and transgression are clearly violations of Divine

Law. It is, therefore, not possible to avoid these three crimes where there is such a violation." (5)

This clearly establishes that those who believe in the Unity of God *(Tawhid)* should not only worship One God, call on Him for all their needs and offer sacrifices to Him alone, but should also leave all the traditions, conventions and way of their forefathers and self-made laws and laws made by other people and follow the Law of God and consider Him the Sovereign and the only Law-Giver. There is no exception to this general rule; even the Holy Prophet was subject to this general principle: "Follow that which is revealed to you by your Lord" (6: 106). And in Surah Al-Tahrim: "O Prophet! why do you forbid that which God has made lawful for you?" (66: 1). This clearly shows that what God has made lawful, no one has the authority to make unlawful; even the Holy Prophet does not possess this authority.

Thus an invitation to *Tawhid* is an invitation to an all-comprehensive and all-pervading revolution which changes not only religion but the entire system and way of living. It provides a new philosophy of life, new values and a new ideology which lift a man far above his fellow-beings. "It is an open invitation to man to be the true embodiment on earth of the excellent qualities of God. When the Qur'an in its upward attention focuses on God, it opens before man new horizons of thought, guides him to unexemplified standards of high morality, and acquaints him with the eternal Source of peace and goodness. Realizing that God alone is the ultimate goal of man is a revolution against the popular trends in human thought and religious doctrines, a revolution whose objective is to free the mind from doubts, liberate the soul from sin and emancipate the conscience from subjugation (to evil)". (6)

5. *The Meaning of the Qur'an*, VOl. 111 pp. 47-48
6. Hammudah Abdalati, *Islam in Focus*, IIFSO, p. 197

With complete belief, knowledge and understanding of the concept of Divinity *(Tawhid)*, a believer finds a perfect and comprehensive concept of the universe ,of life and humanity. He does not falter in the darkness to seek a solution to many of his problems relating to modes of worship, social, economic or political modes of behaviour or judicial decisions because all these matters are based on the fundamental concept of *Tawhid*. (7)

The effects of the belief in *Tawhid* on the life and behaviour of man are manifold. Some of them are explained below:

1. It provides a believer with an ennobling message of advancement in all concepts of his life, physical as well as moral and spiritual, for he regards God as the eternal source of enlightenment and guidance in every matter. He therefore becomes supreme and dominant on earth as regards his Source as well as his support. He goes far ahead of other people in knowing and understanding the nature and reality of the universe because he possesses the master key to the wonders and mysteries of creation (i.e., belief in *Tawhid)*. He is never troubled or confused regarding any matter, event or happening in the universe as are the non-believers, secularists or atheists, for he is fully aware of the Authority, Attributes and all-comprehensives Nature of his Lord, the Sovereign and Master of all creation.

2. A believer also holds a higher and nobler standard regarding those values and measures which determine the nature and significence of various situations, circumstances, things and events in life, as compared to those of a non-believer. (8) Such qualities and attributes of a believer are cultivated and developed only out of a profound knowledge of Divine attributes, because this knowledge

---

7. Syed Qutb, *Islamic Approach to Social Justice, Islam ,its meaning and message,* Islamic Council of Europe, p. 117

purifies a man's mind and soul, his beliefs, morals and actions. (9) This belief enables a man to acquire a standard and vision of human values and human ideas and actions which is far higher and nobler than that of non- believers and atheists. (8)

3. A believer is also at a far higher level than a non-believer in his feelings, ideas, conscience, morals and personal dealings. His belief develops in him feelings of greatness and sublimity, purity and sanctity, modesty and piety. In fact, it enables him to act and behave in the right and most appropriate way in all situations and also cultivates in him the noblest human qualities and fashions his life in virtue and goodness. (9) "Thus his belief makes him virtuous and upright. He has the conviction that there is no other means of success and salvation for him except purity of soul and rightness of behaviour. He has perfect faith in God Who is above all needs, is related to no one, is absolutely just, and none has any hand or influence in the exercise of His Divine Powers. This belief creates in him the consciousness that, unless he lives rightly and acts justly,he cannot succeed."(10)

4. A believer gains superiority over unbelievers and excellence in his attitude to law and other systems of life because he receives inspiration from Divine Law and Divine Attributes. He also bases all his laws and systems on his belief in *Tawhid*, which is the Source of all knowledge, goodness and justice. He compares the diverse and often hostile and changing secular systems which have come and gone in the history of man with the Divine System, and feels sorry for humanity in its helplessness.

8. Syed Muhammad Qutb, *Mu'alim fitariq*, Urdu translation, I. F. S. O. pp. 393-95.
9. Abul Ala Maududi, *Towards Understanding Islam*, p. 21.
10. *Towards Understanding Islam*, pp. 99-103.

5. This also frees man from being enslaved to animate and inanimate objects, to the forces of nature and, above all, from the greatest of slaveries, slavery to other men. It frees him from these slaveries and brings him into slavery to his Lord; takes him out of the narrow valleys of this world into the vast and spacious world of the Hereafter; out of the excesses and shackles of religion into the protection of the goodness and justice of Islam. (9)

Thus all the bonds which restrained and captivated the minds of man have been loosed, and he is again set on his way to progress. Obviously a slave mind cannot achieve anything good or great: "God sets forth the parable (of two men), one a slave under the domination of another; he has control over nothing, and (the other) one on whom We have bestowed a fair provision from Us, and he spends thereof secretly and openly. Are they equal? Praise be to God! But most of them understand not. And God sets forth another parable of two men: one of them dumb, having control of nothing, and he is a burden on his owner; whichever way he directs him, he brings no good. Is he equal with one who enjoins justice and follows a straight path?" (16: 75-76). It was therefore nesessary for the advancement and progress of man that his mind should be freed from the strains and shackles of all kinds of slavery. Belief in *Tawhid* accomplished this objective and opened for man the long road to growth, development and progress.

6. This belief gives self-respect to man and brings home to him his true worth and dignity. One who believes that none but God is his guide and leader in all matters, spiritual or temporal, is told to represent the Divine Kingdom and serve as vicegerent of God on earth. Those who worship and pay homage to persons other than God have degraded themselves. This belief thus stresses the point that no person can claim holiness, authority and overlordship as his birthright and that

no one is born with the stigma of slavery or serfdom on his person. All those who profess belief in *Tawhid* share and represent the Heavenly Kingdom and also share the vicegerency of God on earth: (11) "Shall I seek for you a god other than God when He has made you excel all other creatures?" (7: 140). And again in Surah Al-An'am: "Shall I seek a Lord other than God? . . . He is the Lord of all things . . . . And He has made you rulers (vicegerents) of the earth" (6: 164-165).

7.   Belief also stimulates the idea of the unity of mankind, the   equality of human beings, true democracy and real freedom in the world. Belief in the Lord of the worlds carries another idea of significance, the idea of the unity of the human race. As our Lord is the Lord and Cherisher of all people, He treats all His people alike, and listens to the prayers of all His peoples, whatever their colour, creed or race. He is merciful and kind to all and forgives the sins of all His people. He also rewards the good and punishes the evil alike. And He has created all men of the same nature and from the same parents. "All people are One Community" (2: 213). And in Surah Yunus: "People are but one community" (10: 19). And in Surah Al-Nisa: "O mankind! Be careful of your duty to your Lord Who created you from a single soul and from it created its mate and from them twain has spread abroad a multitude of men and women" (4: 1).

Thus, "This belief broadens his outlook, for a believer can never be narrow-minded. He believes in One God Who is the Creator of the heavens and the earth. He looks upon everything in the universe as belonging to His Lord Whom he himself belongs to. His sympathy, love, and service do not remain confined to any practicular sphere or group. His vision is enlarged, his intellectual horizon widens, and his

11. Abul Ala Maududi, *Vitals of Faith*, pp. 33-35.

outlook becomes liberal and as boundless as is the Kingdom of God." (10)

A person who believes in God and all His Attributes must also believe that all humans have sprung from the same parents and are therefore closely related to one another. This leads to their equality without any reservation of rights or privileges for any sect or group amongst them.

8. Another significant and inspiring effect of this belief on man is that he feels ever conscious of the immense Power, Majesty and Eternal Presence of his Lord, and this gives him strength of character and independence of action and makes him fearless of the powers and influences of persons and institutions other than God. He works and acts honestly and justly on an individual as well as a social level without fear of or favour to anyone. And a society composed of such individuals sets an example of justice, benevolence and goodness for the rest of the people in all matters without regard for the status, influence or power of any person.

It makes a man a responsible and upright person in his behaviour towards other people. The sense of accountability to God for all his acts and omissions in this world is a constant reminder to him that he will face Him One Day. This makes man vigilant and cautious against evil. And the fact that all his actions are watched by God keeps him on guard and on the Right Path and makes him act in a responsible manner.

9. This concept of *Tawhid* also encourages man to look for the vast Kingdom of God, His hidden treasures and mysteries in this world. The deeper you think into the Nature and Powers of God, the clearer become the Signs of the truth of this concept. In fact, "It is this concept which opens up the doors of inquiry and investigation and illuminates the

pathways of knowledge with the light of Reality. And if you deny or disregard Reality, you will find that at every step you meet disillusionment, for the denial of this primary truth robs everything in the universe of its real meaning and true significance. The universe becomes meaningless and the vistas seen on the way get blurred and confused. (11)

10.   Belief also "generates in man a sense of modesty and humbleness. It makes him unostentatious and unpretending. A believer never becomes proud, haughty or arrogant because he knows that whatever he possesses has been given to him by God,and that God can take away just as He can give."(10)

11.   This concept of *Tawhid* also makes man brave and courageous. "There are two things which make a man cowardly: (i) fear of death and love of safety and (ii) the idea that there is someone else besides God who can take away life and that man, by adopting certain devices, can ward off death. Belief in *La ilaha ill'Llah* purges the mind of both these ideas. He gets rid of these ideas because he knows that everything belongs to God Who is the Creator of the heavens and the earth and the Giver of life and death. It is for this reason that no one is braver than a believer." (10)

12.   *Tawhid* "creates an attitude of peace and contentment, purges the mind of the subtle passions of jealousy, envy and greed and keeps away ideas of resorting to base and unfair means for achieving success. The believer understands that wealth is in God's Hands, and He distributes it as He Wills; that honour, power, reputation and authority — everything— is subject to His Will and He bestows them as He Wills; and that man's duty is only to endeavour and struggle fairly. He knows that success and failure depend upon God's Grace; if He Wills to give, no power in the world can prevent Him from doing so; and if He does not Will it, no power can force Him to give." (10)

13. Above all, this doctrine of *Tawhid* makes man very obedient and submissive to the Law of God. One who believes in its truth knows that everything is in God's Knowledge and nothing is hidden from Him. And that He is nearer to him than his own jugular vein. If he commits a sin, whether in secret or openly, God knows it; He even knows our thoughts and intentions and nothing can remain hidden from Him. The stronger a believer's faith in this concept the more observant will he be of God's Commands. (10)

This doctrine of *Tawhid* is the foundation of Islam. It is the bedrock of this Faith and the mainspring of its power and strength. All the beliefs, commands and laws of Islam stand on this concept of Unity and their strength or weakness depends on the strength or weakness of this concept. They all take their strength from this source. If this source were weak, the whole system of the *Islamic Shari'ah* (Law) would become weak. Therefore it is absolutely necessary for the strength and vigour of the *Islamic Shari'ah* that belief in *Tawhid* should be its strong and firm base.

2

Islam in Practice

The entire Islamic system is, in fact, the consequence of its Doctrine of *Tawhid*. It is based on that concept, it receives nourishment and strength from that concept, and is dependent for it existence, endurance and success on that concept. All the Articles of Faith *(Iman)* and all the pillars and elements of Islam are the demands and requirements of this concept; even the problems of *Hillat* what is (permissible), and *Hurmat* (what is forbidden), legal requirements, laws governing economic, social, political, educational and moral matters are based on the Doctrine of *Tawhid*. The source of all these matters is the teaching of the Holy Prophet from his Lord.

The Islamic system is the practical exposition and application of the Doctrine of *Tawhid* and its essential requisites. If *Tawhid* or any part of its requisites is not found in the practical life of any society, that society is not considered to be an Islamic society. Thus the Doctrine of *Tawhid (La illaha illa'Llah)* is considered to be the basis of a perfect system on which is built the life-style of *Millet-e-Islamia* with all its needs and details. The question of building the necessary life-life-style prior to the establishment of this basis does not arise. Likewise, if the structure of life is raised on any other basis than this, or if, along with this, any other basis or a number of other bases are included to build the structure of life, such a life-style or life system can never said to represent the Islamic life: "The Command is for no one but God, Who has Commanded you that you worship (obey) no one but Him" (12: 40).

This verse clearly says that the real Owner and Master of everything is God Who is the Creator and the Lord of the entire universe. He has given no authority or sanction to anyone to be obeyed or worshipped, but, in fact, has reserved all authority, all power and all rights for Himself and commanded people to "serve and worship none but Him".

This brief exposition of the concept guides us in reaching a final decision regarding the Islamic faith and the basic problems of its practical application. First, it guides us in determining the nature of Muslim society. Secondly, it helps in finding the method of building such a Muslim society. Thirdly, it tells us the technique Islam has suggested for dealing with un-Islamic systems. Fourthly, it determines the working discipline of Islam required to change the state of human life in pratice.

The Distinguishing Feature of an Islamic Society

The distunguishing feature of an Islamic society is that the solution of all its problems is based on the concept that God is the Sovereign and man is His servant (*'abd*). The Article of Faith *(la illaha illa'Llah)* is the manifestation of this same concept of adoration of Him and it also determines its nature. The faith of man is also an expression of the adoration and so are all forms of worship *('ibadah)* and use of symbols *(Sha'air)*. The laws and disciplines are its practical demonstrations. One who does not believe in the Oneness of God *(Tawhid)* has, infact, not adopted the worship (obedience) of God: "God has enjoined; "You shall not take to yourselves two gods; for He is the One and only God. So fear Me. To God belonges everything in the heavens and the earth. His Way is being followed in the universe. Will you, then, fear any other than God?" (16: 51-52)

Likewise, anyone who takes others or joins others with God in his worship or use of symbols cannot be a true servant of God: "And declare: My prayer and my rites of worship and my life and my death are all for God, the Lord of the universe, Who has no partner with Him. This is what I have been commanded, and I am the first to surrender to Him" (6: 162-163). And so anyone who leaves the laws and ways given to us by Muhammad the Messenger of God and acquires them from any other source is also departing from the sincere and pure adoration of God: "Or have they partners (in godhead) who have made lawful for them in religion that which God allowed not?" (42: 21) And in Surah Al-Hashr: "And whatsoever the Messenger gives, take it. And whatsoever he forbids, abstain from it" (59: 7).

These are the real and basic values of an Islamic society. Just as the beliefs, ideas and concepts of individuals are coloured in the adoration of God, their worship, symbols and sacrifies also reflect the same adoration. Their social system, its laws and disciplines are a practical reflection of the same concept of adoration. If the colour of adoration fades in any one of these aspects of life, the whole of Islam vanishes from the life of that community. This is because the very first Article of Faith of Islam, *Kalimah Tayyabah*, which is the bedrock and foundation of Islam, cannot materialise in such a society. (1)

Islam is All-Embracing

Thus Islam is not a religion in the traditional sense of being confined to the four walls of a mosque. It is in fact, a way of life which covers and dominates every aspect of man's life, including religious rites, educational or legal decisions, moral or spiritual problems, social or legal requirements or any other practical day-to-day matters — all are governed by the *Islamic Shariah.(Law)*.

Islam has also considerably widened the concept and scope of worship. It considers all actions sincerely performed within the Law of the *Shari'ah* to seek the pleasure of God as acts of worship *('ibadah)*. Thus even eating, drinking, sleeping and other worldly acts to satisfy one's physical needs become acts of worship if they are performed with true religious motives. (2) In this way, Islam has, in fact, brought before man the path of the world and the Hereafter, uniting the good of both. It is related by Abu Hurairah that the Messenger of God said, "Each person's every joint must perform a charity every day the sun comes up; to act justly between two people is a charity; to help man with his mount, lifting him onto it or hoisting up his belongings onto it is a charity; a good word is a charity; every step you take to prayers is a charity; and removing a harmful thing from the road is a charity" (Bukhari and Muslim).

He also narrates that the Messenger said: "Whosoever removes a worldly grief from a believer, God will remove from him one of the griefs of the Day of Judgement. Whosoever alleviates (the lot of) a needy person, God will alleviate (his lot) in this world and the next. Whosoever shields a Muslim, God will aid (His) servant so long as the servant aids his brother" (Muslim). It is also an act of goodness to strengthen one's body by taking exercise, and little rest, recreation or even proper nourishment to enable one to shoulder the burden of his duties, if all these actions are performed within the Code of the *Shari'ah*. According to a hadith of the Holy Prophet, "A believer who is possessed of

---

1. Syed Qutb, *Mu'alim al-Tariq (urdu)*, p. IIFSO, 221-28.
2. Mustafa Ahmad Al-Zarqa,The *Islamic Concept of Worship, Islam, its meaning and message*, P.I.E.O.E. pp.109-15.

strength is better and dearer to God than a believer who is weak. " It is, in fact, the purity of the motive and the intention with which any action is performed that determines whether it is an act of goodness, or charity. (3)

It is possible that a man may advance spiritually and his action may be regarded an act of worship or charity even when he is enjoying the worldly pleasures of life. It is narrated by Abu Dharr that the messenger of God said: "To enjoin a good action is a charity, and in the sexual act of each of you there is a charity." The companions said: "O Messenger of God, when one fulfils his sexual desire will he have some reward for that?" He said, "Do you (not) think that were he to act upon it unlawfully he would be sinning? Likewise, if he has acted upon it lawfully he will have a reward." (Muslim). The Holy Prophet also said: "Even when a person lovingly puts a piece of food in the mouth of his wife to strengthen the bonds of their matrimonial love, he is rewarded for it." (2)

This philosophy of life has been taught by all the prophets of God since Adam, including Abraham, Moses and Jesus. And this is the universal concept which "maintains that religion is not only a spiritual and intellectual necessaity but also a social and universal need. It is not to bewilder man but to elevate his moral nature. It is not to deprive him of anything useful, or to burden him, or to oppress his qualities, but to open up for him inexhaustible treasures of sound thinking and right action. It is not to confine him to narrow limits but to launch him into the wide horizon of truth and goodness. In short, true religion is to acquaint man with God as well as with himself and the rest of the universe . . . It shows that Islam satisfies the spiritual as well as material needs of man. It unties his psychological knots and complexes, sublimates his instincts and aspirations, and disciplines his desires and the whole course of his life." (3)

In short, Qur'anic wisdom is conclusive in all its dimensions. It covers every aspect of man's life in a most balanced way. "It neither condemns nor tortures the flesh nor does it neglect the soul. Everything is carefully placed where it belongs in the total scheme of creation. There is a proportionate relationship between deeds and rewards, between means and ends." (3) Thus an "Islamic ideology does not admit a conflict, nay, not even a significant separation between life-spiritual and life-mundane. It does not confine itself merely to purifying the spiritual and the moral life of man in the limited sense of the word. Its domain extends over the entire gamut of life." (4)

Another feature of this system is that God has created the world for the benefit of mankind and has commanded man to make the best and most productive use of his powers and faculties in utilizing the natural resources that He has created for his benefit. This is why asceticism is forbidden in Islam and man is told in clear words that he will only get what he does. "Has only that for which he makes an effort" (53: 39). He is further asked to better his life in the Hereafter by the proper use of his present resources and not by neglecting them: "But seek the abode of the Hereafter in that which God has given you and neglect not your portion of the world" (28: 77).

There are many verses in the Qur'an which urge man to action and even to compete in the search for the Divine Pleasure by means of good actions. Following the Will of God does not lead to inaction. As man does not know the Will of God, he must always continue his effort, even though failure follows failure, when trying to attain the goal which he

---

3. Hammudah Abdalati, *Islam in Focus,* p. 30, 197
4. Abdul Ala Maududi, *Islamic Concept of Life,* pp. 1-20-24.

conscientiously believes to be good and in conformity with the revealed Commandments of God. This notion of a dynamic predestination, which urges one to action and resignation to the Will of God, is well explained in the following verses of the Qur'an: "No misfortune can happen on the earth or in yourselves but is recorded in a Book before We bring it into existence. That is truly easy for God: In order that you grieve not for the sake of that which has escaped you, nor be arrogant over what God has given you. God loves not prideful boasters" (57: 22-23). Obedient servants of God behave nicely and gracefully under all circumstances and reach the goal of success in this world as well as in the Hereafter: (5) "As for those who strive in Our (Cause), We will certainly guide them to Our Ways, and surely God is with those who do good" (29: 69).

Another characteristic of the Islamic society is that it is formed and shaped in a way conducive to the free growth of good, virtue and truth in every area of human life, and also gives full play to the forces of good in all directions. And at the same time it tries to remove all the obstructions from the way of virtue and goodness. It also tries to eradicate evil from society by prohibiting it and all its possible causes and then takes measures to check its occurrence. Certain directives are prescribed to regulate the lives of people on individual as well as social level, so that they become fully aware of "what is good and what is bad; what is beneficial and useful and what is harmful and injurious; what are the virtues to be cultivated and encouraged in society and what are the evils to be suppressed and guarded against." (4)

Another remarkable feature of an Islamic society is that it is an organic whole. "The whole scheme of life propounded by Islam is animated by the same spirit and hence an arbitrary

---

5. M.Hamiddullah, *Introduction to Islam*, para 222, p. 81

division of the scheme is bound to harm the spirit as well as the structure of the Islamic order. It can be compared to the human body, which is also an organic whole. The same can be said of the scheme of life envisaged by the *Shari'ah*. Islam signifies the entire scheme of life and not any isolated part or parts thereof. Consequently, neither can it be appropriate to view the different parts of the *Shari'ah* in isolation from one another and without regard to the whole; nor will it be of any use to take any particular part and bracket it with any other "ism". The *Shari'ah* can function smoothly and can demonstrate its efficacy only if the entire system of life is practised in accordance with it and not otherwise." (4)

This society is also an ideological society and, therefore, quite different from others based on race, colour or territory. "This society is the result of a deliberate choice and effort; it is outcome of a 'contract' which takes place between human beings and their Creator. Those who enter into this contract, undertake to recognize God as their Sovereign, His Guidance as Supreme, and His Injunctions as Absolute Law. They also undertake to accept, without question or doubt, His classifications of Good and Evil, Right and Wrong, Permissible and Prohibited. In other words, it is God and not man Whose Will is the primary Source of Law in a Muslim society." (6)

This clearly explains the objective of the Islamic society for it is based on a unique opproach to human life and a particular concept of man's place in the universe. Man is considered a servant of God and His vicegerent on the earth. His role is to mould human life on the individual and social level on healthy lines so that the Kingdom of God is established on the earth with peace, contentment, justice and goodness for all His creatures. (4)

---

6. Abul Ala Maududi, *Islamic Way of Life*, pp. 17-21.

The whole scheme of the Islamic society and the Islamic way of life springs from the concept of certain rights and obligations which all believers are enjoined to follow and strictly observe in their daily life. These consist of (a) The rights of God *(huquq Allah)* and (b) the rights of people *(huquq al-'ibad)*. The former, have been fully discussed in Volume 1 of this book while this volume undertakes to explain the latter.

3

Rights of People *(Huquq al-'Ibad)*

Life is a continuous process and worldly life is only a transitory stage of man in his eternal life in the Hereafter. He should therefore utilise every moment of this life for furtherance of his objective of the enternal life. He should consider this life as a test and try to avail himself of this opportunity to achieve success. And according to the Islamic ideology: "The best use of this life is to live it according to the teaching of God and to make it a safe passage to the future life of Eternity." There is no denying the fact that "all men come from God, and they shall return to Him" (1)

God has enjoined man to enjoy his rights but at the same time not to forget other people's rights. The rights of one man are the obligations of another man and thus rights and obligations are reciprocal from the viewpoint of the Islamic Way of Life. These constitute the cornerstone of Islam and it is the primary duty of every believer strictly to observe them. The success of the Islamic society in all areas, including moral spiritual, social, economic, political, etc., depends on the strict observance of these rights and obligations by all Muslims. Any slackness or carelessness in obeying these rules will obviously leave cracks in various areas of Islamic society and gradually weaken and break the entire Islamic system.

---

1. *Islam in Focus*, op. cit., p. 29.

Thus, rights of people *(huquq al-'ibad)* which, in fact, constitute the backbone of the whole way of life of the Islamic society, occupy a unique position in Islam. Rights of people include (a) rights of relatives; and (b) rights of other people.

(a) Rights of Wives

Everyone has obligations first to his own family, parents and other near relatives, and then to society in general. Family comes first in the observance of rights and obligations because "it is not only the cradle of man but also the cradle of civilisation." Islam has given very clear injunctions to build up healthy and cordial relationship between the family members. Man is assigned the job of providing all the necessities of life to his wife and children and woman is required to manage the household, educate and bring up the children and provide comfort and contentment to her husband and children. The children are taught to respect and obey their parents, and, when they grow up, to meet their needs. The husband is the head of the family because no institution, however small, can maintain discipline or work efficiently and properly without some chief administrator in it. The field of operation of the husband is outside the house household for he is the earning member, while the wife most of the time works inside the house as she is to manage the household and looks after younger children as well. (2) Both the husband and the wife enjoy equal social and legal rights and their duties merely reflect a functional distribution between them. It merely points out that the field of work of each member of the family is different from the other and is based on their biological and psychological differences. Both are equal but not similar in the eyes of the law. As human beings, women have equal rights with men: "Women have the

---

2. Abul Ala Maududi, *Towards Understanding Islam*, pp.162-77

same rights as the husbands have over them in accordance with the generally known principles. Of course, men (being active partners) are a degree above them (as senior among equals)" (2: 228)

In order to understand the wisdom and nature of family rights and obligations, it is essential to know the significance and purpose of the matrimonial relationship. Islam recommends marriage to safeguard the morals and chastity of the husband and wife, and the law of marriage strengthes the castle of their mental relationship: "Lawful to you are all beyond those mentioned, provided that you seek them with your wealth in honest wedlock (i.e., chastity), not lust" (4: 24). And again: "So wed them with the leave of their people, and give them their dowries with kindness, they being chaste, not lustful, nor of loose conduct" (4: 25). And in Surah Al-Ma'idah: "And (lawful to you in marriage) are the chaste women of the people of the Book revealed before your time, when you give them their due dowries, and desire chastity, not fornication, nor taking them as secret concubines." (5:6)

These verses of the Qur'an clearly show that the primary object of marriage is to safeguard the morals of the man and the woman. The other object of this relationship is to build and develop a feeling of love and kindness between them so that they are able to enjoy the peace, contentment and comfort of family life and thereby contribute most to the development and growth of a healthy culture and civilization on the earth. (3) "And of His Signs is this, that He created for you mates from among yourselves that you might find rest in them. Aand He has put love and mercy between you (30: 21). " He it is Who created you from a single person, and therefrom did make his mate that he might take rest (and contentment) in her" (7: 189).

The marriage laws of Islam have given full considerations to these mutual feelings of love and peace between husband and wife. And if they cannot live in 'conjugal relationship with love and generosity', they are advised to separate, for in that condition their separation is better than their unity. (3) "If you do good and fear God, God is ever Forgiving, Merciful. But if they disagree (and must part), God will compensate each out of His abundance." (4: 129-130) And even in separation they are advised to maintain good conduct: "And then (a woman) must be retained in honour (on equitable terms) or released in kindness (on equitable terms)" (2: 229). And again in Surah Al-Talaq: "And when they have reached their term, take them back in kindness, or part with them in kindness" (65: 2).

The husbands are warned not to treat their wives unkindly and unjustly when they are separating and are unable to live on good terms: "When you have divorced women, and they have reached their term, then retain them in kindness or release them in kindness. Retain them not to hurt them, or to take undue advantage. He who does that wrongs his own soul" (2: 231). The Qur'an exhorts men to maintain good relations with their wives under all circumstances: "But consort with them in kindness and equity, for if you hate them it may be that you dislike a thing, and God has placed in it a great deal of good for you" (4: 19). And again: "And the remission (of the man's half of the dower) is nearer to piety. And do not forget kindness and liberality between yourselves" (2: 237).

The Holy Messenger of God always advised his companions to be good and kind to their wives. His wife, A'isha, reported God's Messenger as saying, "The best of you is he who is best to his family, and I am the best among you to may family." Abu Hurairah reported that God's Messenger said, "Among the believers who show most perfect faith are those who have the best disposition, and are kindest to their families" (Tirmizi). He also spoke to them about women in his Last Sermon on the occasion of the Farewell Pilgrimage: "O men, to you a right belongs with respect to your women and to your women a right with respect to you. It is your right that they do not fraternize with anyone of whom you do not opprove, as well as that they never commit adultery. But if they abide by your right, then to them belongs the right to be fed and clothed in kindness. Do treat your women well and be kind to them, for they are your partners and committed helpers. Remember that you have taken them as your wives and enjoyed them only under God's trust and with His permission." (4)

Man's Responsibilities

The Islamic *Shari'ah* lays certain duties on the man as head of the family. First, he owes a dower to the woman for the establishment of the marital relationship with her. (3) "And give the women their dower as a free gift" (4: 4). And again in the same Surah: "Lawful to you are all beyond those mentioned, provided you seek (them in marriage) with gifts from your property in honest wedlock, not in lust. And those of you who seek content (by marrying them), give them their dowers as prescribed" (4: 24). And in Surah Al-Ma'idah: "Lawful to you (in marriage) are (not only) chaste women of the believers but chaste women of the people of the Book revealed before your time, when you give them their due dowers and desire chastity, not fornication, nor taking them as secret concubines" (5: 5).

Secondly, man's duty is to provide sustenance to his wife and to meet all her needs while she manages the household and looks after the children. Man is supposed to work and earn a living for the family ("because they spend of their property" (4: 34) and act as the maintainer and provider of the family while the women is the mistress and the queen of the house

---

3. Abul Ala Maududi, *Huquq Az-Zaujain*, pp. 17-28.
4. Muhammad Haykal, *The Life of Muhammad*. pp. 486-87.

("And stay in your houses, and make not a dazzling display, like that of the Time of Ignorance" (33: 33). Man, on the other hand, will be the supervisor and head of the family ("Men are the protectors of the affairs of women" (4;34). The maintenance of the family at a proper standard will depend upon the income and social status of the people concerned and is not dictated by the woman ("Provide for them, the rich according to his means, and the poor according to his means, a fair provision" (2: 236)

The Holy Prophet explicitly fixed the scope and nature of each person's duties and rights. It is reported that God's Messenger said, "The man is the ruler over his wife and children, and is answerable to God for the conduct of their affairs." (Bukhari). He also said, "When a woman steps out of her house against the will of her husband, she is cursed by every angel in the heavens and by everything other than men and jinn by which she passes, till she returns" (Khashf al-Ghamma by Shirani). (4) The Holy Prophet also said, "The woman is the ruler over the house of her husband, and she is answerable for the conduct of her duties" (Bukhari).

Thirdly, he must not misuse his position and the powers God has given him over his wife and must not keep away from her in normal circumstances: "Those who take an oath to keep apart from their wives are given four months (for a final decision). Then if they resume their relations, God is Forgiving and Merciful. And if they resolve on divorce, (let them remember that) God hears everything and knows everything" (2: 226-27). There is no doubt that relations between husband and wife do not always remain cordial, but God's Law does not allow strained relations to continue indefinitely. It lays down the maximum period of four months for a separation in which they legally remain husband and wife but practically live separate lives without any conjugal relations between them. (5) This is necessary to protect and safeguard the conjugal rights of the woman and also that she may not be put to too hard a burden beyond her power regarding her marital desires: "Therefore, (in order to satisfy the dictates of Divine Law) do not lean wholly towards one wife so as to leave the other in a state of suspense. If you behave righteously and fear God, you will find God Forgiving and Compassionate" (4: 129).

This verse clearly demands from man that he must not transgress the rights of his partner under any circumstances. If he does not like her, he must not keep her hanging on in a state of suspense as if she were not his wife. He must fulfil her rights as long as she is his wife, otherwise he must divorce her if he does not like her. The man who does not like his wife but is clinging to her merely to hurt her is severely reprimanded by the Qur'an: "It is transgression to retain them merely for harassment; and whoever does that really wrongs his own soul" (2: 231).

Fourthly, the man who has more than one wife is enjoined to do justice between them or have only one wife: "But if you apprehend that you might not be able to do justice to them, then marry only one wife" (4: 3). "It should be noted that this verse restricts poygamy by the provision of justice to all the wives; therefore whoever abuses this permission without fulfilling the condition of justice and marries more wives than one tries to deceive God. The courts of an Islamic state are, therefore, empowered to enforce justice in order to rectify the wrong done to a wife or wives." (6) In such cases the Islamic Law can rectify the wrong done to the wife or wives.

However, Islam provides all the possible opportunities to

---

5. Quoted by Abul Ala Maududi, in *Purda and the satus of women in Islam,* pp. 45-52.
6. *The Meaning of the Qur'an.* VOl. 1., p. 163.

women to enable them to develop their natural abilities to the maximum limit within the framework of its social life and to be able to play their full role effectively in the growth of civilisation. Therefore it enable women to acquire the necessary education and training so that they can play their part with men in the progress and development of social organisations. But Islam wants women to remain women and work in that capacity. It does not like them to become like men because to become men is not in their rights. It is neither good or useful for them nor for the society to lose their identity and become like men. Otherwise, within its social framework, Islam has given same rights to women as to men: it has raised their social status; given them economic and social rights; and provided them with moral and legal safeguards in law. They have a legal share in the property of their fathers, brothers and husbands. (7)

Women have complete freedom in the selection of their husbands and no one has the right to marry them to anyone without their consent. Likewise, their right to get separation from husbands who are cruel, unjust or impotent and those whom they dislike is absolute. Again, widows and divorced women have complete freedom to marry men of their own choice. And women enjoy absolute equality with men under civil and penal laws. Islam does not recognise any difference between men and women as far as protection of life, property, honour and reputation is concerned. (7) In the acquisition of knowledge and cultural training both men and women are treated on the same level but Islam differentiates between the type of education given to each sex on the basis of their different functional responsibilities and psychological needs in society. It is, in fact, obligatory, in Islam, on every man and woman to acquire knowledge. (7)

---

7. Abul Ala Maududi, *Purdah and the Status of Women in Islam*, pp. 149-58.

(b) Rights of Parents and Relatives

The rights of parents occupy a special place in the Islamic socity. Children are commanded to respect their parents and be polite to them. "O Muhammad, say to them, 'Come, I will recite what limits your Lord has set for you.' Join not anything as equal with Him. . . . and treat your parents kindly" (6: 151). "Kind treatment" is used in a very comprehensive way and is inclusive of respect, honour and obedience. Its purpose is really to develop a willing desire in children to please and serve their parents. Islam has greatly emphasised the right of parents and it is given priority over all human rights. It is considered in importance only next to the right of God.

This loving and kind treatment is specially recommended when the parents have grown old, physically weak and mentally feeble: "Your Lord has decreed that you worship none except Him, and (that you show) kindness to parents. If one of them or both of them attain to old age in your lifetime, say not to them a word of contempt nor repulse them, but speak to them a gracious word. And lower to them the wing of submission through mercy, and say: My Lord! Have mercy on them both as they did care for me when I was little" (17: 23-24).

The Holy Prophet laid special emphasis on the rights of parents. Abu Hurairah told that a man asked the Messenger of God who was most deserving of friendly care from him. He replied, "your mother, your mother, your mother," and the fourth time he replied, "and your father" (Bukhari and Muslim). And Abdullah bin Amr reported God's Messenger as saying, "A man's reviling of his parents is one of the serious sins" (Bukhari and Muslim).

Islam has, however, limited obedience to parents only if they are believers, and if they are non-believers or they enjoin what is unlawful, then the children are advised not to obey them, but to treat them with kindness and compassion: "And We have enjoined upon man (to be good) to his parents. . . . but if they strive with you to make you ascribe to Me as partner that of which you have no knowledge, then obey them not. Consort with them in the world with kindness, and follow the path of him who turns to Me" (31: 14-15). The Holy Prophet gave the same advice to Asma, daughter of Abu Bakr, regarding her unbelieving mother when she visited her at the time of the treaty with the Quraish (Bukhari and Muslim).

The concept of *ihsan* consists of active sympathy, patience, gratitude, compassion and respect. It also includes support and maintenance and provision of a reasonable life of comfort according to one's ability. Along with rights of parents, Islam has also emphasised rights of relatives: "All of you should serve God and associate none with Him . . . and be kind to your relatives" (4: 36). And again: "The people ask, 'What should we spend?' Tell them, 'What ever you spend, spend for your parents, your relatives etc.' "(2: 215). Kind treatment of relatives is considered an act of great goodness and charity. It is third in order of priority in Islam, after *Tawhid* and treatment of parents. And in Surah Bani Isra'il: "And render to relatives their due rights" (17: 26).

There are many verses of the Qur'an and sayings of the Holy Prophet regarding the rights of relatives. Anas reported God's Messenger as saying, "He who wishes to have his provision enlarged and his term of life prolonged should treat his relatives well." Abu Hurairah reported God's Messenger as saying that ties of relationship *(rahim)* is a concept derived from the Compassionate One *(or Rahman)*; and God said, "I shall keep connection with him who keeps you united and sever connection with him who severs you. Abdullah bin Alm Aufa reported God's Messenger as saying, "Mercy will not

descend on a people among whom there is one who severs
ties of relationship." (Mishkat). The Holy Prophet was once
asked who was the best person? He replied that one who
feared God most and kept the best connections with
relatives.

(c) Rights of Neighbours and the Poor

Fourth in order of priority comes the rights of neighbours,
the poor and other Muslims. Islam has given great importance
to the rights of these people and there are many verses of the
Holy Qur'an about them: "Worship (and submit to) none but
God: be good to your relatives, to the orphans and to the
helpless; speak aright with the people" (2: 83). And in Surah
An-Nisa: "Be kind to near relatives, and to orphans, and to
the needy; and be considerate to your neighbours, (be they)
relatives or strangers, and to the companions at your side,
and to the wayfarer, and to the slaves in your possession" (4:
36).

In normal dealings, one is gentle and considerate towards rich
people and those equal in status. It is the poor and weak who
always suffer and do not enjoy any rights in society.
Therefore, it was neccessary that the rights of the weak and
the poor, which are normally trampled underfoot by the
people, should be emphasised and given due consideration in
Islamic society. The Qur'an enjoins people to spend a part of
their wealth on such people: "But virtue is . . . to spend of
one's wealth for relatives and orphans, for the needy and the
wayfarer, for beggars and for the ransoms of slaves" (2:
177).

Then the believers are enjoined to improve their behaviour
towards other people: "Turn not your cheek in scorn
towards people, nor walk in insolence in the land; for God
loves not any arrogant boaster. And be moderate in your
pace and lower your voice; for the harshest of all voices is
the voice of the ass" (31: 18-19). In Surah Al-Hujurat: "You
who believe, do not let one(set of) people make fun of

another set; perhaps they are better than the former. Nor let any (set of) women (make fun of) other women; perhaps they are even better than they are themselves. Nor should you defame yourselves nor insult one another by using nicknames; it is bad to use an evil name after (entering the) faith (of Islam). Those who do not turn away from it are wrongdoers" (49: 11).

Believers are advised to greet and help each other: "Whenever those who believe in Our Signs come to you, say, 'Peace be upon you' " (6: 54). And: "Whenever you are welcomed with a greeting, then answer with something better than it or (at least)return it" (4: 86). And again: "Co-operate with one another for virtue and piety and do not co-operate with one another for the purpose of vice and aggression" (5: 2). And in Surah Al-Hujurat: "Believers are but, brothers, so set things right between your brothers and fear God so that you may find mercy" (49: 10).

(d) Rights of Muslims in General

1. "When you meet a Muslim, greet him with, 'Salam'. When he invites you, accept his invitation. When he sneezes, respond to him (with mercy and blessing). When he falls ill, call on him. When he dies, join his funeral prayer. If he seeks your advice, give him (good) advice. If he is absent, guard his properties. Want for him what you want for yourself and don't want for him what you do not want for yourself." (8) God says: "They (believers) are sympathetic towards one another." (90: 17). Ibn Abbas, explaining it, said, "The pious among them seek forgiveness for the sinners. When a sinner among the Muslims looks to a pious man, the latter should say "O God, grant him the blessing of good of which you have decreed for him and keep him firm in it and grant him benefit therewith. And also say: O God, grant him guidance, accept repentance and forgive his sins." (8)

---

8. Imam Gazzali, op. cit., Book. 11. pp. 145-72.

2.   Want for the believers what you want for yourself and do not want for them what you do not want for yourself. The Holy Prophet said, "The Muslim Society is like a body in respect of mutual love and sympathy. If a limb of the body suffers pain, the whole body responds to it by sleeplessness and fever." He also said, "One believer is to another believer, like a building one portion of which strengthens another portion." (8)

3.   Do not injure a Muslim by your words or actions. The Holy Prophet said, "A Muslim is he from whose tongue and hands other Muslims remain safe." He also said: "It is not lawful for a Muslim to gaze at another Muslim in a way that hurts his feelings."

4.   Be modest to every Muslim. Don't treat him harshly and don't feel pride in front of them for God likes not those who are proud and conceited.

5.   Avoid backbiting and hearing others doing so for the backbiters will not enter Paradise.

6.   Give up disputes and quarrels with your brethren. The Holy Prophet said, "If man pardons the faults of a Muslim, God will forgive his faults on the Day of Resurrection." He also said, "The better of the two is one who greets first with a salutation." (8)

7.   Do good to everyone, deserving or undeserving . The Holy Prophet said, "Do good to everyone, pious or impious. If you do good to one who is fit to receive, it is good. If he is not fit to receive it, you are fit to do good." He also said, "The root of wisdom after religion is to love men and to do good to everyone, pious or impious."

8.   Treat all well and speak to each according to his intellect.

9. Honour the old and show affection to the young. The Prophet said, "To honour an aged one is to honour God." He also said, "He who does not show affection to our young ones is not of us."

10. Live with all people with a smiling and kind heart. The Holy Prophet said, "God loves the simple and those with a smiling countenance."

11. Fulfil any promise which you have made with anyone.

12. Do justice to people because without it your faith is not perfect.

13. Settle disputes between people.

14. Help those who are in distress; save them from oppression regarding their honour, property and life for it will stand as a screen for you from hell.

15. Call on those who are sick, for the Holy Prophet said, "He who visits a patient sits by the side of Paradise and remains immersed in the Mercy of God.

These two kinds of rights, of God *(huquq Allah)*, discussed in the first Volume of this book, and of people *(huquq al-ibad)*, which form the subject-matter of this Volume, determine the nature and composition of the Islamic society. In fact, the Islamic society, which is enjoined to establish a system of justice, piety and goodness on the earth, is a practical manifestation of these rights, and all its disciplines and systems representaing economic, social, moral, spiritual and political aspects of man are manifestations of the same concept.

In order to give a true picture of the practical aspect of Islam and how it establishes justice, virtue and goodness on the earth, it is necessary to discuss the various areas of life which are affected by it. We will therefore explain the working and establishment of the various aspects of the Islamic society in in the following pages. But before we discuss these it will be useful to explain a few things which have helped in the establishment of such an ideal and just social order.

4

Knowledge

Islam attaches great importance to knowledge and considers it the basis of human development and the key to the growth of culture and civilisation. This can be seen from the fact that the first Revelation begins with the subject of learning: "Read! In the name of your Lord Who created - - created man, from a mere clot of blood. Read! And your Lord is most Bountiful, He Who taught the use of the pen, taught man that which he knew not" (96: 1-5). This verse clearly shows that man, who is created from a very lowly and humble origin, can rise to great heights, even higher than angels, only through learning and acquiring knowledge. He can only rise to great heights through knowledge but with the art of writing he can also disseminate and promulgate knowledge widely and thereby preserve and protect his cultural heritage generation after generation. And in Surah Ar-Rahman we have: "The most Gracious (Ar-Rahman) has taught the Qur'an (to Muhammad) and it is He who has created man and taught him speech (and intelligence to learn and distinguish between Right and Wrong)" (55: 2-4).

When man was made vicegerent on the earth, he was equipped with the wealth of knowledge, previously denied to angels, "After this, He taught Adam the names of all things. Then He asked the angels, 'Tell Me the names of all these things if you are right (in thinking that the appointment of a vicegerent will cause disorder)'. They replied, 'Glory be to You! You alone are free from defect. We possess only as much knowledge as you have given us.' Then God said to Adam, 'Tell them the names of these things' " (2: 31).

Knowledge is essential at every stage of man's existence. The first thing man must know is about himself, for if he does not know himself, he cannot know anything else. In fact, knowledge of one's self is the key to the knowledge of God: "We will show them Our Signs on the horizons and within themselves until it will be clear to them that it is the Truth" 41: 53). The Holy Prophet explained it by saying, "He who knows himself well knows God. Obviously this knowledge of man does not refer to his physical needs alone but extends to many of his problems: "What is man in himself and from where is he come? Where is he going, and for what purpose has he come to tarry here a while? In what does his real happiness and misery consist?

"According to Islamic spiritual experience, happiness, the ideal of every human being, is necessarily linked with the knowledge of God. A man would be pleased at being admitted to the confidence of a prime minister; how much more if an emperor makes an intimate of him and discloses state secets to him! Seeing then that nothing is higher than God, how great must be the delight which springs from the knowledge of Him!" (1)

Knowledge of God and His Attributes is essential, because without it man's belief and faith remain meaningless. Then he needs to follow His Guidance in his everyday life. How can he fashion his life according to the Divine Law? Thus it is the knowledge of God and His Attributes which helps man to

---

1. Dr. Ahmad A. Galwash, *The Religion of Islam*, VOl. 11. pp. 208-20.

cultivate his noblest qualities of virtue, goodness and justice and to purify his beliefs, morals and actions. Without this knowledge man can neither know God and His Attributes, nor follow His Way. Again he must also know the consequences of his belief in and obedience of God, as well as those of disbelief and disobedience. Thorough knowledge of these concepts will enable man to safeguard his future interests, whereas an ignorant persom may consider obedience and disobedience of little consequence. (2)

Thus a Muslim's faith stimulates knowledge in all areas of his life. His own creation leads him to the knowledge of God; in his own wisdom and potentialities for diverse actions he finds a miniature reflection of God's Attributes. In this way, knowledge of his own self gradually serves as a key to the knowledge of God and His Attributes. (1) This proves the eternal Truth of the saying of the Holy Prophet that "God created man in His own likeness."

This is why Islam has stressed the importance of knowledge to its followers. God advised the Prophet Muhammad to pray for his intellectual advancement: "And say: O my Lord! Increase me in knowledge' " (20: 114). And the believers should leave their houses (for learning) but why did not some people from every habitation leave their houses in order to learn and understand the way of Islam and to teach their people when they returned to them?" (9: 122). The ignorant are advised: "You may enquire from the people who possess knowledge if you do not know it yourselves" (16: 43). And God selected Saul to be a king for the Jew because of his superiority over others in physique and knowledge: "God has chosen him above you and has increased him abundantly in knowledge and stature" (2: 24). The Prophet Moses was advised to learn from someone who was gifted with

---

2. A. A. Maududi, *Towards understanding Islam.pp.* 20-23

knowledge from God: "Then they found one of Our slaves on whom We had bestowed Our Mercy and whom We had taught knowledge from Our Presence" (18: 65). And God shows the superiority of those with knowledge over the ignorant by saying: "Are those who know equal with those who know not? But only men of understanding will learn" (39: 9). And in Surah Al-Ankabut We have, "These parables, We set forth for mankind, but none understnds them except those who have knowledge" (29: 43). Again: "If they had referred it to the Messenger, or to those charged with authority among them, the proper investigators would have known it" (4: 83). This makes practical decisions dependent upon the investigation of the learned.

In view of the great importance of knowledge the Holy Prophet always stressed that his followers should spend more time in learning and made it a duty of every Muslim, man and woman, to acquire knowledge. According to him, the learned are the heirs of the Prophets of God. The Prophet also said, "The ink of the scholar is more holy than the blood of
the martyr; one hour's meditation on the work of the Creator in a devout spirit is better than seventy years of prayer; to listen to the instructions in science and other learning for one hour is more meritorious than attending the funerals of a thousand martyres, more meritorious than standing up in prayer for a thousand nights; to the student who goes forth in quest of knowledge, God will allot a high place in the Mansions of Bliss; every step he takes is blessed, and every lesson he receives has its reward; the seeker of knowledge will be greeted in heaven with a welcome from the angels; to listen to the words of the learned, and instil into the heart the lessons of science, is better than religious exercises, better than emancipating a hundred slaves; he who favours learning and the learned, God will favour him in the next world; he who favours the learned knows me; whosoever desires to realise the spirit of his teachings must listen to the words of

the scholar." (3)

The Holy Messenger also said, "To rise up at dawn and learn a section of knowledge is better than to pray one hundred rakahs; it is better than the world and its contents; knowledge is a treasurehouse and its key is enquiry. So enquire and there are rewards for it for four persons: The enquirer, the learned man, the audience and their lovers; to be present in an assembly with a learned man is better than praying one thousand rakahs. The Messenger was asked, "O Messenger of God, is it better than the reading of the The Qur'an?" He replied, "What benefit can the Qur'an give except through knowledge." (4) The Prophet said, "The parable of guidance and knowledge from God Who sent me is like that of heavy rain falling on a certain locality. One spot became full of water and consequently abundant herbs and grass grew therein. The ditches and canals in another spot reserved water and with God's Grace benefitted mankind therewith. They drank water therefrom, irrigated their fields and grew crops. Then there was another spot which neither hoarded water, nor grew any grass and herbs. The first spot is similar to that of a man who benefits from his knowledge; the second to that of man who benefits others with his knowledge; and the third to that of a man who is deprived of both the benefits of knowledge. And the Prophet added that one who guides towards somthing good is like one who does good. (5)

The Holy Messenger also said, "Seek knowledge even as far as China; if a man learns a section of knowledge to teach it to the people, he will be given the rewards of seventy siddiqs (righteous men); how exvellent a gift and how exvellent a present is a word of wisdom which you hear, remember and then carry and teach to your brother Muslim; a Muslim gives his brother Muslim no greater benefit than a fair tradition which has reached him and which he subsequently transmits to the other; if a believer hears good advice, and then translates it into action, it is better than his worshipping for one year; there is envy for only two persons, and one of them is the one whom God has given knowledge to which he applies himself and teaches to the people. (5)

All the scholars and sages of Islam have likewise given top priority to knowledge and its acquisition. Ali said to Kamil, "O Kamil, knowledge is better than wealth, it guards you, but you have to guard wealth; it dispenses justice while wealth seeks justice; wealth decreases with expense while knowledge increases with expense. "Ibn Aswad said, "Nothing is more honourable than knowledge. The kings rule over the people while the learned rule over the kings." Ibn Masud said, "You should acquire knowledge before your death. By One in Whose Hand is my life, those who are killed in the way of God should wish that God should resurrect them as learned men, as they will find that honour is meted out to learned men. It is said that learned men are the lights of the ages. Each is a light in his own time giving light to the people of his own time. Hassan Basari said, "But for the learned, the people would have been animals. In other words, learning takes a man to the limit of humanity from the limit of animality." (5)

To summarise the sayings of the Holy Prophet and the teaching of the Qur'an, "Knowledge is a friend on a journey, a companion in solitude, a guide to religion, a light in happiness and misery, a bosom friend to a stranger and a beacon on the path to Paradise. Through it, God exalts a nation, makes them leaders and guides to good. Seeing them, others also become guides to good. Everything, dry and fresh,

3. Ameer Ali, *The Spirit of Islam*, London, 1974, pp. 360-62
4. *Ihya Ulum-id-Din*, English translation, Book 1, pp. 15-19.
5. M. Hamidullah, *Introduction to Islam*, paragraph 447.

seeks forgiveness for them, even the fishes in the sea, insects and worms, beasts, cattle and sheep and even the stars in the sky seek forgiveness for them. Knowledge gives life to the dead heart, it is a light for the eyes in darkness and gives strength to the body in weakness. By its help, man reaches the ranks of the pious. To think of it is like fasting and its study is like prayer. By its help, God is obeyed and worshipped; the Unity of God is understood and faith is strengthened. By its help, ties of blood are maintained and lawful and unlawful things are known." (5)

The study of the Qur'an shows that the object of all the Messengers of God was to impart knowledge of right and wrong to the people in order that they might be able to follow the path of righteousness and to establish a system of justice and goodness on the earth (57: 25). The Prophet Muhammad was also sent with the same objective: "It is He Who has sent among the unlettered a Messenger from among themselves, to recite to them His Revelations, to purify them, and to teach them the Book and Wisdom" (62: 2). It is undoubtedly knowledge that gives clear guidance as to what is right and virtuous and what is wrong and evil. And it is only through knowledge that a believer can gain goodness and virtue and win the Pleasure of God. This is why the Qur'an says that "if you know not then ask those who have knowledge of the Book" (16: 43). and the Holy Prophet said that one learned man is harder on the devil than a thousand ignorant worshippers.

Moreover, "If belief demands the cultivation of the theological sciences, others (i.e. forms of worship) require a study of the mundane sciences. For the service of worship, the face is turned towards Mecca, and the service must be celebrated on the occurence of certain determined natural phenomena. This requires knowledge of the elements of geography and astronomy. Fasting also requires the

understanding of natural phenomena, such as the appearance
of the dawn, the setting of the sun, etc. The Pilgrimage
necessitates knowledge of the routes and the means of
transport in order to proceed to Mecca. Payment of *zakat*
requires knowledge of mathematics, which knowledge is also
necessary for calculations for the distribution of the heritage
of the deceased. Similarly there is the fundamental need of
the understanding of the Qur'an in the light of the historical
facts and allusions and references to the sciences contained
therein. In fact, the study of the Qur'an requires first of all a
knowledge of the language in which it is compiled (lingustic
science); its references to peoples demand a knowledge of
history and geography, and so on and so forth." (5)

Thus Islam and its faith embrace almost all branches of
knowledge and research, from ethics, theology, history,
astronomy and archaeology to madecine, physics, economics
and racial psychology. In fact, "It is an important educator in
all systems of purely human origin and its creed adores,
worships and acknowledges the Creator of the universe in the
most sublime, lofty and divine expression, never to be found
in the liturgy of other religions." (6) This shows very clearly
that a 'Muslims' faith in God is based on knowledge and
research, and it has opened all branches of knowledge to his
intellect for it to penetrate as far as it can go. "It lays down
no restriction against the free thinker who is seeking
knowledge to widen his vision and broaden his mind. It urges
him to resort to all methods of knowledge, be they purely
rational or experimental. By calling on the intellect in this
way, Islam shows its high regard for and confidence in the
intellectual abilities of man and wishes to free his mind from
the right shackles and limits of tangibility. It wants to elevate
the individual and empower him with self-confidence and
Heavenly Authority to expand the domain of his mind into

---

6. *The Religion of Islam*, VOl. 1. op. cit., p. 22.

all fields of thought: physical and metaphysical, scientific and philosophical, intuitive and experimental, organic and otherwise. This is how faith in God nourishes the intellect and makes the intellectual life prosperous and productive. When the spiritual and intellectual activities of man are organised in accordance with the teachings of Islam as mentioned above, the internal nature of man becomes sound and healthy. And when man is internally secure and sound his external life will be of the same nature." (7)

It is this quest for knowledge and learning that really opens a door of research and investigation for man, thereby unfolding unlimited and unending opportunities for him in every field of thought and action. The practical achievements of the early Muslims in every branch of science and art bear strong evidence to this. Wherever they went they took their knowledge with them and enriched the culture and civilisation of that country. Europe and the rest of the world is indebted to Islam for their progress and advancement in knowledge and sciences but unfortunately all their sciences have now taken a wrong turn. The fact is that knowledge is not confined merely to beliefs, religious worship, and religious activities, but covers other activities as well. Its relation with the laws of nature and interest in the wisdom of the Kingdom of God, together with the control and application of those laws, is as strong in these fields as with religious beliefs, worship and other religious activities. However, knowledge and research not based on *Iman* (Faith) is not included in the definition of this knowledge. There is a strong and close relationship between the basis of *Iman* (Faith) and all those sciences which are connected with the laws of the universe and laws of nature, e.g., astronomy, biology, physics, chemistry, etc. All these sciences present a manifest proof of the existence of God, provided they do not

7. Hammudah Abdalati, *Islam in Focus,* pp. 108-09.

come under the control of the misguided desires of man, thereby being completely deprived of the idea of God (i.e., the Creator). This is what happened in Europe during the period of its advancement in knowledge.

It was a time when there occurred very painful differences between the scholars and the leaders of the Church and, consequently, the entire movement of learning and research took a wrong turn, away from God. This movement influenced all areas of life, including the sciences and art, and left far-reaching effects behind it. All its knowledge and sciences developed and grew on a hatred of religion and all that it stood for. (8)

---

8. Syed Kutb, *Mu'alim Eittariq*, urdu translation, pp. 323-24.

5

Reason and the Search for Truth

As man is by nature intellectual, possessing mind, intelligence or power of reasoning, Islam has paid special attention to develop and build his intellectual structure on sound foundations. As explained in the previous chapter, Islam has laid great emphasis on the acquisition of knowledge through experience, experiment, meditation and observation. There is a Divine Injunction making its acquisition compulsory for every Muslim, man and woman, and pointing to the boundless and ever-revealing treasures of knowledge and truth in nature and in all God's Creation. It also teaches him to find the 'truth' and 'reality' of things through reasoning and argument and never accept 'inherited truths' or 'traditional facts' without proof or evidence substantiating them. The Qur'an was the first book to demand proof in support of every conviction or contention and to question every 'conventional truth' or 'historical legacy' and to ask 'why' should it be accepted? What are the bases of its contention? On what authority are such claims made? At the same time, it provides proof and evidence in support of its own claims and contentions.

It may, however, be mentioned that the method and style of reasoning of the Qur'an is quite different from those of philosophers and orators. This is because it is inviting people to believe and have faith in the Truth it has brought from

God. And faith is a positive concept which can be beneficial only when it is fully understood by the people and then firmly established in their hearts. It is therefore essential that it be based on reason and irrefutable arguments. "Without it, faith can neither be a powerful driving force in one's life, nor can it bring into view the details of creed and practice. It can never keep watch over man's activities in his complicated life. Besides, its aim in not to vanquish and silence its listners but to awaken and quicken all their faculties and capacities and direct them onto right path." It also wants to rouse man's nature and intellect to such an extent as to make him aware of the nobility of his objectives as well as the ways and means to achieve them. (2)

Secondly, faith is essential for man to practise right conduct, but such a strong faith cannot be achieved without reasoning and strong and convincing arguments. It is therefore necessary that natural and simple arguments be given that can satisfy and convince an ordinary man in the street and thereby strengthen his faith. This opproach awakens human intellect from its slumber and leads it on to perceive and critically observe every phase of life and every phenomenon in nature. (2)

Thirdly, the Qur'an not only provides reasoning and arguments to prove its point but also develops the faculty of reasoning in man. This is because a total revolution in the individual and social life of man cannot be brought about without fully awakening his faculties of thought. Man possesses a heart and a soul, the physical and the spiritual; he is therefore partly physical and partly spiritual. He needs a philosophy of life that satisfies both his requirements. The Qur'an provides reasoning that prepares the ground for the

1. *Islam in Fucus*, op. cit., pp. 106-09.
2. A. A. .Islahi, *Call to Islam* , pp. 101-17.

creation of this wholesome thought in the heart and soul of man: "He bestows wisdom upon anyone He Wills, and he who is given wisdom is in fact given abundant wealth, but only those who have commonsense learn lessons from these things" (2: 269). The word in this verse which we have translated 'wisdom' is *hikmat,* which stands for the knowledge of discerning what is true and right. Hence anyone who has wisdom will not adopt the narrow ways of Satan but will follow the broad Way of God. And the wise one is he who makes the best use of this short life and makes provision for his prosperity in the eternal life, even if he has been given little wealth here." (3) In Surah Ha Mim, we read, "And no one will be granted such goodness . . . except persons of the greatest good fortune" (41: 35). This wisdom, according to some Hadith of the Holy Prophet, is the greatest and most inexhaustible treasurehouse that is given by God to some of His servants. This gift of God enables man to channel his thoughts on correct lines and to draw right conclusions from his own self *(nafs),* from the universe *(aufaq)* and from human history *(tarikh).* (2)

Fourthly, it appeals to man's sense of reasoning on the basis of common and well-known truths, values and ideals which no reasonable person will deny for they are easily discernable from one's own history, traditions, beliefs and ethics. Good *(ma'ruf)* and *munker* (evil) are commonly recognisable concepts and Islam invites people to reconcile the contradiction between them on these principles. They are asked to think deeply, and if what the Qur'an says is right, accept it; if, on the other hand, they insist that another view is right, they must prove its truth: "Say, O Muhammad, 'Then bring you a Book from God, which is a better guide than either of them, that I may follow it, if you are truthful' truthful' " (28: 49). And in Surah Al-Mulk we read, "Is then

---

3. Abul Ala Maududi, VOl. 1, pp. 196-97.

he who goes grovelling on his face more rightly guided, or he who walks upright on a straight way? Say to them, 'He it is Who has created you, and gave you ears and eyes and hearts. But little thanks it is you give' " (67: 22-23).

It clearly shows that Islam encourages reasoning and argument among the people so that they may not only understand and follow its beliefs and concepts but also because it wants them to find the truth in their own selves and in the world around them, for nothing has been created without a purpose: "We created not the heavens and the earth and all that is between them for sport. If We had wished to find a pastime, We could have found it in Our Presence, if We ever did. Nay, We hurl the Truth against falsehood and it does break its head, and hold! falsehood vanishes." (21: 16-18)

Take *Tawhid* (Unity, the foundation-stone of Islam); even this is not accepted without argument. God invites man to look around and see if there is anyone else other than Him who could be the Creator, Lord and Sovereign of this universe and worthy of worship and obedience. In a beautiful passage of the Qur'an, this challenge is thrown to the non-believers: "Is not He (best) Who created the heavens and the earth and sends down for you water from the sky? With it He cause to grow well-planted orchards of beauty and delight, whose trees it is not in your power to cause to grow. Is there any god beside God? Nay, but they are a people who ascribe equals (to Him)! Is not He (best) Who made the earth a fixed abode, made rivers in its midst; set thereon firm mountains, and set a barrier between the two seas? Is there any God beside God? Nay, but most of them know not!"

Is not He (best) Who listens to the distressed (and wronged) soul when it calls on Him and relieves its suffering, and Who has made you vicegerents on the earth? Is there any god beside God? Little do they reflect! Is not He (best) Who guides you through the darkness of land and sea, and Who sends the winds as heralds of His Mercy? Is there any god beside God? High is God above what they associate with Him! Is not He (best) Who originates creation, then repeats it, and Who gives you sustenance from the heavens and the earth? Is there a god beside God? Say, 'Bring your proof, if you are truthful' " (27: 60-64).

And Prophet Abraham, with extreme compassion and love, appeals to his father: "Dear father! Why do you worship those things which hear not and see not, nor can they profit you anything? Dear father! I have received that knowledge which has not reached you; so follow me and I will guide you on the Right Way. Dear father! Do not serve Satan, for Satan is disobedient to the Merciful. Dear father! I fear lest a punishment from the Merciful afflict you, so that you become a companion of Satan" (19: 42-45).

Man is not only required to worship God but also to obey His Laws and follow His Ways of life because He is the Sovereign and Ruler of the whole universe. Here again man is given a rationale for this concept: "And don't they observe anything created by God, how it casts its shadow right and left, prostrating itself before God? Thus all things express their humility. All animate creation in the heavens and the earth and all the angels prostrate themselves in adoration before God; they do not show any arrogance at all; they fear their Lord Who is above them, and do whatever they are Commanded" (16: 48-50). The reasoning in this verse refers to the fact that everything, animate or inanimate, casts its shadow in obedience to the universal Law of God. The phrase 'casts its shadow' is a symbol of its servitude to God, Who is the Creator and Sovereign of all. As such, the things which are subservient to God and His Law cannot have any share whatsoever in Godhead. Furthermore, not only all things on the earth but also all things in the heavens, including angels, which are considered to be closely related to God, are subservient to Him and obey His Law alone, and have no share whatsoever in His Godhead. (4)

His Law applies equally to all His creation, large or small: "Do you not see that to God pays adoration whosoever is in the heavens and whosoever is in the earth, and the sun, and the moon, and the stars, and the mountains, and the trees, a and the beasts, and many of the people, while there are many who have deserved the torment" (22-18). And again: "For it is God alone before whom everything in the heavens and the earth bows down willingly or unwillingly, and the shadows of all things bow down before Him in the morning and in the evening" (13: 15).

Everything is created by Him and belongs to Him and no one shares in His Creation nor in His Possession; it is therefore His Right alone that all should obey His Law and follow His Way; "Say O Muhammad, 'O God, Sovereign of the Kingdom; You bestow knigdom on whomever you will and You take it away from whomever You will. You exalt whomever You will and You debase whomever You will. All that is good is in Your power; indeed You have power over all things. You cause the night to pass into the day and You cause the day to pass into the night; You bring forth the living out of the dead and You bring forth the dead out of the living and You give sustenance to whom You will without measure" (3: 26-27). A beautiful passage in the Qur'an describes the Majesty of the Lord and Sovereign of the universe: "He is God, than Whom there is no other god, the Knower of the invisible and the visible. He is Most Gracious, Most Merciful. He is God, than Whom there is no other god, the Sovereign, the Holy One, the Source of Peace, the

---

4. The *Meaning of the Qur'an,* VOl. VI, p.

Guardian of Faith, the Preserver of Safty, the Majestic, the Irresistible, the Supreme. Glorified be God from all that they ascribe as partners (associates) to Him. He is God, the Creator, the Evolver, the Bestower of forms (and clours). His are the most beautiful Names. Whatever is in the heavens and the earth glorify Him, and He is the Mighty, the Wise" (59-22-24).

He is also the Lord, Master and Maintainer *(Rabb)* of all His Creation. Therefore all must call on Him alone for all their needs and requirements: "To invoke Him alone is the right thing. As regards the other deities whom they invoke apart from Him, they cannot give any answer to their prayers. It is as if a man were to stretch out his hands towards water and ask it to come to his mouth, when it cannot reach his mouth in this way; likewise the prayers of the disbelievers are nothing but aimless effort . . . Ask them, Who is the Lord of the heavens and the earth? Say, 'God'. Then say to them, 'When this is the fact, have you then made beside Him such deities for your protectors as can do neither good nor harm even to themselves?' Say, 'Is the blind man equal to the one who sees, or is darkness equal to light?' Or do they assign to God partners who have created anything as He has created, so that the creations seem to them alike? Say, 'God is the Creator of all things, and He is the One, the Almighty' " (13: 14-16).

People are told to think carefully of their actions and of their own interests: "Then, instead of God, he invokes those who can do him neither harm nor good; that is straying far indeed (from the Way)! He invokes those who are more likely to do him harm than good. What an evil guardian he chooses and what an evil companion! Such people are told a parable: 'O Men! Here is a parable set forth! So listen to it. Those on whom, beside God, you call, cannot create a fly, even though they may all combine together for this purpose. Nay! if a fly snatches away something from them, they cannot get it back from it.' How weak are the petitioners and how weak those whom they petition! They do not recognise the true worth of God as they should; the fact is that God alone is All-Mighty, All-Powerful" (22-73-74). And in Surah Al-Ankabut, we read: "How many are the creatures that carry not their own provision? God feeds them and you! He hears and knows (all thing). If indeed you ask them Who created the heavens and the earth, and subjected the sun and the moon (to His Law), they will certainly say, 'God'? How are they then deluded away (from the Truth)? God enlarges the provision for whom He pleases of His servants, and straitens it for whom He pleases, for God knows all things" (29: 60-62).

A most beautiful passage in the Qur'an, inviting people to think and reflect on the glorious names of God, is this: "God! There is no god but He, the Living, the Self-subsisting, the Eternal. No slumber can seize Him nor sleep. His are all things in the heavens and on the earth. Who is there that can intercede in His presence except by His Permission? He Knows what is before the people and also what is hidden from them. And they cannot comprehend anything of His Knowledge except whatever He Pleases to reveal. His Kindom spreads over the heavens and the earth and He feels no fatigue in guarding and preserving them. He alone is the Supreme and the Exalted" (2: 255). And the Qur'an appeals to the people to reflect on the Creation which God has created, not in vain but for a definite purpose: "Behold! In the creation of the heavens and the earth, and in the alternation of night and day, there are indeed signs for people of understanding, who standing and sitting and lying down remember God and reflect upon the (wonders) of the Creation in the heavens and the earth. (Then they cry out spontaneously), 'Our Lord! You have not created all this in vain, for You are free from doing such a thing. So save us from the punishment of the hell-fire' " (3: 190-191).

Close observation of the wonderful system of the universe shows everyone who reflects a little that this Creation is not without purpose. "The system itself speaks eloquently of the great wisdom that undelines it, so it follows that the All-Wise Creator must have a definite purpose in the creation of Man. Moreover, the very fact that He placed everything at man's disposal, and has endowed him with a moral sense to discriminate between good and bad, clearly shows that he must be accountable to Him as to whether he has fulfilled that purpose." (5)

This concept of accountablility is explained in greater detail and with convincing arguments from (a) within man's self, (b) in the universe and (c) in human history: "They know but the outer things of the life of the world, and are heedless of the Hereafter. Have they not reflected upon their own selves? God created not the heavens and the earth, and that which is between them, but with Truth and for an appointed term. But truly there are many among men who deny the meeting with their Lord. Have they not travelled in the land and seen the end of those before them? They were stronger than these in power, and they built upon the earth (castles) and flourished on it in greater numbers than these. Messengers of their own came to them with clear signs (which they rejected). Surely God wronged them not, but they did wrong themselves" (30: 7-9).

Then a challenge is given to the unbelievers which also is a convincing proof of the Hereafter. None can deny that One Who can originate the Creation from nothing can reproduce it, which is much easier than the first: "God originates Creation; then He reproduces it, then to Him you will be

---

5. *The Meaning of the Qur'an.* VOl. 1. pp. 80-81.

returned. . . And of His Signs is this: He created you from dust, and behold you human beings are scattered (far and wide)! And of His Signs is this: He created for you mates from among yourselves that you may find rest in them, and He has put love and mercy between you. Verily therein indeed are Signs for people who reflect. And of His Signs is the creation of the heavens and the earth, and the differences of your languages and colours. Verily therein indeed are Signs for men of knowledge. And of His Signs is your slumber by night and by day, and your seeking of His bounty. Verily herein are Signs for people who listen."

"And of His Signs, He shows you lightning for a fear and for a hope, and sends down water from the sky; and thereby gives life to the earth after it is dead. Verily herein indeed are Signs for people who understand (and are wise). And of His Signs is this, that the heavens and the earth stand by His Command, then when He calls you, behold, from the earth you will emerge. To Him belongs whosoever is in the heavens and in the earth. All are obedient to Him" (30: 20-26). And in Surah Yasin, we read: "Has not man seen that We have created him from a drop of seed? Yet behold, he is an open opponent. And he has invented for Us similitude, and has forgotten the fact of his creation, saying, 'Who will revive these bones when they have rotted away?' Say, 'He will revive them Who produced them the first time!' For He is the Knower of every Creation" (36: 77-79).

All the powers and the Creation belong to God alone and there is none who has any share in these: "God is He Who created you and then provided you sustenance, then causes you to die, then gives life to you again. Is there any of your (false) partners who does any one of these things? Glory to Him! and High above what they associate with Him" (30: 40)! Two very common examples from man's birth and from the land's growth in spring are given to appeal to man's sense of reason: "O mankind! If you are in doubt about the Resurrection, then verily, We created you from dust, then from a drop of seed, then from a clot, then from a little lump of flesh partly formed and partly unformed, that We may manifest (Our power) to you. And We cause whom We please to rest in the wombs for an appointed term, then We bring you out as infants, then (foster you) that you attain your strength. And some of you die (young), and some of you are sent back to the feeblest old age, so that they know nothing after having known (much). And you see the earth barren and lifeless, but when We send down water therein, it stirs (to life) and swells and brings forth every kind of beautiful vegetation. This is so because God is the Truth. He brings the dead to life and He has Power over everything and (this is a proof that) the Hour of Resurrection is sure to come and there is absolutely no doubt about it, and most surely He will raise up those who are lying in the graves" (22: 5-7).

These verses of the Qur'an show, first, that what God is telling us is the hard reality of life; secondly, that the existence of God is not a myth but a fact . And that He is not only the First Cause but the only Authority that is Supreme, conducting the affairs of this world according to His Plan, Will, Knowledge and Wisdom; thirdly, that all His Designs and Works are based on Truth and are, therefore, full of meaning and wisdom. (6)

Thus it is clear that Islam invites people even to its basic Article of Faith *(Tawhid)* with reason and arguments. It reveals the essential truth and facts about *Tawhid* and then issues an urgent appeal to the intellect of man to think, reflect and understand. It also provides him with realistic and popular examples from his daily life, from within his self, from his surroundings, from the earth and sky and from his

---

6. *The Meaning of the Qur'an,* VOl. V1, p. 185.

past history; then it wants him to ponder and meditate over these facts of life which provide an open book to him if he has any understanding. This method of reasoning is followed by Islam in all its concepts and ideas so that people may believe and follow the Message of Islam with full conviction and confidence. That is why there is no compulsion in matters of faith, because the Truth is manifestly clear from evil and now it is up to the people to believe in the former and reject the latter (2: 256).

It may here be pointed out that Islam not only invites people to think and understnd but also condemns blind faith, for it cannot carry them to a successful end. A faith based on ignorance or imitation is not very fruitful for such people can not be expected to do any works of excellence in any field. It can also not be very durable and effective in its results, for ignorance can help neither the believer nor others. He can neither enlighten his own soul nor lighten other people's hearts and lives. Therefore Islam has condemned all kinds of blind faith. First, blind faith in one's forefather's tradition and ways of life. Every Messenger of God was told by his people that they were not prepared to leave their father's ways and follow his religion (of *Tawhid*): "Do you forbid us to worship gods whom our forefathers worshipped?" (11: 62). Ignorant people always reject sound reasoning and follow their own blind ways merely because they have inherited them from their forefathers.

The same thing was experienced by Prophet Abraham: "Behold, "he said to his father and his people, "What do you worship?" They said, "We worship idols and are ever devoted to them!" He said, "Do they listen to you when you call (on them), or do they benefit or harm you?" They said, "Nay, but we found our fathers doing things this way" (26: 71-74). This is how all nations have treated their Messengers and rejected the light of Revelation and followed their own ignorant way of blind faith.

Secondly, it also rejects blind following of big but mis-guided leaders. When questioned on the Day of Judgement, the evildoers will reply, "Our Lord! We obeyed our chiefs and our great ones and they misled us from the right path" (33: 67). And again in Surah Ha Mim we read, "And the unbelievers will say, 'Our Lord! Show us those, among jins and men, who misled us: we shall crush them beneath our feet, so that they become the meanest (before all)" (41: 29).

Thirdly, it rejects blindly following one's own self and not caring what the Truth is. This attitude of man is also responsible for his rejection of Truth and following his own ignorant ways: "O believers, obey God and His Messenger and do not turn away from the Message after hearing it. Do not be like those who said, "We have heard," but have not listened to it, for the vilest beasts in God's sight are those deaf, dumb people, who do not use commonsense" (8: 22). And in Surah Yunus we read, "The fact is that most of them are following mere conjecture, whereas conjecture cannot in any way fulfil the requirements of True Knowledge" (10: 36). And again in Surah Al-Furqan we read, "Have you seen him who takes for his god his own lust? Will you then be guardian over him? Or do you think that most of them hear and understand? They are but as the cattle. Nay, but they are further astray!" (25: 43-44).

The Qur'an points out various factors that lead man to ignorant ways of life and throw him into the snare of blind faith from where he finds it difficult, or rather impossible, to listen to any argument based on reason or knowledge. He behaves worse than animals. Islam has totally rejected and condemned this attitude of man and invited him to the world of reason, knowledge and wisdom for his own sake, a world in which he will prosper with the wealth of knowledge and wisdom and enrich himself as well as others. The Qur'an counts the favours of God on His people through His Last Messenger: "He enjoins them to follow virtue and forbids them from evil; he makes pure things lawful for them and impure things unlawful. He relieves them of their burdens and frees them from the shackles (of superstition and man-made laws) that bound them" (7: 157). This is indeed a great blessing of God, that He has relieved man from the burdens of the superstitious restrictions of their religious leaders and forefathers and given them freedom to think and argue the suitability and profitability of anything before bringing it into their lives or systems. Thus Islam has brought him on to the road of wisdom and given him a life of intellegence in place of superstition and of knowledge in place of ignorance and darkness: "Who has created seven heavens in harmony. Do you see any fault in the creation of the Most Gracious? So look again; do you see any flaw? Then look again and again; your sight will come back to you weakened and worn out" (67: 3-4).

6

Freedom of Thought

The paths of good and evil are made plain to man and he is given freedom of choice in following either of the two ways. In the end each will be rewarded for his goodness and punished for his evil deeds. Man is given will and ability to choose without any reservation any way he likes: "Every soul is a pledge for its own deeds." (74: 38). He is plainly told that "On no soul does God place a burden greater than it can bear. It gets every good that it earns, and it suffers every ill that it earns" (2: 286). Thus man is clearly told that he is completely and fully responsible for his own deeds (or misdeeds) but he will not be called to account for not doing anything he could not possibly do. He will also not be punished for not abstaining from something he could not possibly abstain from. However it must be clearly understood by man that he is not his own judge as to what he may do and what he may not do. These matters will be judged by God. (1)

The second principle contained in this verse is that "both the rewards and the punishments are really the result and consequences of the acts and deeds of every individual. One will get a reward only for the good deed one has oneself done and not for the good acts of someone else. It must, however,

---

1. *The Meaning of the Qur'an,* VOl. 1, pp. 209-10.

be noted that if someone has done some good act which goes on producing good results long after his death, all those acts will also be put to his credit in his balance sheet as long as they last. In the same way, if some one has done some evil, which goes on producing evil results long after his death, all those also will be put against his account as long as they last. But all these results, both good and bad, will be the consequences of one's own deeds. In short, a person shall be rewarded or punished only for that thing to which he himself contributed intentionally and actually. There is no transfer of accounts in the Divine Law of Retribution." (1)

This warning is manifestly declared in these verses of the Qur'an: "Say, O Muhammad, 'O Mankind! Now has the truth from your Lord come to you. So whosoever is guided, is guided only for (the good of) his own soul, and whosoever errs errs only against it' " (10: 108). And in Surah Zilzal we read, "And whoso does good an atom's weight will see it then, and whoso does ill an atom's weight will see it there" (99: 7-8). And God will reward everyone according to his deeds for He is always fully aware of what they are doing and nothing is hidden from Him: "And We are also keeping a watch, O people, over whatever you are doing: for there is not an atom weight of anything in the earth and in the sky that is hidden from your Lord, nor what is less than that or greater than that, but is (written) in a clear Book" (10: 61).

This concept of accountability is a guarantee to individuals of their right to freedom of thought and action for without it the idea or accountability is rendered meaningless and purposeless. How can an individual be accountable for his omissions or commissions if he (or she) has no freedom of choice in his (or her) actions? Islam therefore guarantees this right of freedom of thought and action to all its followers, as well as its citizens, irrespective of caste, creed or colour: "There is no compulson and coercion in religion. The right thing has been made distinct from the wrong thing" (2: 256). This verse unequivocally declares the fundamental law of Islam that nothing can be thrust upon anyone forcibly, so much so that even the creed of Islam and its way of life cannot be forced upon individuals. When the light and darkness are made absolutely clear to them and no shadow of doubt is left therein, it is then up to each individual to accept that light consciously with full knowledge and understanding or reject it and follow the ways of darkness, ignorance and evil and bear the consequences of his (or her) action.

This right of freedom is enjoyed equally by all citizens of an Islamic State in their activities in all walks of life. This right of man is recognised as sacrosanct provided he (or she) does not intentionally and deliberately violate the Law of God. However this concept of freedom is given by God and is based on the following principles. First, man with his conscience is subject to God; therefore, he is directly responsible to Him alone. Secondly, he (or she) has been given freedom of choice by his (her) Creator and can follow any course of action he (or she) likes. Thirdly, as a consequence of this freedom of action, every man (or woman) will personally bear the burden of his (or her) own actions, good or bad. Fourthly, man has been shown clearly the right and the wrong, the good and the evil, and now it is up to him (or her) to follow either of these two ways. (2)

"It is a natural right of man (and woman), a spiritual privilege, a moral prerogative and, above all, a religious duty." Without it man can achieve no spiritual elevation, nor moral excellence nor religious faith nor sincerity in his actions. Without it, spiritual life will remain dormant and his moral acttitude dry and without any fruitful result. Under duress and compulsion, his religious excercises would lack

---

2. *Islam in Focus,* p. 34.

fervour and zeal. That is why ' "within the framework of the Islamic concept of freedom, there is no room for religious persecutions, class conflict or racial prejudice. The individual's right of freedom is as sacred as his (her) right of life; freedom is the equivalent of life itself." (2)

There is an other aspect of freedom, in addition to accountability, which is very closely related to the concept of Islam. It is the development and growth of the individual 'ego' or personality. The individual is free to use his right any way he likes and may go against the Law of God (i.e., against his own nature) but in so doing he will be interfering with his own natural growth and development. In other words, he will be damaging his own interest by not following the Law of God. Man has been "the recipient of the gift of freedom "and has been given, within well-defined limits, the capacity to use that freeedom as he likes. Of course he may abuse that trust, but by so doing he will only interfare with his own development. On the other hand, it is also his privilege to submit freely to the Divine Law, and to conform to the mandates of His Master. "Freedom", for man, involves the idea of his capacity to choose between two or more alternative courses of action. The problem of the moral life altimately consists, firstly in being aware as to which of the possible courses of conduct is the right one to follow, and secondly in having the strength of will to be able to execute that which is disclosed by this knowledge to be the right course of conduct. To be able to listen to the call of righteousness, then, is the most important virtue; to know what is right, and knowing it, consciously to abjure the temptation of succumbing to unrighteousness and evil ways is, for man, the *summum bonum* devoutly to be wished for. (3)

---

3. A. K. Brohi, *Islam in the Modern World*, pp. 24-26.

The development or growth of the 'ego' or individuality is retarded or rendered completely dormant if man is not given freedom of action. Growth of the 'ego' or individuality is a consequence of fredom and without it, it can not develop or grow. And as development of the individuality is one of the important aspects of the Faith, Islam has given full opportunity for its attainment through freedom of thought and action: "By the soul and He Who perfected it and inspired it (with conscience of) what is wrong for it and (what is) right for it. He is indeed successful who causes it to grow, and he is indeed a failure who retards or corrupts it" (91: 9-10). And in Surah Al-A'ala: "He is successful who grows (and develops his individuality)" (87: 14). Obviously success or failure of an individual depends whether he has effectively developed his individuality or let it die, rot or even decline or degrade in the wilderness of evil and sin.

It was also one of the important functions and purposes of the Messenger of God to purify and develop the individuality of man: "It is the great Favour of God to the believers that He has raised up from among themselves a Messenger who recites to them His Ayat and purifies their lives" (3: 164). The word *tazkiya* means, first, purification of body and mind; chastening of oneself of all evil and wickedness, in other words, complete moral purity, honesty, integrity and righteousness, and secondly, growth and development of the individuality (or ego). Thus the word *tazkiya* has two basic meanings: one is "cleansing and purifying" and the other growth and development". These aspects of *tazkiya* are complementary inseparable from each other. In fact, the first function leads to the second for without it the attainment of the latter seems imposible. Therefore, the Messenger of God cleansed and purified human souls of evil, corruption and similar other elements which check and retard the growth and development of individuality (or ego). After the process of *tazkiya* it becomes easier for a man (or woman) to develop his (or her) individuality (or ego) because all the impediments and obstacles have been cleared from the way.

But after this cleansing process, the individuality further needs a favourable atmosphere and right motives of action for its positive and healthy growth; if these are not available the desired results may not be achieved at all. First it requires freedom from all kinds of restrictions so that it may grow smoothly and find its natural perfection. Any kind of compulsion or force, no matter from where it comes, will not allow it to attain its natural growth and development. This is why even the Holy Prophet is told by God not to compel people to Islam for this will help them neither in the attainment of purification of their body and mind nor in the development of their individuality (or ego): "Yet it is not your concern if he grows not (in grace and beauty)" (80: 7). And in Surah Al-Gashiya: "So admonish them, for you are only one to admonish. You are not at all a warder over them (88-21-22)." The Messenger is sent to teach people the good things of life for their own benefit. He is not sent to force them to submit to his way of life. It clearly shows that God's Message is meant for all people alike. Anyone who desires to be purified and attain growth can do so of his own free will. If the great people arrogantly keep back from it and do not accept it, they will be the losers for they will attain neither purification nor growth of their individuality. As a consequence, they will neither prosper nor succeed in this world nor in the Hereafter. But for this, they are to blame and not the Messenger, who can guide only those who are willing to accept his guidance. He cannot compel people to accept his guidance for it will not be of any use to them if they are forced to it. It is only a voluntary message of instruction for people's own good and not a compulsory injunction for their submission (80: 11).

Even if the favourable atmosphere of freedom is available, a man (or woman) will not attain healthy growth of individuality (or ego) if he does not follow the right course of action. Unless he follows the Truth as revealed to the Holy Prophet, he can hardly find his true goal. It is therefore absolutely essential that the Divine Message be given to people so that they know what is good and useful for them, but in a voluntary way, as advice. It is up to them to accept or reject this message of their own free will. The Prophet Moses was Commanded by God to go to the Pharaoh and invite him to this Message for his own purification and growth: "And say to him, 'Have you desire to purify yourself and grow (in grace and beauty?)'" But the Pharaoh did not accept this free advice and destroyed his own self.

However, whatever the consequences for people in rejecting the Faith, it is always presented to them in a totally free atmosphere where they are absolutely free to choose. It gives them time to think and ponder over the Message and find out the Truth for their own benefit if they accept and for their loss of they reject it: "And whosoever purifies himself (and grows in grace and goodness) does so for the benefit of his own soul; and the destination of all is to God" (35: 18). Naturally those who willingly accept the message will prosper and achieve greatness: "But those will prosper who purify themselves" (87: 14). And their reward is an eternal life of bliss: "Gardens of eternity, beneath which rivers flow; they will dwell therein for ever; such is the reward of those who purify themselves (from evil)" (20: 76).

Another aspect of faith is the attainment of *taqwa* (fear of God), which also needs freedom. It reflects the moral attitude of man as well as his physical behaviour, which is the consequence of the former, towards other people. Both these aspects of man, i.e., his moral attitude and physical behaviour, are necessary for his spiritual advancement and for his salvation on the Day of Judgement. The importance of

Taqwa is explicitly shown in the following verses: "And whosoever fears God, God will prepare a way out for him. And will provide for him from (sources) whence he has no expectation" (65: 2-3). And in Surah Yunus we read, "Those who believe and fear God, there is nothing but good news for them in this world and in the Hereafter" (10: 63-64). Again, in Surah Al-Hujurat we read, "The most honoured of you in the Sight of God is (he who is) the most righteous (fearful of God) of you" (49: 13). These verses of the Qur'an show that *taqwa* is essential for success and prosperity but attainment of this quality is only possible if the individual is free to do whatever he likes. Negation of freedom of thought and action will, in fact, be negation of *Taqwa,* for without complete freedom no one can acquire any moral excellence or social behaviour of any consequence. And if one cannot attain these two facets of *taqwa,* one will fail to advance any further spiritually or morally. Islam has therefore given freedom to man so that he may have all opportunities to utilise all his talent and potential abilities and powers to develop a healthy moral attitude and to acquire cordial and lovable social behaviour, the two objective signs of taqwa.

Another concept of Islam which is an essential part of faith but cannot be practised by any one without freedom is 'enjoying what is right and forbidding what is wrong' *(amr bi'l-ma'ruf nahy an'l-munkar).* All Muslims, individually and collectively, are duty-bound to God to spread His Message and enjoin what is right (and good) and forbid what is wrong (and evil): "Now you are the best community which has been raised up for the guidance of mankind. You enjoin what is right and forbid what is wrong" (3: 110). This verse points to the fact that the Muslims have been appointed to that office because they possess the moral qualities which are essential for just leadership. These are to establish vertue and to eradicate evil from the earth." (4) They must practise this in their own individual lives and invite others to it, enjoining what is right (and good) and forbidding what is wrong (and bad).

The Holy Prophet himself practised this and also enjoined his followers to do the same: "He enjoins them to follow virtue and forbids them from evil; he makes pure things lawful for them and impure things unlawful. He relieves them of their burdens and frees them from the shackles that bound them" (7: 157). This is the basic function of a Muslim nation, to encourage good and discourage evil in order to establish a system of virtue, goodness and justice in the land. This function cannot be efficiently and effectively performed by individuals or by any society unless there is complete freedom of thought and action. As this was 'one of the cardinal concepts of Islam and an important function of every Muslim, freedom was therefore guaranteed by law to every citizen of the Islamic State so that he could perform his duty freely and without restriction.

This clearly shows why Islam has given so much importance to freedom of thought and action in man's life. There are no dogmas and no dilemmas in Islam which puzzle the mind of the believer which cannot be rationally explained and understood. Islamic faith and all its concepts are simple and logically explainable and they never come into conflict with science. In fact, they are all based on reason, reality and truth, and true science cannot be in conflict with them. This liberality and freedom in Islam gave a tremendous stimulus to the search for knowledg in the early period of Islamic history. Coercion and force is absolutely forbidden in Islam. All matters are decided by mutual consultation and free exchange of views (42: 38) and judgement is given between parties with justice and equity (4: 58) and no one is forced to accept Islamic concepts but by one's own free will and independent decision (2: 256).

The whole history of Islam is full of examples of freedom in practice in the Islamic society. The first Caliph of the Holy Prophet, after assuming authority, said, "Obey me so long as I obey God and His Messenger. But if I disobey God or the Messenger in anything, I shall no longer be entitled to your obedience. And the second Caliph, 'Umar, repeated words to the same effect: "Put me right if you discover any crookedness in me." When he was saying this, one of those present shouted, "By God, if we find any crookedness in you we will put you right with our swords." Thus Islam goes all the way for freedom and condemns tyranny, oppression and dictatorship. According to its philosophy, tyranny and oppression are best fought through the teaching of belief in One God and respect for the freedom of others. It safeguards and defends the right of freedom of people under all circumstances and does not allow any ruler to commit injustice against any of his citizens. It very strictly keeps his authority within the limits of his legal powers and enjoins justice between all his citizens. (5) The Holy Prophet advised his followers to fight against injustice and evil and administer justice: "He who witnesses any vice should change it." He also said, "A word of justice uttered before an unjust ruler is the greatest of jihad (struggle)."

To sum up, the basic concepts of Islam are not only based on the principle of freedom but also require the exercise of this right for the practice and achievements of those very concepts. Besides, administration of justice and eradication of evil and coruption further assist in strengthening this right of the individual against other members of society as well as against the legal authority of the state.

---

4. *The Meaning of the Qur'an*, VOl. 11. p. 54.
5. M. Qutb, *Islam the Misunderstood Religion*, pp. 160-61.

7

Main Systems of the Islamic Society

Our discussion in the previous chapters must have given a clear idea of the Islamic way of life. It is all-embracing and nothing is outside its scope. It is a complete code of life and covers the entire life of man, from the cradle to the grave, including his individual, as well as his social and collective actions. Its chief objective is to organise human society and its main systems and disciplines on the basis of social justice for all, irrespective of colour, creed or race, and to establish concepts of goodness, virtue and benevolence among people so that they are able to enjoy a life of security, peace, prosperity and happiness on an individual as well as a social level. This spirit of unity, fraternity and human brotherhood is equally shared by all its members.

The fundamental purpose of this society is clearly laid down in this verse of the Holy Qur'an: "Muslims are those who, if We give them power in the land, establish regular prayer, and give regular charity *(zakat)*, enjoin right and virtue and forbid wrong and evil" (22: 41). The same principle is expressed in Surah Al-Hadid in these words: "Surely, We sent Our Messengers with clear Signs and sent down with them the Book and the Balance (of Right and Wrong), that mankind may stand forth in justice" (57: 25). The Messengers were given three things for the guidance of mankind: first, manifest Signs, which clearly showed that they were

Messengers of God and that what they had brought was the Truth from their Lord; secondly, the Book containing a complete code of life for human guidance; thirdly, a balance to judge between right and wrong, good and bad and to find Truth from the extreme ways in beliefs, morals and people's affair's and dealings. (1)

The Messengers were equipped with these three instruments for this object: that man's attitude and his life-system, on an individual as well as a social level, must be based on justice. On the one hand, every individual must know, understand and fulfil with full justice the Rights of his Creator, his own rights and the rights of all creatures of God; on the other hand, social life must be organized and built on such principles that all kinds of aggression and oppression are totally wiped out from society and everyone is paid his due with justice and equity. Every aspect of culture and civilisation is fully preserved from the excesses and extremes of both sides. All departments of social life are maintained in perfect balance. And all elements of society receive their rights and fulfil their obligations and duties with justice. In other words, the object of God's Messengers is the establishment of individual as well as social justice. They want to establish justice in the life of every individual in order to achieve balance in his thinking, his attitude, his character and in his behaviour, and also in all the systems of his social life, so that both the individual and society co-operate and assist each other in their spiritual, moral and material betterment and do not obstruct or impede each other. (1)

This explains the real purpose of the Islamic Society: that people adopt piety and virtue in their personal lives and use their economic resources to help others who are not well off

1. A. A. Maududi, *Tafheem al-Qur'an,* VOl. V, pp. 321-22.

and jointly help to eradicate sin, evil and injustice and, instead, promote and establish virtue, goodness and justice in their individual and social relationships. These besic principles must embrace and pervade the whole life-system and cover every area, system and discipline within the Islamic society.

Thus to construct human life on these lines, the *Shari'ah* states its norms of virtues and good *(ma'rufat)* and of avoidance of sin and evils *(munkarat)* to which the individual and social conduct must conform. It not merely provides an inventory of virtues and vices for man but also lays down the whole scheme of life in such a way that virtues may flourish without being polluted or retarded by vices. However, the *Shari'ah* conducts human society towards the free growth of good, virtue and truth in every area of human life. "This gives full play to the forces of good in all directions and at the same time removes all impediments in the path of virtue:" In order to eradicate evil from society, it prohibits vice and closes all possible doors from which it can creep into the social system. (2)

Virtue and Good *(Ma'rufat)*
Virtues are classified into these categaries: (a) Mandatory *(fardh)*, (b) recommended *(matlub)*, and (c) permissible *(mubah)*. The mandatory are obligatory and every member of a muslim society must observe and practise these commandments. The recommended virtues are those which are desirable and the *Shari'ah* wants them to be observed and practised by people. The growth of these is encouraged in a Muslim society but actual observance is left to the discretion of its individual members. All others which are not prohibited are permissible and, again, are left to individual taste and social practice. People have complete freedom of

---

2. A. A. Maududi, *The Islamic Way of Life,* pp. 18-22.

choice, depending upon their own tastes and likes and dislikes.

Prohibited things *(munkarat)* are of two kinds: (a) *haram* (prohibited absolutely) and (b) *makruh* (disliked). Muslims are to abstain totally from forbidden *(haram)* things but in the case of *makruhat,* the *Shari'ah* shows, expressly or by implication, disapproval. There are several things, between these two extremes of *haram* and *makruhat,* which are on the border. The *Shari'ah* has, however, given strict prohibitory orders against those bordering on *haram,* but left the case of those bordering on *makruhat* to the discretion and tasts of individual members of the Muslim society. Both these measures help a great deal in establishing and promoting virtue and good and eradicating and discouraging evil and sin in society.

Now we will study one by one the various systems working in a Muslim society and examine how the concepts of virtue, good and justice operate within those systems.

Spiritual Discipline

The spiritual discipline which educates and trains the inner self of man is the core of the Islamic system. It frees man from the slavery of the 'self' and purges his soul from the lust of material life and instils in him a passion of love for his Lord. He worships Him, obeys His Laws and follows His Code of Guidance merely for His Pleasure. He becomes an embodiment of purity, modesty and sincerity and all his actions are performed in seeking the Love and Pleasure of God. He attains perfection in his actions when his likes and dislikes become subject to and identified with those of God. He really examplifies this verse of the Qur'an: "Say: truly, my prayer and my sacrifice and my life and my death are (all) for God, Lord of the Worlds" (6: 162).

At this stage, he obeys and acts on the Command of his Lord as if he sees Him with his eyes; fears His Anger as if he is in His Presence and pursues his course of action in the service of Islam for His Pleasure alone. He is ever prepared to sacrifice everything in the service of his Lord — his wealth, his family, his comforts, even his life. He considers all that he possesses as a free gift from God and finds complete satisfaction in returing that gift to his Master as a humble offering. The pleasure of God becomes the sole aim of his life. He lives for it, moves for it and dies for it. All his actions become symbols of the Actions of his Lord, because he does not do anything but for the pleasure of God. This level of spiritual attainment represents the highest standard in Islam and is known as *ihsan,* where man does everything as if he is standing and working in the Presence of God, feeling and seeing His Presence all the time.

This attitude completely purifies the ideas, thinking and actions of man from all selfish motives of gain, greed or power. He becomes virtue, goodness and justice personified. Good and virtuous ideas and actions follow automatically from him, for this kind of behaviour becomes natural and ordinary way of life for him. Islam wants to educate and train every believer on these lines so that virtue and goodness should become the common norms and practice of people in their individual as well as social life.

This level of purity and goodness and love for the Divine pleasure is achieved through greater understanding of the Doctrine of *Tawhid* and the exercise of the four 'Pillars of Islam' discussed and explained fully in the first volume of this book. The more you practise those forms of worship (i.e., *'ibadah),* commonly known as the 'Pillars of Islam', and the greater your understanding and devotion, especially in daily prayer *(salat)* and in the anual fasting for a month, the more close you are to your Lord and His Pleasure: "When you remember Me, I will remember you. Be grateful to Me, and be not ungrateful" (2: 152). This is because prayer 'represents' both a solemn ritual and a spiritual state of mind in which the devotee seeks to realise the Presence of God. Regular practise of these forms of worship *('ibadah)* gradually brings the devotee to the level of *ihsan,* when he sees and feels the Presence of his Lord during the act of worship. Thus His Love and Pleasure become the sole object of the worshipper's life, and he tries to attain to them through acts of virtue, goodness and justice, on an individual and social level. And a society composed of such individuals naturally becomes a habitation of goodness, virtue and justice.

Islam has thus proved itself a strong spiritual force and discipline, the equal of which mankind has never known before. It sweeps away the vilest superstitions, grossly stupid ignorance, loathsome immorality and centuries old evil customs and habits in no time. This unparalleled spiritual transformation of man's ideas, feelings, culture, actions and the entire way of life is achieved through the vigorous daily discipline of prayer and other forms of worship *('ibadah).*

Moral Discipline

The Islamic concept of morality is based on certain basic beliefs (i.e., the doctrine of *Tawhid).* God is the Creator, Master and Sovereign of the entire universe, and all truth, goodness and beauty spring from Him. He is the Source as well as the Purpose of Creation. Man is living on the earth as His agent. He is ultimately responsible to Him and his highest prize is the Pleasure of his Lord. God in His Mercy and Wisdom has sent Guidance for him through His Messengers. The code of behaviour suggested by the Messengers forms the basis of Islamic morality. (3) As the moral principles of Islam

---

3. Hammudah Abdalati, *Islam in Focus,* pp. 40-41.

are based on the Divine Revelation, they are permanent: Islam has thus its own standard of morality which is based on its own principles and has its own character. It is based on Divine Judgement and is therefore everlasting and unchangeable. Change of time and space does not have any effect on it.

"This is Islam's fundamental attitude towards life. This concept of the universe and of man's place therein determines the real and ultimate good which is the object of all man's efforts and that is the 'seeking of God's Pleasure'. This is the standard by which a particular mode of conduct is judged and classified as good or bad. This standard of judgement provides the nucleus around which the whole of our moral conduct should revolve . . . It provides us with a stable and flawless set of values which remain unaltered under all circumstances. Moreover, with making the 'Pleasure of God' the object of man's life, the highest and noblest objective is set before humanity and thus unlimited possibilities are opened for man's moral evolution, untainted at any stage by any shadow of narrow selfishness or bigoted race or nation worship." (4)

Thus Islam not only provides a normal standard but also furnishes man with a means of determining good and evil conduct. It does not base human knowledge of vice and virtue on mere intellect, desire, institution, or experience derived through the sense-organs, which constantly undergo shifts and modifications and alterations and do not provide, categorical and unchanging standards of morality. It provides man with a definite Source, the Divine Revelation, as embodied in the Book of God and the Sunnah (way of life) of the Holy Prophet (peace be upon him). This Source prescribes a standard of moral conduct that is permanent and

----

4. A. A. Maududi, *Islamic Way of Life*, pp. 32-39.

universal and holds good in every age and under all circumstances. It guides man at every stage in life, covering even the smallest details of domestic life as well as the broad aspects of national and international behaviour." (3) This morality has abiding value and is not susceptible to any change whatsoever. (5) The character of Islamic morals can be judged from the following Hadith of the Messenger. (6)

Once 'Ali asked the Messenger about the principle governing human behaviour in general, and he replied: "Knowledge is my capital, reason is the basis of my religion, love is my foundation, desire is my mount for riding, remembrance of God is my comrade, confidence is my treasure, anxiety is my companion, science is my arm, patience is my mantle, contentment is my body, modesty is my self-respect, renunciation of pleasure is my profession, cirtitude is my food, Truth is my intercessor, obediency is my sufficiency, sruggle is my habit and the delight of my heart is in the service of worship." (3) The Holy Messenger also said on another occasion: "The sum Total of wisdom is the fear of God. Islamic morality begins with the renunciation of all adoration outside God, be it adoration of the self (egoism) or adoration of our own handicrafts and creations (idols, superstitions) etc., and the renunciation of all that degrades humanity (atheism, injustice, etc.) (7)

The Sanction behind Morality

The moral law without a proper and authentic sanction can have neither force nor support nor co-operation from anyone. It will remain simply a theoretical code of morality without being followed or practised by any group of

---

5. S. D. Islahi, *Islam at a Glance,* pp. 104-6.
6. M. Hamidullah, *Introduction to Islam,* pp. 84-92
7. Dr. Ahmad A. Galwosh, *The Religion of Islam,* VOl. 11. pp. 118-39.

individuals or nations, like the moral ideas of the secularists, humanists and atheists. The Islamic teaching that God is the Creator and Sovereign and Lord of the entire universe and that man is His vicegerent on the earth and accountable to Him for his actions is what gives the proper sanction. Islam engraves in us a strong belief in God Who is Present everywhere, sees every action of man, open or hidden, and from Whom nothing remains hidden. This firmly rooted belief in God and His Attributes is the real and effective sanction behind Islamic moral law. There is no need for police to enforce this code of morality. Although Islam intends to develop a powerful and strong public opinion through moral teaching in favour of its code of morality, and also aims at evolving a political system to enforce it, in fact, its moral code needs no external pressure for this purpose, as faith alone can keep a Muslim individual and Muslim community on the right path of virtue and goodness. (4)

Motive and Incentive

The Islamic ideology also provides a motivating force to inspire individuals and groups of individuals to conduct their affairs in public and private in accordance with the moral code of Islam. This voluntary and willing acceptance of this code of behaviour is far more effective and stronger than any other that can be achieved through the external force of law and order. The believers voluntarily accept the Sovereignty of God and willingly obey His Law and Way of Life. In fact, they strive hard in their efforts to seek the Pleasure of God and try to perform every act, in open or in secret, with great humility and sincerity. All this for no reward in monetary terms but simply to please their Lord. This is perhaps the strongest motive and most effective incentive for the believers to obey the Commands of their Lord.

Furthermore, the belief that whoever obeys His Lord's Commandments and does good deeds will have a happy and peaceful eternal life in the Hereafter, surely provides a strong incentive for a pious and virtuous life, even if one may have to face some hardships and difficulties in the temporary life of this world. On the other hand, the belief that whoever breaks the law of God will suffer eternal punishment, no matter how rich and luxurious a life he may have led in this world, will be a strong deterrent against an immoral and impous life. The stronger and firmer this belief in a good reward for obedience and a severe punishment for violation on the Day of Judgement, the stronger will be the motivating force to inspire one to lead a virtuous life even if the consequences appear to be damaging and harmful, and to abstain from impious and evil deeds even if they appear to be very fruitful and profitable. (4)

A cursory study of Islamic morality and ethics shows that it covers all the moral exvellences known to any advanced and civilized society. But it does not simply enumerate moral principles, it also teaches us how to acquire those moral excellences and shows the straight way to their acquisition. (7) The Qur'an teaches us that there are three sources from which spring forth the three disciplines of physical, moral and spiritual life. The Qur'an lays down for us guidance in matters such as food, drink, dress, cleanliness of the body, etc., because 'the physical conditions of man are closely connected with his moral and spiritual states, so much so that even his modes of eating and drinking play a part in the moulding of his moral and spiritual qualities . . . It is for this reason that in all forms of devotion and prayer and in all the injunctions relating to internal purity and moral rectitude, the greatest stress has been laid upon external purity and cleanliness and the proper attitude of the body." (5)
This is why "The dimensions of morality in Islam are numerous, far-reaching and comprehensive." (3) Islam not only prescribes beliefs and acts of worship for the training of

the soul of man but also gives him rules and a code of behaviour, permitting him certain things and actions and forbidding him certain others, as explained earlier. The Truth and goodness of its moral principles is so apparent and universal that it appeals to everyone. No right-thinking person can ever deny the truth of these principles. Their appeal becomes all the more convincing when one reads the life of the Messenger of God who brought us a perfect practical example. The Qur'an simply states the moral principles which it recommends man to adopt in his practical life and those things which it forbids him, and it was the Messenger of God who showed by his practical example how to adopt the former and refrain from the latter.

Islam has provided an all-comprehensive code of morality, covering man's external behaviour and actions as well as internal thoughts and intentions, laying down strict positive requirements which are to be fulfilled and details of what is to be avoided under all circumstances. The purpose of these instructions, positive or negative, is 'to build in man a sound mind, a   peaceful soul, a strong personality and a healthy body. Carrying them out helps man to acquire peace and prosperity in a just and right way on an individual, national and international level and to establish a system based on justice and goodness. (3) Islam has adopted very practical and effective methods to achieve the desired goal by its moral instructions. It has followed a gradual process of educating and   training   individuals   to   attain   soul   ennobling consciousness of the eternal Presence of God which can greatly help them to perform truly moral actions. To achieve this objective, Islam has given its prescriptions step by step, starting with a simple belief in God and the rules of ordinary social behaviour.

(A) Negative or Preventive Measures
The negative instructions of Islam also cover various fields of

activity, from mere eating and drinking habits to the moral and social behaviour of individuals.

1. Associating a Partner with God

This is the first and foremost prohibitory Commandment regarding the Divinity of God. He is One and no partners should be associated with Him: "Behold, Luqman said to his son by way of advice: 'O my son! Ascribe no partners to God. Surely, to ascribe partners to God is a tremendous wrong' " (31-13). Again: "Say: I am commanded only that I worship God and ascribe to Him no partner. To Him I call and to Him is my return" (13: 36). To ascribe partners to God is a complete negation of His Lordship, Mastership and kingship and open rebellion against obeying His Command. And, as such, the entire ideology and philosophy of life recommended for the benefit and good of mankind is at risk, because denial of the Unity of God *(Tawhid)* strikes at the very root of this way of life. It is why the believers are warned to be aware of this danger lest they wreck the very foundation of their belief which supports the superstructure of the Islamic way of life.

2. Damaging Human Life or Property

Muslims are also forbidden to damage other people's persons, property or honour: "It does not behove a believer to slay another believer except by error . . . As regards the one who kills a believer wilfully, his recompense is Hell, wherein he shall abide for ever" (4; 92-93). They are also forbidden to take over other people's property: "O believers, do not devour one another's property by unlawful means" (4: 29). They are also forbidden to kill their children for fear of hunger" (17: 31).

3. Eating and Drinking

Muslims are prohibited from taking certain foods and drinks: "Forbidden to you are dead meat, and blood, and swineflesh and that which has been sacrificed to (the name of) any other than God; and that which has been killed by strangling, or by beating, or by headlong fall, or by being gored to death, and that which has been partly eaten by a wild animal; unless you are able to slaughter it (in due form); and that which has been sacrificed to idols. And forbidden also is the division (of meat) by raffling with arrows. This is an abomination" (5: 4). But he who is driven by necessity, without wilful disobedience, nor transgressing, it is no sin for him. For God is Forgiving, Merciful" (2: 173). They are also forbidden to drink intoxicating wines, liquors and spirits and to indulge in gambling: "O You who believe! Intoxicants and gambling . . . are an abomination of Satan's handiwork. Leave it aside in order that you may succeed. Satan's plan is (but) to excite enmity and hatred between you, with intoxicants and gambling, and hinder you from the rememberance of God and from prayer. Will you not then abstain?" (5: 93-94). All these measures are taken to protect Muslims from indulgence, weakness, and degeneration. (3)

4. Indecent Behaviour and Shameful Acts

It also prohibits all sexual relations outside the bond of marriage and all ways of talking, walking, looking and dressing in public that may instigate temptation, arouse desire, stir suspicion or indicate immodesty and indecency: "Nor come near to adultery. Surely, it is an abomination and an evil way" (17: 32). To avoid the actual occurrance of indecent acts, preventive measures are taken to preserve modesty and shastity in the individual and social life of the Muslims: "Tell the believing men to lower their gaze and guard their modesty. That is purer for them. And surely God is well aware of what they do. And tell the believing women to lower their gaze and guard their modesty; and not desplay their beauty and ornaments except what (most ordinarily) appear thereof, and to draw their veil over their bosoms, and not display their adornment except to their husbands, their fathers, their husbands' fathers, their sons, their husbands' sons, their brothers or their brothers' sons, or their sisters' sons, or their women or the slaves whom their right hands possess, or male servants free of physical needs, or small children who know nothing of women's nudity. And they should not strike their feet to reveal their hidden ornaments. And turn to God, O believers, in order that you may succeed" (24: 30-1). And the prophet is commanded: "Tell your wives and daughters, and the believing women, to draw their cloaks close around them. That is more appropriate that they may be recognised and not molested. God is Forgiving, Merciful" (33: 59). And marriage of bachelors is encouraged to preverve modesty and chastity in society. "And marry among you those who are single, or the virtuous ones among your slaves, male or female. If they are poor, God will enrich them of His Bounty. God is of ample means, and Aware of all things. And let those who cannot find a match keep themselves chaste till God gives them means of His Grace" (24: 32-33). However, a believer must avoid obscenity under all circumstances: "Do not indulge in indecent acts, be they open or secret" (6: 151).

These preventive or prohibitory measures of Islam are meant for the moral and material benefit as well as the spiritual and mental uplift of individuals and the community. These Divine prohibitory instructions are based on extreme wisdom and do not deprive one of anything good or useful. In fact, they do a lot of good to a person by protecting his interests against harmful and injurious things and by developing in him (or her) a refined taste for the good and better things in life and a greater regard for higher moral values. For this purpose, it is necessary to take care of "man's spirit and mind, soul and body, conscience and sentiments, health and wealth, physique and morals. Prohibition, therefore, is not deprivation but enrichment, not suppression but discipline, not limitation but expansion." (3)

The wisdom of those rules is clearly shown by their relaxation in times of emergency, necessity and other unusual circumstances. Besides, God does not take notice of any evil committed out of ignorance, when proper amends are made by repentance, because God is Forgiving and Merciful" (6: 54-55).

5. Social Behaviour

Believers are advised not to make fun of their fellow believers or ridicule them: "O You who believe, do not let one (set of) people make fun of another set; perhaps they are better than they (themselves) are. Nor let any (set of) women (make fun of) other women; perhaps they are even better than they are themselves. Nor should you defame yourselves nor insult one another by using nicknames; it is bad to use an evil name after (entering the) faith (of Islam). Those who do not turn away from it are wrongdoers" (49: 11). They are also advised to avoid suspicion and other such sins against their brethren: "O you who believe! Avoid suspicion as much (as possible): for suspicion in some cases is a sin. And spy not on each other, nor speak ill of others behind their backs. Would any of you like to eat the flesh of his dead brother? Nay, you would abhor it. But fear God, for God is Forgiving, Merciful" (49: 12).

The believers are cautioned against pride and conceited habits: "And turn not your cheek in scorn towards people nor walk in insolence in the land. For God loves not any arrogant boaster" (31: 18). And in Surah Bani Isra'il we read, "And do not strut about in the land, for you can neither tunnel through the earth nor rival the mountains in height" (17: 37). So against promises for sin: "Do not use God as an excuse in your oaths, to keep yourselves from being virtuous, doing your duty and improving matters among mankind" (2: 224). But God does not take notice of ordinary oaths: "God will not take you to task for any slip in your oaths, but He does take you to task for whatever you have sworn solemnly (and then ignored)" (5: 89). The believers are also advised to be neither niggardly nor lavish in their expenditure. They are also advised not to tresspass on people's private property because it is a negation of their rights. As property and privacy are essential to a refined and cultured life of goodness and modesty, they are told to ask permission of the owner before entering his property: "O you who believe! Enter not houses other than your own, until you have asked permission" (24: 27).

These are the prohibitory or preventive rules of morality which define the scope of action of a believer, and within which he has to adjust his behaviour if he seeks the Pleasure of God. These are the prohibitions *(munkarat)* which must be avoided under all circumstances if one is to win the Pleasure of the Lord. The best course in this respect is to keep away from the border-line of prohibition so that there is no possibility of ever straying into the prohibited zone.

Along with these negative commandments, Islam also gives positive instructions *(ma'rufat)* to the believers to help them develop higher qualities of morality and thus attain the higher order of excellence, goodness and piety reserved for the calm and peaceful soul *(nafs al-mutma'innah)*. These range from instructions concerning ordinary eating habits to high acts of goodness, piety and justice.

B. Positive Instructions

1. Worship of One God *(Tawhid)*.
At the top of the list is the obedience to One God. All believers are commanded to worship, obey and follow the Law of God in all their affairs, be they personal or collective, temporal or spiritual, economic or social, political or moral, legal or educational (29: 17 and 22: 34-35).

2. A Chaste and Virtuous Life

Believers are commanded to be chaste and pure in their private as well as public life and set an example for others to follow: "O Prophet. Tell your wives and daughters, and all the believers' wives as well, to draw their cloaks close around themselves. That is more appropriate so that they may be recognised and not molested" (33: 59). And in Surah Al-Nur we read: "Tell believers to avert their glances and to guard their private parts; that is purer for them; God is aquainted with all that they do. Tell believing women to avert their glances and guard their private parts, and not to display their charms (and beauty) except what (normally) appears of them" (24: 30-31).

Believers are told to attain real virtue and piety but this does not consist in observing merely the forms of worship *('ibadah):* "Virtue does not mean that you turn your faces towards East or West, but virtue means to believe in God (alone), the Last Day, the Angels, the Book and the Prophets; and to give one's wealth away, no matter how one loves it, to near relatives, orphans, the needy, the wayfarer, and beggars, and towards freeing captives; and to keep up prayer and pay the welfare-due. And those who keep their words whenever they promise anything, and are patient under suffering and hardship and in time of violence, those are the ones who are loyal, and those are the heedful" (2: 177).And in Surah Al-Hujurat we read: "O mankind. We have created you from a male and female and set you up as nations and tribes, so that you may recognise one another. The noblest among you before God are those of you who are virtuous; God is Aware, Informed" (49: 13).

3. Eating, Drinking and choice of Clothing

All pure and good things are permitted to Muslims, who are supposed to set an example for the rest of mankind in standards of goodness and cleanliness: "O Believers! If you are true worshippers of God alone, eat without hesitation of the good and clean things that We have provided for you, and be grateful to God" (2: 172). And in Surah Al-Ma'idah we read: "They ask you what has been made lawful for them. Say, 'All the good and pure things have been made lawful for you' " (5: 4). And again: "O Messenger. Enjoy all things good and pure, and do good" (23: 51).

Believers are told to wear clean clothes and keep everything, their body, clothes, houses, etc., clean, for God loves those who are clean and pure: "O children of Adam. We have sent down to you clothing in order to cover the shameful parts of your body and to serve as protection and decoration; and the best garment is the garment of piety" (7: 26). They are further told to observe cleanliness in all their things, from the house to the mosque: "O children of Adam. Dress yourselves fully, properly and decently at the time of every prayer; eat and drink, but do not transgress, for God does not like transgressors" (7: 31).

4. Social Behaviour and Etiquette

Believers are the most polite and decent of people: "Whenever you are welcomed with a greeting, then answer with something finer, or (at least) return it" (4: 86). And Surah Al-Nur says: "When you enter people's houses with their consent, greet them politely; that is best for you, so that you may remember. If you do not find anyone in them, still do not enter them until permission has been granted to you. If you are told, 'go back', then return back; it is more fitting for you,. And God is Aware of anything you do" (24: 27-28). And again: "You who believe, let those whom your rights control, and those who have not yet reached puberty, ask permission from you on three occasions: before the morning prayer; when you take your clothes off at noon (for a rest); and after the late evening prayer. You have three times, for privacy. Outside these times, it is not wrong for you or for them to move about attending on each other. Thus God explains Signs to you; Allah is Aware, Wise. And whenever any children of yours reach puberty, let them ask permission just as those before them have had to ask for such permission. Thus God explains His Signs to you; Allah is Aware. Wise" (24: 58-59).

Believers taught lessons about the best morals: "Be modest in the way you walk, and lower your voice" (31: 19). "Act kindly, just as God has treated you kindly" (28: 77). "Those who act kindly will have kindness and even more besides, while neither gloom nor disgrace shall cover their faces. They will be inhabitants of the Garden, where they will abide for ever" (10: 26). "Let them forgive and over look. Do you not like God to pardon you? God is Forgiving, Merciful" (24: 22). "Practice forgiveness, command decency and avoid ignorant people" (7: 199). "Those who spend their wealth night and day, both privately and publicly, will receive their rewards from their Lord. No fear will be upon them nor need they ever feel saddened" (2: 274). "Whenever you judge between people, you should judge with (a sense of) justice" (4: 58). Whenever you speak, be just, even though it concerns a close relative" (6: 153). "And those who preserve their trusts and their pledge, and who attend to their prayers, will be the heirs who shall inherit Paradise, to live their for ever" (23: 8-10).

And more: "God Commands justice, kindness and giving (their due) to near relatives, while He forbids sexual misconduct, imperiety and insolence. He instructs you so that you may be mindful" (4: 58). "Who is finer in speech than someone who appeals to God, acts honourably, and says, 'I am a Muslim. A good deed and an evil deed are not alike: repay (evil) with something that is finer, and see how someone who is separated from you in enmity will become a bosom friend. Yet only those who discipline themselves will attain it; only the most fortunate will achieve it" (41: 33-35). And the servants of the Merciful (are those) who walk modestly on the earth and say, 'Peace be upon you', whenever the ignorant address them" (25: 36). "Co-operate with one another in virtue and piety, and do not co-operate with one another in sin and aggression" (5: 2). "Whenever two factions of believers fall out with one another, then try to reconcile them" (49: 9).

These are some of the eternal rules of morality provided by the Last Messenger of God to mankind. The grounds and philosophy of sound moral behaviour are summed up by the Qur'an in these words: "O children of Adam! Wear your beautiful apparel at every time and place of prayer; eat and drink, but waste not by excess, for God loves not the wasters. Say: 'Who has forbidden the beautiful gifts of God, which He has produced for His servants, and the things, clean and pure, (which He has provided) for sustenance?" Say: 'They are, in the life of this world, for those who believe (and) purely for them on the Day of Judgement. Thus do We explain the Signs in detail for those who understand'. Say: 'The things that my Lord has indeed forbidden are: shameful deeds, whether open or secret, sins and aggression against truth or reason; assigning of partners to God; and saying things about God of which you have no knowledge' " (7: 31-33).

In the most beautiful words the Qur'an gives fourteen moral Commands to the believers: "Your Lord has enjoined the following: (1) You should not worship anyone but Him. (2) Treat your parents with great consideration; if either or both of them live with you in their old age, do not even say 'fie' to them; nor rebuke them, but speak kind words to them with humility and tenderness, and pray: 'Lord be merciful to them just as they brought me up with kindness and affection.' Your Lord best knows what is in your hearts. If you live righteously, He surely forgives you and turns towards all such people as are penitent and obedient. (3) Fulfil your obligation towards your relatives and the needy and the wayfarer. (4) And squander not your wealth wastefully, because the squanderers are the brethren of Satan and Satan has been ungrateful to his Lord. (5) If you have to turn away from them (the needy persons) seeking mercy from the Lord, then speak to them a kind word. (6) Do not tie your hand to your neck nor stretch it without any restraint lest you should become blameworthy and left destitute. Your Lord enlarges the provision for whom He pleases, and straitens it for whom He pleases. Surely, He is ever the Knower, the Seer of His slaves. (7) Do not kill your children for fear of poverty; for it is We Who provide for them and for you as well. Indeed their killing is a great sin. (8) And come not near to adultery for it is a very indecent thing and a very evil way. (9) And slay not life, which God has forbidden except in justice. And if one is killed unjustly We have granted the right of retribution to his heir. So he should not transgress the limits in retaliation, for he shall be helped. (10) Do not go near the property of an orphan except in the best manner until he reaches the age of maturity. (11) Keep your pledges, for you shall be questioned regarding your pledges. (12) Give full measure when you measure and when you weigh do so with even scales. This is the best way and will prove to be the best in the end. (13) Do not follow that of which you have no knowledge for you shall be questioned on (the use of) your eyes, ears and hearts. (14) Do not walk on the earth with insolence for you can neither cleave the earth nor attain the height of the mountains. The evil (aspect of) all these (Commandments) is hateful in the Sight of your Lord. There are the things of wisdom which your Lord has revealed to you" (17: 23-39).

Thus it is obvious that the range of morality in Islam is very wide and covers all aspects of human activity, from faith in One Supreme Being to ordinary religious and spiritual rituals, from intellectual and economic pursuits to the administration of justice, from simple speech manners to social behaviour, etc. In fact, morality is an essential part of Islam and underlies all its teachings. Every instruction and every rule of Islam bears the colour of its moral principles. It is mentioned in various contexts, sometimes as a single important principle and sometimes as a constituent of the whole system of morality, which itself forms a constituent of the entire religious structure of Islam. It is therefore, very difficult to formulate any simple and brief classification of the moral teachings of Islam. (3)

We give here a brilliant passage from the Qur'an, describing the social behaviour of an average Muslim. Worship (and serve) God, and associate none with Him; and show kindness and affection to your parents, and be kind to near relations, and to orphans, and to the needy; and be considerate to your neighbours − relatives and strangers − and to the companions at your side and to the wayfarer and to the slaves in your possession. Surely, God loves not the arrogant and boastful, . . . nor those who are niggardly and bid others to be niggardly, and conceal the bounty of God that He has bestowed upon them; We have prepared a degrading punishment for such ungrateful disbelievers. And those who spend their wealth to be seen of men, for they do not sincerly believe in God and the Last Day. Whoso takes Satan for a comrade, has very evil company" (4: 36-38).

In the above verses are given the main basic principles of morality on which Islam builds the entire structure of life. These, in fact, form the manifesto of the Islamic society and contain the ideological principles of this society. Islam is not confined to moral teachings but contains in it ideological, moral, cultural, economic and legal principles. The laws of inheritance, of bequests and the rights of orphans are all based on these articles. As a matter of fact, the whole moral system is formed in such a way as to create feelings of generosity, sympathy and co-operation. "So much so that the people begin to realise their importance and observe them voluntarily with out any legal sanction. (8)

Another passage in the Qur'an sums up some of the articles of the Islamic Manifesto: "Say, 'Come, I will recite what limits your Lord has set for you. (He has enjoined): (1) That you should not set up anything as partner to Him (2) Treat your parents kindly; (3) Kill not your children for fear of poverty, for We provide for you and for them; (4) Go not near indecent things, whether open or hidden; (5) Slay not any living being, which God has forbidden, except in justice. These are the things He has Commanded you in order that you may learn wisdom (and understanding). And He has enjoined: (6) That you approach not the wealth of the orphan, except in the best way, until he reaches his maturity; (7) Give full measure and full weight, in justice. We charge not any soul, but with that which it can bear; whenever you speak, speak justly, even though it concerns your own relatives. (9) And fulfil your covenant with God; this He Commands you that you may follow the admonition. (10) And, surely, this Way alone is My Right Way; therefore you should follow this Way and should not follow other ways lest they lead you astray from His Way. Thus does He Command you, that you may be righteous' " (6: 151-153).

This passage sums up the Islamic way of life and mentions the 'Natural Covenant' which God made with every soul that they would follow His Way. This demand of the 'Covenant' is repeated here, according to which 'man should follow the Way shown by God, because any deviation from it into the paths of rebellion or independence or in the worship of someone other than God will be the first violation against that Covenant, and will mislead one into other violations, one after the other. Besides this, no man can fulfil the obligation of this most delicate and vast and intricate Covenant unless one accepts the Divine Guidance and follows it in every aspect of life. 'You should not follow other ways' because they will turn you away from His Right Way, which is the only Way which leads to His Nearness, Pleasure and Approval. Moreover, when the people deviate from His Right Way, each man has to make his own choice out of the hundreds of other ways. Thus all the people are scattered in all directions and there is bewilderment, confusion and disorder among all mankind and this becomes a hindrance in the way of all real progress and development." (9)

The Holy Prophet summed up the fundamental morals of Islam in his last address in the Farewell Pilgrimage: "Your blood and your property are sacrosanct until you meet your Lord, as this day and this month are Holy. You will surely meet your Lord and He will ask you of your works. He who has a pledge, let him return it to him who entrusted him with it; all interest is abolished, but you have your capital. Wrong not and you shall not be wronged . . . you have rights over your wives and they have rights over you. You have the right that they should not defile your bed and that they should not behave with open unseemliness. If they do, God allows you to put them in separate rooms and to beat them but not with severity. If they refrain from these things, they have the right to their food and clothing with kindness. Lay injunctions on women kindly, for they are under your contract. You have taken them only as a trust from God *(fi amanatillah)* and you have the enjoyment of their persons by the words of God, so understand my words, O men, for I have told you. Know that every Muslim is every Muslim's brother, and that the Muslims are brethren. It is only lawful

---

8. Abul Ala Maududi, *The Meaning of the Qur'an*, VOl. V1. pp. 133-37.
9. *The Meaning of the Qur'an*, VOl. V1. p. 171.

to take from a brother what he gives you willingly, so wrong not yourselves." (10)

The Prophet's historic speech after the victory of Tabuk sums up the objectives of his struggle: "The most trustworthy word is the word of piety. The noblest speech is the invocation of God. The best of ways is the one trodden by the Messenger (of God). The best of actions is that which is beneficent. The little that suffices is better than what is abandant and alluring. The tongue which is addicted to false expression is a bubbling spring of sin. Wine is the mother of all evil. The worst thing eaten is one which belongs to an orphan. He who pardons others is himself granted pardon. He who acts only for fame and reputation, God disgraces him. He who shows patience and forbearance, God gives him a double reward." (11)

There are many passages in the Qur'an and the Hadith of the Prophet which throw light on the basic principles of Islamic morality. They are unique in their nature and all-comprehensive in their application. They help an individual to develop his personality and cultivate his character on healthy lines and to build up a close relationship with God. They encourage conscientious action on the part of the believer on every issue. He forgives or retaliates of his own free will in obedience to the Covenant of God. When he forgives, he forgives to please God; and when he retaliates, he retaliates to protect his rights under the Law of God. Both types of actions of a believer are of his own free will, without any compulsion or prevention, and both are within the Law of the *Shariah*. This is the soud morality of Islam, resulting from the Commandments of God, the Source of all Goodness and morality. (12)

---

10. M. Husayn Haykal, *Life of Muhammad,* p. 486.
11. A. Hameed Siddiqui, *The Life of Muhammad,* pp. 268-69

Islam has given especially great importance to the maintenance of good social behaviour with neighbours, relatives and other people: "Hasten to follow the path that leads to forgiveness from your Lord and to Paradise, which is as wide as the heavens and the earth and has been prepared for those pious people who spend their wealth freely in the way of God in ease and in adversity and who control their anger and forgive other people. God loves the doers of good" (3: 133-134). And the Messenger of God remarked regarding relationships with other people: "None of you is a believer if he does not like for his brother exactly that which he likes for himself" (Mishkat). He also said that "the best of men is he who does good to others."

It is a unique characteristic of a believer that he adopts forgiveness in life, prefers others to himself, even if he be poor, and administers justice even to his enemies: "And those in Medinah, who had accepted the faith, love those who came to them for refuge, and entertain no desire in their hearts for things given to the (latter), but gave preference over themselves, even though poverty was their (own lot). And those saved from their own covetousness . . . such are the ones who are successful" (59: 9). And their justice has no parallel in himan history." (6) "O believers, be you the standard-bearers of justice and witness for the sake of God, even though your justice and your evidence might be harmful to yourselves, or to your parents, or to your relatives. It does not matter whether the party concerned is rich or poor; God can best protect both, therefore, do not follow your own desire lest you should deviate from doing justice. If you distort your evidence, or refrain from the truth, know it well that God is fully aware of what you do" (4: 135).

---

12. *Islam in Focus,* pp. 47-48.
13. S. D. Islahi, *Islam at a Glance,* pp. 104-110.

These are in brief, the basic elements of the moral discipline of Islam: to develop a good and virtuous character and cultivate healthy and positive qualities in individuals in order to keep alive its ideological principles in the religious, social, economic and political activities of the people. The individual is the central figure in the scheme of its moral training, for if individuals become righteous and just in their private and public affairs, a society composed of such individuals will automatically become virtuous and just. The individual's moral training starts at home, with his responsibilities to the family, then to his parents, relatives and neighbours; then the sphere of social life extends to other people, including non-Muslims and institutions. He is commanded to maintain all social relations with kindness, liberality and justice. (13)

8

The Economic System

The supremacy of God, as pointed out earlier, is the basis of everything in Islam, no matter of what nature, whether spiritual, economic, political or economic. God is the Creator and Owner of everything on the earth. He has created all things for all mankind: "His is the Sovereignty of the heavens and the earth, and all affairs are referred back to God" (57: 5). And in Surah Al-Baqarah we read: "He it is Who created for you all that there is on the earth" (2: 29). Thus it is the birthright of every individual to make efforts to get his share of this Divine Inheritance and no one can claim this on the basis of his colour, creed or race alone. All individuals enjoy this right equally and no one can be deprived of this by law or otherwise, or can be given precedence over others. There is absolutely no distinction between people or any restriction on any individual, race or group, for making efforts to earn a living in any way they like. All enjoy equal opportunities in the field of economics as to how they earn their living. Likewise, there is no distinction between people on the basis of their colour, creed or race, which can create special rights giving anyone a monopoly of any particular means of production, consumption, exchange or distribution. All people enjoy an equal right to endeavour to get their share of the sustenance of God on the earth. It is the duty of the Islamic State to ensure that all its citizens enjoy equal opportunities and a fair chance to earn their livelihood.(1)

This freedom of work and enterprise to make one's living is secure and guaranteed by the Islamic State so long as the activities are within the law and do not involve any indecency or wrong-doing . There is absolute freedom for honest work and honest business, organised by individuals, agencies or companies. Whosoever strives to make a decent living through honest and hard work will find ample opportunities in this system; but a dishonest person or company will find it difficult, or rather impossible, to prosper in such a system. People who venture into activities involving fraud, dishonesty, unfair means, cheating, corruption, exploitation, smuggling, etc. will not gain anything but punishment. (2)

Main Features of the Economic System

The economic system of Islam is basically different from other economic systems in its nature, form and purpose. It tries to solve the difficult economic problems of man by adopting the Golden Mean between the two extremes of Capitalism and Communism, retaining the virtues of both without including any of their evils. It allows neither unrestricted freedom to damage the interest of the community and the individual, nor does it recommend totalitarian regimentation so as to destroy the personality (ego) of the individual, which is the central figure and source of strength of its system.

The individual is given freedom of enterprise and work so that he may freely exercise his right to earn his living and organise his activities in a manner conducive to the development of a spirit of co-operation and help in place of unhealthy competition and rivalry. Moral education and training changes the entire outlook of the individual. He feels

---

1. A. A. Maududi, *Islamic Way of Life*, pp. 66-80.
2. *Islam in Focus*, pp. 126-30.

no revalry towards other members of society but, instead, regards it as his moral and religious duty to help his co-workers in their economic struggle, or at least not to obstruct them in their struggle for life. This attitude generates feelings of love, co-operation, help, sacrifice and brotherhood among individuals and leads to the maximum productive effort on the part of the community as a whole, with its benefits of prosperity, plenty and betterment for all. This policy meets the desires of the community as well as of individuals, in all areas, without neglecting one or over-emphasing the other. In this system, no rights are lost and no liberty curtailed; no part of wealth is taken away unlawfully by force; consequently, the pests of greed and rivalry — selfishness and self-interest — disappear or are channelled in healthy directions. (3)

Islam has its own philosophy of life, according to which the life of a Muslim in the world is a temporary phase in his eternal life in the Hereafter. He must, therefore, use every moment of this life to improve his permanent life, and this requires him to use all his mental and physical facuties to the maximum possible limit. This is because he cannot improve his eternal life without making the maximum use of this life. In other words, his success in the Hereafter is dependent on the utilisation of the resources of this world in the best and right way. The Holy Qur'an refers to the wealth a man earns by hard and honest efforts as 'blessings of God', 'Favours of God', 'clean things', 'wealth of God', etc. It also recommends him to work hard in this world for the betterment of his life in the Hereafter: "But seek the abode of the Hereafter in that which God has given you and neglect not your share of the world" (28: 77). And God's Messenger made honest effort compulsory for a Muslim: "Next to obligatory prayer is the

---

3. Abdul Azim Mansur, *Islam Allah's Eternal Jurisprudence*, pp. 150-69.

obligation of earning an honest living." (4)

This leaves no doubt that even if the purpose of this life is the attainment of real success in the Hereafter, a Muslim is urged and required to make every effort diligently and honestly to exploit the physical resources of the world for his use and the use of other members of the community. It is only by serving others that he can achieve his goal in the Hereafter. This makes people responsive to the needs of others and encourages them to sacrifice some of their personal interests for the sake of the community, thereby saving them from the misery of selfishness, greed and injustice. This is the true conception and reality of human effort and the wealth it earns. (2)

This is why the Qur'an regards wealth as a trial for people: to see who uses it properly to improve his eternal life in the Hereafter and who spends it on the lustful desires of his worldly self and earns the wrath of God: "It is He, Who has made you vicegerents on the earth, and raised some of you above others in rank so that He may test you in that He has given you. Indeed your Lord is quick in punishment; yet He is also Forgiving and Merciful" (6: 165).

This verse clearly establishes, first, that everything in the universe belongs to God and all mankind together are His vicegerents on the earth. They are holding all possessions in trust from God and must, therefore, use and exploit them according to the Guidance and instructions from God. Secondly, God has placed this trust of property and power in the hands of people in different degrees; some are given more, others less and still others have almost nothing. Thirdly, He has made it quite clear that the worldly life is simply a trial and all the above-mentioned things given to

---

4. S. D. Islahi, *Islam at a Glance*, pp. 122-28.

people in varying degrees are only instruments of the test. Records are kept on how they make use of these things and powers in accordance with the terms and conditions of the trust. The result of this will determine each man's (and woman's) rank in the Hereafter. (5) All this presupposes complete freedom of faith, practice, enterprise, type of occupation and struggle for livelihood of the individual in the economic system of Islam.

This concept also makes struggle and effort for existence on the earth a key factor in the life of an individual.It condemns the monastic attitude to life and encourages positive effort to enter into the economic field with full vigour and power in order to fulfil the terms of the trust and the duties of the vicegerency on the earth. This attitude, therefore, opposes both extreme views, of monasticism on the one hand and of secularism or materialism on the other. It neither lays too much emphasis on the spiritual development of man, regarding all economic activity as a vice and economic struggle as sinful, nor does it confine all its attention to the mere acquisition of material things by fair or foul means, while ignoring or paying very little attention to the spiritual or moral aspect of man. It adopts a balanced course of action in every area of life. It suggests a golden mean between these two divergent views and emphasises that success is neither in in the former nor in the latter but in a true harmony and balance between them. One should neither give one's self entirely to spiritual activities, while disregarding the needs of the body, nor should one judge everything by its economic benefit while ignoring the moral value of life.

It emphasises that the success of the individual and of society depends upon adjustment between the spiritual and the material needs of man. It must keep a right balance between

---

5. *The Meaning of the Qur'an,* VOl. 111. p. 174.

the needs of the body and the soul in order to protect its personal interests, as well as the welfare of society and must not forget that human progress depends upon the successful co-operation of, and harmony between, the spiritual and material aspects of life. When the spiritual life is separated from the economic struggle of man, he loses the balance which is essential to maintain stability in the economic system. As a result, people experience rivalry and antagonism, instead of co-operation and mutual love, between the two concepts of life, thus causing disruption and chaos in society.

Islam teaches him to keep the balance and to maintain his moral and spiritual values while continuing to strive on the economic level. But it condemns the other two opposing views. Monasticism is rejected as the unworkable philosophy of life: "But monasticism they invented . . . We did not prescribe it to them . . . (We Commanded) only seeking the Pleasure of God; and they observed it not as they should have done" (57: 27). The words, "We did not prescribe it to them" clearly shows that this conception of life is unnatural and that God has not created man with this instincts but that he forced it upon himself. God certainly requires that man should renounce the idle pleasures and vain desires of this world and turn to the path which leads to God's Pleasure. But God does not recommend or require gloomy lives in the darkness of caves, nor perpetual engagement in the corners of mosques or churches. Service to God is given in pure and chaste lives in the struggle and turmoil of this world. (6)

And again: "He has chosen you for His service and has not laid on you any hardship in your religion" (22: 78). This means that "the Creed you have been given is very simple and straightforward and the Laws and regulations you have to

---

6. A. Yusuf Ali, *The Holy Qur'an*, p. 1507.

obey are practical. You are free within their bounds to make as much progress as you can. This verse points out that the lives of the Muslims were free from all those useless and unnatural restrictions which had been imposed upon former communities by their priests and law-givers." (7) In Surah Al-Al-Araf we read: "He relieves them of their burdens and frees them from the shackles that bound them" (7: 157). This relief was from the burdens that had been laid on them by the legal hair-splittings of their jurists and by the exaggerated piety of their spiritual leaders, and by the superstitions, restrictions and regulations imposed by their common people." (8)

The Holy Messenger of God categorically stated that there was no room for a life of asceticism in Islam. It is narrated by Abu Hurairah: "Islam is very easy and simple and whosoever creates difficulties in it will be overpowered by them. Adopt the middle way in life and remain close to moderation and be happy" (Bukhari). It is reported that the Holy Messenger said, "I am sent to you with an easy and convenient religion" (Mishkat). And he was also reported to have said that "the best religion is that which is easy and covenient" (Mishkat).

These verses of the Qur'an and sayings of the Holy Messeger of God show that asceticism is not the right approach to human life for it is not only unnatural but also retrogressive. It destroys the natural instincts of man and thereby hinders the progress of his culture and civilization. "The problem of the natural relationship of man and woman is the most fundamental problem of civilisation, and on its right and rational solution depends the well-being prosperity and stability, or otherwise, of man's communal life on the earth. One kind of relationship between the sexes is of animal or

---

7. *The Meaning of the Qur'an*, VOl. V11. p. 227.
8. *The Meaning of the Qur'an*, 1V, p. 77.

purely sexual nature: its only object is the propagation of the race. The other relationship is the human one, which aims at bringing the two sexes together for co-operation in attaining the common goals of life according to the inherent abilities of each. To secure this co-operation, sexual love acts as a binding force between the male and female; and, thus, the animal and human factors not only impel man to work for the advancement and preservation of civilisation, but also to supply individuals to carry out this function. Hence, the prosperity and stability, or otherwise, of civilisation wholly depends on a balanced and proper co-operation of the two elements." (9) A life of asceticism is a complete negation of this purpose of life.

Likewise, Islam also condemns the other exereme view of life namely, that mere gratification of economic needs is the whole object of life: "And those who desire nothing but the life of the world, such is their sum of knowledge" (53: 30). And in Surah Yunus we read: "The fact is that the ultimate abode of those who expect not to meet Us, and are well pleased and satisfied with this worldly life and pay no heed to Our Signs, shall be hell, in consequence of the evils they earned (because of their erroneous creed and wrong conduct" (10: 7-8). There is no doubt that "if a man leads his life on the presumption that there is no other life, he will have no fear that he shall have to render a full account of all his deeds in this world. Therefore his sole aim in this life will be to win, by hook or by crook, prosperity, happiness, fame and power in this world." (10) This attitude will naturally lead men to wrong ways and incur God's Displeasure. Islam suggests a balanced course between these two divergent conceptions of life: "O Lord, give us what is good in this world and also what is good in the Hereafter and save us from

---

9. Maududi, *Purdah and the Status of Women in Islam,* p. 87.
10. *The Meaning of the Qur'an,* VOl. V. p. 12.

the punishment of the Fire" (2: 201). Good *(hasanah)* here refers to economic prosperity which is acquired by rightful means and without exploiting one's fellow-beings. It is earned through just and honest means and is also for the satisfaction of personal needs and the betterment of society. Man is advised in this verse to pray to God to give him the best of both worlds: prosperity and happiness in this world and success in the Hereafter.

Man is plainly told in the following verses of the Qur'an to benefit from the Treasures of God to the fullest extent and thereby enjoy the physical pleasures of life which may add to his spiritual life as well: "Eat of the pleasant and pure things that God has bestowed on you" (5: 5). Again: "O Muhammad, ask them, 'Who has forbidden the decent garments that God has created for His servants and (who has forbidden) the good and pure things of life bestowed by Him? ' " (7: 32). The argument implied in the question is this: As God Himself has created all the pure, good and nice things for His servants, it cannot be His Will to make these unlawful for His servants. Therefore, if a religious, moral or social system makes these things unlawful or detestable or considers them impediments in man's spiritual evolution and progress, this very thing is a clear proof of the fact that that system is not from God." (11)

The Holy Prophet explained this principle in these words: "The best of you is one who leaves not this world for the Hereafter, and the Hereafter for this world, and is not a burden on the people." The Messenger of God has here impressed upon the believers the desirablity of true harmony between the moral and economic sides of the struggle for life. A man should neither be so entirely of this world, that, in the acquisition of the material means of life he forgets God, nor

---

11. *The Meaning of the Qur'an*, VOl. 1V. p. 23.

should he incline so much towards the spiritual life that he ignores the economic struggle, but should keep everything in its proper perspective. It is also reported from the Holy Prophet: "Do your work in the world in such a way as if you were going to live for ever; and work for the Hereafter as if you were going to die tomorrow." He rejected all the wrong conceptions of religion which people had formed for themselves and remarked that religion did not teach hatred of the world and, furthermore, that hatred of the world did not in itself make a man pious or righteous.

Thus Islam tries to co-ordinate in a most balanced way the economic and spiritual aspects of man, for a defect in one leads to a defect in the other. As a result, we find men who, while engaged in the economic pursuits of life, are not unmindful of the existence of God in their life. The Holy Qur'an praises these men: "Men whom neither merchandise nor sale can divert from God's remembrance, nor from regular prayers, nor from practising regular charity" (24: 3). The Messenger is advised to maintain this true harmony in life in these words: "And keep yourself wholeheartedly content with those who call on their Lord morning and evening; and do not let your eyes overlook them, seeking the pomp and glitter of this life" (18: 28).

This is the true conception of life which teaches the believers to maintain true harmony and balance in life; neither to hate nor to love this world too much. It makes economic satisfaction of economic needs a prerequisite for the moral and spiritual uplift of man; for so long as the common man does not have his basic needs satisfied, he can neither become a good citizen nor can his moral standards improve. It is also a fact that poor peoplehave neither religion nor moral standards. Therefore Islam has made provision for the basic needs of every individial in its economic system. The words of the Holy Prophet that 'poverty takes man to the boundary lines of disbelief' refer to the needs of each individual.

This is undoubtedly the most important contribution of Islam to the civilisation of man. It teaches man to improve his material life in order to improve his spiritual life. This moral conception of life has given a workable mean between diametrically opposed views of life. On the one hand, it declares that everything of this world is for the use of man, and, on the other, it lays emphasis on the responsibilities of man; just as he is responsible for himself, so is he responsible for his family and for his relations, and then for his nation and all humanity. When he himself benefits from his own wealth he must, in like manner, let others benefit from his wealth. Thus, by diverting the selfishness of man into unselfish channels, and by harmonising the material with the spiritual aspects of life, Islam has given humanity a practical solution to the most complex and difficult problem. It has enabled man to profit from the material and spiritual aspects of life in order to establish an economic system on the basis of justice and equity; and this objective is achieved in so simple a manner by moral education and training that the individual, instead of indulging in rivalry and greed, becomes a co-operating and useful member of society.

Islam also imposes moral duties upon both the employee and the employer. The employee is commanded by God to do his work diligently, efficiently and honestly. It is reported that the Messenger of God said that if anyone undertakes any work, God loves to see him do it nicely and efficiently for He is Good and Beautiful and He Loves to see things done in a beautiful and nice way. When the work is finished, the employee is entitled to a just and reasonable wage for his work. The employer is bound by law to pay a fair wage as soon as the work is done. It is reported by Abdullah bin Umar that God's Messenger said, "Give the labourer his wages before his sweat dries". (Ibn Majah). And Abu Hurairah reported God's Messenger as saying, "There are those whose adversary I shall be on the Day of Resurrection; one of them is a man who hired a worker and, after receiving full service from him, did not give him his wages" (Bukhari). (12) With these comments, however, the basic features of the economic system of Islam are summarised below:—

1. Individual Liberty

The individual enjoys complete liberty to do anything or adopt any profession or use his (or her) wealth in any manner he (or she) likes within the law of the land. "Islam allows a person to create as much wealth as he can by his knowledge, skill and labour, through means that are not unsocial and immoral, and it envisages a natural inequality of energy and aptitude which necessarily results in the inequality of material or social rewards. But as all society is one organism, it prohibits all those means that lead to the concentration of wealth in a few hands. It is a Qur'anic injunction that economic life must be so organised that too much wealth does not remain locked up in private treasures. Like all religions, Islam inclucates charity, but it goes further than any other creed by imposing a capital levy on all surplus that remains unutilised in single hands for a whole year. Then the Islamic Law of Inheritance is used as a means of dispersion of capital, creating a comparative equality of opportunity for a number of individuals to start life again on the basis of individual initiative and personal effort." (13)

And there is absolutely no doubt that "if the system, as visualised by Islam, is truly and wholly established in society and all its departments are organised in the right places, a social system will grow in which there will be neither big

---

12. For details see *Economic Doctrines of Islam*, VOl. 1.
13. Khalifa Abdul Hakim, *Islam and Communism*, pp. 167-68

millionaires nor paupers and destitutes. The great mass of people will be moderately well off." (14)

2. Right to Property

Islam has recognised individual's right to own property, but subjects it to such limitation as to render it absolutely harmless to the common good of society. It has, however, established and developed such an intimate relationship between the individual and society that they work together without any apparent clash between them. It maintains that the individual has two simultaneous capacities: his capacity as an independent individual and his capacity as a member of the community. His response to either capacity may at times be greater than his response to the other one, but he will finally combine and harmonise both. The social concept based on such a belief does not separate the individual from his community nor does it regard them as two conflicting forces trying to overcome one another." (15)

This system is based on the concept of harmony between capitalism and communism, combining the merits of both without having their drawbacks. It allows private ownership in principle with certain restrictions which make it quite harmless. Islam gives full play to individuals' natural desire to ownership and tries to satisfy the propensities of human nature in a way that is best for both the individual and the community. (16) Thus Islam has set a pattern of private ownership that is compatible with the public interest. It has given due consideration to the instinctive tendency towards ownership that is common to all mankind and that gives meaning to life and creates for man an aim and an end

14. Abdul Kalam Azad, *Tarjaman-ul-Qur'an*, VOl. 11. p.132
15. M. Kutb, *Islam the Misunderstood Religion*, pp. 154-56.
16. A. A. Mansur, *Islam Allah's Eternal Jurisprudence*, pp. 150-52.

towards which he strives." (16) Man is naturally inclined to wealth in its various forms and this is recognised by Islam: "Beautiful for mankind is love of the joy (that comes) from women and children, and hoarded heaps of gold and silver, choicest horses, cattle and cornfields. That is the comfort of the life of the world" (3: 14). And in Surah Al-Hadid we read: "And know that the life of this world is . . . rivalry in respect of wealth" (57: 20).

Islam recognises the individual's right to ownership, and this concept forms the basis of economic life in a Muslim society. This right of the individual is fundamental and is recognised by the Qur'an: "And in their wealth and possession the beggar and the needy have due share" (51: 19). And in Surah Al-Nisaa we read: "And for men is the benefit of what they earn; and for women is the benefit of what they earn" (4: 32). And again in the same Surah: "And give to the orphans their property, and substitute not worthless (things) for (their) good ones" (4: 2).

These verses explicitly recognise the right of the individual to own, inherit and sell his property as and when he likes. It also recognises all other rights which go along with the right of ownership, e.g., the safety of the property from theft, dacoity and other forms of unlawful possession of someone's property by force or deceit. It gives a guarantee for the safety of the property of individuals and recommends heavy punishment for offenders: "And for the thief, man or woman, cut off their hands as a punishment for what they have earned, and an exemplary punishment from God" (5: 41). Again, the individual who owns property also enjoys the right to inherit property from his relatives. This right of inheritance is recognised by Islam and, obviously, it can only be recognised if people have the right of ownership: "There is a share for men in what has been left by parents and near relatives, and there is a share also for women in what has been left by parents and near relatives, whether it be little or much; for this share has been prescribed (by God)" (4: 7).

Islam regards possession and ownership of property as a natural instinct in man and therefore it does not think it proper or equitable to destroy or suppress it. It feels that there is no harm in private ownership because it will stimulate individual efforts for the acquisition of wealth and will thereby greatly benefit society. And it is also the natural corollary of the soul of justice that society should also play its part in benefiting the individual. It would be injustice to the individual if he were left to toil and sweat to benefit society without any reciprocal compensation from the latter. If social justice is to be established in society, it is absolutely essential that its rights and duties be equally shared by the individual and society. If the individual works for the uplift of society, it is the obligatory duty of the latter to provide necessary facilities to the former so that he may not be hampered in his work. And obviously the ownership of property is one of those things which can greatly assist the individual in his efforts to acquire more wealth.

However, it may be pointed out that this right of wonership is not absolute. Islam recognises this right of the individual but does not leave him entirely free to use this right in any way he likes. It does not favour the expansion of private property to an extent that may endanger the very foundation of the Islamic system and thus destroy its real object. Therefore, it has allowed private ownership in principle, as pointed out earlier, but has subjected it to such limitations as to render it absolutely harmless. It has authorised the community to enact the necessary legislation to organise private ownership and to change it whenever the public interest demands it. (15) The individual enjoys certain rights but has also certain obligations and duties to society which has conferred these rights on him. He has undoubtedly the right to own property, to purchase or to sell it and to inherit it; but this right is accompanied by certain duties and obligations which he owes to society. In other words, the individual's right to property is not absolute but restricted and limited by the obligations which it carries with it.

The individual must realise that he is only a trustee who is holding the property, which, in fact, belongs to the community; as such he must willingly accept the restrictions placed by the latter on its use. The individual is, however, free to use, and benefit from his property, provided, in the enjoyment of his rights, he does not encroach upon others' rights or damage the common good of society. The limitations are merely to check such tendencies on the part of rebellious or evil-minded owners in society. The gentle and honest property owners enjoy their rights freely and without restrictions, unaffected by these limitations.

This is how real balance is established between the two conflicting views of individual and public ownership; the individual enjoys his right of ownership, while the community reserves the right to forfiet or limit this right in cases of abuse or misuse. And, in fact, it is the only policy that can really guarantee complete social justice in the proper use of property and other forms of wealth.

Another principle likely to affect the use of wealth is its sphere of circulation. Islam wants wider circulation of wealth so that it is spread out in the community and not confined to a small group of people. The laws of inheritance and charity (compulsory as well as optional) partially assist in widening the area of circulation of wealth but still there ia a likelihood of centralisation of such resources. Therefore, Islam has issued instructions and empowered the community to take the necessary steps whenever it feels the need of such measures: "Whatsoever God may restore to His Messenger. . .

is due to God and to His Messenger. . . the orphans and the needy . . . so that it may not be confined to the (few) rich among you" (49: 7). As society is one organism, Islam likes to keep a steady flow of wealth in all the parts, in order to maintain its vigour and strength, like the circulation of blood in a healthy body. It is a sign of a healthy society. This is why Islam organises it in such a way that the wealth remains in wider circulation and is not locked up in private treasures. It encourages people through moral education to give away their wealth (above their needs) to the poor and the needy in the community, merely for the Pleasure of God. Then it imposes a compulsory levy of *zakat* on all surplus wealth for the use of the poor and the destitute. The law of inheritance further helps by spreading wealth among the relatives of the deceased. (17)

It may be added that both private and public ownership are limited within their respective spheres but are linked in a well balanced and equitable manner so that the former is neither unnesessarily suppressed nor let loose so as to damage the interests of others or endanger the common good of society. Private ownership is generally allowed to a great extent in the field of production but is restricted in the field of distribution, especially when it is likely to interfere with the rights and interests of other members of the community. But no private ownership is permitted in things of great value and benefit to the community. On the whole, the entire superstructure of the Islamic system is built upon the freedom of the individual to create and possess wealth, and state interference is very much limited to things of extreme necessity to the community. (17)

3. Economic Inequality within Natural Limits

---

17. For details see *Economic Doctrines of Islam,* VOl. 1. of the author.

Islam recognises economic inequalities among people but does not let them grow wider; it tries to maintain the differences within reasonable, equitable and natural limits. The existence of economic inequalities among people is not only natural but essential for the purification of 'self' and the development of the human personality (ego); without its existence, the individual would be deprived of an important but basic means of achieving this goal. He is left free to achieve the highest possible ideal through helping others, without expecting any reward except the Pleasure of God. There are immense opportunities for him to develop high qualities of love, fraternity, spirit of natural help and co-operation. Islam, therefore, permits private ownership and economic inequalities within reasonable limits in society in order to provide an opportunity to the individual for the development and utilisation of his noble qualities.

The people whose means of sustenance is scarce should thereby learn to be patent, tolerant and content; while others who have abundant resources should develop their hidden qualities of gratefulness, kindness, benevolence and sacrifice. If economic inequalities were abolished by artificial means, as the communists would have it, the individual would not get any chance to develop these noble qualities in himself, and, in fact, a very great stimulus in economic struggle would be removed; and as a result, the individual would be deprived of a vast field of action which nature has provided for his development.

It is said that inequitable distribution of wealth can be remedied through equal redistribution. But this hypothesis, as has been proved even under the communist system, is unnatural and impracticable. It is absolutely essential for the success and progress of every society that the natural differences in ability, intelligence and efficiency which are found among people, in the nature of their work, in the responsiblities of their effice, in the service which they have rendered to the community, and its nature, and in their economic needs should be maintained, up to a limit, in their remuneration. Just as there is variation in nature and its manifestations and in the ability and intelligence of different persons, similarly the maintenance of this difference, to the same degree, in their remuneration is indispensable. There cannot be equality in the physique, ability,intelligence and other qualities of people, and, naturally, there cannot be any possibility of economic equality. (18)

The Holy Qur'an recognises these economic inequalities: "It is He, Who has made you the vicegerents on the earth, and raised some of you above others in ranks so that He may test you in what He has given you" (6: 165). And in Surah Al-Zukhruf we read: "And We raised some of you above others in ranks, so that some may take others in service" (43: 32). These verses of the Qur'an have stated three fundamental realities clearly visible in the life of man. First, it is a reality that everything of the earth and of the universe belongs to God and that man is His vicegerent on the earth who has been entrusted with many things here for his use and proper exploitation. Secondly, God has assigned different ranks to His representatives regarding His trusts. Some are entrusted with huge fortunes and endowed with greater ability and capacity for work and some with lesser fortunes and lesser ability for work than others. Thirdly, it has also been made clear to them that this life is merely a trial. Through the things and powers He has bestowed upon men, God will one Day judge them concerning those trusts and how they used them.

The Holy Qur'an refers to this fact of life as a trial for the individual; to see how far he is able to utilise the opportutities and the powers provided to him for the refinement of his 'self' and the betterment of the community. And this is the real purpose for which Islam maintains economic gradation in society and does not favour its abolition. It may here be pointed out that Islam does not recommend or recognise the class system as such; it is merely stating the facts of life. There is no doubt that people differ in rank and livelihood in every society; even in communist countries people don't all receive the same wage, and conscripted people do not all get equal rank in service. The inevitable fact is that differences among people in rank, in earning and, consequently, in wealth do exist everywhere.

So long as difference in wealth and rank do not lead to the emergence of class systems, the rulers and the ruled, the masters and the servants etc., and all are treated alike before the law of the land; and do not create an unbridgeable gulf and inequitable barriers between the rich and the poor, it is permissible and lawful in Islam. (19) Islam recognises these natural differences among people, but tries to maintain them at a reasonable level, and does not allow them to outstrip the natural limits so as to divide society into two sections, where the prosperity of one means the poverty of the other, and thus become the cause of natural tyranny and oppression among the people. It takes certain moral and legal measures to keep these inequalities within their natural limits. It teaches people to regard the existence of differences in wealth as a means by which God may try them in this world. It is a part of their faith that they are on trial here in the respective economic gradations. God, by granting abudance of wealth and power to some, observes how they spend and use it; whether they regard it as their personal property acquired through their own efforts and intelligence, or think of it as a blessing of God and that others also share in it. On the other hand, the poor are also under trial in their

---

18. *The Meaning of the Qur'an*, VOl. 111. p. 174.
19. Muhammad Qutb, op, cit., pp. 162-64.

straitened circumstances, a trial as to whether they lose their faith in God and become ungrateful and also hateful and envious towards the rich or keep their faith and remain patient and tolerant in their present condition.

Equitable Differences

Islam permits differences in wealth within reasonable limits but does not allow these differences to grow so wide that some people spend their life in luxury, while the great majority of people are left to lead a life of misery and hunger. This difference in wealth and rank must not exceed natural and reasonable limits, because if it does, it will be the beginning of the end of that society, as referred to in the Qur'an in these words: "And when We wish to destroy a town, We give Commands to its well-to -do people who transgress therein; thus the word proves true against them, so We destroy them utterly" (17: 16). These people widen the gulf between the rich and the poor and cause the growth of inequalities in wealth beyond natural and equitable limits. As a result, mutual rivalries and hostilities of the groups within the community gradually destroy the economic life of the people.

The Holy Prophet was referring to this condition of society, which leads to unnatural inequalities and thereby to its destruction when he said: "If anyone spent a night in a town and remained hungry till morning, the promise of God's protection for that town came to an end" (Masnad Imam Ahmad). He is also reported to have said that, "No one's faith among you is reliable until he likes for his brother (in Islam) what he likes for himself" (Bukhari). There is no doubt that Islam does not like differences in wealth or rank between different people beyond a certain point. This is because it breeds enmity and hatred and leads to a bitter class conflict among the various sections of the community which ultimately shatters its foundation. When economic inequlities turn into inequitable trends and the 'have nots' become powerless slaves in the hands of the 'haves' of society, it is a signal for the destruction of those people. Islam would under no circumstances allow such a situation to arise, much less to continue for any length of time in a society. It would take the necessary steps to keep economic inequalities from going beyond reasonable and natural limits. In fact, such a situation would never arise in a fully functioning Islamic society, where the law of *zakat* and the Law of Inheritance are in operation, along with an abudance of charitable funds from the surplus wealth of people *(Al-Afw)*.

To sum up, though Islam accepts natural differences in wealth among people, it favours equality in their basic needs and advocates a 'right to a livelihood' for all its members. The wealth of the rich is not meant to aggravate the poverty of the poor, for it is on trust from God and should be used under His Guidance, as reflected in the Qur'an and the Sunnah, for removing or lessening the poverty of the poor. In fact, the prosperity of the rich should be considered a boon and not a burden for the poor members of the community. If the rich do not show any sense of responsibility in the use of their wealth, then it is the duty of the state legally to force them to abide by its principles; and if the state treasury is not enough to meet the needs of the poor, then it has the legal right forcibly to take a part or whole of the surplus wealth *(Al-Afw)*, as the case may be, in order to meet the basic needs of the people, even though they had paid all thei their economic obligations. For, according to the Hadith of the Holy Prophet, "in one's wealth there is a due share besides *zakat."* It may, however, be pointed out that it is not necessary that all should have the same or similar means of livelihood; what is required, and is absolutely necessary, is that all should have sufficient to meet their basic needs. (17)

4. Social Security:

The Islamic state is legally and morally responsible for the provision of basic needs to its members. And it is the distinctive feature of the state that, along with social utility services, it takes the responsibility of public maintenance as well. Every citizen is guaranteed his basic needs. The principle of public maintenance pervades the whole fabric of Muslim society. The individual is held responsible for his person, his family, his near relatives, the society in which he lives and, finally, for the whole of humanity. Islam gives such moral education and training to its members that they seek wealth not only for themselves, but also to help other members of their families and the poor destitute members of the community. The Holy Prophet described the individual responsibility for protecting social welfare in these words: "Those who honour the boundaries ordained by God and those who don't are like the people who together bought a boat. Some of them occupied the upper part of the boat and some the lower part. Those who were occupying the lower part of the boat had to go upstairs to fetch their water; they thought that it would be much better if they were to make a hole in their part (to get the water); thus they would be saved from the trouble of going upstairs and disturbing the people living there. If the people would let them do what they wanted, they would all be destroyed; but if they stopped them from doing this, they would not only save themselves, but also save all the other people occupying that boat." (20)

The Holy Prophet has in these words very explicitly described the relationship between individial welfare and the common good of society; the action of a few individuals can, sometimes, ruin the whole community. If a few individuals were allowed to accumulate the greater portion of the wealth of the community and waste it on the luxuries of life or hoard it, and thereby deprive the vast majority of the people

---

20. *Bukhari* and *Muslim,* quoted by S. Qutb, op. cit., p. 130.

of their due share, it would be bound, sooner or later, to wreck the entire economy. The Islamic state, under these circumstances, has a duty to perform. In fact, no one can be absolved of his responsibility to the community, for every individual is regarded, at one and the same time, as a guardian and as a ward in an Islamic society. The Holy Prophet described this dual responsibility of the individual in these words: "Everyone among you is a guardian and, as such, is accountable for his wards (on the Day of Judgement)"(20)

Likewise, society is also accountable and answerable to God for the weak and the poor living in its fold. It is responsible for strengthening the weak and providing adequate means to the poor to enable them to meet their basic needs. It is also the duty of society not to let the gap between the rich and the poor widen beyond natural limits; and if it does, it must take necessary steps to narrow down the differences in wealth to the natural and equitable limits. It must also protect the wealth and property of the weak and the orphans from the hands of aggressors.

The Islamic society is also responsible for providing the necessities of life to the poor and the destitute in the community. If there are not sufficient funds in the treasury, the state can levy taxes on the wealthy to meet the requirements of those in need; for if one individual is left hungry or naked or shelterless on any day, the whole community will be answerable to God on the Day of Judgement. It is, therefore, absolutely necessary that the community should endeavour to develop a spirit of brotherhood, natural love and co-operation among its members in order to eradicate poverty. It is a grave sin and a crime to leave the poor and the destitute in their wretched condition: "Have you seen one who denies the (Day of) Judgement? That is he who repels the orphan and encourages not the feeding of the needy" (107: 1-3). It is one of the qualities of the sinful, who will be thrown into hell: "This was he that would not encourage the feeding of the needy! So no friend has he here this Day" (69: 33-35).

These verses of the Qur'an merely point out the apparent signs of the grave situation of a community, where poor and destitute people starve while the rich indulge in luxuries, for such a situation, if left unremedied, will ultimately destroy the entire community. Therefore, it cannot be tolerated by a Muslim society, which takes every possible step to eradicate such evils. The Holy Qur'an emphasises that the poor have a right in the wealth of the rich (51: 19) and the Holy Prophet explained this right of the poor by saying that all the riches and luxuries of the wealthy are the products of the labour of the poor workers. Therefore, it is required of every individual to help those of his fellow men (and women) who stand in need of such help. When individual resources are spent or found to be inadequate to meet the needs of the poor and the destitute, Islamic society must mobilise its resources to help them. Thus Islam endeavours to organise social maintenance in all possible forms on the basis that individual and social objectives are the same. Therefore, those in different areas of activity also co-operate, which increases their effectiveness in solving problems.

5. Social Justice

The establishment of a system of social justice on the earth was one of the important functions of the Messengers of Allah. They were sent from time to time for the guidance of man to enable him to establish such a society. Muhammad was the last of the line of Messengers: "We surely sent Our Messengers with clear Signs and revealed with them the Book and the Balance (of Right and Wrong), that man may stand forth in justice; and We sent down iron, in which is (material for) mighty war and many uses for men" (57: 25).

Three things are mentioned in this verse. These are the Book, the Balance and iron, which represent respectively Divine Guidance, Justice and the authority of the Law to maintain sanctions against those who break the laws. In other words, this verse explains the great function of God's Messengers, and to achieve their objective, they are given the Book and the Balance, so that they may check any unnecessary excesses of the people and keep them evenly balanced. It should not be forgotten that balance (justice) is not merely moral and spiritual, but covers every aspect of human life. It is necessary to establish justice throughout the entire social life of man; and as the maintenance of harmony and moderation in the economic field is almost impossible without strength, the importance of political power is emphasised in this verse.

Just as Islam wants to maintain a balance in the relation between God and man, similarly, it wants to establish a balance (i.e. justice) in regulating the relations of human beings, in order to protect it from the evil consequences of excesses in the economic field. This is why Islam wants to establish justice in the entire social life of man, and not just in any one aspect of it.

Production: Islam forbids its followers to exploit other people or to use unjust methods in acquiring wealth, but it allows them the use of all good means to acquire wealth. It also admits the right of the individual to own property and work in freedom, but does not tolerate the misuse or abuse of these rights. In other words, it does not discourage people from earning wealth and getting rich through just and lawful means; what it does not like is the use of wrong and unjust mens to earn wealth.

The Holy Qur'an makes it obligatory for every Muslim to struggle hard according to his ability and power to earn his living. It tells him that the whole world is full of the means of sustenance and it is for him to find them out through his own efforts. The Holy Prophet exphasised the importance of human endeavour by saying, "Seeking lawful livelihood is the greatest duty of the Muslim after the duty of (daily) prayers." And on another occasion, he said, "When you have finished the morning prayer, do not rest until you have worked for your living." While demanding hard and constant effort from men in seeking their livelihood, Islam enjoins them to adopt just and equitable means and to avoid unlawful and wrong ones.

Islam adopts the same attitude towards capital formation. It does not forbid saving; what it prohibits is hoarding or accumulation of wealth for anti-social activities. It advises people to keep their wealth in circulation either by consuming it, or by investing it, or by giving it over to others who have little or no means of livelihood. The levy of *zakat* is a strong preventive measure against those who merely want to hoard their wealth.

Consumption: The same principle of justice governs activities of people in the fields of consumption. It forbids both miserliness and extravagance and suggests a middle course between the two extremes: "And do not tie your hand to your neck nor stretch it without any restraint lest you should become blameworthy and left destitute" (17: 29). And again in Surah Al- Furqan we read: "And they who, when they spend, are neither extravagent nor miserly, and there is ever a just mean between the two" (25: 67). The Holy Prophet explained this in these words: "Moderation between income and expenditure is half the pleasure of the economic life." In order to achieve its objective in this field, Islam forbids all methods of expenditure which cause moral or social injury. It suggests that surplus wealth of people is better spent in the service of virtue, righteousness, public welfare etc, instead of on luxuries.

Distribution: The main principle governing the field of distribution is justice and benevolence in order to achieve a two-fold objective; first, that wealth may not be concentrated in few hands but continue circulating in the community; secondly, that the various people who have participated in the production of national wealth should be justly and fairly rewarded. It does not permit inequalities of wealth to grow beyond a certain point and tries to keep them within reasonable limits. And, in order to check the growth and concentration of wealth, it prohibits accumulation and hoarding of wealth and insists upon its expenditure on the welfare of the community.

Its basic concept of wealth is that all "the means of living which God has created on this earth are meant to satisfy the real needs of mankind. If, therefore, by sheer good luck one finds himself possessing more of these means than his requirements justify, it only implies that a surplus which was really the portion of others has reached him. Why should he therefore hold it for himself? He should transfer it to those who need it. Islam demads that this surplus should be given over to the community for meeting the needs of the poorer people, so that the national wealth may continue circulating among all classes of people. Moral education makes people conscious of this fact of life, while legal measures ensure the balanced flow of wealth in the community and check its undue concentration at any particular point. (21)

Exchange: Islam applies the same principle to all the forms of exchange. It allows those forms of exchange which are based on justice and fairplay and prohibits others which are either unjust or are likely to lead to quarrels and litigation, or

21. A. A. Maududi, *Economic Problem of man,* p. 25-26.

resemble gambling, or contain an element of interest *(riba)* or deceit, or where the gain of one is based on the loss of another. These measures are recommended partly to purify all the forms of exchange from unhealthy and socially harmful elements and partly to introduce very strictly the principle of justice in the entire field of exchange.

6. Social and Individual Welfare

Islam recognises social and individual welfare as complementary rather than competitive and antagonistic and accordingly it tries to harmonise their conflicting but complementary interests. It considers the good of the individual as the good of society and vice versa; if the individual prospers, society prospress, and if society prospers, the individual is better off. But this is possible only when individuals maintain complete harmony between their individual good and the social good, so that in acquiring their individual needs they do not, directly or indirectly, damage the good of others. If they themselves benefit, they also let others share in that benefit; and if they cannot derive any benefit from any enterprise, they complete it for the sake of others, who may benefit from it. This is how every individual shares in the welfare of others and how individual and social welfare become complementary in the economic system of Islam. In other words, individual and social welfare is closely linked.

Thus the economic system of Islam is based on the concept of complete harmony between individual and social good. It neither separates the individual from society, nor does it regard his welfare as conflicting with that of society. As the objective of the Islamic state is equitably to provide and distribute the means of sustenance among its members according to their needs, it finds no difficulty in determining the form of its organisation of distribution. It matters little whether the means of production are entrusted to the individual or to the community. Whoever is entrusted with the means of production is supervising it as a trustee and has the right to benefit from it along with others, so long as he co-operates with the state in attaining its above-mentioned objective and is helpful in creating that atmosphere which guarantees social welfare and progress for all. It is not important in this system who owns the means of production; what is important is the objective. If it can be achieved by distributing the means of production, etc., among individuals, then they are distributed among them; on the other hand, if it is better achieved through communal ownership, they are entrusted to the community. (22)

Islam adopts practical methods of educating and training its members in order to maintain harmony in its system and tries to sublimate the human instinct of selfishness. Greater stress is laid on moral reformation and the creation of the right moral attitude towards life among its members, so that the evil of greed in their minds should be not only subjugated but sublimated to the heights of spiritual joy and material success. Along with moral teaching, it also introduces certain restrictions to check the uncompromising forces and evil desires in society. But the main reliance is placed on the moral training of the people. (23)

---

22. M. Qutb, *Islam the Misunderstood Religion,* pp. 154-55
23. For details see *Economic Doctrines of Islam,* VOl. 1.
    of the author.

9

The Political System

The political system of Islam is entirely different from other systems in vogue in various countries of the world. Unlike other systems, it is based on spiritual and moral foundations and is guided by Divine Revelation; but it is not theocracy, as known to political thinkers, for it does not confer Divine Rights on any elected or hereditary class. It is also not a revengeful proletariat or like a modern democracy but is a system of Government based on quite different principles and having an entriely different nature, structure, function and purpose.

1. Nature of the Caliphate

The political system of Islam is based on three main principles: *Tawhid* (Unity of God), *Risalat* (Prophethood) and *Khilafat* (Caliphate). It recognizes the enternal reality of the universe, that it is created, maintained and governed by One God (Allah) Who is the Creator, Master and Sovereign of the whole creation. He alone has the right to command and He alone has the right to obedience from all His creation, including human beings. His Will or Law is received through His Messengers in the form of the Book containing the Law and the interpretation and exemplification of it by the Messengers, who by their example, in word and deed, set up a working model of the system. And *Khilafat* implies representation. Man acts as a representative (vicegerent) of

God on the earth and excercises the Divine Authority, by
virtue of the powers delegated to him by God, within the
limits prescribed by God. (1)

Vicegerency implies four conditions as essential to the
function of representation. First, the real authority remains
vested in God; secondly, man merely administers His Law;
thirdly, the adminstration of the Law is strictly in accordance
with , and within the limits prescribed by, Him; and fourthly,
in the administration of His Law, man will execute His Will
and fulfil His object and Purpose. Thus the human Caliphate
is established under the Sovereignty of God in order to fulfil
His Purpose and Object within the limits prescribed by Him.
(2) The whole of mankind is vested with the authority of
vicegerency and not any one class or group of people.
Whoever is prepared to accept the conditions of the
vicegerency will shoulder the responsibility of the Caliphate
for the whole of society. This is the starting point of Islamic
democracy, in which every member enjoys the rights and
powers of the vicegerency of God. All the members enjoy
this right equally without any distinction. The agency to
settle the affairs of the state will be formed with the approval
of the members and its powers and authority will, in fact, be
delegated powers by the authority of the members.

(a) Forms of Democracy:

What form this democracy will take in practice will depend
on the prevailing circumstances and the requirements of the
time and place. The Qur'an and *Sunnah* are silent about this
matter. There is no specific form of agency recommended or
approved by the Qur'an or by the Holy Prophet. The Holy
Prophet wanted to settle this issue, as it implicitly seems
from his behaviour during his illness, but he deliberately and

1. Hammudah Abdalati, *Islam in Focus*, pp. 130-38
2. A. A. Maududi, *Islamic Way of Life*, pp. 42-52.

intentionally, perhaps by Divine Commandment or Instruction, left it open for the community to settle by mutual consultation. Therefore, it can be said with certaintly without any shadow of doubt that no form of democracy or Government is sacrosanct in Islam. Any form which fulfils the condition of the vicegerency and is approved by the members of the community can be adopted by the Muslims to manage the affairs of the state at any particular time and place. And so long as this form of democracy can fulfil the purpose and object of the vicegerency effectively and successfully, it can remain in operation, but the actual form of democracy is not an important issue in the Islamic political system.

The fundamental issue is the fulfilment of the conditions of the vicegerency of God and the form of agency (or Government) in whatever way it is established is not important, so long as it has the effective approval of the members and is not established by coercion or aggression. This does not, however, give licence to every military dictator or mob damagogue to take over the affairs of the community and then get approval through coercive and repressive measures. The approval of the members is a basic factor after the conditions of the vicegerency in the political system of Islam. The will or the approval of the members cannot be ignored or suppressed without infringing the basic principle of the vicegerency. The agency or Government as such is functioning on behalf of the members. If it comes into power without their approval or, after gaining power, loses their confidence, it ceases to be a legally representative Government of the community. Likewise, an hereditary form of Government, by itself, has no sanction in Islam, for Islam does not recognise privilege or power on the basis of race, family or wealth. However, these factors neither promote nor hinder the merits of any individual who gains the approval of the members and becomes their representative in the true sense.

The Government or the ruler is the representative of the members and is chosen by them in any manner they approve, but he does not derive authority from them. He derives his authority from obedience to the Law of God, to which both the ruler and the ruled are bound. The political contract of Islam is not made between the ruler (or Government) and the ruled but between these two combined and God; and both the ruler and the ruled are morally and legally bound to fulfil their obligations to God. The ruler is bound to administer the Law of God, and the members are bound to support him and co-operate with him so long as he is observing the Divine Code. If the ruler deviates from the Law of God, he loses his right to support and loyalty from the members; and, on the other hand, if he observes the Law of God, he is entitled to support and co-operation from the members. If the members or any individual fail to give him such support and co-operation, they are committing an offence against the administration as well as against God. "O Believers, obey God and obey the Messenger and those entrusted with authority from among you. Then if there arises any dispute about anything, refer it to God and the Messenger, if you truly believe in God and the Last Day. This is the only right way and will be best in regard to the end" (4: 59).

Thus it is an obligatory duty of a Muslim to obey those invested with authority, whether he likes it or dislikes it, provided they are observing the conditions of the vicegerency and are not ordering obedience in sinful things. Obedience to the rulers is obligatory only in right things. The Holy Messenger is reported to have said, "There will be rulers over you who will practise right things as well as wrong things. (In such a case) whoso protests against the wrong things shall be absolved of the responsibility and whoso dislikes the wrong things shall also escape punishment. But whoso approves and follows them shall incur punishment." The companions asked, "Should we not fight against such rulers?" The Holy Prophet answered, "No, so long as they offer salat (prayer)." Salat here means the establishment of salat in the system of Government. This hadith explicitly lays down the minimum condition that makes a Government Islamic in principle. If it fulfils this condition, then obedience is obligatory on the Muslims. If Government has discarded Islam, then the Muslims are fully justified in overthrowing such a Government. (3)

(b) The Concept of Consultation

The concept of consultation has great significance in the political system of Islam. The Holy Prophet himself always consulted his companions concerning important matters of administration and his practice has immensely enforced the importance of this concept. The political leaders in various Muslim countries have recently made very high claims to fit the apparel of modern democracy onto the body politic of Islam. It is therefore quite relevant to examine the various aspects of this concept before attempting to say anything else about it. The Qur'an advises the Holy Messenger in these words: "O Messenger, it is a great mercy of God that you are very gently and lenient towards them for, had you been harsh and hard-hearted, they would all have broken away from you: so pardon them and implore God to forgive them, and take counsel with them in the conduct of affairs; then, when once you make up your mind (to do a thing), trust in God (and do it). God likes those who trust in Him in whatever they do" (3: 159). The Qur'an mentions this as one of the qualities of the Muslims: "Those who answer the call of their Lord, and establish prayer; and who conduct their affairs by mutual consultation" (42: 38). This is explained by the Holy

---

3. *The Meaning of the Qur'an*, VOl. 11. p. 133.

Messenger, when Ali said to him, 'O Messenger of God! What should we do if, after your demise, we are confronted with a problem about which we neither find anything in the Qur'an nor have anything from you?' He said, "Get together the obedient (to God and His Law) people from amongst my followers and place the matter before them for consultation. Do not make divisions on the basis of the opinions of any single person." (4) It is also reported from him, "The man who gives counsel to his brother knowing full well that it is not right does most surely betray his trust." (5)

The Qur'an has mentioned 'consultation' but has not suggested or prescribed any specific method. The Holy Messenger always consulted those of his companions gifted with wisdom and knowledge and the representatives of the tribes of his followers before taking any final decision. But there are neither in the Qur'an nor in his Sunnah any hard and fast rules regarding the number of consultants, the form of their election or selection, or the duration of their office, etc. All such matters are left entirely to the discretion of the Muslims. This seems to show that the form of representation by itself is neither very significant nor fundamental to the basic concept of consultation. Consultation may take any shape or form, it may be direct or indirect, through proper representatives, selected or elected in general elections or through electoral colleges; the consultative body may consist of a few members, or one or two houses having a large number of members representing every section or area of the Islamic state. (5) All such matters are left to each society to determine according to the needs of the time and place. However, one thing is important, that consultation, whatever its form, must be the basis of every Islamic Government. The

4. Alusi, *Ruh al-Ma'ani*, quoted in *Concept of Islamic state* issued by Islamic Council of Europe.
5. Abu Da'ud, quoted in *Concept of Islamic state*, op. cit.

ruler or the Government must always have representatives, possessing integrity of character and enjoying the confidence of those whom they represent, for consultation on state matters of importance affecting the lives of the people in general.

A cursory study of the verses of the Qur'an and the sayings of the Holy Messenger mentioned above shows that the concept of consultation implies, first, that all affairs of the Muslims must be decided by consultation. There is supposed to be a ruler or Government which conducts the affairs of the state. It is commanded never to conduct any affairs of state without consulting the people whom it represents. This automatically rules out Government by a family, or any dictator or autocrat. It also denies any power of supervision of the constitution to the ruler or the Government, for it is against the spirit of the concept of consultation. Secondly, the people are to be consulted directly or indirectly through their official representatives. The Qur'an and Sunnah are silent about the form this consultation may take. However, there are indirect references which seem to suggest some form of proportional representation that can be adopted by the Muslim: "And Moses chose from among his people seventy men (to accompany him)to attend a meeting appointed by Us." (7: 155). And again in the same Surah we read: "And We had divided them into twelve tribes and made them distinct communities. When his people asked him for water, We directed Moses to strike a certain rock with his staff. Twelve springs gushed for forth from it and each tribe was specified its drinking place (7: 160).

These are two examples in the Qur'an which suggest that every situation must be properly appreciated before taking a final decision on any matter. The Prophet Moses, after taking stock of the whole situation and through Divine Guidance, adopted these measures which fully satisfied his people's desires and feelings. Moses was able effectively to know their wishes through their representatives and this is the main object and aim of representation, that the ruler or the Government should always remain in touch with public opinion. (6) Thirdly, it requires free, genuine and impartial consultation, without any duress or persuasion. In cases of duress or persuasion the purpose of consultation is nullied, for in reality it is a consultation in name only. (7) These three principles must always be observed very strictly, no matter what the form of representation of the people. However, every effort must be made to find a proper and effective method of slection or election so that the community is able to play its proper role as the consultative body of the ruler or the Government. Furthermore, the community must so devise its constitution as to close all doors which would allow any ruler or government to administer its affairs without consulting the people or their proper representatives. And if such a ruler or government is established without proper authority at any time, there must be a viable procedure or machinery to dislodge it without much trouble or bloodshed.

The Covention of the Consultative Process: Let us examine the form and nature of the Government in the early Caliphate *(Khilafat)* in order to find some form of convention in this matter. The Holy Messenger himself became the first ruler and head of the Islamic State. He was not elected or selected by anyone but was chosen by God, the absolute Sovereign, as Messenger as well as ruler of the State for ten years but decided all matters relating to the State by consultation with his colleagues. Those very people who had strived hard and sacrificed everything for the sake of their faith became the first members of his consultative

----

6. M. Hamid Ullah, *Indroduction to Islam,* pp. 93-105.
7. *Concept of Islamic State,* op. cit.

committee. This included learned men from the Muhajirun as well as from the Ansar, who enjoyed the full confidence of all the Muslims. Thus they became members of the consultative committee of the Holy Messenger through a natural process of selection. The whole community trusted them and honoured them, and they accompanied the Holy Messenger in every compaign.

Abu Bakr, the first Caliph, was elected in public by a popular vote. He consulted the same people on state matters who were prominent from amongst the Muhajirun and the Ansar during the time of the Holy Messenger. Before his death, he consulted the prominent memebers from amongst the Muhajirun and the Ansar and from other important sections of the Muslim community present in Medinah, and found Umar the most trustworthy, suitable and acceptable and, therefore, nominated him for the office of *Amir* (head) of the Muslim state. Abu Bakr, after great deal of consideration and thought and consultation with diverse groups of people, severally and jointly, addressed the Muslims in these words: "Are you willing to accept him as your *Amir* whom I nominate as my successor? God is my Judge that I have left no stone unturned in coming to (the best) conclusion in these matters. I am not nominating anybody related to me. I nominate Umar, son of Khattab, as my successor. Therefore, listen to him and obey him." The people gathered there cried, "We have heard and we accept." (8)

Thus Umar's name was suggested and recommended by Abu Bakr after consultation in confidence and then put before the Muslims for their approval. When they approved, Umar was officially declared *Amir* (i. e., head) of the State. When Umar reached the last moments of his life, he appointed a

---

8. *Tabari*, VOl. 11. p. 618, quoted by Abul Ala Maududi. *The Islamic Law and constitution*, 00. 223-224; 618.

consultative committee consisting of six most righteous and trustworthy men from amongst the Muslims to select the next *Amir* from amongst themselves within a definite period. The consultative committtee, in its turn, delegated this task to one of its most trusted and righteous members, Abdur Rahman bin Auf. He went round the city finding out the general opinion of the public. He consulted various sections of the community, men, women, and even students of schools and pilgrims who were visiting the city from other parts of the state after their pilgrimage to Makkah. After a thorough fact-finding survey, he found that Ali and Uthman, two members of the consultative committee had the massive support of the public; and of these two, Uthman was slightly more popular than Ali. Abdur Rahman bin Auf, therefore, finding the greatest support of the Muslims to be for Uthman, declared him the *Amir,* and the people accepted him as their leader.

After the tragic event of Uthman's death, some companions of the Holy Messenger went to Ali and asked him to accept the office of the *Amir* because there was no better and more suitable than him to shoulder this responsibility. Ali at first refused to accept their request, but when they insisted, he said, "If you wish it to be so, then come to the Mosque, for my acceptance as *Amir* cannot be secret, nor without the approval of the Muslim masses." (8) When they went to the Prophet's Mosque, where people had assembled, Ali was accepted *Amir* by great majority of the people, though not unanimously. When Ali was inflicted with a fatal wound and was dying, he was asked if he would allow them to accept his elder son Hassan as their *Amir,* and he replied, "I neither ask you to do so, nor forbid you from doing so. You can decide according to your wishes." (9)

---

9. Quoted by Abul Ala Maududi, *The Islamic Law and constitution,* pp. 222-30.

This is the sum total of the entire convention of the selection of the *Amir* and the consultation process. This, however, clearly points to the facts, first, that the appointment, selection or election of the *Amir* of the Muslim State depends wholly on the will of the people and no one has the authority or right to impose himself by force as *Amir*. Secondly, this office is not a monopoly or birthright of any individual, class or family. Thirdly, the matter must be decided with the free will of the Muslim public without any compulsion or force. (9)

Almost the same is the convention of chosing the consultative committee of the *Amir* (i.e. head of the State). From the time of the Holy Prophet to Ali, the fourth Caliph, those people formed the consultative committee who were either associated with him from the very beginning of the struggle for Islam or who subsequently came to prominence owing to their great sacrifices, wisdom, ability and knowledge. These people were most righteous and trustworthy and they enjoyed confidence of the Muslims as well as the Holy Messenger and, later on, of his Caliphs. These people were chosen both from the Muhajirun and from the Ansar for their services to the cause of Islam and for their knowledge and ability, and all had the full support and backing of the Muslims from all sections of the community. After the death of the Holy Prophet, these representatives of the people were automatically included in the consultative committee. There was no election or voting in the modern sense, nor was there any need for it, because those very people were known for their services, ability and knowledge, and had the confidence of the entire Muslim community.

What is required, according to the concept of consultation, is that the Government and its affairs should be conducted with the approval of the people or their representatives. As long as the representatives have the confidence of the people, no matter how they are selected, the Government is fully representative of the people and its form of selection does not in any way affect its nature and function. The procedure of taking new members onto the consultative committee by virtue of their services, experience, knowledge or outstanding intellectual achievement had the universal approval of the Muslim community. It enabled the Government continually to add new and fresh vigour and intellect to the consultative body by accepting younger members and also to inspire confidence and trust in it among the new generation. All decisions of the Government were taken with the advice of this body. It may here be pointed out that the Amir could not and did not appoint anyone he liked as a member of the consultative committee. Only men who were universally known to the people for their great reputation, intelligence and integrity served on this committee during the time of the Holy Messenger and his Caliphs. (9)

This clearly shows that the *Amir* has absolutely no authority or right to pick his own yes-men for the consultative committee, for they must be persons of great ability and knowledge and also enjoying the confidence of the people. Now the question arises as to how to select for this purpose men who possess not only knowledge and ability but also enjoy the full confidence of the people. Islam has not set any definite hard-and-fast rules for any particular form or method of selection or election; therefore any system which enables us to select such men as can do their job efficiently and effectively and who possess the confidence of the people, can be adopted in the political system of Islam. However, the western election system is neither conductive nor suitable to the genus of Islamic ideology in the present circumstances, now that the masses are absolutely ignorant of the basic teachings of Islam. If we want to use this system, we must first educate the masses and acquaint them with the purpose and intention of the Islamic state. If we put the cart before the horse, as is happening in many Muslim countries, we are likely to destroy the very thing we intend to achieve. The modern election system is more suited to the interests of the capitalist secular society, where wealthy demagogues can use their wealth and power of speach to gain power. If this wild and vicious horse is brought under control through education and training, perhaps it may then be used to find the right solution to our political problem, but not in its present form. Until the ferocity and wildness of this horse is tamed, we must find another effective method to give practical shape to the concept of consultation in our political system.

It may, however, be pointed out, that though the Qur'an and the Sunnah are silent about the form of selection or election of the Head of the State and his consultative body or legislature, certain rules and principles can be deduced from them regarding the nature and quality of the people who are worthy to serve in these two capacities. The office of the *Amir* (Head of the State) carries great responsibilities and, obviously, these can not be efficiently and effectively fulfilled by an ordinary man. It requires not only ability, experience and great knowledge of the practical affairs of the State but also needs honesty, integrity of character and strong faith in God. A man of great ability and skill may prove a useful and successful administrator for a secular state but is not fit even to be an office boy in the Islamic State, if he has no faith in God, nor integrity of character. Likewise the members of the consultative committee and legislature must be persoms of great integrity and knowledge, having strong faith in God.

What is the best way to select or elect such persons to hold high office in the Islamic State? It is a very difficult job and can only be entrusted to people who are capable of understanding their obligations as electors or selectors. Obviously, such an important job cannot be entrusted to ignorant people who can be easily misled by the demagogues of modern times. They must have the ability and knowledge to judge the suitability of each candidate for the office for which he is being elected as a true Muslim; for without it the whole procedure will become a farce and the State will fall into the hands of ignorant and evil persons. In the words of the Holy Prophet: "The ignorance of an ignorant man is more harmful than the transgression of a sinner." (10)

If the work of electing or selecting persons to high offices is given to unworthy people, it will have very grave consequences both for the state and the people. That is why the Holy Prophet made the acquisition of knowledge compulsory for every Muslim man and Muslim woman. He did not specify any particular kind of learning but emphasised the importance of knowledge. It is therefore the duty of all Muslims, men and women, to learn the science of action. They must learn and acquire more knowledge and information about the activities and offices which are entrusted to them. As different responsibilities are laid on them, the acquisition of knowledge about the duties of those offices and the kind of action required of them also become compulsory. (10) And there is no substitude for knowledge. The Qur'an emphatically states: "O Muhammad, are those who know equal with those who know not? But only men of understanding pay heed" (39: 9). In this verse, two kinds of people are compared: those who in their ordinary lives disobey the Command of God but turn towards Him when in trouble; and others who obey the Commands of God and follow His Way in their ordinary lives. The first group of people are called 'ignorant', even though they may have acquired degrees in sciences and law from Western-type universities; the second type of people are called 'men of learning and knowledge', even though they may never have

---

10. Gazzali's *Ihya Ulum-id-Din* Book 1., English. pp. 109-13

attended any university or obtained any degrees. This is because the real knowledge is the knowledge of Truth and Reality and the action required according to that knowledge, which is the basis of man's ultimate success and prosperity. This verse emphasises the point that these two types of people can never be equal.

This point is further stressed in another Surah in these words: "The blind and the seeing are not equal; nor are the depths of darkness and the light" (35: 19-20). Again, these verses compare two types of people and emphasise that they cannot be equal. There are those who are blindly following their own course of life and completely ignoring Reality and there are those who clearly see the Reality of God's manifestation and direct their lives according to the teachings of His Messenger. These two groups of people cannot be alike, either in their conduct of affairs or in their ultimate end. Here blindness is compared to ignorance and seeing to knowledge. The Qur'an often mentions light and blindness (or darkness) to mean knowledge and ignorance respectively: "Light has come to you from God and the Book which guides to the Truth, whereby God leads to the Path of Peace those who seek His Pleasure and brings them out of darkness into the light of His Grace and guides them to the Right Way" (5: 16).

The Holy Prophet explaining the significance of this knowledge, remarked: "O People, acquire knowledge from your Lord and advise one another using your intellect. Know what you have been enjoined to do and what has been prohibited. Know that intellect will give rank to your learning, and know that the intelligent man is he who obeys God, although his face may be ugly, his body dwarfed, his rank low and his appearance shabby. And an ignorant man is he who disobeys God, though his appearance may be beautiful, his body tall, his conduct good and his speech fluent." (10) He also said, "The good conduct of a man does not become perfect till his intellect is complete and when his intellect becomes perfect he obeys God and disobeys His enemy, the devil." (10) This clearly shows that intellect and knowledge by itself is of no use unless it is used for obeying God and following His Way of life. Mere possession of intellect without proper knowledge of God is of little avail for it does not lead to the right course of action in life.

Thus it is obvious that the common people who are to elect or select persons to high offices should themselves possess not only intellect and knowledge but must also have a sound and clear understanding of the basic principles of Islam in theory and practice: unless they are equipped with both these qualities they will not be able to perform their duty properly. It would therefore be utter folly to adopt Western type of electoral system and entrust the duty of selection or election to people who are totally unfit to perform it rightly.

It is most essential that the people must be educated and brought to the level where an individual has, first, the ability and intelligence to take decisions on his own; secondly, the integrity and character to know the Truth and to support it under all circumstances, no matter whether Truth comes from him or from his adversaries; thirdly, a knowledge of his duties and full consciousness of it as a true Muslim; and fourthly, adequate knowledge of the candidates. (8)

The candidates for the high office of the State and for the consultative body or legislature should possess these qualities to a much higher degree, especially in knowledge, strength of character and integrity. Besides, they must be well-known to the people and enjoy their full confidence. The practice of the Holy Prophet clearly shows that only knowledgeable persons with great intelligence and service to the cause of

Islam, and enjoying a great reputation and the confidence of the people, were consulted by him on state matters. He never consulted ordinary people or people with mere knowledge and no intelligence or ability to take decisions on important state matters. Even the Qur'an advises people not to take important state matters into their own hands but to refer them to the Messenger or to the people of knowledge and understanding: "Whenever these people hear any news concerning public or danger, they make it known to all; instead of this, if they had only referred it to the Messenger, or to the responsible people of the community, the people with knowledge from amongst them would have drawn the right conclusions from it" (4: 83). The first four Caliphs followed very strictly the way of the Holy Prophet in their consultation process and always appointed men of great integrity, knowledge and wisdom on their consultative committees. They were very careful in their selection and always picked very pious men who also had the support of the community.

Thus, in principle, there is no objection to any form of Government or to the procedure of its selection (or election) in Islam, so long as its purpose and aim is fully and effectively realised. However, history, past and present, bears irrefutable testimony to the fact that the aim and purpose of the ideological state of Islam cannot be realised unless the above-mentioned principles regarding the qualities of the selectors (or electors) and the candidates for these high offices are observed in the process of consultation. Any leniency or carelessness in this matter can do great damage to the ideology of Islam and the state. Moreover, seeking any office or running for any post on the part of any one is in itself a disqualification for him because the Holy Prophet, in replying to the request of Abu Musa for an office, said, "I swear by God that I will not put in charge of this work anyone who asks for it, or anyone who is eager for it." In another version, he said, "We will not employ in our work one who wants it." (11) And Abu Hurairah reported God's Messenger as saying, "You will find among the best people those who have the strongest dislike of this command till they fall into it." (11) Once Abu Zar asked the Messenger to make him a governor; he said, "You are weak, Abu Zar, and it is a trust which will be a cause of shame and regret on the Day of Resurrection except for him who undertakes it as it ought to be undertaken and fulfils his duty in it." (11)

It is hard to find people who do not seek any office of responsibility for themselves and when burdened with such a heavy responsibility, are fully conscious of their duties and do them honestly to the best of their ability in the interest of the community, merely seeking the pleasure of God. Past experience with the present Western democratic form of elections in Muslim countries has clearly shown that this method of election not only does not bring really able, intelligent, knowledgeable and good people to the top office or offices but also corrupts people at various levels and enables corrupt people to come to the top positions in the State. Therefore, it can be said without any fear of contradiction or doubt, that the Western form of electoral system is not at all suitable for Muslim countries under the present circumstances. It has awefully failed in the past and has actually aggravated the deterioration of people's state of affairs, morally as well as economically,spiritually as well as politically. And, if the Muslims do not learn a lesson from their past mistakes, their future seems absolutely dark. It is high time that they disregard the past decisions of their politicians and scholars, however great they may have been in the field of theology, jurisprudence, Islamic knowledge and Qur'anic science. After all, they were men, though great, and, as such, liable to make mistakes, especially in the field of

---

11. *Mishkat,* VOl. 1. English translation, pp. 783-84.

interpretation of the text and its application to the practical problems of politics. There is need for new thinking and a new approach to the problem of consultation and the various practical forms that can be adopted to solve our politacal problems in the light of the practice of the Holy Prophet and his rightly-guided Caliphs, and of our past experience in wholly depending on the Western style of democratic forms of government. Insha'allah, if efforts are made sincerely and wholeheartedly by all people and all parties to find the right solution to solve our fundamental problems as Muslims, there is every hope that some suitable form of consultation can be devised which can meet our present political needs without limiting or restricting its field of operation or functioning in any way.

2. Sovereignty

The concept of sovereignty is based on two realities: first, that God is the Creator, the Supporter, the Master and Sovereign of the whole universe, including man; secondly, that man is a humble servant and vicegerent (representative) of God on the earth and obeys the Laws of His Sovereign for his own benefit. The root cause of all evil and disorder on the earth is the belief in the wrong philosophy that man is his own master and sovereign, which, in fact, he is not. The real Master and Sovereign is God. The Prophet Joseph announced this concept in these words: "Verily I have abandoned the creed of a people who believe not in God and who are disbelievers in the Hereafter. And I have followed the religion of my fathers, Abraham and Isaac and Jacob. It was never meant for us to attribute anything as a partner to God. This is the Blessing of God on us and on all mankind; but most people give not thanks. . . Are diverse lords better, or God, the One, the Supreme? Those whom you worship beside Him are but names which you have invented, you and your fathers. God has revealed no sanction for them. Sovereignty belongs to none but God alone. He has commanded that you obey none but Him. This is the Right Way, but most men know it not" (12: 37-40).

It is also explained in another verse of the Holy Qur'an: "Verily, your Lord is God alone, Who created the heavens and the earth in six days, and then mounted upon the Throne of His Kingdom; Who makes the night cover the day and then the day follows the night swiftly; Who created the sun, the moon and the stars, all of which are under His Command. Verily His is all Creation and His is all Sovereignty. Blessed be God, Lord of the world" (7: 54). This establishes beyond any shadow of doubt that there is only One Master Creator Who is in full control of His Creation. He is also its Sovereign and all beings obey His Law. He is, in fact, the real and virtual Ruler and Sovereign Who controls and commands the entire Kingdom Himself without any help or assistance in any form. This concept is further explained in many other verses of the Qur'an: "Say, O Muhammad, 'I seek refuge in the Lord, the Sustainer of mankind, the Sovereign (Ruler) of mankind, the Lord (Judge) of mankind' " (114: 1-3).

And again, "Say, O God, Sovereign of the Kingdom, You bestow kinghead on whomever You please and You take it away from whoever you please" (3: 26). And in Surah Al-Kahf we read: "None is a partner in His Sovereignty" (18: 110). The people are commanded in very clear words: "O people, follow what has been sent down to you from your Lord and do not follow other partners beside Him" (7: 3). This verse explicitly invites man to accept and follow the Divine Guidance sent through God's Messengers. This alone can provide him with true knowledge about himself and the world, and explain the aim and object of his life and then teach him how to establish his social system with its culture and civilisation based on high spiritual and moral principles. (12) This verse also warns him not to follow the ways of any others than God because to do so would utterly ruin his entire social system with its culture and civilisation: "Those who do not judge by the Law which God has sent down are indeed the disbelievers" (5: 44), "unjust" (5: 45) and "transgressors" (5: 47). So, O Muhammad judge between these people by the Law that has been sent down to you, and do not follow their vain desires, turning away from the Truth that has come to you" (5: 51-52).

Thus the political and legal Sovereignty is the exclusive prerogative of God, and no one shares it with Him. This concept of Sovereignty is one of the fundamental principles of the political and legal system of Islam and it is recognised as most sacrosanct and beyond compromise. And, obviously, no state can become truly Islamic unless it recognises and declares categorically the political and legal Sovereignty of God, and acknowledges Him as the Supreme Power Whose Command must be obeyed under all circumstances and also binds itself to obedience to Him with the words: "Know that none but God is the Sovereign and no Command is worthy of obedience except that which is given by Him." And in the words of another scholar: "As Command is the exclusive prerogative of God, none is entitled to give any Command but He." And all Muslims agree on this point. (12)

3. Sovereignty and Vicegerency

As explained before, all political and legal sovereignty belongs to none but God. The political Sovereignty of God means that He is the Real Head of the State, and all its administration is directly under His Command. It also implies that God's Authority and Sovereign Power is neither limited by any power other than His Own Free Will, nor bound by any law imposed from outside. The legal Sovereignty of God signifies that the Source of all law and legislative power is none other God. He is the Law-Maker and Law-Giver, and all

----

12. *The Meaning of the Qur'an,* VOl. 1V. pp. 8-9

such Powers belong to Him alone and there is none who shares with Him in His Law-Making Power or who can restrict His Legislative Powers by his will or authority. Both politically and legally, He is far above the posibility that anyone should share with Him or restrict Him in His Authority or Sovereign Power. All executive, legislative and judical power belongs to Him.

As soon as any society or state acknowledges the Sovereignty of God and His Messenger in all matters affecting human relationships in their wider context, it becomes a representative or vicegerent of God and His Messenger on the earth. As a vicegerent of God, it has a two-fold status. First, its position in relation to God and His Messenger is that of a state with limited sovereign power, because all Sovereign Powers belong to God and His Messenger. Any assertion of sovereign power in the real sense means open rebellion against God and His Messenger and a clear negation of its Islamic character. Secondly, the vicegerent's status in relation to other states of the world is that of a state exercising absolute Sovereign Power in all administrative matters involving other states.

Another aspect of vicegerency is that it does not belong to any particular class, group or family but to all the members of the Islamic State. All citizens of the Islamic State share equally the office of vicegerency. This concept of vicegerency, which is vested in the people and rests on their common support, is the basis of democracy in Islam. On the other hand, 'popular sovereignty is the basis of a secular state in which all sovereign authority is vested in the people and they can do whatever they like. In the former, people enjoy vicegerency because the authority that is vested in the state and the community is delegated to them by God. But their authority is limited and is exercised within the limits prescribed by God. As the authority is delegated to the community as a whole, the Ruler or the Government can be established only with the consent and approval of the community as a whole, or of their approved, elected or selected representatives, and can function and remain in office as long he or it has their confidence.

Thus the Islamic State acts on behalf of God as His vicegerent on the earth and executes His Will and Law within the prescribed limits. Its sovereign power is exercised within the Divine Law. Besides, it exercises its right of vicegerency on behalf of the people because, in fact, they are the recipients of this right, although they have nominated some people or some person to act on their behalf. Their office lasts as long as they enjoy the confidence of the community (the real vicegerents) . (12).

4. Theocracy and Vicegerency

Vicegerency in nature and function is quite different from the so called 'Divine Right of Kings' or the 'Papal authority'. The vicegerency of God belongs to the community as a whole and not to any particular individual or class or tribe. It is, in fact, the collective right of the Muslim community which has accepted God as its Sovereign and adopted His Divine Code as its Way of Life: "God has promised to those of you who believe and do good deeds that He will most surely make them His vicegerents in the earth" (24: 55). The vicegerency (or *Khilafat)* is democracy in the true sense and, therefore, in essence and function, the antithesis of the monarchical, theocratic and papal form of government. It is also different from Western secular democracy, under which people possess absolute power of sovereignty. Their will is the supreme authority in the land. On the other hand, under the *Khilafat,* the people enjoy only the vicegerency (or *Khilafat)* of God, Who alone is the Sovereign. (13)

---

13. A.A. Maududi, *The Islamic Law and Consitution,* p. 210

Western writers, knowingly or unknowingly, have confused the nature and junction of vicegerency (Caliphate) and compared it to the Western concept of 'theocracy', with all the memories of the long struggle between State and Church and a dark background of evil and horror. In fact, the whole philosophy of theocracy as known to the Western mind is "alien to Islamic thought; for Islam does not authorise any material form, human or institutional, that could claim to be representative of God. God is God and man is man. The Prophet was a bearer of Revelation, and both were terminated by the Prophet's passing away." (14) The Prophet left behind God's Laws, but they are not God. All Muslims now follow and obey these Laws. No one can claim special privileges in Islam because they are all equal in the sight of God. Everyone has the right to speak on the Divine Texts without claiming a special privilege for it. The final word rests with the Divine Texts.

Another feature of the struggle between the State and the Church in the West was that religion became a private affair between man and his Lord. And gradually this established a kind of sanctity for certain men or classes of men as saints who enjoyed a special position and privileges in religious matters. There is no such concept in Islam. There is privacy in optional prayers, but it constitutes the real 'essence of all religious experience'. However, even in optional prayers offered in privacy, Muslims are governed by a Divine Code which is binding on all. This kind of 'privacy' does not establish any type of 'sanctity' for a man or group of men in Islam. The supremacy of the Divine Law is paramount, so that even Muhammad's actions as a man were subject to it and, under no circumstances, could he override the former: (13) "O Prophet! Why do you ban that which God has made

---

14. Dr. Said Ramadan, Theocracy Ruled out, an article in *Concept of Islamic State*, pp. 29-31.

lawful for you, seeking to please your wives? And God is Forgiving, Merciful" (66: 1).

This clearly shows that the Divine Code of Law is Supreme and no one has any authority to go outside its limits. Even the Prophet himself could not do so. What God's Law forbids no one can make lawful and what It allows no one can make unlawful. This applies to all and no one is considered to be above the Divine Law. The rule of the Law is fully operational and none can escape the consequences of his (or her) actions in a truly Islamic State because no individual or class of individuals enjoys any special privileges or holds any kind of sanctity above the Divine Code of Law. All obey God and are subject to His Code of Law.

5. The Purpose of the Islamic State

According to the Qur'an and the Sunnah, the aim and purpose of the Islamic state is to establish, maintain and develop those virtues among its members which God likes and to prevent and eradicate from their lives the evils which He utterly dislikes. Thus, qualities of modesty , goodness, virtue, peace and prosperity, which God likes, should be evolved, developed and encouraged by all means in the life of the people, while exploitation, injustice, obscenity and disorder, which are detrimental to human progress and welfare, should be prevented, suppressed and discouraged in society by all possible methods. In order to achieve this high ideal, Islam launches its moral discipline to educate and train its members in self-discipline, self-culture and self-purification. (2)

The great emphasis is on the constant observance of those moral principles which are dear to God and are the 'basis of a good, virtuous and successful society'. "These are the people who, if We give them power in the land, establish *salat* (worship and prayer) and pay zakat (poor due), enjoin right and virtue and forbid wrong and evil" (22: 41). Again, in Surah Al Hadid we read: "Certainly We sent Our Messengers with clear Signs, and sent down with them the Book and the Balance, so that people may conduct themselves with equity" (57: 25). The Holy Prophet explained this principle by saying that "God brings to an end through the State (i.e. authority) what He does not eradicate with the Qur'an." This shows that the main purpose of the Islamic State is to enforce and implement the reforms which Islam has recommended for the betterment and welfare of the community. Its distinguishing feature is its programme of popularising good and virtuous things and ways of life and discouraging bad and harmful things and ways of life. (14)

This verse explicitly spells out the purpose of the Islamic State and the fundamental characteristics of the rulers and administrators who are supposed to be the architects of this system. When they are granted power and authority in the land, they act in the following way: (15)

(a)   "In their personal lives, they adopt the way of piety and obedience. Their character is free from the blemishes of sin, disobedience to God, vanity and arrogance. They behave like gentlemen, offer prayer to their Lord, act humbly and establish the system of *salat* in the collective life of the people.

(b)   Their wealth and resources are not wasted on sensuality and luxury. Instead, they establish the institution of *zakat* and organise it so that the wealth of the community may be equitably distributed and the state fulfil its welfare function.

(c)   They use the powers of the state for the eradication of evil and of sin and for the promotion and establishment of virtue and goodness."

---

15. Abul   Ala   Maududi, *The Islamic Law and Conctitution*, pp. 176-92.

To sum up, the fundamental aim and object of the Islamic State is to establish and promote honest, truthful and fair principles among the people and to eradicate and discourage evil and corruption from their lives so that all may live a virtuous, happy and peaceful life.

6. Basic Human Rights

Islam attaches great importance to the maintenance and protection of human rights and the basic freedom of the individual in society. But the concept of freedom in Islam is fundamentally different from that of Western society. The Western concept of individual liberty is based on the notion that man is the measure of all things. In Islam, God is Supreme and Paramount and man exists only to serve His Creator. He is responsible to Him for all his actions. His duty to God embraces both his duty to other individuals and his duty to society. Thus, paradoxically, in Islam the rights of individuals are preserved by the obligations of each individual to God. Duties to God are expressed by the Qur'anic concept of *huquq Allah* (duties to God) and *huquq al-'ibad* (duties to society). The former embraces the various forms of worship necessary for purity of mind and body and has an individual colour, while the latter embraces man's relationship to his fellow-beings and has a social aspect. And consciousness of accountability for all actions to God on the Day of Judgement constitutes the sanction for the protection of these rights. It is the quality or strength of this consciousness or realisation *(niyyat)* which determines the actions of believers. However, as the Islimic State is also responsible to God, it has the authority to protect human rights and the basic freedom of the individual.

Thus human rights and individual liberty in Islam are secured through negative, but conscious, efforts of the people, which is much better than the Western mechanical approach by man made law. Islam attaches more importance to right belief and right conduct, because human action can never be right unless it is based on right belief and is consciously and knowingly performed. "This 'conscious intention' is the core of the matter, and the Prophet said that the *niyyat* (intention) of the mu'min (believer) to do something, in obedience to the Law of God, was better than mere external conformity with the terms of the conduct prescribed by such Law *(al-niyyat 'l-mu'min khairun minal-amallin)*. Since it is in the inwardness of a man's being that such a conscious willing intention can be formed, Islam takes good care to insist that its primary purpose is to produce *salihin* (rightous people), *muttaqis* (self-controlled people) and *siddiqin* (people who adhere to Truth). (16) On the other hand, the procedure of the Western World "is to attempt to influence from outside the inner condition of man, believing that social, political, economic and other institutions are capable of influencing the individual character." (16)

The approach of Islam is the most natural and best. It gives man his human liberty, but only within a religious framework which insists on him being fully aware of his accountability and responsibility to God. (16) It may here be pointed out that Islam gives freedom of expression and action but not licence to apostasy, obscenity and corruption. All such irresponsible behaviour is strictly restricted by law as in any other state. Beside this, human rights in Islam are not restricted to any geographical boundaries or any state but are universal in nature and are enjoyed by all human beings. They are to be observed and respected under all circumstances, in peace or in war. The basic rights laid down by Islam are as follows: (17)

---

16. A. K. Brohi, *Islam and Human Rights*, article in the Challenge of Islam. pp. 176-92.
17. Abul Ala Maududi, *Islamic Way of Life*, 47-50.

(a) The Right to Life: Human life is sacrosanct and cannot be taken without justification (i.e., in return for killing): "And you should not take life, which God has made sacred except by law" (6: 151). And verse 17: 33 also forbids the taking of life. These verses declare the sanctity of human life, which is an inviolable right of man, except in five cases, three of which are mentioned in the Qur'an and two in the Sunnah of the Holy Prophet: (i) murder, (ii) obstructive opposition to the establishment of Islam, (iii) causing disorder or rebellion against the established Islamic State, (iv) adultery, and (v) apostasy.

(b) Protection of Property and Honour: It is the duty of the Islamic State to protect the property and honour of every member of the State, irrespective of his colour, creed or race: "Do not eat up one another's property by unjust means nor offer it to the judge so that you may devour knowingly and unjustly a portion of the property of others" (2: 188).

The Holy Prophet, in his last Pilgrimage to Makkah, stated the basic principles of the Islamic State in these words: "Most surely, your life, your property and your honour are as sacred as this day of pilgrimage – they will save their lives from me (i.e. the State) except when they commit a crime against the Law of Islam . . . their lives and their properties are sacred to us except when they violate the sanctity of the life and property of others, and God alone is the Judge of their intentions." (18)

(c) Religious Freedom: Every member of the state is free to practise any faith or religion he (she) chooses and is allowed complete freedom of conscience: "If they turn away, We have not sent you as a guard over them. Your duty is but to

---

18. *Bukhari,* quoted by A. A. Maududi, *Islamic Law and constitution,* pp. 256-57

convey the Message" (42: 48). Truth and falsehood has been clearly shown to people and no doubt has been left in their minds in regard to them. The wisdom of reward for good deeds and punishment for evil deeds depends on willing acceptance or rejection of the Truth, otherwise the very purpose of religious freedom would be completely lost. That is why there is no compulsion in religion snd everyone is entitled to practise his religion according to his own beliefs (2: 256). The Holy Messenger granted complete freedom of faith to the Jews of Medinah and to the Christians of Nejran, and this practice was strictly adhered to by his successors. Umar, the second Caliph, granted the same right of faith to the Christians of Palestine.

The Islamic Faith invites all mankind to live together as a family of God or as a "fold, every member of which shall be a shepherd or keeper unto every other and be accountable for its welfare." (19) All believers in the Sovereignty and Lorship of One God (Allah) are members of the Islamic community, where distinctions of race, colour, creed and birth melt away and all live as brothers: "O Mankind! We created you from a single (pair) of a male and a female, and made you into nations and tribes, that you may know each other. Surely the most honoured in the sight of God is he who is the most righteous among you" (49: 13).

(d)   Freedom of Speech: This is another basic right of every member of the Islamic society. He enjoys complete freedom of thought and expression, provided he does not openly propagate opinions against the fundamental concept of Tawhid (Unity) or encourage abscenity. Even non-Muslims are free to express their opinions openly: "O believers, obey God and obey the Messenger and those entrusted with

19. A. K. Brohi, article read at the London Conference 1976.
organised by the Islamic Council of Europe.

authority from among you. Then if there arises any dispute about any thing, refer it to God and the Messenger, if you truly believe in God and the Last Day. This is the only right Way and will be best in regard to the end" (4: 59). This verse clearly gives people the right to differ with their rulers. All Muslims, the rulers and the ruled, must obey God and His Messenger, but obedience to the rulers is conditional that they themselves obey God and the Messenger.

The Holy Messenger made it absolutely clear: "It is obligatory on a Muslim to listen to and obey the orders of those invested with authority, whether he likes it or dislikes it, provided that they are not sinful." On an other occasion, he said, "Obedience to anyone in a sinful thing is forbidden. Obedience is obligatory only in right things." (20) Thus the people enjoy not only complete freedom of thought and expression, but also full liberty to hold different opinions from the people in authority. This was made clear by Ali, the fourth Caliph, when the Kharijites rose in revolt against him: "You may live and move about whereever you like, provided you do not shed blood or spread choas and resort to terrorism. But if you are guilty of any of these, I will go to war against you." (21) It undoubtedly establishes the fact that Islam allows freedom of thought, expression and action in all those matters about which the Qur'an and the Sunnah are silent. In other words, every member enjoys complete freedom of speech in every matter, provided it is not against the basic creeds of Islam.

Another concept of Islam which strengthens and adds weight to this right of freedom is Amr 'l-ma'ruf and nahi an'l-munkar (enjoining good and right and forbidding wrong

---

20. *Muslim* quoted in *The Meaning of the Qur'an*, VOl. 11. p. 133
21. *Concept of Islamic State* op. cit., 26-28.

and evil). This duty can only be performed effectively if a person enjoys complete freedom of thought and expression. No one can enjoin good and forbid evil under a totalitarian state or dictatorship because he cannot exercise his right to do so. Thus freedom of speech and action is prerequisite to the fullfilment of this essential duty. (22) In this connection, it is interesting to note that even the Holy Messenger himself never forced his opinion on his companions in matters not strictly relating to Faith. When he came to Medinah, and found that the people fecundated their palm trees, he expressed his surprise and did not like it. People did not fecundate their palmtrees that year but found that non-fecundation resulted in a loss of the crop. When they told the Holy Messenger about this, he said, "This was my personal opinion, and my personal opinion in such matters is liable to be right or wrong." He further added that "my personal opinion pertaining to all worldly matters should be taken in this light and the people have the right to discuss their worldly affairs and to treat them as directed by their experience and knowledge; in some cases it may be that they have more knowledge than myself and the matters which I am commissioned by God to transmit to the people are beyond any doubt, confined to religious affairs relating to belief and to the law of Islam." And he declared: "I am but a human being. Whenever I order you concerning some religious matters, then obey it. But whenever I tell you my opinion then I am only a human being, and you may know better about your worldly affairs." (23)

(e) Freedom of Work: Islam also recognises man's right to do any lawful work and to adopt any profession he likes. It does not place any barrier of race, colour or creed in matters

---

22. For further details see *Muhammad, Blessing for Mankind*, of the author, pp. 216-17 and 301-304.

23. Dr. A. A. Wahid Wafi, *Human Rights in Islam, pp. 3-12*

of service or professions but gives complete liberty to individuals to take up any lawful work which they like and for which they qualify according to the rules of the profession. It regards all kinds of labour, physical or mental, as honourable and respectable. In fact, it gave real dignity and respect to manual work and completely abolished any distinction between man and man (or between woman and woman) on the basis of his (or her) work.

Islam has greatly emphasised the importance of work and effort in exploiting the natural resources of the earth: "It is He Who has made the earth manageable for you, so walk through its tracts and eat of His provision" (67: 15). All the Prophets of God worked as shepherds. It is narrated by Abu Hurairah that the Holy Prophet said, "God has not sent a Prophet who did not work as a shepherd." His companions asked whether this was also true of him and he replied, "Yes, I used to be a shepherd for the people of Makkah for a payment of some qirats." (Bukhari). The Prophet Moses also worked for years as a shepherd in Midain. The Holy Prophet once said, "Never has one of you eaten better food than that which he has earned with his own hands." Thus Islam encourages work and respects the individual's right to undertake any kind of work without any distinction.

(f) The Right to Basic Needs: Every individual is entitled to have the minimum basic requirements of his family. This is one of the fundamental rights of every citizen of an Islamic State: "In their wealth the beggar and the destitute have their due" (51: 19). The righteous and the truthful consider it a right of the poor and the destitute to share in their wealth and they are always ready to give a share of their surplus wealth to them. In cases of emergency, the Islamic State has the legal duty to take this surplus from the wealthy to meet the basic needs of the poor in their society. Again in Surah Al-Tawbah we read, of the evil doers: "purify them (or vice) and develop them (in virtue) by taking *zakat* from their wealth, and pray for them (9: 103)."

This principle is further clarified by the Holy Prophet in these words: "God has made *zakat* obligatory upon the Muslims. It is to be collected from the wealthy among you and distributed among the needy ones." (24) And he also clearly stated the duty of the Islamic State: "The Government is the guardian of anyone who has no other guardian." (25) He also said, "If anyone dies while he owes a debt and does not leave behind any property for its payment, then the responsibility for its payment is mine (as head of the State). But if anyone leaves any property behind, (the responsibility devolves upon) his inheritors." (24) And also, "When one dies in debt or leaves behind dependants who are in danger of becoming destitutes, the latter should come to me because I am their guardian (as head of the State). (24)

These verses of the Qur'an and sayings of the Prophet leave no doubt that one of the main duties of the Islamic State is to shoulder the responsibility of providing the basic needs of those individuals and families who are unable to do so for themselves.

(g)   Right to Equality Before the Law: Islam has conferred equal rights on all individuals, irrespective of their race, cast, creed, colour, class, nationality or sex and has removed all artificial and man-made distinctions between man and man and between woman and woman: "O Mankind! We have created you from male and female and have made you nations and tribes that you may know one another. Surely the noblest of you, in the sight of God, is the most righteous of you" (49: 13). And the Holy Prophet clarified this in his

---

24. *Bukhari* and *Muslim*.
25. *Abu Daud, Tirmizi, Ibn Majah, Darmi, Masnad Ahmad.*

address in his Last Pilgrimage: "O people! Surely your God is One, and surely your Father is also one; you have all descended from Adam and Adam came out of dust. The noblest of you, in the sight of God, is the best in conduct. No one is superior to any one else by reason of his race, his nationality or his colour.

Islam also established complete equality between Muslims and non-Muslims with regard to civil rights. Non-Muslims enjoy equal civil rights with Muslims and the same laws apply to both, excepting their personal and religious matters which are decided by the laws of their own religion. There is absolutely no difference between a Muslim and non-Muslim in respect of civil and criminal law. And in respect of personal law and religious matters, they enjoy complete freedom and there is no interference with these: in respect to those rights there is a covenant between the Islamic State and the Zimmi (minorities). As long as they abide by the conditions of the covenant and don't go against it, they cannot be deprived of their rights. These rights are of irrevocable nature and are guaranteed by the Islamic constitution. (26)

Another important point with regard to civil rights is that Islam does not differentiate or discriminate between a ruler and an ordinary citizen or between rich and poor in matters of law. The same law applies to all its citizens irrespective of their social or political status. There are no exceptions to this rule. Even the Holy Prophet and his offspring were subject to the same law. It is reported that before his death, the Holy Prophet offered his own self for the satisfaction of any claim that anyone might have against him. And, according to 'A'isha, his wife, when Usama tried to intercede regarding one of the punishments prescribed by God, the Holy Prophet

26. *Islamic Way of Life*, op. cit., pp. 47-50.

said, "I swear by God that if Fatimah, daughter of
Muhammad, should steal, I would have her hand cut off."
Likewise, Umar, the second Caliph, forced Jabalah bin
Aiham, the ruler of a native state, to satisfy the claim of a
common man against him. He also totally refused to agree to
the request of Amr bin al-As for legal safeguards for the
governors. (27)

7. Relations with Other States

The basis of the foreign relations of the Islamic State with
other states is justice and equity: "O Muslims! God
commands you to give trusts into the care of those persons
who are worthy of trust and judge with justice when you
judge between people" (4: 58). God warns Muslims in this
verse against the injustices practised by their predecessors and
enjoins them always to judge between people with justice,
whether they be friends or foes. And in Surah Al-Ma'idah:
"O believers! Be steadfast in righteousness and just in giving
witness for the sake of God; the enmity of any people should
not so provoke you as to turn you away from justice for it is
near to piety" (5: 8).

These verses of the Holy Qur'an emphasise the importance of
justice and enjoin Muslims to do justice on an individual and
collective level as well as on the national and international
level. It is, therefore, the duty of an Islamic state, the
collective institution of the Muslims, to be just in all its
matters whether relating to its own citizens or to other states,
both in peace and in war. If it avoids justice in any of its
dealings, then there can be no justice in that society. (28)

The fundamental principle of foreign relations in Islam is that
Muslims and non-Muslims are absolutely equal *(sawa)* in

27. *Mishkat*, VOl. 1. English translation p. 769.
28. *The Islamic Law and Constitution*, pp. 258-59.

respect of state matters. And in the history of international law, Muslims are the first to admit the rights of foreigners without any discrimination or reserve, during both war and peace." (29) As the basic ideology of the Islamic state is the sovereignty of God, Who is the Creator and Lord of all the worlds and all peoples, religious tolerance and justive to all is indispensable.

Another point to remember in this respect is to fulfil the terms and conditions of international agreements and treaties. The Qur'an emphasises in the strongest of terms the necessity of adherence to the conditions of contracts made with foreign powers, whether friend or foe. No matter what happens, Muslims are not to be the first to break their trusts or promises with their enemies. The Holy Prophet is enjoined to act with justice under all circumstances: "Then, O Muhammad, We sent this Book to you which has brought the Truth . . . Therefore, judge between the people by the Law sent down by God and do not follow their desires by turning aside from the Truth that has come to you" (5: 48-50). And in Surah Al-Hadid we read: "We have sent Our Messengers with Signs, and sent the Book and the Balance down with them, so that mankind may conduct themselves with all fairness" (57: 25).

Muslims are always the first to advance the claims of peace and friendly relations between states. Even though the enemy is treacherous and not trustworthy, Muslims are enjoined to make peace with him if he so desires and to place their trust in God: "And, O Prophet, if enemies incline to peace, you should also incline to it, and put your trust in God; indeed He is All-Hearing, All-Knowing. And if they intend to deceive you, God is sufficient for you" (8: 61-62). This shows that Muslims' relations with other nations are based on their trust

---

29. *Introduction to Islam,* op. cit., pp. 102-105.

in God. They boldly face the enemy, both in war and in peace. When the enemy is willing to make peace, the Muslims are enjoined to make peace and not to reject it for fear of insincerity or treachery on their part, because the enemy's intentions are known only to God. (30)

Muslims are forbidden to fight those enemies who are inclined to peace: " . . . those who come to you and are averse to fighting either against you or against their own people. Had God Willed, He would have given them power over you and they would have fought against you; therefore if they leave you alone and desist from fighting against you and make overtures for peace to you, then God has left you no cause for aggression against them" (4: 90).

Muslims are allowed to fight only against those who commit agression against them and create conditions of persecution in the land: "And fight in the way of God with those who fight against you but do not commit aggression because God does not like aggressors. Fight against them wherever they confront you in battle and drive them out from where they drove you out. Although killing is bad, persecution is worse than killing" (2: 190-191). This is a clear warning to Muslims that "the aim of their war should not be self-interest, nor national gain nor retaliation. They should not, therefore, go to war against those who are neither opposing them nor hindering them from their work. Besides, the Holy Prophet gave detailed instructions for keeping the war humane. Muslims were asked to refrain from using barbaric methods in warfare and from hurting or injuring children, women, old people and the wounded. They were also instructed not to mutilate dead bodies, not to cause wanton destruction of crops, fruit trees, animals etc., and also not to indulge in any form of cruelty, barbarism and vandalism. (31)

30. *The Meaning of the Qur'an,* VOl. 1V. p. 147.

They are enjoined to maintain friendly relations with central powers: "God does not forbid you to act generously or to act fairly towards those who have never fought you over religion nor have evicted you from your homes. God loves the fair-minded. God only forbids you to be friendly with those who have fought you over religion and evicted you from your homes, or who have helped others in your eviction. Those who make friends of them are wrongdoers" (60: 8-9). They are allowed only just retribution: "Attack anyone who attacks you to the same extent as he attacked you. Heed God and know that God stands by the heedful" (2: 194). And in Surah Al-Nahl we read: "If you should punish them to the same extent as you have been punished. Yet if you are patient, it is certainly better for you (16: 126)."

The Muslims are forbidden to wage war on, or interfere with, the affairs of any state with whom they have a mutual alliance, even for the purpose of helping and protecting those of their own people who are living there. They must honour their agreements under all circumstances: "It is your duty to help them (your people living abroad), except against a people with whom you have a treaty of mutual alliance. And remember God sees all that you do" (8: 72). This shows that Muslims' international relations are based on goodwill and justice, seeking equality among peoples, irrespective of caste, colour, creed or race. They endeavour to establish peace and order on the earth, so that mankind may enjoy a life of peace, prosperity, virtue and justice. (29)

Muslims have also taken a new approach to the problem of prisoners of war. They are commanded by God to treat them with kindness and reasonableness: "Is there any reward for kindness except kindness itself?" (55: 60) And again in Surah Yunus we read: "Those who act kindly will have kindness

31. *The Meaning of the Qur'an*, VOl. 1. p. 147.

and even more besides, while neither dust nor any disgrace will cover their face. Those will be the inhabitants of Paradise; they will live in it for ever " (10: 26). The Holy Prophet and his companions set an everlasting example of generosity and kindness towards the prisoners of the Battle of Badar. (32)

---

32. For details see under 'Muhammad As a Commander and Soldier', in the book entitled *Muhammad, Blessing for Mankind*, of the author.

10

The Legal System

Law is essential for the maintenance and development of the healthy and peaceful civilised life of any society and no civilised life can be imagined without some sort of regulation. Every nation has contributed its share to the world legal system and Islam is no exception, but its contribution to the international system of law is so rich and valuable that it needs special mention.

1. Source of the Law

The source of Islamic Law is the Qur'an and the Sunnah of the Holy Prophet. Any law clearly stated in the Qur'an is eternal and unchangeable because it is the Ultimate Source of all law: "The Authority is for none but God. He has ordered you to obey Him alone; that is the Right Way, even though most men do not understand it" (12: 40). And in Surah Al-Kahf we read: "They have no partner besides Him, nor does He let any one else share in His Authority" (18: 26). These verses categorically deny the authority of any other than God to make laws for mankind: "They said, 'Have we any say in the (conduct of) affairs?' Say; 'All (authority to conduct) affairs lies with God (alone)' " (3: 154).

Legal authority belongs completely to God and to no one else. He is the Creator, the Sovereign and the Lord: "Surely Creation and Authority belongs to Him" (7: 54). And again in Surah Al-Baqarah we read: "God (alone) holds control over heaven and earth" (2: 107). Thus, all mankind must obey Him and follow His Law: "Follow whatever has been sent down to you by your Lord and do not follow any sponsors besides Him" (7: 3). And those who do not obey and follow His Law are aggressors: "Such are God's Limits, so do not exceed them; those who exceed God's Limits are wrongdoers" (2: 229). And : "Those who do not judge but what God has sent down are disbelievers . . . wrongdoers . . . rebels" (5: 47, 48, 50).

The second source of law is the practice (Sunnah) of the Holy Prophet. The Holy Qur'an gives only broad or essential principles of religion and the Holy Prophet provides the details by his example or explanation, and these, being part of the Law, are as binding as the Law itself: "We have not sent any Messenger unless he was to be obeyed with God's Permission" (4: 65). And again in the same Surah we read: "Anyone who obeys the Messenger has obeyed God (Himself)" (4: 80). And whoever does not follow the way of the Messenger follows the way to Hell: "Anyone who opposes the Messenger after Guidance has been clearly explained to him, and follows some way other than the believers, We shall turn over to what he himself has turned to, and lead him to hell. How evil is such an end!" (4: 115)

This is clearly stated in this verse: "Accept anything the Messenger may give you, and keep away from anything he forbids you to do. Heed God (alone); God is severe in punishment" (59: 7). And again: "Yet, by your Lord, they can never become believers until they accept you as judge concerning what they are quarrelling over among themselves, and then surrender to your decision with entire submission without feeling the least resentment in their hearts." This clearly lays down that 'the way of life taught by the Holy Prophet under the Guidance of God, and the rules and regulations practised and taught by him, shall remain the final authority for ever. And the Holy Prophet explained this in these words: "None of you can claim to be a believer unless he subordinates his desires to the way of life I have brought." (1).

These are the two principal and basic sources of law in Islam and if anything or any problem is not covered by these two, then, in the light of these instructions, the Muslim jurists will judge each case exerting all their ability to the maximum possible limit to reach a decision.This is called *ijtihad* (the exercise of judgement). The source of *ijtihad* is a tradition narrated by Muadh bin Jabal: "On being appointed governor of Yeman, he was asked by the Holy Prophet how he would decide cases; he replied, "By the law of the Qur'an." "But if you do not find any direction therein? " asked the Holy Prophet. "Then I will act according to the Sunnah of the Prophet," was the reply. "But if you do not find any direction in the Sunnah? " he was asked again. "Then I will exercise my judgement and act on that," came the reply. The Holy Prophet raised his hands and said, "Praise be to God Who guides the Messenger, His Apostle, as He Pleases."

The scope of *ijtihad* is very wide because it is a method of meeting the needs of the community which are not met expressly in the Qur'an and the Sunnah of the Holy Prophet. Qiyas (i.e., reasoning based on analogy) is an important method of *ijtihad,* through which jurists have tried to meet the needs of the Muslim community since the times of the Holy Prophet. When all, or the overwhelming majority of, the jurists agree, it is called *ijmah* (i.e., consensus of opinion among the jurists). But the source of all Law remains the Qur'an and the Sunnah of the Holy Prophet for all time to come, and if any problem is not covered by them, then the

---

1. *The Meaning of the Qur'an,* VOl. 11., p. 138.

jurists use their discretionary powers in the light of the two principal sources of the Islamic Law, i.e., the Qur'an and the Sunnah.

2. Inviolability of the Authority of Law

Islam established, for the first time on earth, the rule of one Law for all, irrespective of race, colour, creed or nationality. All citizens of the state were subject to the same law and no one was regarded as being above the Law. Citizens with wealth, status or privilege were treated the same as the humblest of the citizens of the state in subordination to the law. All stand equal in the eyes of the law, with no privileges or reservations for anyone. The Caliph and the beggar stand together for judgement before the law: "No believing man nor any believing woman should excercise any choice in their affairs once God and His Messenger have decided upon some matter. Anyone who disobeys God and His Messenger has clearly wandered into error" (33: 36). And in Surah Al-Nur we read: "The only statement believers should make when they are invited to God and His Messenger, so that He may judge between them, is: 'We have heard, and we are at your orders.' Those persons will be successful" (24: 51).

The Law of God is Supreme in the land and all are subordinate to it without exception: "O you who believe, obey God and obey His Messenger and those from among yourselves who hold authority; then if there is any dispute between you concerning any matter, refer it to God and His Messenger if you really believe in God and the Last Day. This is the best course and better as regards the final end" (4: 59). Thus the authority of God and His Messenger is the final authority in the Islamic State and no one is outside the Divine Law. If there is any dispute between the ruler and the ruled, both will be judged by the same Law on an equal basis, without giving any special favours to the former. The Holy Prophet explained this fundamental principle in these words :

"Even if Fatimah, daughter of Muhammad, had committed a theft, I swear by God, I would have cut off her hands." (2)

No one in the Islamic State has any power or authority to stop the enforcement or operation of any Law expressly stated in the Qur'an and the Sunnah of the Holy Prophet. In the enforcement of Law, the ruler and the ruled are alike, both being subject to it. Umar punished his son who committed adultery with a hundred stripes and he died during the punishment and a few remaining stripes were lashed on to his dead body. The law does not discriminate between the high and the low or between friend and foe but treats them all alike. "He is God Who has sent His Messenger with Guidance and the Right Way so that He may make it prevail over other ways, even though the unbelievers may not like it" (9: 33). This verse establishes the inviolability of the Law for all time and no one can oppose this Supreme Authority of the Divine Law in an Islamic society.

3. General Features of the Law

The most distinguishing and outstanding feature of the Law is that it covers every aspect of man's life, material as well as spiritual, individual as well as social, and leaves no area of his life unaffected. It deals with his personal duties to God in the form of worship, and also explains his duties to other human beings, e.g., to be polite, generous, friendly, etc. It discuss matters of law, trade and taxes as much as rules for the performance of prayer and pilgrimage; and then proceeds to give a long discourse on laws of war and peace and international law; and , further, it goes on to laws governing affairs of inheritance and wills. Thus the law deals with need of man, be it spiritual or material, legal ro social, and leaves no area of his life outside the scope of its regulation. In other words, it is all-comprehensive, and treats man as a whole, and

---

2. *Bukhari.*

gives instructions governing every field of his activities. It provides a complete code of life for man from the cradle to the grave. It meets the needs of his body as well as his soul and issues directions for the welfare of both, in private as well as in public. It discusses his problems as a member of one State, as well as international problems affecting various States, and gives directions for the right conduct of such affairs with justice and equity.

International relations have existed since older days but their relations have been governed more by politics and the discretions of the kings and rulers than by any set of rules. The Muslims were the first to separate international relations from politics and 'place them on a purely legal basis'. They collected all the forgotten international rules and developed them into a complete science. In times of war, very grave and barbarous acts and brutalities were committed by civilised nations against their enemies and no rule of conduct was adhered to by anyone. It was left to the Muslims to formulate the rights and obligations of the belligerents, which were enforceable by Muslim courts. They codified the rules and made them into a science of international law dealing with the behaviour of sovereign states in war and peace. (3)

Another feature of the Law is the importance given to a man's motive and intention *(niyyah)* in the performance of any act. This concept is based on the Hadith of the Holy Prophet: "Acts are not to be judged except by motives." And in a Hadith narrated by Umar ibn al-Khattab, the Holy Prophet is reported to have said, "Actions are but by intentions and every man shall have only that which he intended. Thus he who migrated for God and His Messenger had a different intention from him whose migration was to achieve some worldly benefit or to take some woman in

---

3. *Introduction to Islam,* op. cit., pp. 106-20.

marriage." (4) This concept has entirely changed the nature of the treatment for acts committed involuntarily as compared with those committed intentionally.

Another point to note is that the whole system of law is all written down. .The Holy Prophet received Revelations over a period of twenty three years, covering regulations with regard to multifarious problems, ranging from marriage and divorce to international relations and state matters. He handed it over to his successor and since then it has formed the basis of the Islamic Law.

4. Legislation and Interpretation of Law

As pointed out earlier, the Source of all Law in Islam is God, the Almighty, Perfect and Eternal. He Knows all, the present as well as the future and the hidden as well as the open. Therefore His Law is eternal and without any discrepancy and needs no amendments or abrogation. But the rules composing the Law are not all of the same nature and degree in application. Some of these rules are obligatory and must be obeyed under all circumstances, like those relating to murder, theft, fornication, etc. Some are only recommendatory, only suggesting certain action as good and beneficial, but not making it obligatory; while others are merely optional, leaving everything to the discretion or liking of the individual. In the last category of regulations, the Law gives great latitude to the individual to perform or abstain from them. It is left entirely to his personal choice. (3)

A cursory study of the Qur'an and the Sunnah will show that the first category of laws, i.e., obligatory ones, are very few in number; the recommendatory ones are a little more than those, but the third category of laws, which allow a wide range of choice in action to the individual, are numerous.

---

4. *Bukhari* and *Muslim* quoted in *Forty Hadith*, p. 26.

Another point with regard to these laws is their interpretation. Though the law themselves are unchangeable and eternal, they can be interpreted and adapted by the jurists according to circumstances. The last Messenger having gone from this life, there is no possibility of new Divine Law to settle problems in cases of a difference of interpretation on any issue. As the jurists are human and bound to differ in the interpretation of the Law of the *Shariah*, this provides opportunities for open and free discussion among them to find the most suitable solution of particular problems. (3)

Besides this, Divine Law exists in the original Arabic language as revealed to the Holy Messenger. The Arabic language itself is very eloquent, rich and profound in meaning and scope and when it comes from the Creator Himself, its richness and eloquency is increased many times, bearing a wide range of meaning and interpretation, thus unfolding innumerable opportunities for the jurists to find relevent and appropriate meanings and interpretations of the text to suit the changing needs of time and place. Thus the Islamic Law, though itself unchangeable and eternal, provides ample opportunities to the experts through interpretation and divergence of opinon to develop a system of law and adapt it to changing circumstances. This also opens up new vistas of research in law, thereby keeping the spirit of investigation fresh. And even though the source and basis of the Law are permanent, this process of interpretation and investigation will not let it become obsolete, out-dated or rigid. (3)

On the other hand, the fact that the Law is of Divine Origin itself inspires great respect, confidence and a sense of reverence for it in the people who observe and follow it conscientiously and scrupulously. And jurists' decisions made from a desire to find the truth will carry the same respect, because 'what Muslims consider good is good in the eyes of God'. (3) It is narrated by Abdullah bin Amr and Abu

Hurairah that the Holy Messenger of God said, "When a judge gives right decision, having tried his best to decide correctly, he will have a double reward; and when he gives a wrong decision having tried his best to decide correctly, he will have a single reward." (4) This establishes the superiority of the Divine Law over man-made law, first because of its infallibility, second, because of its great eloquence and profoundness; third, because of its popularity and conscientious and voluntary observance by the great mass of people; fourth, because of its natural sanction due to the great respect and awe it inspires in man; and fifth, because it offers great scope for investigation and research in its interpretation and adaptation according to the changing circumstances of time and place. This gives it great strength and stability, as well as the dynamism which leaves room for investigation to interpret the Divine Law to the best of their ability. They deal with the problem referred to them in the way in which, in their own judgement, it would have been dealt with by the Messenger of God, if it had been presented to him. (5)

5. Administration of Justice
Islam accords complete judicial autonony to the various sections of the community in order to protect and preserve their own personal and religious affairs. It allows every community to have its own tribunals to judge its civil as well as criminal cases and leaves it to the discretion of the parties to take the case to their own judicial tribunal or to the Muslim judiciary: "If they do come to you, either judge between them, or decline to interfere. If you decline, they cannot hurt you in the least. If you judge, judge in equity between them. For God loves those who judge in equity" (5: 45).

In order to administer justice fairly and equitably, Islam not

---

5. S. D. Islahi, *Islam at a Glance,* 134-37.

only eliminates long procedural intricacies and makes it simple and expeditious, but it also takes the necessary steps to purify the 'institution of witnesses.' This is the responsibility of every local tribunal which keeps a record of the conduct and habits of the people. The Qur'an renders all accusers who cannot prove their charges unworthy to testify before the judicial tribunals: "And those who accuse chaste women but bring not four witnesses (to support their allegation), flog them with eighty stripes; and never accept their testimony" (24: 4). (3)

The Islamic Law admits no exemptions in favour of anyone, including the Caliph (i.e., Head of the State). He is as much subordinate to the Law of the *Shariah* as any ordinary citizen of the State. Likewise, no exemptions are found in the Islamic Law in favour of foreign diplomats, ambassadors, rulers, etc. All are subject to the Law and no one is held to be above the Law. (3) Moreover, justice is administered free to everyone without any cost whatsoever.

The judiciary is completely independent of the executive. The judges or the *qadhis* are appointed by the executive but they are not subordinate to it. As soon as they are appointed they act independently of the executive and are responsible to God. Their only function is to administer justice within the Law of the *Shariah* without outside interference. (6)

The Nature of the Islamic Legal System

Islam has laid down universal and most equitable laws for mankind, covering all aspects of human activity, including protection of life and property, honour and religion, family life, inheritance and wills, marriage, divorce, war and peace, international relations, and every other sphere of human life. For a Muslim, religion is everything; if prevades his whole life, his home, his work and his business. His entire life is governed by Islamic principles, from the cradle to the grave. And this is precisely what non-Muslims, especially a Westerner entrenched in his own cultural and religious prejudices, finds hard to understand, much less to appreciate.

(i) There is a fundamental difference of approach to religion between a Muslim and Christian. A Muslim, unlike a Christian, believes that every word of the Holy Qur'an is the Word of God and that every word of Revelation to the Holy Prophet Muhammad 1400 years ago has been preserved without any change in the original text right down to the present

(ii) Every true Muslim obeys the Commandments of God and feels pleasure in the very act of obedience. Obedience to the word of God comes from within, spontaneously, and without external compulsion.

(iii) No Muslim can interpret the injunctions of the Holy Qur'an to suit his own ends. First, because the Holy Qur'an can be fully understood only with reference to the corresponding explanation or elaboration by the Holy Prophet; second, because every injunction of the Qur'an or Tradition of the Holy Prophet is fully explained in detail and supported by long established historical practice. Third, if any problem needs further elaboration or interpretation, it has to be explained and interpreted by those Muslims who are well versed in the Qur'an and the Sunnah of the Holy Prophet. Just as a lawyer is needed in matters relating to law and a doctor for medical problems. Only a Muslim scholar is competent to explain or interpret the injunctions of the Qur'an.

(iv) If some individuals express their views about Islam, they merely express their personal opinions; such isolated individual opinions can by no means be treated as genuine interpretations of Qur'anic injunctions. The fact that some Muslim men and women have adopted the social norms and

---

6. For details see under 'Muhammad as a judge, in the book entitled *Muhammad, Blessing for Mankind'* of the author.

ways of Western society does not make their behaviour Islamic.

11

The Educational System

The Meaning of Education

Education has been defined differently by different people each according to his own point of view. However, all agree on one point: that it is a process through which a nation trains its younger generation in the art of living and in fulfilling their purpose in life effectively and efficiently. This shows that education is more than mere public instruction. It is, in fact, a process through which a nation develops self-consciousness among its individuals and is able to pass on its cultural and intellectual heritage to future generations and inspire them with its ideology of life. Thus education is really a physical, mental and moral training of individuals to make them highly cultured men and women who will be able to discharge their duties as decent human beings and become worthy citizens of a state. This is the true nature and object of education and is fully supported by leading educationists of all times. (1)

According to John Stuart Mill, "Not only does education include whatever we do for ourselves and whatever is done for us by others for the express purpose of bringing us nearer to the perfection of our nature: it does more in its largest acceptation: it comprehends even the indirect efforts produced on character, and on the human faculties by things of which the direct purposes are quite different." And John

Milton said, "I call a complete and generous education that which fits a man to perform justly, skilfully, and magnanimously all the affairs, both private and public, of peace and war." A famous American educationist considers education as " the process of forming fundamental dispositions, intellectual and emotional, towards nature and follow men." (1)

According to Professor H. H. Horne, "Education is the eternal process of superior adjustment of the physically and mentally developed, free, conscious human being to God, as manifested in the intellectual, emotional and volitional environment of man." And professor Niblett writes that " the end of education is not 'happiness' but rather to develop greater capacity for being aware; to deepen human understanding, perhaps inevitably through conflict, struggle and suffering . . . to make right action natural." (1)

Thus education is a continous process of learning and assimilating by the younger generations of the cultural values and ideals of society. It is comprehensive process which embraces all aspects of the life of the younger generation and prepares them for the life-struggle ahead of them.

Liberalism and Religious Education
Religious education in the West has been greatly affected by liberalism. And in view of these developments, religious education is not to be regarded as a means of instructing young children in religious dogma, but rather as a way helping them to face their disappointments and problems by presenting them with opportunities to explore their emotions, thus enchancing and developing their feelings of wonder, joy and awe. Many teachers of religious education do not believe in religious education because, according to them, it is indoctrination and not open to critical study and leads to the point of view that it is impossible to find rational

grounds for the continued inclusion of religious education in the curriculum."

This line of approach has completely divorced education from the cultural aspect of life in Western society and rendered it absolutely impotent, meaningless and purposeless. Generation after generation have been coming out of schools and universities without any aim in life. All emphasis has been on the growth and development of the individual, to the detriment of religious aspects, which are as important as, if not more important than the individuality. This freedom in education and neutrality towards religious and moral issues has done more harm than good to humanity. Moral bankruptcy, obscenity and anarchy are the three popular fruits which society is reaping from its liberal concept of education.

It is obvious that education cannot be neutrat towards the culture and ideals of a people, as is advocated by the supporters of liberal education. If education is divorced from religion and moral values, it will lead to the disintegration and destruction of the social fabric of that society. This may be seen from the achievements of liberal education in the West as well as in the East. In the words of Walter Lippman, "The schools and colleges have been sending out into the world men who no longer understand the creative principles of the society in which they must live. Deprived of their cultural tradition, the newly educated Western men no longer possess in the form and substance of their own minds and spirits, the ideas, the premises, the rationale, the logic, the method, the values of Western civilisation —the present education is destined, if it continues, to destroy Western civilisation and is, in fact, destroying it." (1)

---

1. Lippman, Walter, *"The state of Education in this Troubled World"*, Speech, January 15, 1941 p. 200.

Professor Harold H. Titmus writes, "Even more serious than the lack of a common store of knowledge is the lack of common ideals and convictions. Education too frequently fails to build up any vital affirmations, convictions and discipline. There has been a dangerous separation of science and research from human values and loyalties — education has divorced itself from the spiritual heritage of the past but has failed to supply any adequate substitute. Consequently, even educated persons are left without convictions or sense of values, as well as without a consistent world-view." (2) According to Mr. M. V. C. Jeffreys, "The most serious weakness in modern education is the uncertainty about its aim. A glance over history reminds us that the most vital and effective systems of education have envisaged their objectives quite definitely, in terms of personal qualities and social situations. By contrast, education in the liberal democracies is distressingly nebulous in its aims." (3)

The Western liberal education has totally failed to give definite and precise objective or even to develop social ideas among students. It has also failed to inspire the new generation with moral and cultural values. It deals with material things and fails to provide the needs of the soul. Further, it has failed to organise knowledge into one consistent whole, with the consequence that students see life in small, unrelated parts and fail to understand its meaning and significance as a whole. Above all, modern liberal education has failed to produce men of understanding who fully grasp the fundamental issues of life. (4)

These weaknesses of modern education are becoming

2. Titmus, Harold H., *Living Issues in Philosophy,* pp.420-21.
3. M. V. C. Jeffreys, Glanon, *"An Inquiry into the Aims of Education"*, Pitman, London 1950, p. 61.
4. Khurshid Ahmad, *Principles of Islamic Education,* pp.2-27.

increasingly manifest and responsible persons in the West are beginning to feel its drawbacks. Dr. Albert G. Sims, Vice President, Institute of International Education, writes, "The central problem in U. S. education, to which all others are tangent, is that of defining and giving effect to objectives and philosophy. It is no answer to say to this that the educational system mirrors in these respects the society which it serves. Education is also the means by which a community must deliberately project the image of its future." (5)

The same thing is clearly pointed out by Rockefeller reports on U. S. education, in these words, "They (the students) want meaning in their lives. If their era, and their culture and their leaders do not or cannot offer them great meanings, great objectives, great convictions, then they will settle for shallow and trivial meanings. People who live aimlessly, who allow the search for meaning in their lives to be satisfied by shady and meretricious experiences, have simply not been stirred up by any alternative meanings – religious meanings, ethical values, ideas of social and civic responsibility, high standards of self realisation. This is a deficiency for which we all bear responsibility."

"We must assume that education is a process that should be infused with meaning and purpose, that everyone will have deeply held beliefs, that every young man will wish to serve the values which have nurtured him and made possible his education and his freedom as an individual." And Sir Walter Moberly writes, "Our predicament is this: most students go through our universities without ever having been forced to exercise their minds on the issues which are really momentous. Under the influence of academic neutrality, they are subtly conditioned to unthinking acquiescence in the social and political status quo and in a secularism on

5. Current History, September 1958, p. 174

which they have never seriously reflected. Owing to the prevailing fragmentation of studies they are not challenged to decide responsibly on a life-purpose or equipped to make such a decision wisely . . . . Fundamentally they are uneducated." (6)

Thus the experience of modern liberal education has clearly shown that the concept of neutrality in education is harmful to human values, culture and society and to its progress. Dicidedly, this concept takes society to secularism and gradually, but surely, to an irreligious and immoral life. It replaces all positive and moral values by material and immoral ways of life. And man becomes, in fact, a slave to his self and its desires.

Education in the Islamic system plays a positive role in moulding the character and influencing the morals of younger generations so that they can take an active and effective part in spreading the ideals and values of Islamic culture, both inside and outside their own social circles. It widens their horizon and vision of life and opens up unlimited opportunities of attainment: "And surely God is your goal and limit" (Qur'an). "This verse embodies one of the deepest thoughts in the Qur'an; for it defintely suggests that the ultimate limit is to be sought not in the direction of the stars, but in an infinite cosmic life and spirituality."

The system of education of each nation and each people represents its own social ideals, national traditions, cultural values and norms which are based on a positive view of life; it is therefore suicidal for others to imitate it. There is no harm or danger in learning new teachings and methods of education from other people's experiences. What is harmful is copying other people's educational systems. For in this way,

---

6. Moberly, Sir Walter, The *Crises in the University*. 1949, p. 70

you not only copy their educational system but their cultural values and social norms, which are part and parcel of their educational system. Whether it is done consciously or unconsciously, it is suicidal for a nation to copy another nation, especially for its younger generations.

The Purpose of Education

Education is not an end in itself but a means to an end. The end is to become something or achieve some objective. Most Western scholars also agree that it is through education that a people pass on their cultural and intellectual heritage to the future generation and inspire them with their own ideals of life. According to Dr. Iqbal, "The life of the individual depends on the relationship of the body and the soul. The life of the nation depends on the preservation of its traditions and culture. Individual dies if the life flow ceases and nation dies if the ideal of life is ignored. (4)

Parents generally give education to their children so that they may be able to secure a good job to earn their livelihood. Such education is only for livelihood. Some regard the acquisition of knowledge as the purpose of education. Others consider the service of the community or to make good citizens as the purpose of education. There are many others who enumerate different purposes of education about which there is no agreement.

But the end of education in Islam is to become an obedient and righteous servant of God. Education should turn the natural trends of the students in the right direction and enable them mentally, physically, morally and practically to become grateful servants of God. A person should be moulded through education in such a way that he always thinks, plans and acts according to the Will of his Creator and Sovereign — God. This in Islam is and should be the right, comprehensive and basic objective of education.

Education must instil in students the beliefs and ideals for which Islam stands. It must also try to preserve and promote the culture and basic principles of Islam. Even some Western scholars realise and emphasise this aspect of education. A. N. Whitehead was emphasising this point when he said that "the essence of education is that it should be religious." (7)

According to Dr. Iqbal, Islam should be the purpose of our life and education. He explained the meaning of *ilm* (knowledge) in a letter to one of his friends. He says, "By *ilm* I mean that knowledge which is based on the senses. This knowledge yields physical powers which should be subject to *din* (i.e., the religion of Islam). If it is not subject of *din* then it is evil, pure and simple. It is a duty of Muslims to Islamize knowledge. . . If it (knowledge) becomes subject to *din* then it will be a great belessing to mankind." (8)

This clearly shows that Islamic ideology is the purpose of education, according to Dr. Iqbal. He is of the opinion that education should be ideologically orientated and any education which is neutral towards religion is evil and satanic. His advice to the Muslim nation is that if they seek inspiration from Islam, they will assemble their scattered forces, regain their lost integrity and thereby save themselves from complete annihilation. (9)

The Qur'an has very clearly laid down this objective of Islam in these words. "It is He Who has sent among the unlettered ones a Messenger from among themselves, to recite to them His Signs, to purify them and to teach them the Book and

7. Vide, Hughes, *"Education: Some Fundamental Problems*, p. 86.
8. Dr. Muhammad Iqbal, *The Reconstruction of Religious Thought in Islam*, 131-32.

Wisdom, although they had been before in manifest error."
(62: 2) Then the Qur'an further clarifies this point while
explaining the function of the Prophets. "We indeed sent Our
Messengers with clear proofs, and sent down with them the
Book and the Balance (of right and wrong), that mankind
may stand forth in justice." (57: 25)

Thus the mission of the Prophets was to educate the people,
lead them to the Ways of God, teach righteousness and
establish a just and healthy society. The Holy Prophet was
also sent to improve the quality of life of the people: to
purify their morals, their habits and their customes of all evil
and to adorn their life with the best of attributes. The
purpose of education is, therefore, to discharge this prophetic
function − to educate the people in the religion of Islam,
inspire them with its Message and ideals and prepare them for
a full adult life. (4)

The Islamic Ideal of Education
The acquisition of knowledge and purification of the self are
the two essential ingredients of the Islamic system of
education. The source of all knowledge is God, who gives
knowledge to mankind through His Messengers. The
Messengers educate people in Islamic ideals and purify them
and prepare them to establish justive, benevolence and
goodness in society. This is the basic principle of Islamic
education. It gives importance to both knowledge and
training and regards both as indispensable to its objective. It
considers knowledge and purification of the self (through
training) as essential elements in its system of education.
Knowledge and character-building are considered to be two
sides of the same picture. Islamic education inspires young
men with deep convictions of the philosophy and ideology of

9. Saiydain, K. G., *"Iqbal's Educational Philosophy"*, Lahore
Lahore, 1942, p. 99, quoted by Khurshid Ahmad, op. cit.

Islam on an individual as well as on a collective level. It prepares the young generation, through Islamic ideology and Islamic philosophy, to fulfil the mission of the Prophet – to propagate the Message of Islam and establish a pure, just and healthy social system.

Thus the main function of Islamic education is to educate the young generation in the Divine Religion of Islam, develop in them the spirit and ideals of this religion and prepare them for a missionary life in the service of Islam. In the pursuit of this ideal, it is necessary to explain to students the Islamic viewpoint in the teaching of each and every subject. Particular care must be taken in the teaching of Western languages and sciences to scrutinise material so that un-Islamic (i.e., immoral, obscene, irreligious, etc.) matter is removed before teaching to the Muslim young generation.

Islamic culture, history and ideals should be described and depicted at each stage in the teaching of foreign languages and sciences so that Muslim students are not influenced by Western culture and Western ways of life. If the need is felt, such portions as depict or describe immoral or obscene stories or incidents or present irreligious and liberal views, will be deleted from the text books as well as supplementary reading books.

Likewise, in the teaching of the sciences, the concept of Tawheed that God is One and that He is the Creator as well as the Controller of all the Universe and its physical laws will be emphasised at every stage. They should be reminded at each stage that He is the Final Cause of all the causes.

The Main Characteristics of the Islamic Educational System;
The Islamic educational system has the following chief characteristics:

1. Acquisition of Knowledge: Basic Islamic teaching is compulsory for every man and woman. Every Messenger of God was given knowledge of this before everything else. The very first Revelation Muhammad received commanded him to acquire knowledge. "Read: In the name of your Lord and Sustainer, Who created – created man out of a mere clot of congealed blood." (96: 1-2)

Thus in very simple words, the basic message of Islam was given to the Prophet Muhammad in his first Revelation, which proclaims it the duty of the Messenger and all his followers to acquire knowledge of their Lord (i.e., Islam) and spread it among other people. The Holy Prophet himself declared that, "the acquisition of knowledge is the duty of every Muslim man and Muslim woman." (10)

2. Imparting Knowledge: The first leads to the second, which is the teaching of knowledge. It is also a salient feature of the Islamic educational system that it makes it essential for Muslims to impart the knowledge they have acquired to other people. "Acquire knowledge and teach it to other people." (11)

3. Moral Values: Spiritual and moral values are emphasised and given extraordinary importance. No efforts are spared to uphold and maintain these values under all circumstances. This was emphasised by the Holy Prophet when he said, "I am sent to perfect all moral values." (12) And on another occasion, the Holy Prophet said, "People will come to you to acquire knowledge from all directions; teach them good morals." (13)

4. The Pleasure of Allah and the Public Good: Knowledge is acquired and imparted to others not for any monetary

---

10. *Hadith.*
11. *Hadith.*
12. *Hadith, Muatta, Imam Malik.*
13. *Hadith, Tirmizi.*

compensation but for the good of society, and also merely
for the Pleasure of God. This view is based on many sayings
of the Holy Prophet quoted by Abu Daud, Ibn Majah,
Ahmad, Tirmizi, Darmi, etc.

5.   The Quest for Knowledge must become widespread: All
people, children and adults, literates and illiterates, are
encouraged to seek knowledge. Educational facilities in the
form of libraries, reading rooms, educational debates, ect.,
are provided so that people can continue their studies till the
last days of their life. It is reported that the Holy Prophet
said, "A believer's belly never becomes full with knowledge;
he keeps on storing it until he reaches the end of his life."

6.   Education according to the Suitability of the Pupil: In
the early days of Islam, education was imparted according to
the age, ability and aptitude of the child and every effort was
made to render the process of education easier for him. The
Holy Prophet has established the basic principle by saying,
"Provide ease and do not put people to hardship; give good
news and do not make them abhor you." (14) Ali, the fourth
Caliph, elaborated the same principle in these words, "heart
of people have desires and aptitudes; sometimes they are
ready to listen and at other times they are not. Enter into
people's hearts through their aptitudes. Talk to them when
they are ready to listen, for the condition of the heart is such
that if you force it to do something, then it becomes blind
(and refuses to accept it)." (15)

7.   The Development of Personality: The natural talents and
personal skills of each student are given ample opportunity to
develop and to become useful to the community. And each
child is regarded as a trust from God, and all his physical and
mental capacities and powers as gifts from Him. No stone is
left unturned to provide facilities for the proper and full
growth and development of the personality of each child.

---

14. *Hadith.*
15. *Kitab-al-karaj*, Abu Yusuf.

The whole Islamic system and its various organs are empolyed to direct each child to its right course – Islam.

8. Emphasis on Action and Responsibilities: Every student is inspired and pursuaded to put into practice his knowledge, for mere theoretical knowledge is of very little use, as point out by the Holy Prophet, "Knowledge is of two types, one that goes straight from the tongue into the heart. This is beneficial and useful knowledge. The other stays upon the tongue and will testify against man in the Court of God."(16)

The Islamic educational system also imparts true knowledge of individual, family and social responsibilities to each student and trains him to fulfil them in accordance with the Commandment of God and His Messenger.

Problems of the Curriculum and Syllabus
The purpose of education determines the nature and contents of the curriculum and syllabus. If the purpose of education is secularism, then the basis of its whole syllabus will be irreligious and secular and God and His Guidance will form no part of it. If the purpose of education is Communism, then atheistic philosophy will colour the entire curriculum, without any mention of God. Purpose of education of a people determines the content of its curriculum and syllabus.

As Islamic education is ideologically orientated, the nature and contents of its curriculum and syllabus will also be ideologically orientated. The beliefs and ideals of Islam will, therefore, determine its nature and contents.

1. *Tawheed* (Unity of God). God is the Creator, Cherisher, Master and Sovereign of the earth and the whole Universe.

----

16. Darmi.
17. Professor Smith, W. O. Lester, *"Education,* p. 25.

All human beings are His servants and, therefore, subject to His Laws. They are not independent beings who came into existence without any Creator. They are obliged to obey Him.

2.   *Risalat* (Prophethood). God sent His Messengers for the guidance of man. Muhammad was the last Messenger of God. Mankind can receive true and everlasting guidance only from His last Prophet and only thus establish a system of truth, justice and goodness on the earth.

3.   *Akhirah* (Life Hereafter). All human beings are destined to die and one day stand trial before their Lord for their omissions and commissions. The obedient and righteous will be awarded with permanent life in the Paradise, while the rebels and wicked will be punished with permanent life in hell.

4.   Concept of *Khilafat* (Vicegerent). The earth and the universe and all that is in it belongs to God and man is His vicegerent on earth. Therefore, the right attitude and course for him is to live here as His obedient servant and obey His Commands, encouraging good and forbidding evil and establishing justice, benevolence and goodness on earth.

The curriculum and syllabus should be designed on these lines. The basic doctrines of Islam should be taught in a way that their meaning, purpose and bearing upon individual and social life is fully understood by the students. They should also be taught the Islamic values of morality, the nature and content of Islamic culture and the duties and nature of their mission as Muslims. It should give special emphasis to the development of the individual personality of the student on proper and balanced lines. Islam stands for the golden mean and its ideal is the development of a balanced personality — the growth of the individual personality along with a sense of social responsibility.

Another feature of this curriculum should be emphasis upon the character-building of the student for "character-training is closely linked with the conception of school as a society." (17) Islam lays great stress on good deeds and unless education goes to build up good character, it will never achieve its real purpose. One of the fundamental functions of the Prophet was to purify human life and build good character.

As basic character traits are formed in the early stages of life, school education can play an important role in building up the character of the child. It is, therefore, absolutely necessary that the school curriculum should be designed to mould the character of the child on the Islamic pattern. Imam Ghazali has rightly pointed out that, "Education must not only seek to fill the young mind with knowledge, but must, at the same time, stimulate the child's moral character and stimulate him to the properties of social life."

The ideal character for a Muslim is that of the Holy Prophet. "Indeed in the life of the Prophet of God you have the best example to follow." (33: 21) It is thus desirable that important incidents from the life-style of the Holy Prophet should be quoted at all stages of school education. This could be supplemented by examples from the lives of the Companions of the Holy Prophet.

Islam stands for life-fulfilment and induces its followers to seek the best of both worlds. Islamic education, therefore, prepares the young generation for the struggle of life. It gives them education to earn an honest and decent living, trains them in the arts and crafts of living and caters for the multifarious economic, social and scientific needs of the community.

12

The Social System

Introduction:

The social order of Islam is based on the universal principle of human brotherhood and it endeavours to secure happiness, prosperity and goodness for both the individual and society. There is absolutly no place for class-war of any kind between individuals or between individuals and society in this system. Both individuals and society are responsible to God, Who created man from a single pair and will take account of their actions in this world. This philosophy of a common parentage and a common goal governs people's relationships and therefore calls for social solidarity and mutual responsibility. Thus the role of the individual is not contradictory but complementary to social welfare. He tries his utmost to work for the maximum good of society because he is responsible not only to society but also to God. Society looks after his interests and welfare, for which it is answerable to God. It is because of this sense of responsibility on the part of individuals and society that both work in great harmony, the former trying his best to enrich the latter while the latter provides security and care to the former. There is neither domination of the state over individuals to usurp their rights nor of individuals over the state to exploit and corrupt it. Mutual responsibility leads to an harmonious balance between rights and duties and results in constructive interaction between the individual and society. (1)

Another feature of this social order is co-operation of individuals in goodness and piety: "Co-operate with all in what is good and pious but do not co-operate in what is sinful and wicked" (5: 2). This enhances the importance of the role of the individual in society. The individual does not remain neutral or indifferent to society but plays a very effective role in spreading and establishing sound and high morals by inviting people to good and advising them to refrain from sin and evil: "Who enjoin what is right and forbid what is wrong and remain earnestly engaged in good deeds; these are the righteous people" (3: 114). People fully realise their responsibilities and therefore work harder to fulfil them by all the available and lawful means at their disposal. Their efforts towards the maximum good of society are encouraged by the knowledge that their reward is based on their own efforts in this world as well as in the Hereafter: "That man has only that for which he makes effort" (53: 39). And in Surah al-Baqarah says: "every soul is credited with whatever it has earned, while it is debited with whatever it has brought upon itself" (2: 286). And to further encourage positive behaviour of the individual, he is promised: "Anyone who comes with a good deed shall have ten times as much to his credit, while he that does evil shall be rewarded but the like thereof; and they shall not be wronged" (6: 160).

This points to another distinguishing feature of this social order. It is the value pattern set for the individual and society. At the top of the list comes the worship and obedience of One God; other values come after it and follow from it. All good and evil springs from this doctrine. Whatever God likes us to do is good for us and for society

1. *Islam in Focus*, op. cit., pp. 123-26.

and whatever He dislikes is bad for us and for society. Therefore the individual will endeavour to direct his efforts in accordance with the Divine Guidance; encouraging good and piety and discouraging evil and obscenity in society.

Thus the religious and social areas of the individual's life are very closely and inextricably bound together and it is impossible to separate the one from the other without destroying both. Islam offers a comprehensive social system, containing a complete code of life for man's conduct in every field of activity. It not only lays down rules governing his relation with God but also gives instructions regarding his relations with his fellow-beings. In fact, the worship of One God provides an opportunity to the individual to develop higher and finner moral qualities in himself, such as justice, kindness, forgiveness, generosity, and love of truth etc. What a miraculous change this philosophy of life brings into people's ideas and behaviour is shown by the speech of Jaafar, a leader of Abyssinian emigrants and a cousin of the Prophet, before the Negus: "O King, we lived in ignorance, idolatry and unchastity; the strong oppressed the weak; we spoke untruth; we violated the duties of hospitality. Then a Prophet arose, one whom we knew from our youth, with whose descent and conduct and good faith we were all acquainted. He told us to worship the One True God, to speak the truth, to keep good faith, to assist our relatives, to fulfil the duties of hospitality and to abstain from all impure, ungodly and unrighteous things. And he ordered us to say prayers, give charity and to fast. We believed in him, we followed him; but our countrymen persecuted us, tortured us and tried to cause us to forsake our religion." (2)

In the words of Sir William Muir: "What a change those thirteen years (in Makkah) has now produced — they now

2. Dr. A. A. Galwsh, *The Religion of Islam,* VOl.1. pp.105-7

lived under the constant sense of the ommipotent Power of God and of His providential care over minutest of their conserns. In all the gifts of nature, in every relation of life, at each turn of their affairs, individual or public, they saw His Hand. Muhammad was the minister of life to them, the source, under God, of their new-borne hopes, and to him they yielded an implicit submission."

This type of education and training of individuals helps to organise human relationships on the basis of co-operation, justice, mercy, love and goodness for the benefit of all people. The life-style of the people is built on moderation, while ostentatious luxuries and extravagance are condemned. They are also advised to abstain from futile and vain actions, for the Prophet said, "One of the hallmarks of a Muslim is that he abstains from useless things" (Tirmizi). This will keep them away from obscene and shameful acts which tend to impair their morals. And all sources of obscenity and licentiousness which are likely to encourage and spread sexual immorality are prohibited. In other words, this social order accepts and encourages everything that is good, right, useful and serves humanity but condemns and fights against all such cultures and civilizations which "consist of alcholic liquor-drinking, gambling, prostitution and oppression of the weak" (3)

The main characteristics of the social system of Islam are as follows.

1. Equality of Man

All mankind has the same parents. Adam and Eve . . . the first human pair on the earth and all human beings have sprung from this first father and mother. They originally had one religion and spoke one language. There were no differences of any sort between them and they all equally

---

3. M. Qutb. *Islam The Misunderstood Religion*. pp. 138-41.

enjoyed life and its benefits. There were no social prejudices or social injustices or special privileges for any person or group of persons or families in the beginning, for they were fully conscious of their common parentage and that they were the creation of One Supreme God: "O Mankind, fear your Lord, Who created you of a single soul, and of the same created his mate, and from that pair spread countless men and women over the earth; fear that God in Whose Name you demand your rights from one another, and abstain from violating relations between people." (4: 1)

But as time passed, their number increased and they gradually spread to different lands and different geographical areas. They became divided into different tribes and nations and adopted different customs and different ways of life. Geographical factors and climatic differences slowly changed their colours, physical features and languages. As a natural consequence of their diversification, they grew into different peoples and different nationalities, with almost different features and different manners and cultures, speaking different languages.

These differences are natural variations and Islam fully recognises them as a matter of fact. They help in knowing different peoples and distinguishing one from the other but should not lead to prejudices and privileges on the basis of colour, creed, race or nationality. Islam regards all such views as sheer manifestations of people's ignorance, for all come from the same parents and are brothers and, therefore, equal as human beings. The Holy Qur'an and the Sunnah of the Prophet Muhammad remind us of the eternal truth of the unity of Mankind by nature and origin. (4) This helps in completely eliminating racial pride and prejudices and claims of ethnic superiority, etc., and gives way to the growth of

---

4. Abul Ala Maududi, *Islamic Way of Life.* pp. 53-65

genuine feeling of human brotherhood among peoples of different regions.

Islam further stresses that there can be differences between people, not on the basis of their colour, race, nationaality and language, but on the basis of their beliefs, principles and ideologies. Thus two children of the same parents may have different ways of life according to their own beliefs and principles, though they are equal from the viewpoint of their common parentage. Likewise two persons living poles apart, and speaking different languages, and having different ethnic traditions and dress may follow the same way of life if they have identical beliefs and principles.

This forms the basic concept of the social system of Islam on which it aims to build an ideological society totally different from merely national and parochial societies. The basis of this society is neither colour nor race nor nationality but a moral code of life. Those who believe in One God as their Sovereign, Master and Lord and accept His Guidance, as revealed to His Prophet, as the law of their life, are members of this society, no matter what the colour of their skin, black, white or brown, what race they belong to, where they live and what language they speak. All these differences fade away when they declare their allegiance to One God and follow the teachings of His Messengers in their whole life, leaving no area of activity unaffected by their belief and moral code.

All members of this community enjoy equal rights and equal status. There are no social or racial prejudices or class privileges or any other kind of distinctions for any person or group or family in this social order, for all are equal members of the Islamic society: "The believers are but a single brotherhood." (49: 10) The Holy Prophet said: "Muslims are like a building; each constituent of which is a support for the others" (Bukhari). "In respect of natural love, compassion and kindness, Muslims are like a body which is in fever and feels discomfort if any of its parts is ailing" (Bukhari). And again: "Do not be envious of each other. Nor give a higher bid in auctions to raise the price, nor foster any ill-will against each other, nor abandon contacts with each other, nor interfere in the sale deeds of others to promote your interest — but be a good bondman of God and treat each other as brothers. Each Muslim is a brother unto the other. Neither does he commit any excesses on the other nor leave him helpless in the lurch, nor look down upon him. It is the bounden duty of each Muslim to respect the blood, property and honour of every other Muslim." (5)

This shows the nature of mutual relationships among people in the Islamic social order. They are one, like a strong concrete wall, one part strengthening and supporting the other part. This is because of their identical ultimate and final aim of life — belief in One God and in their final return to Him. Therefore, the sole purpose of their life is to worship and obey Him and follow His Way of life — establish a system of truth and justice on the earth, based on love, mercy and goodness and on brotherhood: "They are those who, if We establish them in the land, establish prayer, and give charity, enjoin right and forbid wrong; with God rests the end of all affairs." (22: 41). Again, in Surah Al-i-Imran: "Now you are the best community which has been raised up for the guidance of mankind; you enjoin what is right and forbid what is wrong and believe in God." (3: 110) Thus, in this community one's development will depend on one's moral conduct in excelling others in piety and goodness and not on one's social status or family connections.

This philosophy of life outstrips all geographical boundaries and limitations of colour, race, language, and nationality and

5. S. D. Islahi, *Islam at a Glance*, pp. 112-115.

is able to establish a cosmopolitan society based on human brotherhood. But this society will be quite different from racial or national societies, which are open only to the members of their own race or nationality and are closed to people who do not belong to their race or nationality. Islamic society is an ideological society and anyone who accepts its ideology and creed can become a member of it. Thus it can form a world-wide society whose members believe in one creed and follow one code of life, though belonging to different nationalities, races and ethnic groups. They all live in one way and enjoy the same rights but are scattered all over the world. In all their apparent diversifications and variations, they have unity of faith, unity of purpose and unity of final goal: "Those who embraced the faith and emigrated from their houses and expended their possessions and their lives in the Way of God, and those who gave refuge to the emigrants and helped them, are indeed the guardians of one another." (8: 72).

People who do not accept this creed and ideology are not of members of this society but are treated very liberally and generously. It gives them all the basic human rights as members of the human brotherhood and treats them with tolerance. Its relationship with such people is exactly like that of the two brothers, who have different views and ideas and follow different patterns of life yet nevertheless remain real brothers. Likewise, Islamic society will differ from other peoples and societies in its fundamental creed, ideology and organisation of its social order but will continue observing the common ties of human brotherhood. Hence it will develop all kinds of relationships with them and give them all the cultural and social rights on the basis of the common bonds of humanity.

2. The Structure of Social Life:
Islam has built the structure of social life on very high,

sound, rational and comprehensive principles. The structural edifice of social life, is pervaded by very deep and sincere feelings of love, goodness and brotherhood. The whole social life is a true picture of co-operation and mutual help. The Islamic ideology presentaed by the Holy Prophet through his unique personal example inspired his companions to great heights in social conduct and behaviour. The Holy Prophet said: "Whoever relieves a human being from grief in this world, God will relieve him from a grief on the Day of Judgement." He also said: "Anyone who has no mercy on the juniors nor respect for the seniors is not one of us Muslims." And: "None of you is a true believer in Islam until and unless he loves for his fellow men what he loves for himself." And his address at the Last Pigrimage gives eternal guidance for social scientists in matters of social behaviour.

The Family

In the Islamic social order, the family is the first and real unit of humanity and the real cohesive force which makes civilisation possible. A family is established through marriage and then it grows through ties of kinship into groups of tribes, clans and nations. It is the family which prepares and trains, with love and affection, the members of the young generation to discharge their social obligations with devotion, sincerity and enthusiasm and to maintain and develop human civilisation. It earnestly desires the future members of society to be better educated and trained than themselves and to be better equipped to maintain, develop and guard the cultural heritage of mankind.

Thus family is truly fountainhead of the progress, richness and strength of human civilisation. And all this owes its existence to marriage; without marriage, there would be no family and no ties of kinship to unite the different members of humanity, and, therefore, no civilisation. It is the family which holds humanity together and thereby makes human civilisation possible. It is because of the family's importance that Islam pays special attention to the social problems relating to the family and makes every effort to establish this primary scial unit on firm, strong and healthy foundations. (4)

In Islam, marriage is the only right form of relationship between man and woman, for it establishes a family and enables them to undertake and fulfil their social responsibilities conscientiously, with devotion and sincerity. The purity, goodness and richness of human civilisation depend on the goodness, piety and purity of the members of the primary unit of the social order, which is the family. Therefore Islam lays great stress on it and takes various practical legal and other measures to build the family on a sound and proper footing.

First, it ensures that social life starts with the establishment of a family through marriage, for it considers it not only a physical necessity but also a religious duty. It therefore encourges marriages of young people and condemns the life of celibacy: "Marry those among you who are single, or the virtuous ones among your slaves, male or female; if they are in poverty, God will give them means out of His Grace." (24: 32). Again in Surah al-Nisa we read: "Marry, of the women who seem good to you, two or three or four." (4: 3) And those who are unable to marry are advised to be virtuous (24: 33). The Holy Prophet greatly strengthened this institution by encouraging marriage among young people: He said: "Marriage is my way (Sunnah); whoso loves my conduct should follow my way; and whoso strays from may way is not for me." Again, he said: "Whosoever amongst you can afford to marry must marry, for it makes a man modest and chaste." (5) He also said: "Marry women who will love their husbands and be very prolific, for I wish you to be more numerous than any other people." And again: "All young men who have reached puberty should marry, for marriage protects them against intemperance." On an other occasion he remarked: "When a Muslim marries he perfects half of his religion, and he should practice righteousness to secure the remaining half."

Secondly, Islam forbids all sexual relationships outside marriage and takes measures to stop this happening, and if it has happened, then it prescribes severe punishments for the offenders. It condemns adultery in very severe words (25: 68), and takes preventive measures against it. It advises men and women to be modest and lower their gaze and to women not to display their adornment and beauty in public (24: 30-30-31. Women are further advised not to entertain and talk unnecessarily to men who are not their close relatives (33: 32). Free mixing of men and women is forbidden (33: 59) and, in general the sphere of women's activities is limited to their homes (33: 33). Both men and women are commanded not to enter other people's houses without permission (24: 27). The propagation of obscenity and evil is prohinited (24: 19). Other instruments and means of obscenity and sensuality, such as gambling and drinking, are also prohibited (5: 90). (6) Instead, a moderate style of living and eating is encouraged (25: 67). When the crime against the sanctity of marriage has occurred, Islam prescribes a very severe punishment as a lesson for other and as a deterrent (24: 2-3 and 4-10).

The aim of all these measures is to purify society of all activities which encourage irresponsible actions and provide opportunities for them, so that the institution of the family is protected and strengthened. Any action which is likely to damage, harm, cause friction or split the family is condemned. For this purpose, Islam has laid down very

---

6. For details see the author's book entitled, *"Economic Doctrines of Islam*, VOl. 111.

accurate, profound and exhaustive rules and regulations to protect the family against any infringement of its rights. This strong surrounding fence of laws and guidance provides proper and desirable security and safety to the family, so that its members are able to lead a life of goodness, piety and prosperity. As the family is the foundation-stone of society and human civilisation, its goodness and prosperity will enhance the goodness and richness of society and human civilisation.

In view of its importance, Islam does not merely regard family life as desirable but considers it virtuous and an act of worship *('ibadah)* and dislikes celibacy and urges young persons to shoulder the social responsibilities of married life. Likewise it does not merely regard asceticism as no virtue but condemns it as unnatural and a deviation from the natural course of man and an act of rebellion against the Divine Way of life. At the same time, it makes marriage easy and simple and strongly disapproves of those ceremonies, rites and restrictions which tend to make marriage a long and difficult affair. In this respect, it has destroyed all myths of noble birth, caste, family and wealth and allowed marriage between any Muslim man and Muslim woman provided they both agree and give their consent. In a simple ceremony in front of two witnesses, they can become husband and wife, but they must publiscise this news so that people know that they are now living a matrimonial life. (4)

In order to further strengthen the bonds of family and develop love and affection between husband and wife and cement relations between them, Islam has given various instructions and directions. These are also meant to preserve their morals and enable them to live in comfort, peace and happiness so that they are able to fulfil to the maximum the aims and objectis of human culture and civilisation by their joint actions (30: 21, 7: 187). In cases of mutual disputes and differences, they are advised to resolve them with affection and understanding and not to take any hasty action (4: 129-130). In all such circumstances kindness and equity is recommended, especially to the husbands (2: 229 and 4: 19). They must try their best to live with love and affection and show kindness towards each other, even in disputes, but if they cannot continue to live amicably, they are advised to separate on equitable terms (2: 231 and 65: 2). Husbands are especially advised to be generous and liberal in their dealings with their wives (2: 237).

In order to maintain discipline, the husband is assigned the position of protector and maintainer of the family (4: 34), but is given very strict instructions to be just and benevolent (2: 226-227) and fulfil his duties with equity and willing co-operation (4: 4) and never to keep his wife merely to injure her or take undue advantage of her (2: 231). He is allowed to take more than one wife, provided he can do justice between them. Otherwise he must keep only one wife (4: 3). But if he marries more than one wife, he must treat them all alike and must not keep any of them in a state of suspense (4: 129). Likewise, wives are advised to be loyal and obedient to their husbands (4: 34) and should not let anyone enter their houses whom their husbands do not like. Taking into account the practical problems of life, both the husband and the wife are given due rights based on equity, justice and benevolence.

The object of all these instructions and rules is not only to strengthen and protect the bonds of matrimonial relationship, but also to build it on the sweetness of love, understanding and mutual respect. When this spirit of companionship and affection is missing, both the husband and the wife are given the right to separate (2: 226-227)

Parents and Relatives:

The limited family circle widens into kinship through the blood relationship with common parents, to include brothers, sisters, uncles and aunts and relations by marriage. Islam enjoins fair and friendly treatment of all relatives within the limits of justice and considers this an act of great virtue and goodness. Again and again the Qur'an emphasises kind and liberal treatment of one's near relatives. First in importance in the line of relatives come the parents.

Parents: The Qur'an enjoins good treatment of parents: "We have enjoined every man to look after his parents; his mother bears him in travail upon travail" (31: 14). And in Surah al-Ahqaf: "And We have commanded man to be kind to both his parents. His mother bears him painfully, and give birth to him painfully." (46: 15). And again in Surah Bani Isra'il: "Your Lord has decreed that you should worship none except Him, and show kindness to your parents . . . Serve them with tenderness and humility." (17: 23-24).

Relatives: Islam has also given detailed instructions to Muslims to be kind and friendly to their relatives: "God commands justice, kindness and giving their due to near relatives." (16: 90). And in Surah sl-Baqarah we read: "It is righteousness . . . to give one's wealth away in charity, no matter how one loves it, to near relatives . . ." (2: 177). The Prophet was once asked, "Who is the best person?" He replied, "One who fears God and keeps the best connections with his relatives." Abu Zar reported that the Prophet said, "Keep good relations with relatives, even though they treat (you) badly." The Prophet also said: "Charity to a poor man counts as one merit and charity to a poor relative counts as two marits." (7)

Neighbours: After obligations to relatives, come obligations to one's neighbours. Islam has also enjoined fair treatment, affection and courtesy to one's neighbours: "And worship

God and ascribe no partners to Him. And show kindness to parents and to neighbours." (4: 36). Abu Hurairah reported that the Holy Prophet said, "Let him who believes in God and the Last Day be generous to his neighbour." (8)

The Holy Prophet said that the rights of neighbours were so strongly emphasised to him by the Angel Gabriel that he feared that they might have a right to share in one's inheritance. He also said, "Treat your neighbour well, be a (good) Muslim." He also said, "Do you know your duties to your neighbour? Help him if he seeks your help; give him a loan if he wants it; remove his need, if he is in need; follow his funeral if he dies; give him joy if he gets good news; show him sympathy and express sorrow if he is in danger; don't erect your building without his permission so high as to obstruct his air; don't give him trouble. If you purchase some fruits, give him something. Don't give him trouble by the smoke of your cooking." (7)

This shows how close and loving a relationship Islam wants to build between neighbours, so that they may share their joys and sorrows and their wealth and poverty. This deep, loving relationship can go far in building a society on a healthy and strong foundation.

The General Community:
After family and neighbours the circle of relationships widens to cover the entire community. Islam lays great stress on its members fulfilling the duties they owe to the community and caring for the rights of its members. They must co-operate with all in acts of virtue and goodness, and not co-operate in acts of vice and injustice (5: 2). And they must act as friends to one another (9: 71) and say kind things to other people

7. *Mishkat.*

(2: 83). They are required to greet others with peace and blessings (6: 54) and return other's greeting with something even more courteous, or at least equally courtesy (4: 86). They are also advised to set things right between their brother Muslims (49: 10) and to remain a united family by means of the rope God holds out and not to be divided (3: 103).

Respect for other people's feelings and honour is enjoined; "O believers, do not let one set of men make fun of another set of men; perhaps the latter are better than the former. Nor let any set of women make fun of other women; perhaps the latter are even better than the former. Nor should you defame yourselves nor insult one another by using nicknames; it is bad to use an evil name after entering the faith of Islam. Those who do not desist from it are wrongdoers." (49: 11) The Holy Prophet said: "None of you truly believes until he wishes for his brother (Muslim) what he wishes for himself." (8) He also said: "The Muslim society is like a body in respect of mutual love and sympathy. If a limb of the body suffers pain, the whole body responds to it by sleeplessness and fever." And he said: "The relationship of one believer to another believer is like that of a building one part of which strengthens another."

Many similar traditions are reported which describe the duties of a Muslim to other Muslims and their mutual love and brotherhood: "Don't give trouble to a Muslim by your words and actions and treat him with kindness; be modest to one another and don't be proud to one another; give up disputes and quarrels; do good to everyone, deserving or undeserving; speak nicely with everyone; live with people with a smiling face and a kind heart; fulfil your promises to people and do justice to them and help them at a time of distress and calamity." (7)

---

8. *Mishkat.*

Such teaching helps to build a society to very high standards of goodness, benevolence and justice and guarantees peace and happiness to its members, who work with great devotion and love for the enrichment of its culture and civilisation.

The International Community:

At the top of the ladder come human relationship on an international level. As someone has rightly said, if the first brick is wrongly placed the whole building right up to the sky will be crooked. When the first unit of human civilisation (i.e., the family) is established, developed and brought up on sound, healthy and right foundations, the whole civilisation prospers and develops on healthy lines.

Islam, which cares so much for the goodness and richness of the first and primary unit of human civilisation, cannot be expected to ignore or undermine the value and importance of the whole of humanity. It has put great emphasis on right and proper conduct to purify international relationships of all injustice and other evil, in order to establish peace and security in the world, so that mankind may live in peace, goodness and happiness.

Islam's international relations are based on the fact that all mankind have a common origin and therefore as human beings are equal. Islam, therefore, respects other people's interests and rights and tries to maintain friendly and cordial relations with them (4: 1, 2: 190-193 and 42: 42).

Islam enjoins mutual respect for agreements and pacts between nations and peoples (16: 91; 9: 4) and emphasises honesty and intergrity in all dealings, whether personal, national or international (16: 92). It commands justice and equity to enemies, and a policy of neutrality to non-combatants is respected (4: 89-90). At the same time, every effort is made to establish and maintain peace (8: 61).

This shows clearly that an Islamic society truly believes in God and endeavours to establish His Law and His Way on the earth. Its members themselves work righteous deeds, practise justice and goodness in their personal lives and invite others to truth, goodness, benevolence and justice (103: 1-3; 3: 110), and they say: "I believe in what God has sent down in the form of the Book, and have been commanded to deal justly with all of you. God is our Lord as well as your Lord. We have responsibility for our actions and you for yours; no quarrel exists between us and you. God will bring us (all) together; to Him is the return (of us all)" (42: 15).

The Position of Women:

At the time of the dawn of Islam, women all over the world were degraded, subjected and without any rights and were considered as non-entities. Since the beginning of the industrial revolution, they have been asserting their rights in the Western countries and have now been given certain political and economic rights. But Islam recognised women's position fourteen hundered years ago and granted them their due rights and privileges, which are not enjoyed by women in other faiths and societies even in this modern industrialised age.

Social Life

Islam recognises women as an equal and full partner to man in their matrimonial relationship. Man is the father and woman is the mother in the household and the role of both is equally essential for this life. Both enjoy equal rights and undertake equal responsibilities: "O mankind! Be careful of your duty to your Lord Who created you from a single soul and from it created it mate and from them twain has spread a multitude of men and women." (4: 1). They are equal in nature and in origin: "And God has given you mates of your own nature, and has given you, from them, children and grandchildren, and has provided good things for you." (16:

72; 42: 11).

Woman's Rights as a Wife

She enjoys absolute equality as an equal member of the family unit. In certain ways her position as wife and as mother is unique and of great honour and distinction. As a wife she is the queen and mistress of the household and the status of the husband is determined by the way he treats her: The Holy Prophet said, "The best among you is the one who is best to his wife, and I am the best among you to my family." (Mishkat). He also said: "Among the believers who show most perfect faith are those who have the best disposition to, and are kindest to their families" (Mishkat).

In the Farewell Message on the occasion of the Last Pilgrimage, the Holy Prophet spoke of the rights of women at great length and said: "O people! Surely there are rights in favour of your women which are incumbent upon you, and there are rights in favour of you which are incumbent upon them." And he ended the message with the words: "Have therefore fear of God with regard to women, and I enjoin you to treat them well." (9) The Qur'an clearly states: "And they (women) have rights similar to those of men over them according to what is equitable (2: 228).

As wife, a woman is the source of joy, pleasure, delight and comfort for her husband and the center of all worldly attractions for him. He seeks peace and happiness through her and she enjoys comfort, peace and security in his company: "Among His Signs is the fact that He has created mates for you from among yourselves so that you may console yourselves with them. He has planted affection and mercy between you; in that are Signs for people who reflect." (30: 21). And in Surah al-A'raf we read: "He is the

9. *Mishkat.*

One Who has created you from a single soul, and made its mate from it, that he might find comfort with her." (7: 189).

And the Holy Prophet has wonderfully summed up the mutual relationship between husband and wife in these words: "Abu Hurairah said that when God's Messenger was asked which woman was best, he replied, ' The one who pleases her husband when he looks at her, obeys him when he demands (something), and does not go against his wishes regarding her person or property by doing anything which he disapproves' " (Mishkat). In fact, as his help-mate and comforter, she makes man's stay on earth a pleasanter, easier and more worth-while experience.

Marriage is a sacred contract and is formed by the free consent of both the man and the woman. The woman can refuse if she does not like or approve of the match. The parents may, and do, suggest and select the life-partners for their young sons and daughters, but the final word in the matter rests with the latter. "No widow should be married without consulting her; and no virgin be married without her assent, and her assent is her silence" (Bukhari and Muslim).

In all kinds of family disputes, men and women are treated alike: "If you fear a split between a man and his wife, send for an arbiter from his family and an arbiter from her family. If both want to be reconsiled, God will adjust things btween them." (4: 35). Other family matters, regarding their children, are also decided by mutual consultation and agreement: "If the (husband and wife) desire to wean the child by mutual consent and after consultation, there is no blame on them." (2: 233).

Just as she has the right to decide her marriage, so she enjoys the same right to seek to end the marriage that has not been successful. However, at all moments, husbands are advised to treat their wives politely, even if they don't like them, because it is just possible that you dislike something but God placed some good in it for you. (4: 19). They are enjoined to be kind to their wives even when they have finally decided on separation (2: 231).

Woman's Rights as a Mother

Woman's position as mother is unique in a Muslim society. She is the focus for all members of the family. She enjoys great esteem and respect from all and all come to her to pay their respects on all important occasions, and her opinions and suggestions carry great weight in all family matters. According to one tradition: "Even Paradise lies beneath the feet of your mothers." According to a report of Al-Bukhari: "Someone asked the Prophet which work pleased God most. He replied, "The offering of prayer at the appointed time." When the question was asked and what after that pleases God most?' the Prophet replied: 'Your parents.' "

It is reported by Abu Hurairah that a man asked the Prophet of God: "Who is the most deserving of friendly care from me?" He replied: "Your mother." Again he asked who came next and the Holy Prophet replied "Your mother."The man again asked who came next and the Holy Prophet replied, "Your father." (Mishkat).

The Qur'an regards kindness to parents as next to the worship of God (17: 23). but has laid special emphasis on the treatment of mothers: "And We enjoined upon man (to be good) to his parents: his mother bears him in travail upon travail." (31: 14 and 46: 15).

Rights of the Female Child:

Female children used to be buried by some Arabian tribes but this is condemned by Islam. "When news is brought to one of them of the birth of a female child, his face darkens and he is filled with inward grief. With shame does he hide himself from his people because of the bad news he has had. Shall he retain her on sufferance and in contempt or bury her in the dust? Ah! What an evil choice they decide on!" (16: 58-59) Such parents will suffer their fate on the Day of Judgement: "And when the famale (infant) buried alive is questioned, for what crime she was killed . . . " (81: 8-9)

Islam stopped this practice and instead enjoined kind and fair treatment to girls. The Prophet said: "Whoever has a daughter and does not bury her alive, does not insult her and does not favour his son over her will be received by God into Paradise." And he also said: "Whoever supports two daughters till they mature, he and I will be on the Day of Judgement like this (and he put two fingers close together)" (Ibn Hanbal).

Women and Spiritual Life:

Islam regards both men and women as equal and promises equal rewards to them for their efforts: "So their Lord accepted their prayers, (saying): 'I will not suffer to be lost the work of any of you, whether male or female. You proceed from one another.' " (3: 195). And in Surah al-i-Imran we read: "Whoever works righteousness, man or woman, and has faith, surely to him We give a new life that is good and pure, and We will bestow on such their reward according to the best of their actions." (16: 97 and 4: 124).

And again in Surah Al-Ahzab: "Lo! Men who surrender to God, and women who surrender, and men who believe, and women who believe, and men who obey, and women who obey, and men who are truthful, and women who are truthful, and men who persevere in righteousness, and women who persevere in righteousness, and men who are humble, and women who are humble, and men who give charity, and women who give charity, and men who fast, and women who fast, and men who guard their modesty, and women who guard their modesty, and men who remember God, and women who remember God — God has prepared for them forgiveness and a great reward." (33: 35).

These verses of the Qur'an explictly state the absolute equality of men and women in matters of the reward for their efforts — each will earn the reward for that he or she has done in this world, for in the sight of God they, as human beings, are equal and will reap what they have sown. "O mankind! Lo! We have created you male and female . . . The noblest of you, in the sight of God, is the best in conduct." (46: 13).

Women and Economic Life:
Islam recognises woman's right to inherit, to have money and own property, whether single or married. She can buy, sell, mortgage or lease any or all of her property. She inherits property, including land and real estate, from her parents, brothers and husbands: "To men (of the family) belongs a share of that which parents and near kindred leave, and to women a share of that which parents and near kindred leave, whether it be little or much — a determinate share." (4: 7).

She keeps her property acquired before marriage and has no legal obligation to spend on her family out of her personal wealth. She is also entitled to a dowry *(mehr)* from her husband. She may invest her property in any way she likes or thinks best. She is quite independent and even keeps her maiden name and does not merge it after marriage with her husband's, as happens in Western, African and Asian countries.

Women And Education:
Women have the same rights as men in the acquisition of knowledge and education. The Holy Prophet said: "The

search for knowledge is a duty for every Muslim, male or female. Seek knowledge from the cradle to the grave."

And knowledge in Islam is not divided into religious and secular knowledge. It is the duty of every Muslim man and Muslim woman to acquire any knowledge which is useful and not futile in order to benefit them and to enrich human culture and civilisation with its applications to life. The acquisition of knowledge is essential for both men and women, not only to know God with all His Attributes, but also to learn His Teaching so that they may find out what is the right and proper way of life for them. And this duty falls as much upon women as it does upon men, because they are equally responsible and accountable for their omissions and commissions on the Day of Judgement. Unless they acquire this knowledge how can they possibly follow the Way of God?

Thus both men and women are equal as far as the learning of knowledge in general is conserned. However, in the actual selection of professional or technical subjects women may have to learn different subjects from those of men, to suit their own physiological, biological and practical needs and functions. This is only reasonable in view of their functional differences.

Legal and Civil Rights:
In the eyes of law, both sexes are equal and are treated alike, the same legal penalties being imposed on both men and women for breaking any moral or legal laws. Both enjoy equal rights and privileges as members of the Islamic society. In civil life, women lead exactly the same life, with the same rights and obligations as men. However, women enjoy certain privileges and exemptions because of their physiological and biological functions. They are exempt from some religious duties, such as prayer and fasting during menstrual periods

and during confinement and are permanently exempt from obligatory congregational prayer on Friday. They are also exempt from all financial liabilities.

Conclusion:
The above clearly shows that the rights and duties of women are equal to, but not necessarily indentical with, those of men. In certain areas women enjoy privileges denied to men. However, the fact of being a woman does not in any way affect her human status, or independent personality, nor does it justify any prejudice against her or injustice to herself. Islam has granted women rights and duties in a most balanced way that match and suit her functions in society and she is held in great esteem and honour in all her positions, from childood to motherhood. She enjoys certain rights over men and men have certain rights over her (2: 228) and the overall position of woman is honourable and noble in the sight of God as well as in the eyes of Islamic society.

It may, however, be pointed out that although woman, as a human being, occupies equal status with man and is treated as equal, and enjoys equal rights, privileges etc., the fact remains that there is a difference between the sexes. No amount of debating or discussion, physical excercise or hard industrial work can change her sex. As woman, her special function in life is different from that of a man and she is naturally equipped with a different physical, physiological, biological, and even psychological structure. Islam has taken these natural differences between the sexes into accout in differentiating roles and allotting functions to each sex. Therefore to talk of absolute equality between men and women is complete nonsense. Their general equality as human beings is quite natural and reasonable because men and women are two complementary parts of humanity proceeding from common parents. But to assign them equal or similar functions in life is preposterous because it is physically impossible to interchange their functions, e.g., men sharing in conception, birth, suckling, etc. Islam has therefore given due allowance to these factors and treated men and women on the basis of equality where there is a natural scope for it, and differentiated between them where such differentiation is in accordance with nature. (10)

Let us discuss in what respect Islam differentiates between men and women. First, take the case of inheritance, where Islam allows the male to inherit as much as two females (4: 11). It is an established fact that man alone has to shoulder all the financial responsibilities of the family. He is legally and morally responsible for maintaining his wife and family. The wife has no legal obligation to spend any part of her personal wealth on the family. She need spend it only on her own personal needs and may use it as pocket-money. It is therefore natural that a man should get more than a woman, to enable him to meet his extra financial obligations. However, in earnings there is absolute equality; in wages for labour, profit from trade or revenues from real estate, etc., Islam maintains equality between men and women. But it would be wrong to conclude from this inequality in inheritance that Islam regards woman as no better than half a man.

Second, there is the problem of headship of the family. Like any other institution, the family needs a responsible head who can control and maintain proper discipline in the house. Now the question is, which of the two parents is better equipped and more suited to shoulder the responsibilities of headship? Woman is, by her very nature, emotional, fickle-minded and susceptible to outside influences, especially during menstruation. She is also physically and constitutionally weak and so less able to fulfil the demands of this position. Besides it would be too heavy a burden to give her extra responsibilities over and above the function of being a mother. But this does not make man an absolute dictator over his wife and the family, because this relationship is a personal relationship and its success depends more on their personal conduct and attitudes than on outside factors. It depends, first, on the personal and physical harmony between the husband and the wife. If one of them does not like the countenance of the other, no matter what the other does, they will find it difficult to come to terms. Second, on the psychological and rational level, harmony between them is necessary. Sometimes, the couple cannot manage to live together because they are temperamentally different and, therefore, cannot accommodate each other. The Law cannot secure any of these things for them. Third, it requires love, mutual understanding and perpetual sympathy for each other, especially of the man for his wife (4: 19). And, above all, success in such personal relationships depends on mutual consultation, love and co-operation rather than on the dictatorial powers of one partner. (10)

Woman can, however, play her proper and constructive role in the family, as well as in society, only if she responds to her natural instincts; if she tries to equate herself with man and endeavours to express manly instincts in her conduct, she will fail in playing the role which nature has assigned to her. But if woman par excellence fails in her duty to play her role as a mother in the development of human personality, it will indeed be a loss to the entire human race,especially if she wastes her energies in the futile and irrelevant effort to find the answer to the old-age question: "Who is superior — man or woman?" (11)

Islam has given woman her true position and put her on a

---

11. A. K. Brohi, *Islam in the Modern World,* pp. 126-129.

level with man, where both are treated as one in honour, influence and love, where children are a common bond of concern, attention and affection and where family matters are decided by love and mutual consultation and not by sheer force. And this way of life proceeds from the understanding of the family relationship, with the full realisation that men and women are different but complementary. Both need each other and depend upon each other. She provides him with comfort and in turn receives love and comfort from him. Thus she is there to co-operate and not to compete with him. The more she realises this and plays her natural role the more will she become indispensable to her partner. This natural, healthy and constructive, co-operative role between man and woman will enrich society, as well as human culture and civilisation in general — it is the human ideal. (11)

Social Justice:
The concept of social justice in Islam is very comprehensive and covers every aspect of human activity, but it cannot be properly understood until the meaning of the basic concept of Islam, i.e., *Tawhid* (Unity), and its implications concerning man and his relationship with the universe and humanity, is thoroughly grasped. This is because social justice is a part of the whole concept of *Tawhid,* which is the basis of the entire teaching of Islam. The Islamic concept of life is all-comprehensive and treats all areas of human activity as a unity and not as unrelated parts of human life, as explained earlier in this book. The concept of life presented by Islam is a complete whole which revolves round the fundamental concept of *Tawhid.* A knowledge of this universal concept enables man to understand the basic principles of Islam and its laws and thereby the relationship between any particular aspect of human life and the fundamental principles of Islam. It will be far easier to understand particular problems of social justice, politics, economics or the relationship between man and society if an effort is first made to understand

the all-embracing concept of *Tawhid,* the universe, life and humanity. And this must be studied and sought for in the original and only true sources of the Islamic concept, i.e., the Qur'an and the *Sunnah* (lifestyle) of the Holy Prophet. (12)

The Basis of Social Justice

Islam has clearly explained the nature of the relationship between the Creator and His creation, between man and the universe and between man and man. It has also thrown sufficient light on his relationship with society and the state and the relationship between different societies and nations. According to Islam, all these relationships are based on the fundamental and universal truth of *Tawhid* (Divine Unity) (12): "Everything in the Universe is running its course to its fixed term. And God alone is directing the whole affair. He makes His Signs plain, that you may be convinced of meeting your Lord." (13: 3). This points to two signs. First, that there is only one Creator and Administrator of the Universe; second, that there will be a Day of Judgement when rewards and punishments will be given to people according to their merits.

God is incharge of the whole Universe and organises, conducts and sustains all affairs and things Himself and there is no intermediary between the Creator and His creation: (12) "Blessed be He in Whose Hands is the Kingdom, and He has Power over all things." (67: 1). Thus everything in the world is controlled and directed by One Supreme Power, forms a perfect unity and works in perfect harmony. The whole scheme of creation is based on Wisdom and every part of it fits in to this perfect order: "He has created everything and ordained for it a measure." (25: 2). In Surah al-Qamar we read: "Surely We have created all things in proportion

---

12. S. Qutb, *Islam, its meaning and Message,* pp. 117-30.

and measure." (54: 49). Again, Surah al-Malik says: "He Who created seven heavens in harmony (one above another). You do not see any fault in the creation of the Beneficent. So look again; can you see any fault? Then look again and yet again; your sight will come back to you dazzled and weary." (67: 3-4).

All these verses of the Qur'an show the great wisdom behind Creation and the perfect harmony in which everything operates and fits into the same scheme and purpose and that everything is constantly under the direct control and direction of God's Absolute Will and Power, Who makes it exist in harmony with, and for the benefit of, all His Creation. As such, the universe and all that is in it cannot be hostile to life or to man; nor can nature be considered opposed to him and working against him. Everything, being the Creation of God, is rather helpful and friendly because its aims and purposes are the same as that of the life and mankind. Likewise, it is neither the purpose nor function of man to compete and fight with nature because he has grown up in her bosom, and both form an integral part of the Creation of God. There is no doubt, therefore, that man lives in very friendly surroundings, among the forces and powers of a friendly and co-operative universe. When God created the earth, "He set therein firm mountains over it, and blessed it, and measured therein all things to give them sustenance in due proportion." (41: 10).

All things on the earth and in the heavens are a part of the Creation of God and, therefore, each is very co-operative, friendly and harmonious with other parts of God's creation. Man, being a part of the Creation, undoubtedly receives this co-operation from all other parts of the Creation: "He it is Who has made the earth submissive (and manageable) for you, so walk in its tracts and eat of His Provisions." (67'15). And in Surah al-Naba'a we read: "Have We not made the earth a wide expanse, and the mountains as pegs? And We have created you in pairs, and have made you sleep for rest; and have appointed the night as a covering and the day for livelihood. And We have built above you seven strong heavens, and placed therein lamp. And We have sent down from the rainy clouds abundant water, thereby to produce grain and vegetation, and gardens of luxurious growth." (78: 6-16).

Thus God has created man in very friendly and helpful environment; now it is up to man to study the forces of nature, co-operate with them and find out how to seek their co-operation with him in building up human civilisation and culture on a sound and proper foundation. This is the Islamic concept of the universe, in which there is complete harmony in all its parts. Likewise mankind is an essential unity in its origin and purpose. All its component parts, though varying and living in different ways, are by nature meant to work in harmony. This is how mankind can work in co-operation with the unified Creation: (12) "O Mankind, We have created you male and female, and have made you nations and tribes that you may know one another." (49: 13). Unless mankind can work together in co-operation and harmony in the manner God has ordained for it, there is no possibility of achieving its true welfare and good. The only right guidance for its success is turning back to the Way of God.

Islam has given humanity the hope to partake of the harmonious working of the universe and to fulfil its real aim and purpose in life. It has given it a perfect and coherent concept of life which brings all its powers and abilities, spiritual, physical and mental, into one comprehensive unity. It aims at uniting all areas of human activity into one whole, in which body and spirit, worship and work, this world and the Hereafter, are all seeking one common goal – the Way of God – subjecting their energies to His Authority: "This is the real and true unity between the various parts of the universe and its powers, between all the diverse potentialities of life, between man and his soul, between his actual life and his dreams. This is the unity which can establish a lasting harmony between the universe and life, between life and living beings, between society and individuals, between man's spiritual aspirations and his bodily desires and , finally, between the world and faith, between the temporal and the spiritual." (12)

It may, however, be mentioned that this harmony is not achieved at the expense of any one area of human activity. No field of activity is over-emphasised at the expense of another one. Likewise, the interest of the individual is not emphasised at the cost of society, or vice versa. Complete and perfect harmony is established between all the fields of human activity without disadvantage or undue favour to one or other. All activities of the individual and society are performed in complete freedom according to the law of God, without any conflict between them. This helps to establish justice and equality in human affairs in consequence of their conformity with the true unity of the universe: (13) "Surely this community of yours is one community, and I am your Lord; so obey and serve Me." (21: 92).

The Principle of Social Justice:
Islam is a comprehensive and all-embracing human viewpoint that encompasses every aspect of human life and is not the limited economic justice of the Communists or the satisfaction of mere spiritual aspirations, as with the Christians. Islam looks at all the desires, demands and aspirations of man. It looks at man as a whole, including his material needs, his spiritual aspirations and his physical demands. It deals with universe and with life in a comprehensive way, without separating or dividing any part of it from the whole. (12)

Another thing to remember in this regard is that Islamic justice is based on feelings of mutual love, respect and co-operation and a sense of mutual responsibility between Muslims, on the one hand, and between all human beings on the other. (12)

Thus social justice in Islam has two distinguishing features; its just and coherent unity and its insistence on the mutual responsibilities of individuals and societies. However, it gives due consideration to differences of human virtue, and does not ignore differences of human ability. Man's love for worldly wealth is described in these words: "Had the treasures of your Lord's Blessings been in your possession, you would have held them back lest they should be spent. Indeed man is very narrow-minded and niggardly." (17: 100).

This niggardliness and avarice could become dangerously hostile to the Divine scheme of Unity if not properly disciplined and educated: "But if you show generosity and fear God in your dealings, you may rest assured that God will be fully aware of all that you do. If you behave righteously and fear God Forgiving and Compassionate." (4: 128-129). And again in Surah al-A'raf we read: "But My Mercy embraces everything. So I will prescribe it for those who refrain from disobedience." (7: 156).

Islam takes full account of human love for self interest and natural greed for wealth in its code of behaviour and demands from man only what he can bear: "But none shall be burdened with more than he can bear." (2: 233). It does not ignore the welfare of society nor does it disregard the freedom and high ideals of society. It considers both encroachments by ambitious individuals upon society, or by the latter upon the ability and nature of the former, as a kind of oppression not consistent with the principle of justice and equity. Suppression of individual liberty will deprive both the individual and society of the benefit of the maximum use of former's abilities. Islam regards mutual co-operation and mutual responsibility as essential to human life. Therefore, it guarantees freedom of the individual and condemns all kinds of repression or deprivation. Everything and every action explicitly not forbidden is permissible and lawful in Islam and every person is rewarded for those of his actions which are performed within the boundaries of the Divine Law for the Pleasure of God. (12)

Islam has a very wide vision of justice, in which all human values, including the economic ones, are properly adjusted. It tries to establish justice in the entire field of human action and not just one field of action. Therefore it does not impose or recommend equality in the economic field alone. This concept is considered against nature, because individuals are endowed with varying abilities and talents. It would check not only the development of individual ability but would also prevent able individuals from using their abilities. This would deprive individuals as well as the community and mankind of the benefits of their abilities. Islam fully recognises this natural difference in people's abilities and talents and gives full allowance for it in its laws. However, in order to establish justice, it recognises equality of opportunity to use individual talents within the limits of the law. Thus it guarantees the fruits of hard work and of exceptional talents for all people and also disciplines them with higher and nobler ideals and values beyond the material level; (12) "Surely the noblest among you in the sight of God is he who is the most righteous of you." (49: 13).

And in Surah al-Kahf we read: "Wealth and children are an ornament of the life of the world. But good deeds which endure are better in your Lord' Sight for reward, and better in respect of hope." (18: 46). Thus Islam makes it clear that there are other values, more important than material values in real terms. And it is through these real values that a proper balance can be established in society, in spite of material differences resulting from the varying natural talents of different people. It also emphasises that material needs and material values must not be given high priority, such as they are given in human societies which attach less or no importance to religious values. But at the same time it recognises the right of individuals to own private property and indulge in enterprise. However, it forbids luxurious living, which encourages obscenity and sensuousness in society and creates gross disparity in the living standards of people. (12)

In order to establish social justice for the less fortunate members of society, it not only recognises the rights of the poor in the wealth of the rich according to their needs, but also guarantees, first, that they do get their share to meet their needs, and second, that the wealthy fully know and understand their moral and social responsibilities to the poor and needy members of the community. They are explicitly taught through moral education that a life of overflowing wealth, while a part of the humanity is dying in starvation or leading a life of extreme poverty, is not a joy but a chastisement and misery for them in the Sight of God. A description of the attitude of such men will give some idea of the importance of this concept: "Lo! he would not believe in God Most High, and would not encourage the feeding of the needy." (69: 33-34). And in Surah al-Fajr we read: "Nay, but you honour not the orphan. Nor do you encourage the feeding of the poor." (89: 17-18). And again in Surah al-Ma'un we read: "Have you seen him who denies the (Day of) Judgement? That is he who repels the orphan, and urges not the feeding of the needy." (107: 1-2).

The references to these two outstanding examples of evil

conduct and bad morality are merely to show how disbelief in the Unity of God leads people to acts of immorality. This does not mean that only these two evils result from disbelief in God and the Day of Judgement, i. e. repelling orphans and not feeding the needy. But the aim is to present two of the many evils of this attitude that every noble-minded and right-minded person considers as most heinous and atrocious. At the same time, it is also intended to impress upon people that if this man had believed in God and the Day of Judgement, he would not have indulged in such mean actions as to repel orphans and deprive the needy of their basic needs. This shows how Islam has endeavoured to achieve its aim of social justice in the economic field through moral education, moral persuasion, moral culture and moral discipline, instead of using external compulsion, which tends to destroy the very object which it wants to achieve.

Islam tries to keep economic inequalities within natural and reasonable limits and takes positive legal and moral steps to keep wealth in circulation so that it may not remain among the few rich people (59: 7). Its laws of zakat (poor-due) and inheritance tend to check the concentration of wealth and help to increase its distribution to the poorer members of society. Its moral education encourages people to spend their surplus *(al-afw)* on meeting the needs of the poor and the needy: "Virtue is that one should sincerely believe in God . . . and, out of love for Him, spend of one's wealth for relatives and orphans, for the needy and the wayfarer, and for the beggar." (2: 177). The truly righteous in the Sight of God are those "in whose wealth and possessions is (remembered) the right of the needy and the poor." (51: 19). (13)

---

13. For details of social justice in consumption, production, exchange and distribution see *Economic Doctrine of Islam,* VOl. 1. of the author.